I, Anatolia
and other plays

Middle East Literature in Translation

Michael Beard *and* Adnan Haydar, *Series Editors*

Selected titles from Middle East Literature in Translation

I, Anatolia

and other plays

◆ ◆ ◆

An Anthology of

Modern
Turkish
Drama

VOLUME TWO

◆ ◆ ◆

Edited by

Talat S. Halman and Jayne L. Warner

Syracuse University Press

First Edition 2008
08   09   10   11   12   13   6   5   4   3   2   1

Front cover: Yıldız Kenter as Andromache in *I, Anatolia,* Kent Players Theater, Istanbul, 1986.
Courtesy of *Skylife,* Year 6, no. 72 (May 1989), pp. 30–31.

The paper used in this publication meets the minimum requirements of American
National Standard for Information Sciences—Permanence of Paper for Printed Library
Materials, ANSI Z39.48-1984.∞™

For a listing of books published and distributed by Syracuse University Press,
visit our Web site at SyracuseUniversityPress.syr.edu.

ISBN-13: 978-0-8156-0935-3   ISBN-10: 0-8156-0935-3

Library of Congress Cataloging-in-Publication Data

I, Anatolia and other plays : an anthology of modern Turkish drama / edited by Talat S.
Halman and Jayne L. Warner.
p. cm. — (Middle east literature in translation)
"Volume Two."
Includes bibliographical references.
ISBN 978-0-8156-0935-3 (pbk. : alk. paper)
I. Halman, Talât Sait.   II. Warner, Jayne L.
PL237.I22 2008
894.35'2308—dc22
2008033409

Manufactured in the United States of America

Contents

◆　◆　◆

Preface

I, *Anatolia and Other Plays*, with its companion volume *İbrahim the Mad and Other Plays*,[1] represents the first major collection of Turkish plays to be published in English translation.[1] The nine plays in *İbrahim the Mad* span the decades from the 1940s through the 1960s, and those in *I, Anatolia* cover the 1970s through the end of the millennium.

For these volumes, the editors chose a representative selection from the vibrant and varied modern Turkish dramatic writing—a Western genre adopted and adapted by Turkish playwrights beginning in the latter part of the Ottoman Empire and the early period of the Turkish Republic. The selected plays include settings that are historical (*I, Anatolia; The White Gods*), village/rural (*In Ambush*), small town (*Bald Mehmet of Atça*), urban (*The Mikado Game; Old Photographs*), and international/universal (*Vladimir Komarov; A Ball for the Imaginative*). The principal locale of two of the plays is the small-town or neighborhood coffeehouse found throughout Turkey (*The Neighborhood; Fehim Pasha's Mansion*). The plays address a range of social, economic, and political issues and run the gamut from ribald comedy to dramedy to historical tragedy. Examples of musicals and vaudevilles have not been included because of the problems inherent in rendering these forms into another language. The plays range from one act (*In Ambush; My Lovely Scarf*) to four acts (*Man of the Hour*) and from a one-woman play (*I, Anatolia*) to two-character plays (*The Mikado Game; Old Photographs*) to those with more than thirty characters plus extras (*İbrahim the Mad; Bald Mehmet of Atça*). Several of the plays are written primarily in free verse (*İbrahim the Mad; The White Gods; I, Anatolia*).

The selections in these two volumes generally reflect the work of the leading Turkish playwrights from the period covered. The translators, many well known for their translations of Turkish literature, include some of the playwrights themselves.

The plays are arranged in chronological order by date of their original Turkish publication or production. The cast of each play is presented in the order of stage appearance. The editors have checked each translation against the Turkish original line by line and word by word—in some cases making substantial revisions (submitted when possible to the translators for approval) and frequently opting for more colloquial English.

1. A shorter collection is Talat S. Halman, ed., *Modern Turkish Drama: An Anthology of Plays in Translation*, which contains four plays. Published by Bibliotheca Islamica in 1976, it received wide critical acclaim.

By providing a representative sampling of the genre over six decades, the editors intend that *I, Anatolia* and its companion volume will help address the nearly complete omission of Turkish drama from general surveys of world literature and drama. It is also hoped that these volumes will spark an interest in Turkish theatrical arts in the English-speaking world, as well as provide enjoyable reading and scripts for possible staging.

Jayne L. Warner

Guide to Turkish Spelling, Pronunciation, and Monetary Terms

Throughout this book, Turkish proper names and special terms conform to standard modern Turkish spelling. The pronunciation of the vowels and consonants is indicated in this guide:

a	(like *gun*); var. â (like *are*)	m	(as in English)
b	(as in English)	n	(as in English)
c	(like *jade*)	o	(like *eau* in French)
ç	(*ch* of *chin*)	ö	(like *bird* or French *deux*)
d	(as in English)	p	(as in English)
e	(like *pen*)	r	(*r* of *rust*)
f	(as in English)	s	(*s* of *sun*)
g	(*g* of *good*)	ş	(*sh* of *shine*)
ğ	(makes preceding vowel longer)	t	(as in English)
h	(*h* of *half*)	u	(like *pull*); var. û (like *pool*)
ı	(like second vowel of *portable*)	ü	(like *tu* in French)
i	(like *it*); var. î (like *eat*)	v	(as in English)
j	(like *measure*)	y	(*y* of *you*)
k	(*k* of *king*)	z	(as in English)
l	(as in English)		

Of the twenty-nine characters in the Turkish alphabet, six do not exist in English: ç, ğ, ı, ö, ş, ü. The letters *q, w,* and *x* are not in the Turkish alphabet, although they may occur in foreign names. The letter ğ has its own capital, Ğ, but it never starts a word. The undotted ı and the dotted *i* are separate vowels whose distinctions are strictly observed in pronunciation and spelling. These two letters have their individual capitals as well: I and İ, respectively.

The few exceptions to authentic Turkish spellings are words that have found their way into the English language and appear in standard English dictionaries often in anglicized forms—for example, *rakı, paşa,* and *efendi* are anglicized as *raki, pasha,* and *effendi*—as well as words that keep their Turkish spellings in English, such as *bey.* Exceptions include *molla, hacı,* and *ağa,* which have been kept in Turkish. *Ağa* has numerous meanings and connotations, and the specific use has been provided in plays where the term occurs.

Proper names have been kept in modern Turkish with two major exceptions: İstanbul and İzmir have been rendered with normal English spelling using *I* rather than *İ*. Names of Muslim Turks and members of ethnic minorities appear in the translations exactly as they are spelled in modern Turkish.

MONETARY TERMS

The plays in this collection and in its companion volume *İbrahim the Mad and Other Plays* cover a period of about sixty years during which currency values dramatically fluctuated. The changes owing to inflation, in particular the rampant increases in later decades, render the monetary references virtually meaningless. To give the reader an idea of the relative values, prices, and salaries, all the original numerical amounts have been kept, but lira and kuruş (one hundred kuruş equal one lira) have frequently been dropped (and *penny* is occasionally substituted for *kuruş*). References to gold and silver coins have been left as they appear in the original texts.

◆　　◆　　◆

Introduction

The Turkish Theater Since 1970

TALAT S. HALMAN

The impetus for modernization that characterized the political and cultural life of the Republic of Turkey, born in 1923, continued with full vigor from the 1960s onward. Its founding father, Mustafa Kemal Atatürk, had launched a spectrum of legal, institutional, and educational reforms. Social and cultural life underwent swift, European-style changes, especially in the urban areas. The moving spirit was nationalism reinforced by secularism, and the ultimate goal was democracy. A multiparty system was introduced after World War II. The year 1950 saw free elections that installed a democratic regime. By 1960, the experiment had faltered, and a military coup ended it. Parliamentary democracy, however, was resumed—only to be interrupted again by military takeovers in 1971 and 1980. By the beginning of the twenty-first century, Islamic sentiment had gained momentum in the country's political life. Yet cultural transformation maintained itself based on the artistic models and intellectual currents from western Europe and the United States.

Notwithstanding the setbacks, Turkish modernization gained strength over time, especially in such performing arts as the cinema, opera, and ballet. An established tradition since the mid–nineteenth century, the legitimate theater took impressive strides from the 1970s onward. In the first decade of the Turkish Republic, there were only several dozen performing artists. In the first decade of the twenty-first century, Turkey boasted several thousand. At present, it probably leads Europe in the numbers of performing artists on public payrolls. The conservatories and drama departments increased from one in the 1940s to scores in the 2000s.

The quantitative growth has been truly impressive. The State Theaters network, active in thirteen administrative provinces, is expanding its operations to all eighty-one provinces. The State Theaters opened their 2006–2007 season with a total of sixty-three new

For information on the evolution of Turkish theater prior to 1970, refer to the introduction "An Overview of Turkish Drama" in *İbrahim the Mad and Other Plays: An Anthology of Modern Turkish Drama, Volume One* (Syracuse, N.Y.: Syracuse Univ. Press, 2008), pp. xi–xxiv.

productions (thirty-six Turkish plays and twenty-seven foreign plays, including works by Sophocles, Ibsen, Ariel Dorfman, and Shakespeare).

In terms of the production quality and the level of acting, Turkish theater is generally above that of the rest of the developing world and arguably stands on a par with some of the world's best, an opinion with which some impartial observes tend to agree.

The plays in the present volume demonstrate the diversity of Turkish dramatic writing from the 1970s through the 1990s. The coverage of these selections, representing only a very small portion of what was written and produced in this period, ranges from late Ottoman history to Spanish colonial rule over the Aztecs; from a congeries of Anatolian women, mythic and historical, heroic and ordinary, to a man and a woman caught in conflict and confusion; from the first Muslim actress to appear on the Turkish stage to the Soviet cosmonaut lost in space. They attest to the vitality of Turkish drama and the versatility of the playwrights at work in Turkey.

I, Anatolia

AND OTHER PLAYS

Bald Mehmet of Atça

ORHAN ASENA

Translated by Yeşim Salman

An Editor's Note

Orhan Asena (1922–2001) is remembered as a virtuoso playwright who left behind a diversity of creative work with a dazzling range—from Ottoman tragedies depicting Süleyman the Magnificent and his queen Hürrem Sultan to a play focusing on the assassination of Salvador Allende in Chile, from a dramatization of the Gilgamesh epic to the story of a Turkish village girl, from horror stories of lies and fear to a portrait of the modernization of the Turkish theater. His originality is evident in virtually every one of these diverse themes and techniques.

Asena led a life of double careers. A doctor by profession, he practiced pediatrics for nearly five decades, but at the same time was also a writer who turned out more than thirty plays and published poetry and books about medical and social topics. He was also an accomplished television screenwriter and a librettist whose work included the script for an opera about Vincent van Gogh. For his contributions, he was given the honorific title "State Artist." Many of his dramatizations won awards in Turkey, and one of them was honored in Germany, where he lived for eight and a half years, working as a pediatrician.

Bald Mehmet of Atça is a dramatization of an actual historical episode that took place in rural Anatolia during the weakening of the Ottoman state's tight grip. The Ottoman system was not conducive to the rise and entrenchment of an aristocracy or even a semblance of landed gentry. It did, however, generate a fairly large number of feudal lords who wielded enormous and often ruthless power in some rural areas. Asena's play depicts the confrontation between a feudal lord and an archetypical rebel. The historical event has very little in the way of reliable documentation, but the story has survived in the oral tradition. Asena used the basic story line as his plot and added numerous imaginary episodes. Needless to say, all the dialogue is fictitious. A lifelong idealistic socialist, Asena shaped the play as an analogue for the socioeconomic inequities and feudal oppression in some regions of his country as well as in the underdeveloped world in general.

Bald Mehmet of Atça had its premier in Ankara in 1970, and it came out in book form during that year. In 1971, it won one of Turkey's major awards.

Yeşim Salman (1940–2007), who translated the play into English, was a graduate of Robert College. She worked many years as a chemistry teacher. Her translations into English include two plays by Çetin Altan and three other plays by Orhan Asena. She published two collections of her original poems.—TSH

Characters

ŞERİF HÜSEYİN, one of the notables of Atça, about forty-five

OSMAN BEY,[1] lord of Arpaz, about fifty

WOMEN

FATMA, Şerif Hüseyin's daughter, about eighteen

SERVANTS/HIRELINGS, including some that are individually named

WRESTLER (CHAMPION) BEKİR

WRESTLER SÜLEYMAN

BALD MEHMET OF ATÇA, first a hireling of Şerif Hüseyin's, later renowned as an *efe*, that is, a *zeybek*,[2] about twenty-five

AYŞE, Şerif Hüseyin's daughter, about fifteen

MAHMUT, Şerif Hüseyin's bailiff, about forty

TURNA ALİ, one of Mehmet's men, about twenty-five

YÖRÜK AHMET, one of Mehmet's men, about twenty

MUSA, Osman Bey's bailiff, about fifty

CAZGIR, wrestling referee

BEKİR'S MEN

ELVAN, Mehmet's mother, about fifty, but looks older

MAHMUT'S MEN

CROWD

DEPUTY VOYVODA (HACI MEHMET ALİ),[3] governor of Kuyucak

İSMAİL EFFENDI, tax collector

CLERK

NOTABLES (including Osman Bey and Şerif Hüseyin)

PEASANTS

TWO POLICE OFFICERS

CRAZY YANİ, a very old yet robust Greek

HACI AHMET EFFENDI, one of the notables

ÇAKMAKOĞLU ŞECERELİ, one of Mehmet's men, about thirty

ÇAKMAKOĞLU MEHMET, one of Mehmet's men

PALABIYIKOĞLU, one of Mehmet's men, about thirty-five

HASAN, Fatma's fiancé, about twenty

ZELİHA, Şerif Hüseyin's wife, about forty

---

1. *Bey:* Honorific; in this context, roughly signifies a minor lord.

2. *Efe, zeybek:* A swashbuckling hero of southwestern Turkey's Aegean region; can be used as a form of address for a *zeybek*.

3. *Voyvoda* (sometimes seen as *vaivode, voivode, voivod*): A Slavic term for a governor of a province or district; sometimes used for the military commander of the area.

4. *Ağa:* A landowner and minor feudal lord.

ABDURRAHMAN AĞA,[1] Hasan's father, about fifty

CROWD/VOICES, residents of Aydın

JEW, seal engraver

ACT I

Scene 1

[*The year 1829.* ŞERİF HÜSEYİN, *one of the notables of Atça, is giving a big feast at his farm in honor of* OSMAN BEY, *lord (bey) of Arpaz. A large open area; in the left fore-ground a plane tree, half green, half struck by lightning. In the background,* MEHMET'*s simple one-room cottage and the façade of* HÜSEYİN BEY'*s mansion. The mansion has a projection with a bay window toward the open area. The windows are bolted.*

The two BEYS *with their esteemed guests have gathered at a table with drinks. At one side are the* WOMEN *of both* BEYS' *harems.* ŞERİF HÜSEYİN'*s daughter* FATMA, *a ravishing beauty, glitters like a star among them. At the end, the* HIRELINGS *and* SERVANTS *of both* BEYS. *Center stage, a violent wrestling match. Drums and flutes are heard. As the curtain opens on this uproar,* BEKİR, *the champion of the* BEY OF ARPAZ, *has laid his opponent down and is turning him over.*]

EXCITED VOICES (from the group of HIRELINGS):

—Long live!

—Turn him, Bekir!

—Expose his navel to the sun!

—Resist him, Süleyman!

—Don't let our bey down!

[WRESTLER SÜLEYMAN *forms a bridge, but it is obvious he won't be able to resist.*]

OSMAN BEY: [*Sips his drink and teases* ŞERİF HÜSEYİN.] Do you feed your champions with bread or with hay, neighbor? [ŞERİF HÜSEYİN *keeps quiet.*] Caught in a pinion, they kiss the ground; in another hold, the sky.

ŞERİF HÜSEYİN: [*Sullen.*] We're not beaten yet, so wait!

OSMAN BEY: It's near. I hear your bridge chatter. [SÜLEYMAN'*s bridge is actually shaking.*]

EXCITED VOICES (from the group of HIRELINGS):

—Come out!

—Get him, champ!

—Come on!

—Come on!

—Come on!

—Ohhh! [*This "oh" is produced by everyone at the same instant. It shows a general relief.* SÜLEYMAN's *back is stuck on the ground.*]

OSMAN BEY: [*A bit more sardonic.*] You feed your champions with hay, neighbor, it's obvious.

ŞERİF HÜSEYİN: [*Upset, stands up, calls toward the direction of the* HIRELINGS.] A purse of gold to the brave young man who can beat Champion Bekir! [*Not a sound is heard. It is clear no one has taken a fancy to* WRESTLER BEKİR, *who swaggers about.*] Come on! Isn't there a brave one among you? [*Not a sound to be heard.* BEKİR *makes salutations to left and right.*] Two purses of gold! [*Not a sound to be heard.*]

BEKİR: [*Roars.*] Come on, boy!

OSMAN BEY: [*Pulls* ŞERİF HÜSEYİN's *garment.*] Hey, neighbor, sit down. When the lion roars, the jackals piss blood.

ŞERİF HÜSEYİN: [*Anger and drink gone to his head, yells.*] I shall give my daughter to the brave man who beats Champion Bekir.

[*With bated breath, everybody looks at* ŞERİF HÜSEYİN's *ravishingly beautiful daughter* FATMA. *The girl turns crimson, lowers her head. Commotion is suddenly heard in the back.* BALD MEHMET *breaks through the lines of* HIRELINGS *and comes forward. He is of medium height, with a slender, wiry, well-muscled body; on his head is a bald spot the size of a child's palm. He walks toward* ŞERİF HÜSEYİN *with confident steps.*]

SURPRISED VOICES (from the group of HIRELINGS):

—Hey, this is Bald Mehmet!

—Has the boy gone crazy?

—Who does he think he is?

—He'll be flattened with one hold!

AYŞE: [*Whispers in her sister* FATMA's *ear.*] That boy's in love with you. Did you know that? [FATMA *shakes her head no.*] Pity, he'll let himself be smashed by that boor for you.

FATMA: He should have known his rank. Am I to be left to a mere baldy?

MEHMET: [*Comes up to* ŞERİF HÜSEYİN *and kneels slightly in front of him.*] With your permission, I'd like to wrestle Champion Bekir.

ŞERİF HÜSEYİN: [*Perplexed.*] You? But he is twice your size.

MEHMET: [*Indicates* SÜLEYMAN *with a movement of his head.*] But he was twice Champion Bekir's size.

ŞERİF HÜSEYİN: Have you ever wrestled before?

MEHMET: I have—with friends on the meadow.

ŞERİF HÜSEYİN: Do you think you can match Champion Bekir?

MEHMET: I do.

ŞERİF HÜSEYİN: Look and then speak.

MEHMET: [*Looks and turns away immediately.*] Before getting to grips on the wrestling ground, no one knows who anyone is.

ŞERİF HÜSEYİN: They say that man is very cruel.

MEHMET: So I've heard.

ŞERİF HÜSEYİN: Did you see how he pulled down our great Süleyman?

MEHMET: I saw it.

ŞERİF HÜSEYİN: What gives you such confidence then?

MEHMET: [*Stops for an instant, then without being boastful he points to his heart.*] This.

ŞERİF HÜSEYİN: Look, you, let me tell you, if you disgrace me, too . . .

MEHMET: I won't.

ŞERİF HÜSEYİN: All right, let's try you once. [*Calls to* MAHMUT, *his bailiff.*] Mahmut, see that he finds some trunks.

> [MAHMUT *beckons to both* SÜLEYMAN *and* MEHMET. *They exit together. Now there is excitement among the* HIRELINGS.]

ASSERTIVE VOICES (from the group of HIRELINGS):
> —Our baldy can't resist that boor for two minutes.
> —What d'you mean "two"? He'll be wiped out in one minute.
> —Let's hope Bekir won't injure the boy or something.

TURNA ALİ: [*A very slender youth,* MEHMET'*s close friend.*] Never mind his appearance. What a terrific baldy he is.

YÖRÜK AHMET: [*A man of thirty, a bit pockmarked;* MEHMET'*s second friend.*] He's a "tough nut," one not every tooth can break.

OSMAN BEY: [*Asks his* BAILIFF.] Musa, isn't that our bald boy?

MUSA: It's him, sir.

OSMAN BEY: The one we used to send on errands?

MUSA: That's right.

OSMAN BEY: Well? Why did we dismiss him?

MUSA: He was a fool. If I'd give him a basket of eggs, tell him "take these to town and sell 'em," he'd break half of them, and the other half he'd let clever boys steal from him, and then he'd come back sniffling. Though we fed him and his mother, I saw that not even half the job was getting done, so with your permission I gave them their walking papers.

OSMAN BEY: He's gained courage, though.

MUSA: A little too much courage. Now Champion Bekir will flatten him.

> [MEHMET *comes forward. Since* WRESTLER SÜLEYMAN'*s trunks are very loose on* MEH-MET, *they have tied them onto him with rope around the waist and legs. Next to* CHAM-PION BEKİR, *he looks like a scrawny mouse in front of a fat cat. General merriment and laughter take hold of the gathering.*]

CAZGIR: [*Comes, says his prayers, and announces the rules of the wrestling match.*]
> Allah Allah mashallah!
> There are two stout lads in the ring,
> Both are brave, neither is a sapling.

One should not look down upon the other,
Nor seek help from another.
The one you see on the right here
Is Champion Bekir.
The one on the left
Is Champion Mehmet.
No boasting if you get on top;
Many a time that one will flop.
Don't give up if you go under;
Many a time he becomes the winner.

Champions, you know the rules of the game. All's well if his back is on the ground. If it isn't—if you take your opponent by the leg and drag him three steps on the ground or uncover his navel—you win the game. Let the best man win! [*Withdraws.*]

[*The wrestling begins. It is obvious from the start that one relies on his brute force, the other on his agility. One is impatient with the desire to get on top of his opponent, press him down, and defeat him. The other looks for his chance, intends not to enter the struggle before he sees fit. That is why at first the wrestling looks like a game of tag.*]

IMPATIENT VOICES:
    —E-e-ey? Is that what you'd call wrestling?
    —Is tag to be played in a man's field?
    —Leave the arena to the men!
    —Go lean on your mama's knee, Son!
ŞERİF HÜSEYİN: [*Yells with fury.*] You're disgracing me, you baldy! If you're going to wrestle, do so!
TURNA ALİ: [*To* YÖRÜK AHMET.] What's that baldy of ours up to?
YÖRÜK AHMET: Don't look at what he's doing, think about what he will do.
TURNA ALİ: Can't he see the bey is furious?
YÖRÜK AHMET: He wants to time his opponent, can't you see? Tire him out and get him loosened up.

[*In fact, at that moment, when a general boredom has come over everyone and* CHAMPION BEKİR *has gotten tired of chasing his opponent,* MEHMET *suddenly plunges in and grabs* BEKİR's *legs.* BEKİR *places him in a headlock.*]

EXCITED VOICES:
    —What a plunge that was!
    —He grabbed Champion Bekir's legs.
    —Bekir really squeezed the baldy's neck, too.
    —That one attacks, the other presses . . .
    —The wrestling has come alive!

TURNA ALİ: [*Shouts excitedly.*] Come on, Mehmet, come on, my boy, put 'em to shame!

YÖRÜK AHMET: You've got him now, don't let him go!

BEKİR'S MEN: Crush him, Champion! Make mincemeat out of him! He's got only a breath left anyway.

[*The fight really looks terrible.* BEKİR *squeezes;* MEHMET *resists.* MEHMET *charges;* BEKİR *resists. In the end, blood spurts out of* MEHMET's *nose in streams. A deadly silence takes over.*]

CAZGIR: [*Wants to get between them.*] Enough, Champion, you'll kill the man.

MEHMET: [*Cries in a furious, hoarse voice.*] Get away, you!

[*Something unbelievable happens.* MEHMET *upsets the huge man's balance with a last effort.* BEKİR *goes down on his two hands in order not to get pinned.* MEHMET *drags him, not just three steps, but all the way to* ŞERİF HÜSEYİN. *Only there does he let him go. As* BEKİR *stands up on his two feet,* MEHMET *kneels down where he is.*

The defeated wrestler, shocked at what's happened to him, stands up straight now. The victor has collapsed, breathlessly wiping the blood off his nose and mouth with his arm.

Only later do the spectators remember to shout "long live." The BEY OF ARPAZ *gets up angrily. It is obvious he cannot take this defeat in stride.*]

ŞERİF HÜSEYİN: [*Watching his guest with pleasure, he whispers to* MAHMUT.] Good for the baldy. He brings us honor. Give him five purses of gold. [*Exits.*]

MAHMUT: [*Goes to* MEHMET, *who is still panting.*] Well done, Baldy! You've vomited blood, but you've earned five purses of gold.

MEHMET: [*Spits out two bloody teeth.*] I don't want it.

MAHMUT: [*Shocked.*] What? You don't want it? It's five purses of gold, boy . . . five purses of gold! If you wanted to, you could buy yourself a little farm; you could be your own master.

MEHMET: [*Still out of breath.*] I want the bey's daughter.

MAHMUT: [*His eyes wide open.*] What did you say? [*Laughs are heard left and right.*] Have you gone crazy, you ignoramus? You never said that, and we have not heard it. [*Looks around him.*] We have not heard it, have we? [VOICES *say,* "We have not, we have not."]

MEHMET: [*Looks at him with vacant eyes.*] I want the bey's daughter.

MAHMUT: Is a bey's daughter ever given to a pauper? Where does this ever happen?

MEHMET: [*Takes a deep breath.*] He promised.

MAHMUT: [*Convincingly, while leaning down to help* MEHMET *rise.*] A promise is the easiest thing to give, yet you ought to know which promises are kept and which ones aren't. You take those five purses of gold, Son, and be grateful.

MEHMET: I want the bey's daughter. [*Laughs are heard from left and right. The stage gets more and more crowded.*]

MAHMUT: [*Rises angrily.*] Look here, you baldy! You're making me mad. Didn't you ever hear the saying, "Everyone to his own kind"?

MEHMET: [*Breathless.*] He promised.

MAHMUT: He did, but so what? Is he obliged to keep his promise to a bastard like you?

MEHMET: [*So drained he can do nothing but say the same words over and over like a broken record.*] I want the bey's daughter.

MAHMUT: You bastard! Don't let the bey hear that. He'd have your head chopped off and let your carcass be eaten by bird and beast.

MEHMET: I want the bey's daughter.

MOCKING VOICES:

—What . . . what does he want?

—He says he wants the bey's daughter.

—The bey's daughter?

—He has big ideas.

—While the baldy dreams, it is not a phoenix that lights on his head, but the droppings of a crow.

[*The giggling and joking suddenly stop.* ŞERİF HÜSEYİN *is back. He obviously overheard what was said.*]

ŞERİF HÜSEYİN: [*Stands near* MEHMET.] What is it? What's going on?

MAHMUT: Have mercy, my bey! Champion Bekir squeezed this one's neck too much. He doesn't know what he's saying.

ŞERİF HÜSEYİN: What does he want?

MAHMUT: I can't say it, my bey, my tongue would drop out.

ŞERİF HÜSEYİN: Say it!

MAHMUT: God forbid, God forbid. "The bey's daughter for me," he says. He says nothing else.

ŞERİF HÜSEYİN: [*Comes to his senses in an instant. He is no longer drunk or full of joy.*] That right, boy? [MEHMET *is so weak, he can barely nod yes.*] How dare you think like that?

MEHMET: You promised.

ŞERİF HÜSEYİN: [*Draws* MAHMUT *back, whispers in his ear.*] Add my bay mare to those five purses and shut his mouth. [*Is about to leave.*]

MEHMET: [*Has heard the* BEY's *words.*] I don't want it.

ŞERİF HÜSEYİN: Well, what do you want, Boy? God's curse?

MEHMET: [*Raises his gaze to the sky.*] God was there as you promised, God was there.

ŞERİF HÜSEYİN: Are you right for my daughter?

MEHMET: God has seen you as well as me, as well as your daughter.

ŞERİF HÜSEYİN: [*Turns to* MAHMUT; *his face looks upset.*] He's talking nonsense; take him away.

MEHMET: God will judge you and me and your daughter.

MAHMUT: [*From his waist, he draws his lead-tipped whip.*] Shut up, dog, you've howled enough.

ŞERİF HÜSEYİN: [*Stops his* BAILIFF *with a movement of his hand.*] Take him home, deliver him to his mother. If he does not pull himself together tomorrow, I know how to make him. Tell that to his mother. Either he gives up my daughter, makes do with what I've given him, or I'll have him publicly thrashed so thoroughly that he'll be notorious all over the country. [*Exits. As the others bend down to take* MEHMET, *he becomes unconscious.*]

Scene 2

[*The inside of* MEHMET's *simple hut. The sun is rising. A ray of light comes through the high, glassless window and falls on* MEHMET *and his mother,* ELVAN. *She has leaned against her son and fallen asleep. A herd of cows is heard mooing nearby.*]

MEHMET: [*Opens his eyes.*] Mother!

ELVAN: [*Springs awake.*] My son, my Mehmet . . . you've opened your eyes, thank heaven!

MEHMET: Go ask for the bey's daughter for me, right now, by God's will. I want the bey's daughter.

ELVAN: Don't be crazy, my baldy son. From this we would get only curses from the bey's mansion, no bride.

MEHMET: I want the bey's daughter, Mother.

ELVAN: You were unconscious, my dear. You didn't hear what that villain, that Mahmut, said. If you go on this way, think what will befall us.

MEHMET: I want the bey's daughter.

ELVAN: They say they'll give you a thrashing.

MEHMET: I want the bey's daughter.

ELVAN: They say they'll break every bone in your body.

MEHMET: The bey's daughter . . .

ELVAN: They say they'll even take this modest hut from us.

MEHMET: The bey's daughter . . .

ELVAN: If you don't die, but survive, they say they'll throw us out.

MEHMET: The bey's . . .

ELVAN: They say they'll disgrace us before everyone.

MEHMET: The bey's . . .

ELVAN: They won't give her, my falcon. They'll give five purses of gold in return for the blood you vomited. They'll give you the bay horse in return for your bravery. But they won't give you the girl.

MEHMET: You used to tell me a tale when I was a child, remember? A bald boy's tale . . . if I haven't forgotten, that bald boy got the sultan's daughter in the end.

ELVAN: That was a tale, my brave son, such things happen only in tales.

MEHMET: I know it was a tale and that such things happen only in tales. That is why I restrained myself and kept quiet then. I burned with obsession, yet I didn't confide even in you. Say so if I did!

ELVAN: You didn't, you were as quiet as a deep well, Son.

MEHMET: Had my tongue given me away, I'd have broken it off. Had my eyes given me away, I'd have gouged them out. If my dreams went too far, I would have sprung up from my sleep. But now?

ELVAN: Now?

MEHMET: I have no secret anymore, Mother. I haven't got a secret. My secret is on every tongue, and that kills me.

ELVAN: My poor son . . .

MEHMET: Don't think that it's my love that makes me speak madly like this. I've kept this secret for a long time. Now my secret's out in the open. I want the bey's daughter, Mother!

ELVAN: It's no use, my brave son. Those words are spoken only between you and me. They don't listen. Even if they did, they wouldn't understand.

MEHMET: They used to make fun of my baldness and my serfdom, and I'd make fun of them. That way I escaped from both my baldness and my serfdom. But now what they keep on and on about is neither my baldness nor my serfdom . . . it's the secret I've guarded against everyone, that I've kept even from you. I want the bey's daughter, Mother!

ELVAN: Let's take the five purses of gold, my dear son, let's also take the bay horse, let's then go off without notice. It's a big world, there are many pretty girls, the heart is brave.

MEHMET: A purse of gold isn't my heart's wish. It isn't five purses or ten purses of gold. Now everyone knows my heart's wish. I can't hide it. That kills me.

ELVAN: These words you're saying bring tears only to my eyes, my hero, my son. Not to somebody else's. What you're telling me is, "Make a fire out of the ashes in that hearth and keep me warm." How can I turn ashes into flames?

MEHMET: We talk a lot, yet we do nothing. The day has rushed by and come all the way to our door, and we are still talking. If you won't go, I will, Mother. [*Gets up to leave.*]

ELVAN: [*Rushes.*] I'm going . . . I'm going . . . [*Puts on her coat.*] I hope to God they won't kick me out after my first words, but will hear me out. [*Exits.*]

MEHMET: [*Moaning, he puts his head down on his pillow. His eyes are fixed beyond the ceiling on the invisible sky.*] My God! I know you're trying me . . . trying me in an ordeal of fire. You're putting me through that ordeal to see if I'm truthful or not. That which I keep deep inside, which I let none touch, that which sirs and lords call pride, that which they don't think us worthy of . . .

Scene 3

[When the stage gets bright again, the sun is quite high. In the diffuse light, MEHMET *is seen in deep sleep; his face, having been through a storm, looks serene.* ELVAN *dashes in, runs to her son, wakes him up by shaking him.]*

ELVAN: Wake up, my Mehmet. All sleep is forbidden for us now.

MEHMET: *[Opens his eyes.]* What happened, Mother?

ELVAN: Get up, my Mehmet. It's no day to stand still. Before Şerif Hüseyin's dogs attack us, let's run away.

MEHMET: *[Calm.]* What happened? Tell me.

ELVAN: *[Crams some pots and pans into a saddlebag covered with patches.]* I went to the bey's lady's doorstep. They thought I brought your apology. They showed me in. They asked after my health, even offered something to me. But the moment I started to speak . . .

MEHMET: The moment you started to speak . . .

ELVAN: Try to see, my intelligent son. Don't let me speak bitterly.

MEHMET: What did she say? I want to know exactly. Don't mind the harshness of what she said. Whatever she said can't be harsher than what I say about myself.

ELVAN: *[Stops for an instant, looks at* MEHMET *with her heart shattered.]* Well . . . she said this, "Tell that stupid son of yours that if he's that hot, let him wait; in a few days our dog will bear her young, and I'll give him the bitch for a wife."

MEHMET: *[Still amazingly calm.]* And then?

ELVAN: Then they threw me out. As I was coming back, I heard the town crier call. He asked the people to assemble. They obviously want to get you into trouble. Let's run away, my baldy son, let's run away.

MEHMET: *[With a bitter laugh.]* Where to? To the end of the earth? Don't you see, Mother? We ran away from the bey of Arpaz, and what happened? We got caught by Şerif Hüseyin. Which one is less cruel than the other? And how can you, ruined the way you are at this old age and in this weary state, run away from his hounds and mastiffs?

ELVAN: Let's run away, my brave son! It's not what you expect. They want to kill you, give you a thrashing and kill you.

MEHMET: They can't.

ELVAN: *[Gives her son a curious glance.]* How can you say that with such assurance?

MEHMET: After you left, I thought hard, Mother. I feel that God wants to test me. He wants to test me with trouble, with fire, with flood.

ELVAN: You? God?

MEHMET: If that were not the case, would He have dropped that fire in my heart? Would He have revealed my secret to some evil tongues?

ELVAN: What are you saying, my confused son?

MEHMET: I say that God wants to prepare me . . . prepare me for much tougher days.

ELVAN: Yours is a vanity that one day they will beat out of you.

MEHMET: God, who has pulled this mountain down on me, can grant me the power to lift it if He so wills. Nobody will be able to say, Mother, that the bald boy had big, big words but a tiny heart. We raised our eyes very high; we can't lower them down to the ground, Mother.

ELVAN: [*Sits on the saddlebag.*] What will happen now?

MEHMET: They'll come, they'll take me, tie me to a post, whip me hard so that it may be a warning to others.

ELVAN: [*Springs up with fear, starts to squeeze some items into the saddlebag.*] I can't stand that.

MEHMET: You will, just as I will. If I survive, I'll be the winner.

ELVAN: You? Why you? How?

MEHMET: Everyone will then know where I get this strength. Everyone will understand that it is such endurance that made Ferhat bore through the mountain.[5] Then no one will be able to make fun of my secret.

ELVAN: What do you expect from Şerif Hüseyin? Do you suppose that cruel heart of his will feel pity?

MEHMET: Pity? Who wants pity from him? [*There is pounding on the door, followed by an eerie silence.*]

TURNA ALİ: [*From outside.*] It's me, Mother Elvan! Turna Ali. Open the door!

[ELVAN *looks into* MEHMET's *eyes.* MEHMET *motions with a nod for her to open the door.* ELVAN *opens the door.* TURNA ALİ *rushes in with lightning speed, watching his back as he enters.*]

[*Happy to see that* MEHMET *has gained consciousness.*] Thank heaven you look OK! How did you manage to get that huge man's feet off the ground?

MEHMET: You certainly have not come here, risking all the danger, just to speak those words.

TURNA ALİ: [*Hesitates.*] No. The bey's daughter sent me.

MEHMET: [*Springs up.*] What did you say?

ELVAN: What? What did you say?

TURNA ALİ: The bey's daughter says: "I saw, I realized that your friend is a brave man, a fine man. However, I wouldn't want him to incur my father's antagonism. Terrible is my father's slap. Your friend should give me up. He should just tell you . . . that would be enough. I could make my father forgive him."

ELVAN: [*Rushes forth with excitement, kneels down, and holds* MEHMET's *knees.*] This is an opportunity, my Mehmet. Why do you hesitate? Our safety depends on a couple of

---

5. Refers to the story *Ferhat ile Şirin* (Ferhat and Şirin), a popular tale of star-crossed lovers in which Ferhat makes the heroic attempt to dig through a mountain in order to reach his beloved Şirin.

words. See, the bey's daughter comes to you; her words come, if not she herself. Her heart comes; her wish comes.

MEHMET: That is pity, Mother. Alms of the rich to the poor. Just like something occasionally thrown to a dog.

ELVAN: You mean . . . ?

MEHMET: [*Turns to* TURNA ALİ.] Tell the bey's daughter, "What God wills will happen."

TURNA ALİ: Have you thought this through?

MEHMET: I have, I've thought hard. I've been thinking for years.

TURNA ALİ: Aren't you at all afraid of the bey's wrath?

MEHMET: I'm afraid, I'm very much afraid. I've been afraid for years.

TURNA ALİ: So?

MEHMET: My fear continued until . . . until I reached this point.

TURNA ALİ: The bey's daughter says: "He can expect nothing good from me anyway. That he should know."

MEHMET: I've reached such a point that from here everything looks a little different—the bey and his daughter and life and death.

TURNA ALİ: I don't understand.

MEHMET: God is in my heart and my mind. I can see none but Him. I can listen to none but Him. I can obey none but Him.

ELVAN: They're going to kill you.

MEHMET: I'm being tested with death, Mother. Either he wins, or I do. [*Knocks are heard on the door.*] They've come. If they happen to find you here . . . [*Moves his searching eyes around him for an instant, sees the top window, rushes forward, stands underneath the window.*] Jump on my shoulders. [TURNA ALİ *jumps on* MEHMET's *shoulders.*] Leap onto the roof! [TURNA ALİ *climbs onto the roof.*] Don't let your breath be heard until they come and take me. [*Furious blows are struck on the door.*]

MAHMUT: [*From the outside.*] Open the door, or I'll knock it down.

MEHMET: Open the door, Mother! [ELVAN *opens the door.* MAHMUT *rushes in with a few* MEN. *By that time, a* CROWD *of people has gathered outside.*]

MAHMUT: [*Mockingly.*] I've come to ask about your health, Baldy.

MEHMET: [*Stands in front of them.*] The day will come when I'll ask about your health.

MAHMUT: [*Drags him outside.*] Don't be hopeful; that day will never come. [*They exit.*]

[*One of the* MEN *also drags* ELVAN *out.*]

MEHMET: [*Shouts furiously.*] Let go of her . . .

MAHMUT: [*Pushes* MEHMET *forward.*] No-o-o-o-o! She has to be present at the festival. She should see her son. She should see her son's bravery so that she'll be happy and proud.

MEHMET: [*With disgust.*] You dog.

MAHMUT: Soon it will be my turn to speak. Let's see if you'll bluster so then. If you'll even be able to.

MEHMET: [*Calm.*] I'll kill you, Mahmut. If I survive, I'll kill you. Not because of what you have done or will do to me, but because you see fit to make that poor woman suffer this torture. [*Takes courageous steps.*]

[*The front door of the* BEY's *mansion is opened, and* ŞERİF HÜSEYİN *comes out. They tie* MEHMET *to the trunk of the old plane tree. One of the windows of the* BEY's *mansion is partly open.* FATMA's *presence is felt there.* MEHMET's *shirt is removed.* MAHMUT *unties a whip from his waist and waits for* ŞERİF HÜSEYİN's *order. Sobbing,* ELVAN *embraces her* MEHMET.]

[*Harshly.*] Don't cry! Don't show your tears to the coward. [*At that moment, the woman's tears dry up in her eyes.*]

ŞERİF HÜSEYİN: [*Approaches* MEHMET.] I ask you once more. Do you give up Fatma, or don't you?

MEHMET: [*Soft but final.*] Fatma's mine. [*With a nod from* ŞERİF HÜSEYİN, MAHMUT's *whip cracks on* MEHMET's *back.*] God has written her on my brow. [*The whip cracks.*] It is God who has caused you to do wrong. [*The whip cracks.*] God who has caused your tongue to slip. [*The whip cracks.*] God who has rendered me superior to my opponent. [*The whip cracks.*] God who has rendered the impossible possible. [*The whip cracks.* MEHMET *faints.*]

[*The window of the* BEY's *mansion is closed. Just as nobody notices when it was opened, nobody except the audience notices that it is shut.*]

ŞERİF HÜSEYİN: [*Stops* MAHMUT *with a signal and turns to the spectators.*] That's what happens to someone who raises his eyes over the threshold of the bey's house. Keep that in mind. Everybody go home now! [*The* CROWD *disperses quietly, without saying anything. It is impossible to tell whether they are happy or sad about what they have seen.*]

MAHMUT: [*Takes hold of* MEHMET's *drooping head by the hair, pulls it left and right.*] What shall we do with this one? Shall we feed his carcass to the dogs?

ŞERİF HÜSEYİN: Leave him where he is! [*Turns to* ELVAN.] And you, woman, if a miracle takes place and your son remains alive, both of you clear out. If you're wise, you'll go way to the other end of the world. [*Beckons* MAHMUT. *They exit together.*]

ELVAN: [*Goes to her son after everyone has left, kisses his bloody back.*] My son, my Mehmet! See, I didn't cry. You said, "Don't cry," so I didn't cry. I'll cry later, when I'm left alone with you.

Scene 4

[*When the stage is bright again, a slope covered with tiny trees is seen, and far away on the distant horizon farm houses are barely visible.*]

MEHMET: [*Enters.*] What an impudent, unabashed fool you are, Baldy. Boy, you went round and round and ended up where you were chased away from. What d'you expect? Supposing she came across you suddenly, could you lift your eyes off the ground and look at her face? Could you understand what she means if she speaks? Then why does your heart pound like this? [*Lies down on the ground, places his arm under his head, and gazes at the sky, plunged in thought.*] They couldn't understand. They came upon you with a whip, came by force. If they had let her come upon you, if they'd said, "There she is, there you are, what could you manage to do, you bald one?" But they tried to quiet you down by force. They can't see that violence begets violence, violence arouses violence, violence forces violence. [*Sits up suddenly.*] Flee, Mehmet, flee from here. What can you say to anyone if you're caught? Will you say, "I've been carrying some fire within me for months, but it has never burned as violently as today"? Will you say, "It never blinded my reason as much as it has today"? Will you say, "There is nothing I hope for, nothing I expect"? Even if you say no, will you be able to convince them? [*Darkness sets in slowly.*]

[*Lies face up and gazes absently into the distance.*] Here comes evening; darkness sets in; soon the lights of the bey's house will go on. It always used to be like that around this time, you crazy boy. You'd hide at the base of that bush, you'd watch the lights of the bey's house, you'd not even be able to dream while looking at them. You had forbidden yourself the dreams. You'd just gaze. Sometimes you'd be seething, sometimes you'd be drained. [*All of a sudden* MAHMUT *enters with his six* MEN. YÖRÜK AHMET *and* TURNA ALİ *are among them.*]

MAHMUT: [*Roars upon seeing* MEHMET.] Isn't that our bald one, boys? [MEHMET *springs to his feet.* MAHMUT *unties his whip from his waist, snickering.*] You're in my hands, you baldhead! [*Slowly walks toward* MEHMET.] There is no bey to protect you, to say, "This is enough for him." [*Cracks his whip, but* MEHMET *is on guard and springs backward, avoiding it.*]

[MAHMUT *approaches again, still snickering nastily.*] You cleverly warded that off, you baldhead. Let's see if you'll ward off this one. [*Cracks the whip.*]

[MEHMET *jumps back once more, escapes the whip, but in doing so comes up against one of* MAHMUT'S MEN. *He will not be able to back up anymore.*]

[MAHMUT *attacks* MEHMET.] You're in my hands, you baldhead. Not even God can take you out of my hands. You wish to become famous, do you? Famous you'll become, then . . . but not alive; your dead body will get the fame. [*Cracks his whip. This time* MEHMET *escapes the whip by jumping sideways.* MAHMUT *turns toward him.*] There's no escape, you scoundrel! If I don't kill you, you said you'd kill me, remember that? [*Cracks the whip, and this time it hits its target with a blow that hurls* MEHMET *a few steps.*] Therefore, you must die.

[*Just as he is about to collapse,* MEHMET *feels that someone standing behind him is supporting him almost imperceptibly and has pressed a dagger into his hand. He senses that behind him is a friend. Holding the dagger tightly, he waits for his enemy with nervous tension.*]

[MAHMUT *approaches* MEHMET *with mockery.*] So you didn't fall. You didn't die! I'll kill you, you bastard. I'll chop your head off and take it to the bey. Here, I'll say, is the head of the scoundrel whose life you spared on the condition that you would never see him again. Where did I find it? Plucked it off a field and brought it. Why was it there? You should ask him that. [*Raises his whip to crack it.* MEHMET *springs like an arrow, and thrusts the dagger into* MAHMUT's *belly. The whip falls from* MAHMUT's *hand; he holds his belly and collapses. Now two guns point toward* MEHMET, *who shuts his eyes and waits for death. Two gunshots . . .* MEHMET *opens his eyes and sees* MAHMUT's *two armed* MEN *fall down.* YÖRÜK AHMET *and* TURNA ALİ *have guns still smoking in their hands. They have killed two of the* MEN *in a tacit agreement. The other two are scared and flee.*]

[*Only* MEHMET, YÖRÜK AHMET, *and* TURNA ALİ *are left on the stage now.*]

MEHMET: [*Embraces his two, brave friends, one by one.*] Thanks, friends, you've saved me, yet you've become the enemy. Şerif Hüseyin won't let you survive.

TURNA ALİ: It wasn't with Şerif Hüseyin's command that we loved you, so would we abandon you on his order?

YÖRÜK AHMET: Had we been in trouble, you'd do the same.

MEHMET: [*Looks at the purple hills in the distance and sighs.*] Now only the mountains can harbor us.

CURTAIN

ACT II

Scene 1

[HACI MEHMET ALİ, *the deputy* voyvoda *of Kuyucak;* İSMAİL EFFENDI, *the tax collector; a* CLERK; *a few* NOTABLES, *including* HACI AHMET EFFENDI; PEASANTS; *and two* POLICE OFFICERS *have taken their place on the stage.*]

İSMAİL EFFENDI: [*As someone inside leaves.*] Come, the next one! [*Enter the next one, who is a poor old* PEASANT. *He stands respectfully in front of the* DEPUTY VOYVODA, *the* TAX COLLECTOR, *and the* CLERK.] Your name?

PEASANT: Veli.

İSMAİL EFFENDI: [*To the* CLERK.] Look and see how much this one owes.

CLERK: [*Looks in the black-covered notebook, finds the man's name.*] One hundred and twenty silver coins.

İSMAİL EFFENDI: You owe 120 coins, old man.

PEASANT: How can I have 120 coins? Even if you cut me up into 120 pieces, I still couldn't find the money.

İSMAİL EFFENDI: What? Are you standing up against the imperial rescript?

PEASANT: Have pity, İsmail Effendi! If you don't understand our condition, who will? Write to our sultan. Tell him what the drought has done to us this year. Our fields are dried up, our hands are empty, our tables are bare.

İSMAİL EFFENDI: Your debt is now 150. If you object again, I'll make it 200. Keep that in mind.

CRAZY YANİ: [*A very old, short, and stunted Greek who mingles among the* CROWD. *Angrily.*] What's all this, you sons of bitches? [*A moment of tense silence. Then his voice becomes stronger and more striking.*] Are you trying to squeeze blood from a stone?

İSMAİL EFFENDI: [*To the* DEPUTY VOYVODA, *who makes a motion to quiet* CRAZY YANİ.] Who is this man? [*To the* POLICE OFFICERS.] Catch him.

HACI AHMET EFFENDI: [*Tries to go between the* OFFICERS *and* CRAZY YANİ.] Excuse him, İsmail Effendi. He is a harmless lunatic. The people call him "Saint." For that reason, he can go in and out of places without being invited and speak without being called upon. Nobody takes offense at his words.

İSMAİL EFFENDI: Saint who? That infidel ass whose tongue should be torn out?

CRAZY YANİ: [*Between the* POLICE OFFICERS, *who try to restrain him.*] May a stone as big as that infidel ass fall upon your head, you grave robber, you!

İSMAİL EFFENDI: [*To the* POLICE OFFICERS.] Take him away, give him a lashing. We'll think of the rest later.

HACI AHMET EFFENDI: Have pity!

İSMAİL EFFENDI: Look here, Hacı Ahmet Effendi, we'll take no notice of your rank. We now think differently about you. We know you have been playing games for a long time. The letter you wrote to Hasan Pasha, the warden of Izmir, has ended up in our hands.

DEPUTY VOYVODA: How?

İSMAİL EFFENDI: Yes, in the letter this man has written to the warden of Izmir, Hasan Pasha, he says, "Don't leave the people in the hands of some *voyvoda*s and tax collectors who exploit them cruelly; be the protector of the people." Who are those cruel tax collectors and those *voyvoda*s? Surely you and I.

DEPUTY VOYVODA: That's absurd!

İSMAİL EFFENDI: That's not all; there's more to it. "Because of those cruel tyrants," he says, "the people get so afraid and so poor that they see no alternative but to take refuge with the bandits up in the mountains."

DEPUTY VOYVODA: Is that so, Ahmet Effendi?

HACI AHMET EFFENDI: [*Calmly.*] Yes, I said so. I still say that if we weren't coerced all the time, the mountains would not be so full of bandits. When Mehmet of Atça went up to the mountains, there were hardly eight or ten men with him. Now the men are said to run in the hundreds. They are the ones that go around with guns. But what about their men in the villages or towns, their followers who'd rather die than reveal their secret, their supporters?

İSMAİL EFFENDI: Who knows? Maybe you are one of their supporters.

HACI AHMET EFFENDI: God forbid. If I were one of their supporters, I would not have written that letter to Hasan Pasha. By speaking the truth, I tried to open the eyes of those who diagnose the problem from afar, to explain that it is not a simple case of banditry, and thereby to submit the most reliable information to our sultan.

DEPUTY VOYVODA: Oh, is that so? So you, too, go against the sacred law. [*To the* POLICE OFFICERS.] Seize this one, too. So, we've been harboring a snake in our bosom.

CRAZY YANİ: [*Appears to be in ecstasy at this moment.*] My God! At the time when you made our Lord Christ descend to the earth to come, see, correct, and, if not able to correct, atone for its sins, was the world as corrupt as this? Had eagles become food for grasshoppers, and lions for scabby dogs? Were kings begging among Gypsies? Had wisdom fallen to the level of bats, scorpions, centipedes, and salamanders?

DEPUTY VOYVODA: Shut up, you infidel! Why do you keep rambling on?

CRAZY YANİ: I will, I will. Yet when I am quiet, the grass in the fields will begin to speak . . . the birds in the sky and the leaves on the trees will begin to speak. We've seen days when lies, slander, and fabrications have leaped to the value of gold or silver among the beys and sultans. We've seen days when human worth has all but vanished, days when the honest have fled to the mountains while the dishonest have served as judges.

DEPUTY VOYVODA: [*Roars.*] Chop his head off! [*All of a sudden, shots are heard, apparently fired by horsemen riding at full gallop.*]

İSMAİL EFFENDI: [*Jumps up in fear.*] What's that?

DEPUTY VOYVODA: [*Runs to the window.*] Could that be the cursed bald man of Atça? [*A tense pause.*] Let me go and see. If we're subject to a raid, let me go and get my men ready.

İSMAİL EFFENDI: Wait! I'm coming with you. [*While he squeezes money into a saddlebag, the* DEPUTY VOYVODA *flees.*]

CRAZY YANİ: [*Acts like Michael announcing Judgment Day.*] I called the Messiah, but instead the Antichrist came to burn and destroy, to strike and crash. [*Gunshots come nearer. Still in ecstasy.*] He came to shatter the earth to pieces. Woe unto you who worship silver and gold! Woe unto you who make God a partner in your transgressions! Those who forget their humanity . . . what's the difference between you and me at this feast? You'll be a glorious, dressed-up corpse, and I a naked corpse. [*A horse gallops away.*]

HACI AHMET EFFENDI: [*Breaks free of the* POLICE OFFICERS, *who have let go of his arms as a result of the general confusion, and runs to the window to look out.*] It's the deputy running away.

ISMAIL EFFENDI: [*Runs to the window.*] What did you say? [*Terrified and lost.*] Oh, the scoundrel! Oh, that crook. He was supposed to be gathering his men.

CRAZY YANI: When the day comes, the good and the bad can be told apart, says the Book. That day is here. Woe unto you, the evil! Woe unto you who take the share of the good!

ISMAIL EFFENDI: [*Confused and desperate, to the* POLICE OFFICERS.] Guard the window, don't let the bald hound step inside. [*The two* POLICE OFFICERS *take their places next to the window.*]

HACI AHMET EFFENDI: [*Lunges forward between the* POLICE OFFICERS, *and pushes their guns aside.*] Don't . . . if a single one resists, he'll turn the town upside down.

ISMAIL EFFENDI: [*Takes* HACI AHMET's *hands and pleads.*] I'm at your mercy, Ahmet Effendi. Save us from this calamity!

HACI AHMET EFFENDI: [*Has become the leader.*] Get away from the window. Let him come, and let's find out what he wants.

CRAZY YANI: First, scorpions and centipedes will attack your corpses until you're rotten and turn to dust. Later, the scorpions and centipedes will eat each other up, and then the soil will gobble up the others. When the black earth emerges victorious, I ask you, what's the worth of your rank and your lordship? Who's ever been able to carry his possessions to the other world? You idiots! You blind men! You fools! You who feed upon one another's guts!

[*The door is thrown open. Enter* MEHMET *and his men,* ÇAKMAKOĞLU ŞECERELI, ÇAKMAKOĞLU MEHMET, PALABIYIKOĞLU, *and* YÖRÜK AHMET, *armed and dressed as zeybeks.*]

MEHMET: [*Slowly walks toward* ISMAIL.] You weren't expecting me, were you? [*Walks forward, puts his hand into the saddlebag, and rattles the coins.*] It's clear you weren't. [*Turns to* ISMAIL *again.*] You must be the tax collector. [*Roars.*] Where's that bastard *voyvoda*?

ISMAIL EFFENDI: [*His chin rattling from fear.*] He ran away, Baldy Mehmet Efe!

MEHMET: [*Looks at him with disgust.*] "Bald," not "Baldy"! [*Turns to one of his men.*] Çakmakoğlu Mehmet, you go get him. [ÇAKMAKOĞLU MEHMET *rushes out.*]

ISMAIL EFFENDI: [*Meanwhile.*] You shouldn't say that about yourself.

MEHMET: [*Turns to him with fiery eyes.*] Why not? Is baldness something to be ashamed of? [*Removes his cap, shows him his bald spot.*] See, bald! Bald!

ISMAIL EFFENDI: [*Trembles.*] Pardon me, sir.

MEHMET: [*His eyes still spitting fire.*] Fear not, I'm used to being called "bald scoundrel" or "bald curse" by men like you. [*Takes the money bag in his hand and hefts its weight.*] From whom have you collected this . . . all this money?

ISMAIL EFFENDI: Sir, the state's in trouble, you know it, too; the Russian war . . .

MEHMET: [*Roars.*] Which Russian war? As far as I know, the Russian war was over a long time ago. With such disgrace, too.

İSMAİL EFFENDI: It's over, sir, it's over. However, it's left the treasury absolutely empty.

MEHMET: And the treasury needs to be filled. Not only the treasury, but many other chests, large and small . . . yours, for example.

İSMAİL EFFENDI: God forbid, not at all, sir.

MEHMET: How much of what you've collected will reach the sultan, I wonder?

İSMAİL EFFENDI: [*Bathed in sweat.*] All of it, sir, all of it, our Baldy Mehmet Efe! I swear by God, all of it.

MEHMET: [*Turns to him furiously.*] Shut up, you sissy! How many times have I told you my name is "Bald Mehmet," "Bald Mehmet"! [*Stares absently for a moment, affectionately.*] My mother, only she can call me "Baldy Mehmet." Only to her am I not bald, but baldy. [*Roars.*] How much of this goes to the royal treasury?

İSMAİL EFFENDI: All of it, sir . . . all of it.

MEHMET: Let me tell you. [*Empties the bag on the table. The coins that are poured out form heaps; only one or two fall off the table.*] As many as those that have fallen off, true?

İSMAİL EFFENDI: By God, sir!

MEHMET: [*Spreads out the heap of gold on the table with his hand.*] These are your god. A god that does punish anyway. [*Turns around and goes to* İSMAİL, *who has been trembling. With a calm but commanding voice.*] From whom did you collect this gold? According to what regulations?

İSMAİL EFFENDI: According to the law code.

PEASANT: [*Has been following the scene excitedly. Can't restrain himself any longer and breaks in.*] Not true, Efe, not true! All he says is lies. They tell the man, "You owe 120 silver coins for agricultural tax." He says, "No, I don't." "Then it's 150," they say. "Oh no, don't," he says. "It now comes to 200," they say. They enforce the tax not according to law, but according to whatever they fancy.

MEHMET: [*To* İSMAİL.] What do you say?

İSMAİL EFFENDI: [*Suddenly throws himself at* MEHMET's *feet.*] Forgive, Efe! We have to obey orders, too. The more we take to the tax officer, the more pleased he will be. The more he sends, the more content the palace is. If there is something wrong somewhere, if there's a fault, it is beyond us. Don't sacrifice me, Efe!

MEHMET: Is that so? Get up, then! [İSMAİL *gets up.* MEHMET *points to the table.*] Go over there! [İSMAİL *goes to the table.*] Sit down! [İSMAİL *sits down.*] Take that pen and ink in front of you! [İSMAİL *takes them.*] Now write: "To his Majesty, the Sultan, our Lord." [*A moment of tense silence.*]

İSMAİL EFFENDI: [*Moves his eyes with fear.*] But!

MEHMET: Write, you scoundrel! "I, who collect the revenue here by His Majesty's grace . . ." [*Asks.*] What's your name?

İSMAİL EFFENDI: Your servant, İsmail of Atça.

MEHMET: [*With disgust.*] We come from the same town. [*Dictates.*] "I, İsmail of Atça, your servant who collects the revenue of Kuyucak and the surroundings by His Majesty's order have seen the people suffering in poverty everywhere I've been." [İSMAİL *writes.*] "The war is over. Even so, the tax imposed to meet the war expenses has been raised twofold, threefold."

İSMAİL EFFENDI: [*Again throws himself at* MEHMET's *feet.*] Mercy . . .

MEHMET: [*Holds* İSMAİL *by the nape of his neck and lifts him almost off the floor, sets him on his chair.*] Write, you coward! [İSMAİL *writes helplessly.* MEHMET *dictates.*]. "The people are weary, exhausted, hungry. They are pressed under the weight of ceaseless taxes." [İSMAİL *raises his eyes to* MEHMET *with a desperate look.* MEHMET *roars.*] Write! [İSMAİL *writes.*] "Our mountains are full of bandits lately. Among them is a villain named Bald Mehmet of Atça."

İSMAİL EFFENDI: God forbid! You shouldn't say things like that!

MEHMET: Write, man! Write down exactly what I say! "A villain named Bald Mehmet of Atça, taking advantage of the people's poverty and suffering, is inciting trouble and provoking them into action. He is urging them not to pay the taxes collected from them by coercion."

İSMAİL EFFENDI: [*Moans.*] How can all these things be written to His Majesty?

MEHMET: [*Takes out his pistol, aims it at* İSMAİL's *head.*] Write, I say. [İSMAİL *writes these lines in mortal fear.*] "He provokes the people to resist against this clear injustice." [İSMAİL *writes.*] "I, İsmail of Atça, charged with the duty of collecting the revenue of Kuyucak and surroundings, pray thee, sir, have mercy on the people. Save them from the temptations of this bald devil. We are ready to comply with anything, sir." [İSMAİL *writes.*] Have you finished writing? Now put your seal on it!

İSMAİL EFFENDI: [*Trembling.*] I can't, sir.

MEHMET: Stamp it, I tell you!

İSMAİL EFFENDI: I can't, sir. Even if you're going to kill me, I can't.

MEHMET: Why?

İSMAİL EFFENDI: I . . . I don't know how to tell you, sir. It's not what you know, what you could understand. It's . . . it's . . . how d'you say . . .

MEHMET: [*Takes the paper from* İSMAİL's *hand.*] All right, so I'll say it. These taxes, which you say you collect in the name of our sultan and which you've increased from once a year to two or three times, have actually been abolished. Because the war has ended, they have been abolished. [*Roars.*] Is that not true? [İSMAİL *moans.* MEHMET *turns to* PALABIYIKOĞLU.] Take this fellow, Palabıyıkoğlu; we'll figure out what to do later. [PALABIYIKOĞLU *takes* İSMAİL *and leaves.* MEHMET *addresses everyone.*] Do you know anybody to whose fairness and conscience I can entrust you?

PEASANT: We have complete trust in Hacı Ahmet's honor and conscience, Efe.

MEHMET: [*Looks at the man whom they introduce as* HACI AHMET.] I appoint you mayor of Kuyucak, Hacı Ahmet Effendi. Do you swear you will not part from the canonical law?

HACI AHMET EFFENDI: Excuse me from this appointment, Efe!

MEHMET: [*Startled.*] Why? Or do you consider me one of the low-breed bandits, too?

HACI AHMET EFFENDI: [*Proud.*] No. However, what I know changes nothing. However justified the causes that made you go to the mountains, your action is regarded as perverse. I never overlooked what they did, but I know that your course has no way out. [*A moment of terrible silence.*]

MEHMET: [*Pensively.*] You're right. We can't force you to share our destiny. [*Turns to* YÖRÜK AHMET.] Again we have to do it, Yörük! I appoint you the *voyvoda* of Kuyucak. Return the money to whomever it has been collected from! I've abolished the land taxes that crush the people. You'll collect the other taxes according to the law. Let the amount for our sultan be sent regularly every year; the rest should be spent for the poor. Land should be provided for those without any land, homes for the homeless, workshops for the unemployed. Those who can't marry the ones they love because they haven't the money should be helped. Hacı Ahmet Effendi should be the one you appeal to whenever you're in trouble, whenever you're confronted with difficulty. [*In that instant,* TURNA ALİ *brings a trembling youth inside.*]

TURNA ALİ: I've found and brought the boy whom Şerif Hüseyin picked out for a son-in-law, Efe! He was enjoying himself in a house by an orchard. When he heard us come by, he hid in the chicken coop.

MEHMET: [*Turns to the young man, who trembles in great fear.*] What's your name?

HASAN: Hasan. [*Running suddenly, he drops to his knees, takes the* EFE'S *hands, kisses them.*] I'm not guilty, Efe, I'm not guilty. Have mercy on me! My father and Şerif Hüseyin talked and came to an agreement between themselves. However, I don't even know your Fatma.

MEHMET: [*Orders.*] Stand up.

HASAN: [*Gets up, still trembling.*] Pardon me, Efe.

MEHMET: Take your cap off! [HASAN *takes it off.* MEHMET *holds the young man's chin, turns it to the left, to the right, examines his head from the front and the back, from the left and the right.*] He has no bald spot. [HASAN, *unable to show any resistance, has left himself in* MEHMET'S *hands.* MEHMET *takes* HASAN'S *pocket watch and swings it by its gold chain.*] Rich, respectable, aristocratic, dashing. [HASAN *grins.*] However, in his chest is a piece of dung for a heart. The moment our name gets around town, he runs to the chicken coop.

HASAN: [*Almost moaning with fear.*] Have mercy on me, Efe!

MEHMET: [*Orders his men.*] Give him a dagger. [*One gives a dagger to* HASAN.] You'll fight me. If you survive, Fatma is yours. The way is clear. My men won't touch you, I swear. Come on, attack!

HASAN: [*Tosses the dagger away; throws himself at the* EFE'S *feet.*] I'll kiss your feet, Efe. I'm innocent. It happened exactly as I said. Her father and my father . . .

MEHMET: Stand up! [HASAN *doesn't stand;* MEHMET *pulls him up.*] Even if you're a dog, be a wolf. I'm disgusted even by a dog if he's cringing. [*A moment of tense silence.*] We tried to test you—to test you against hardship, to test you for courage. If you'd ventured to fight me, if only you'd ventured to, we'd say we've been wrong; we'd kiss you on the forehead; we'd take comfort from the fact that even though Fatma isn't and won't be mine, at least she now belongs to a brave young man. Yet you're not even worthy of pouring water over her feet. [*Turns to* TURNA ALİ.] Take this fellow; he'll come with us. [*Exit* TURNA ALİ, *pushing* HASAN *out.* MEHMET *addresses everyone.*] I'm going, comrades! Not very far . . . I'll always be close enough to hear your voices. Don't let me hear any news of your bad behavior. I won't come like this on my next visit. [*Turns to* YÖRÜK AHMET.] Yörük, it'll be very hard for me to leave you, but I couldn't entrust these people to anybody else except you. So long now.

CRAZY YANİ: [*Calls.*] Efe! [MEHMET *turns around while leaving, and so do his men.*] Take me along, Efe!

MEHMET: [*His eyes wide open.*] What did you say?

CRAZY YANİ: I said take me, too.

MEHMET: [*At the peak of his amazement.*] You? [*Breaks into laughter. The men, too, start laughing.*] How old are you?

CRAZY YANİ: Don't know. I been alive as long as I can remember.

MEHMET: What's your name?

CRAZY YANİ: Yani. Around here they call me "Crazy Yani."

MEHMET: Why do they call you "crazy"?

CRAZY YANİ: I confront the thief with his theft, the villain with his misdeed. Whoever doesn't like it calls me "crazy."

MEHMET: Do you know how hard our job is?

CRAZY YANİ: I do, but it's no harder than living among these parasites.

MEHMET: A clash any minute, a fight every moment.

CRAZY YANİ: And here it's another lie every minute, another shame every moment.

MEHMET: Sometimes for an entire night we sleep on horseback.

CRAZY YANİ: That means you can sleep, even if it's on horseback. As for me, here I can't go to sleep many a night in my comfortable bed.

MEHMET: Why?

CRAZY YANİ: I see, I cannot point out; I hear, I cannot tell; I tell, I cannot convince. The tyrant's slap always lands on my face, even if it's not meant for me.

MEHMET: Don't you have anyone, any kin, old man?

CRAZY YANİ: I'm as alone as a shrub that sticks out of a crack in a rock.

MEHMET: You are some talker.

CRAZY YANİ: I'm a thinker, too.

MEHMET: You look like you've seen many a day.

CRAZY YANİ: I took my loneliness, my restlessness, my discomfort around land after land. I saw man was the same everywhere: slave to the mighty, brutal to the weak. I'm tired, Efe, I'm tired. I selected this place to die, then I saw you. I saw that I have much more to do before I die.

MEHMET: Oh, is that so? What is it that you have to do? What is it that you're capable of doing?

CRAZY YANİ: I don't know if it's considered a skill or not, but I swear a lot. I swear without taking anybody's feelings into account. I even curse God if I catch any indecisiveness, an injustice, a naughtiness on His part. [*Some laugh.*]

MEHMET: [*Looks askance at his men, then turns to the old man.*] Come, Baba,[6] come! I'll take you around on the back of my saddle all the time. We won't be separated for a moment, so that I won't be far away from you when you curse. The truth is, we have a great need for a curser like you, a very great need. [*They exit.*]

Scene 2

[*A large room in* ŞERİF HÜSEYİN's *mansion. His wife,* ZELİHA, *is sitting in front of the window embroidering.* FATMA *enters.*]

FATMA: Mother, I had a dream.

ZELİHA: [*Motions for* FATMA *to sit beside her.*] I hope all is well.

FATMA: You won't reproach me?

ZELİHA: Reproach you? Why should I reproach you, my darling girl?

FATMA: I did something foolish. I went to the bank of a brook. I saw that the moonlight was milky, the water calm, the leaves not rustling, not a sound heard, the birds and insects asleep. I pulled off what I was wearing and plunged into the water.

ZELİHA: [*Her eyes wide open.*] Well?

FATMA: You said you wouldn't get mad.

ZELİHA: [*Bearing the same expression of fear.*] When did you do that, girl?

FATMA: In a dream, Mother, in a dream.

ZELİHA: [*Relieved.*] Oh, well, that comforts me. I'd thought that . . .

FATMA: The water was cool; it took away the burning in my body.

ZELİHA: What kind of burning was this in your body, girl?

FATMA: [*Blushes.*] That's just a figure of speech, Mother.

ZELİHA: Tell me, then.

FATMA: [*Absorbed in the excitement of her dream.*] Then suddenly I see in the dark of the water something darker . . . a monster coming toward me, coming with such fury, though . . . that I cast myself on land, look for my clothes, but can't find them. Then he

---

6. *Baba:* Literally "father"; used in referring to or addressing an elderly and respectable male; on occasion, the leader of a sect or small section of a sect.

comes on land. I run, he runs; my cries mix with his roars. Then I see a white bird in the sky; what a fast bird, what a big bird, what an attractive bird . . .

ZELİHA: God's angel probably.

FATMA: He attacked the monster . . . attacked him in the eyes . . . the eyes that scared me stiff, those flaming red eyes. Then I saw that one eye of the monster grew dark, a terrible howling covered earth and sky. Then the second eye went dark as well. The monster became still. So all his life was in those eyes. I turned around to find my clothes, and I saw that the huge monster had dissolved and flowed into some mud on the bank of the brook—some filthy, dark, inauspicious mud. My clothes were there behind the smoldering mud. I took a step; as soon as I took it, I sank into the mud up to my neck.

ZELİHA: Oh my God.

FATMA: As I struggled to get free, the mud pulled me down. Then that white bird came to my rescue, pulled me out of the mud.

ZELİHA: Then?

FATMA: Then we flew over green fields, passed through red poppy fields, went in and out of a lake in the moonlight. I opened my eyes, and I was in my bed, and the bird had turned into a brave young man standing before me, his face covered.

ZELİHA: Were you by any chance naked, girl?

FATMA: Oh, Mother, how can I know if I was naked or not? When he was distracted, I pulled the cover off his face, and who do I see?

ZELİHA: [*Excited.*] I'm very curious, girl. Who?

FATMA: [*Carefully watching her mother.*] I see Mehmet Efe, Mehmet Efe of Atça.

ZELİHA: Wha-a-at? That bald scoundrel?

FATMA: Don't you understand, Mother? Don't you see the sign here, the heavenly sign?

ZELİHA: What sign? It's just an ordinary dream.

FATMA: No, it's a sign, Mother. It's a heavenly sign that goes together with the other signs.

ZELİHA: What other signs?

FATMA: I should have known then, but vain pride blinded my eyes. I couldn't see. "I'm a bey's daughter," I said, "how dare he!"

ZELİHA: Of course. Who are you? And who is he?

FATMA: So I said. However, Mother, in the course of time I came to disbelieve my own words.

ZELİHA: Disbelieve? In what?

FATMA: There exists such a chasm between us, but he made the impossible possible with his faith. I ask myself: What's greatness? Is it to be clothed in silk? Or is it to lie in satin beds? Or is it to give orders to hundreds of men? And now someone has come forward from among them.

ZELİHA: The times belong to the villains, my girl!

FATMA: I've felt at times that if it had been Mehmet who held the whip in his hand, he would have made my father forsake you and me and even his God.

ZELİHA: What are you saying, girl?

FATMA: It's not easy, Mother, not easy . . . to feel a love so intensely, yet still have to smother it inside you for so long until that secret comes out spontaneously at a moment of fun. I thought that this fancy arose within him suddenly at that moment . . . at that inauspicious moment when my father promised his daughter to the one who would beat the champion wrestler, yet I now realize that it was no passing fancy, but an obsession that surfaced then, broke its chains. Thinking we would have fun, we opened a lion's cage.

ZELİHA: So, girl, have you fallen for that bald dog?

FATMA: [*Turns crimson.*] Fallen for him? No. [*Pauses for an instant.*] Or, rather, I don't know, Mother. I felt some pain from that unbearable day of the whipping. Then one day I saw that the pain within me had changed into a hardly perceptible delight as the news of his successes came one by one.

ZELİHA: [*Appalled.*] Delight?

FATMA: A vague delight. I started to think all those triumphs were meant for me.

ZELİHA: We made an agreement with Abdurrahman Ağa about you and his son. How can you forget that?

FATMA: That's your decision. What about God's decision?

ZELİHA: [*Furiously.*] Hush! Enough now! You'd better get this—if your father were to hear what you're saying, he'd do anything to send that dog to hell and let his carcass be eaten by vultures.

FATMA: [*Obstinate.*] He couldn't.

ZELİHA: [*Tongue-tied with fury and shock.*] He couldn't?

FATMA: Maybe he'd try, but he couldn't. Have you forgotten? Only last month Mehmet sent word to the bey of Arpaz saying, "I need two thousand gold coins, send them at once." The bey didn't send them, and what happened? Mehmet himself came and took twenty thousand gold coins instead of two thousand. If he doesn't levy a tribute on us, it's not because he's afraid of my father.

ZELİHA: Oh no? Then why?

FATMA: [*Lowers her eyes shyly.*] You know why, Mother. [*Horses are heard whinnying outside.*]

ZELİHA: [*Looks out the window.*] Your father's coming . . . together with Abdurrahman Ağa and Osman Bey. I hope everything is all right. [ZELİHA *and* FATMA *exit. The stage remains empty for a moment.*]

ŞERİF HÜSEYİN: [*Enters with his guests.*] Welcome. Won't you sit down.

OSMAN BEY: [*Sits down where shown.*] Well, well. That bald fellow of yours is said to have turned Kuyucak upside down, and he appointed Yörük *voyvoda*. What a fine *voyvoda* that pockmarked rascal will make.

ABDURRAHMAN AĞA: [*With a sullen face, sits down where shown.*] Our boy's in their hands, have you heard that?

ŞERİF HÜSEYİN: I have.

ABDURRAHMAN AĞA: [*Gnawing his lips in his fury.*] You know why?

ŞERİF HÜSEYİN: I can guess.

ABDURRAHMAN AĞA: It's not enough to guess. You've got to be sure. [*Produces a letter from his vest. With shaking hands, extends it to* ŞERİF HÜSEYİN.] Take it, please, read it. One of his men brought this to my house, left it, and went off.

ŞERİF HÜSEYİN: What? And you let him? You let him leave?

ABDURRAHMAN AĞA: [*Nervous.*] You forget that my son is captive in the hands of that brute. I even played host to that son of a bitch, Yörük, so that he'd ask that bald monster for mercy for our son.

ŞERİF HÜSEYİN: This is your son's statement, written in his own hand and bearing his signature.

ABDURRAHMAN AĞA: Not written, but forced to be written. Won't you read it . . . read it out loud, please?

ŞERİF HÜSEYİN: [*Hands the letter back.*] You read it since it's written to you.

ABDURRAHMAN AĞA: [*Takes the letter with shaking fingers and reads with a trembling voice.*] "Father, I am in the hands of Mehmet Efe. No harm has been done to a hair on my head. If you don't want any harm done, you must undo the engagement between myself and Fatma, whom you have tied to me with a contemptible agreement. No good will come of this, neither to me nor to her. I want to live, Father, to live." [*Chokes, cannot read.*]

OSMAN BEY: [*Takes the letter, reads the rest.*] "P.S. To the man who brings this letter to you give ten thousand gold coins as ransom." [*Raises his head.*] And those lines are from the demon of Atça.

ŞERİF HÜSEYİN: And so?

ABDURRAHMAN AĞA: [*Sulking.*] And so I collected the ten thousand gold coins and sent them.

ŞERİF HÜSEYİN: That is, you accepted the bald scoundrel's conditions.

ABDURRAHMAN AĞA: [*Peevishly.*] What would you have done if it had been you?

ŞERİF HÜSEYİN: I'd probably not have surrendered to my former servant in such a way.

ABDURRAHMAN AĞA: In what way?

ŞERİF HÜSEYİN: Under such disgraceful conditions.

ABDURRAHMAN AĞA: [*Madly.*] Sir! If that bandit whom you call "the bald scoundrel" is wandering about the mountains today, robbing on highways, kidnapping, and levying tribute on the unfortunate, it's your fault.

ŞERİF HÜSEYİN: My fault?

ABDURRAHMAN AĞA: Of course! When you've wounded the snake, you kill him. You don't leave him wounded. Yet you did what? First, you wounded him to prove your power, you struck him at his most sensitive spot, and then supposedly to prove that you're forgiving, you released him, wounded like that, to the mountains.

ŞERİF HÜSEYİN: How could I have known that inside that incapable, that sluggish boy there slept such a monster?

ABDURRAHMAN AĞA: So you've learned. Good for you, but I can't let my son pay the penalty for your mistake.

ŞERİF HÜSEYİN: You mean to say that the agreement between us is no longer valid?

ABDURRAHMAN AĞA: [*Bows his head.*] Do I have any other choice?

ŞERİF HÜSEYİN: Very well, that's up to you. Anything else?

ABDURRAHMAN AĞA: [*Gets up.*] With your permission.

ŞERİF HÜSEYİN: [*Gets up.*] Good-bye.

ABDURRAHMAN AĞA: [*Turns to the* BEY OF ARPAZ, *who still sits.*] And you?

OSMAN BEY: I have some business to talk over with my neighbor. Now that we're here . . .

ABDURRAHMAN AĞA: Well, good-bye then!

OSMAN BEY: Good-bye.

[*Exit* ŞERİF HÜSEYİN *to see* ABDURRAHMAN AĞA *off. The* BEY OF ARPAZ *remains alone on stage, takes out his tobacco case, rolls up a cigarette, and sets it in his cigarette holder. A smile both mocking and frightening is on his face.* ŞERİF HÜSEYİN *returns, his face sullen.*]

[OSMAN BEY *puts his cigarette in his mouth and smokes.*] What do you think about this, neighbor?

ŞERİF HÜSEYİN: I don't know what to think.

OSMAN BEY: Shall we let the guy roam around out of control like that?

ŞERİF HÜSEYİN: What can we do, neighbor? First we sent Black Efe after him, then Tall Efe. Both are the most fearless heroes of this area. He crushed both of them. As far as the state goes, it's struggling with its own problems. The people have no master, the herd no shepherd.

OSMAN BEY: [*A mocking smile on his lips.*] I say the only way out is to get at him from his side.

ŞERİF HÜSEYİN: Which man of his do you suppose you can buy? They all have taken the death oath with him. He points to the fire, they jump into it. What I can't understand is how that bald scoundrel can manage to bind people to himself in such a manner.

OSMAN BEY: I also know that we can't lure his men away, but what if we have one of our own men join them? You know he needs men, many men, very many men.

ŞERİF HÜSEYİN: [*Thoughtful.*] Do you think that would work?

OSMAN BEY: I sounded out Champion Bekir. He has a never-ending grudge against the fellow, way back from that day of the defeat. He can never rest; it still bothers him. I'll go to him and say, "Shame on you. You let that bald cock get your legs; you made a fool of yourself."

ŞERİF HÜSEYİN: And then?

OSMAN BEY: And then this. [*They move closer to one another. The lights intensify on the two for an instant.*]

Scene 3

[*The inside of* ELVAN's *house at Köşk, consisting of an entryway and a single room, with an outside door that goes to a small yard. The entry is also used as the kitchen, a hearth at the back. Steam rises in clouds from soup in the kettle that hangs over the hearth. A very low table, a pillow on the floor, and so on.* ELVAN *is spinning wool. There is a knock on the door.*]

A VOICE: [*From outside.*] It's the peddler, the peddler . . . I've got silk shawls from Lahore . . . rose oils distilled in the gardens of Isfahan. I've got prayer beads brought from holy Mecca!

ELVAN: [*Yells from where she sits.*] Don't want any! [*Another knock on the door.*]

A VOICE: [*From outside.*] Come on, European combs for flaxen hair!

ELVAN: [*From where she sits.*] Take them to those with flaxen hair!

A VOICE: I've got kohl for velvety eyes.

ELVAN: Take it to those with velvety eyes. [*There is another knock on the door.*]

A VOICE: [*Husky and meaningful.*] Open, Mother! Open! Maybe we'll find something fit for you, too.

ELVAN: [*Gets up, grumbling.*] Is he crazy or something? [*Opens the door.*] What do you want, eh? [*Suddenly almost tongue-tied.*] You! You! You! [*At once, a hand extends and covers her mouth; strong arms lift up the old woman and carry her inside. Then we recognize* MEHMET *in a peddler's outfit.*]

MEHMET: Hush, Mother! Don't you know what a dangerous name we've got?

ELVAN: [*Raves as though in a dream.*] You! You! You! [*Strokes her son's face and hair one minute, mumbles meaningless words the next.*] How was I supposed to know? I thought that . . . I said that . . .

MEHMET: You took me for a shameless peddler, didn't you, Mother? Some impudent Gypsy.

ELVAN: [*Only then has the sense to embrace her son.*] My son-n-n!

MEHMET: That's better! I risk death to kiss my mother's hand, and she turns me away.

ELVAN: [*Keeps kissing her son.*] But you look no better than a peddler, my poor son. What kind of clothing is this? I always dream of you on a rearing black stallion.

MEHMET: Oh yes, wouldn't it be spectacular to storm through the streets of Köşk on my black stallion, with guns on my chest, then pull in the reins at your doorstep? To enter proudly in front of friend or foe, but be taken out between two policemen half an hour later with my tail between my legs?

ELVAN: [*Suddenly panics.*] Wait, let me put your donkey inside; we left the poor animal outside. [*Goes outside.*]

MEHMET: That's right, put it inside. Or else what would they say? They'd say, "Elvan has taken a peddler inside and will not let him go."

ELVAN: [*Her voice comes from outside.*] You, devil, you! Now, have you come merely to kiss your mother's hand, really?

MEHMET: Of course? What else could it be?

ELVAN: Isn't there another reason, a small reason?

MEHMET: There is another, a small one, Mother dear, an insignificant one.

ELVAN: [*Comes back inside.*] I should hope so.

MEHMET: I've heard that Şerif Hüseyin's men came down to Köşk, is that right?

ELVAN: It is. But what's on your mind, my baldy son?

MEHMET: Nothing.

ELVAN: Well, well.

MEHMET: My heart is such a scoundrel, so crazy that I can't control it, Mother. My voice can move rocks, but cannot tame my heart.

ELVAN: In the marketplace once, I came face to face with Ayşe, Şerif Hüseyin's younger daughter. Like the devil, she recognized me, even took a step toward me, but I walked on. After that, I had no peace of mind for quite a while. I feared they would come one day and make life difficult for me.

MEHMET: Don't worry, Mother, I've put such fear in their hearts that if they saw you, they'd lose sleep.

ELVAN: Why have you come?

MEHMET: [*Lifts up the lid of the kettle. Sniffs deeply as if a delicious smell is wafting through the air.*] I missed your soup, Mother! Ohhh! How wonderful it smells. Everyone makes that soup, yet no one can make it quite like you. I'm so hungry.

ELVAN: [*Hastens to set the table.*] Right away, my Mehmet, immediately, my Mehmet . . . [*Brings bread, onions, the soup, and arranges them on the low table.*] Let me fry some eggs for you.

MEHMET: [*Attacks the food.*] Don't bother, Mother. This is enough for me.

ELVAN: What d'you mean "don't bother"? Who am I going to serve if not you? [*Puts a little butter in a pan, breaks two eggs.*] But, do you know, my son, sometimes I get a lump in my throat. I wonder whether, in God's presence, that lump will turn into molten lead and burn my throat.

MEHMET: [*Petrified, spoon in hand.*] Believe me, Mother, that mouthful is much more honorable than the mouthfuls that pass down Şerif Hüseyin's throat because the real pillage is theirs . . . what a merciless pillage at that. I used to believe that only my bey was unfair, that only I have been unjustly treated, yet how tiny my problem is. How insignificant are the things that have happened to me.

ELVAN: Insignificant, eh? Tiny, eh? They'd have killed you if you hadn't been alert.

MEHMET: I've seen those who died, Mother, those who died because they couldn't be alert. I've seen how human pride is played with. They first ask for your shirt. You take it off and give it. Then they ask for your skin. If you don't give it, they call you a rebel. They report to our sultan that you've rebelled.

ELVAN: What venom you have within you that you poison me with just this little bit.

MEHMET: Well, they plunder like that. They've gotten organized; they've got pen, they've got paper in their hands. You don't know what a terrible weapon pen and paper make. Our flintlock guns remain toys next to them. With our rifles, we can shoot what's a hundred steps or, at the most, two hundred steps away, but with their pen and paper they aim at what's at the other end of the world.

ELVAN: But you . . . how is it that you can cope with those men?

MEHMET: You see a tax collector before you. You grab him by the collar. You see that he's not guilty, that there's the governor who orders him. You get that fellow by the throat. You realize he takes orders from a pasha somewhere. This time you say, "I've found my enemy." Then you see that *this* fellow's got some papers in his hand—stamped, signed, bearing the imperial seal.

ELVAN: Enough, my crazy son. Ask God's forgiveness. Don't talk against the sultan; at least, don't talk against the caliph.

MEHMET: [*Exuberant.*] If only I knew, Mother, if only I knew he was really responsible, my job would be simplified. There's a man with me they call "Crazy Yani." Now I don't know if he's ninety or a hundred. He's been around a lot, read a lot, seen many a day, is not without foresight. He says that in the West they've been fighting because of this for years. They've chopped the king's head off, and still evil is everywhere. [*Yells in despair.*] Where's evil, Mother, where? Let me confront it, let me say, "Here we are, you and I." If necessary, let me give my life for this cause.

ELVAN: Who knows, maybe we all share some of the evil.

MEHMET: There, that's what's keeping me back. While I was working on Şerif Hüseyin's farm, I used to believe that evil ended at the boundaries of the farm. I became an outlaw, went up to the mountains, and I saw that there were other Mahmuts on other farms, other Şerif Hüseyins giving orders to those other Mahmuts. I raided Kuyucak. I heard bitter screams. I left Yörük Ahmet with them as my deputy so that he'd put an end to their cries. Now their cries come from Nazilli, from Güzelhisar, from Tire, from Turgutlu, from Bayındır, from Ödemiş . . . saying, "Come here, come here!" I sent Çakmakoğlu Şecereli to Tire, to Turgutlu, to Bayındır. The revenue farmers, the mayors run away, the people rejoice. I sent Çakmakoğlu Mehmet to Ödemiş, to Sart, to Yenipazar. However, I know the cries won't come to an end. Every day they'll call me from a little farther, a little farther . . . a little farther, a little farther.

ELVAN: [*With pain.*] Where will you stop? I wish I knew at least that.

MEHMET: How do I know, Mother, where those cries will end?

ELVAN: [*Suspicious.*] What if they don't?

MEHMET: [*His face overcast.*] They won't. Where one ends, another will begin. I wonder if Almighty God wants to punish me by making me run after something impossible to reach.

ELVAN: In the end, you'll rebel against the sultan.

MEHMET: I don't know, Mother, I don't know. [*Pushes away the dish in front of him.*] Whether I'm the game or the hunter, I don't know. [*Stands up.*] Do you remember? I told you one day that God wants to test me, to test me for much tougher days.

ELVAN: [*Absentmindedly.*] And I asked you if there were any tougher days.

MEHMET: Those days have come now. Mother, I can't turn back, I can't stop. I can only walk, walk not knowing where my road will take me. Only, about that lump, that lump you get in your throat . . . you can comfortably swallow that because it's not smuggled from the table of a poor man . . . it is taken by force from a tyrant.

ELVAN: [*Swallows her food, then looks at the unfinished food on the table.*] You haven't finished your meal!

MEHMET: I don't know, my appetite's gone. Wish I hadn't come. I'm worried.

ELVAN: Son, you've come to kiss Mother's hand.

MEHMET: To kiss Mother's hand, yes. I left the boys with Turna Ali and came. We're not very far away.

ELVAN: You said there was another reason why you came.

MEHMET: Did I? Maybe I did. Well, in my heart there's a pain that comes and goes. It neither kills nor heals. [*Suddenly there is a sharp knock on the door. They both jump to their feet. To his* MOTHER.] Who is that? Were you waiting for someone?

ELVAN: No. [*Points to the single room.*] Get in there! [MEHMET *goes. His* MOTHER *quickly collects the dishes on the table while insistent and nervous knocks are heard at the door. Anxiously.*] Coming . . . coming . . . I'm coming right now. [*Opens the door.* FATMA *is on the doorstep, very pale.* ELVAN *cannot believe her eyes.*] You?

FATMA: Ayşe described the house to me. You met one another in the market once, and she secretly followed you—supposedly to play a joke on me.

ELVAN: But this visit?

FATMA: I was desperate, Mother Elvan, I was desperate, that's why I came. I thought I'd notify you of a great, a terrible danger. Mehmet Efe's life is in danger.

ELVAN: What did you say?

FATMA: I said Mehmet Efe's life is in danger. They want him to fall into an ambush. Those who set the ambush are the bey of Arpaz and . . . the bey of Arpaz and . . . [*Cannot bring herself to say it.*] the bey of Arpaz and my father.

ELVAN: On one side your father, on the other my poor Mehmet, my humble Mehmet, my lonely Mehmet.

FATMA: [*As though aware of* ELVAN's *suspicion.*] How come I give up my father, my family, myself for your poor Mehmet? [*Bows her head. In a barely audible whisper.*] Don't you understand at all, Mother Elvan?

ELVAN: Do you?

FATMA: [*Full of shame.*] Yes! As you've guessed, Mother Elvan!

ELVAN: My God!

FATMA: If only you knew, Mother Elvan, if only you knew your Mehmet's worth to me!

ELVAN: Wasn't it you who said, "Am I to be left to a mere baldy?" I've heard an expression like that.

FATMA: It wasn't me, Mother Elvan. The person who said it was a conceited . . . a presumptuous, stupid girl.

ELVAN: Wasn't it you who sent word with Turna Ali saying, "We are not for each other, let him give me up, and I'll make my father forgive him"?

FATMA: It wasn't me, Mother Elvan! The one who said it was a silly girl who interpreted the most beautiful stirring inside her for misplaced compassion.

ELVAN: [*Absentmindedly.*] He told me, "It's pity, Mother. Alms of the rich to the poor. Just like something occasionally thrown to a dog."

FATMA: Then I saw them tie him to a tree. I saw the welts left on his shoulders by the strokes of the whip. But I still heard him say, "Fatma is mine, Fatma is written in my destiny." I was crying, yet I said to myself. "It's pity I feel." I was fooling myself, Mother Elvan! Actually, I thought I was, but I wasn't really able to.

ELVAN: I was praying to God just at that moment: "My God, do what you will, drop a fire in the merciless girl's heart so that her heart is aflame, so that she'll burn, she'll take to the mountains, crying, 'My Mehmet!'"

FATMA: I didn't go to the mountains, Mother Elvan, but look, I've come to you. [*Grabs her hand.*] Let me kiss your hand. Be my mother, too.

ELVAN: [*Withdraws her hand suspiciously.*] What if this too is a trick?

MEHMET: [*Comes out.*] It's not a trick. Give your hand to her to kiss, Mother.

FATMA: [*Turns to him with a shudder.*] My God!

MEHMET: [*Walks toward her.*] Forgive me, I heard your secret unintentionally, just like my own was unintentionally revealed. [FATMA *covers her face with her trembling hands.*] I wasn't given the right to cover my face with my hands, Fatma. It was as if they'd undressed me so I was stark naked, and most of all I was ashamed for you.

FATMA: [*Her face still hidden in her hands.*] They want to ambush you. I've come to warn you.

MEHMET: So I've heard.

FATMA: [*Still troubled and uneasy.*] What will happen now?

MEHMET: I must get going at once. They could ambush Turna or someone else instead of me. [*Kisses his* MOTHER's *hand.*] Wish me luck, Mother!

FATMA: [*Suspicious.*] You won't hurt my father, will you?

MEHMET: [*Exuberant.*] Your father? No, I've forgiven your father . . . I've forgiven him a hundred times. Not only for what he's done, but also for what he'll do from now on. Now good-bye. [*Is about to leave.*]

FATMA: [*Rushes to him breathlessly.*] Efe! [MEHMET *stands still.* FATMA *is shy and timid.*] Take me with you, Efe.

MEHMET: You know what they're going to say if I take you?

FATMA: [*Still shy.*] Let them say whatever they will. Let them say Şerif Hüseyin's daughter eloped with Bald Mehmet of Atça.

MEHMET: They won't say that. They'll say Bald Mehmet of Atça kidnapped Şerif Hüseyin's daughter, kidnapped her by force, took her as an insult. They'll defame what remains as the best, the holiest, the purest in me.

FATMA: But do you know what's going to happen now? Everything will be known. I shall be accused of everything. I shall hear endless insults. They'll keep me away from you, but who knows, maybe we'll come together in the other world.

MEHMET: [*Embraces* FATMA *tightly.*] We will come together, I swear we'll come together. I swear I'll find you wherever you are! [*Runs outside without looking back. The two women remain motionless for an instant. Then* ELVAN *opens her arms, and* FATMA *seeks shelter in those arms like a little child.*]

FATMA: [*As though seeking refuge on* ELVAN's *chest.*] Why? Why? Why? Please, do you understand?

ELVAN: [*Strokes* FATMA's *hair.*] No. Anyway, I haven't understood him since he was a child.

CURTAIN

ACT III

Scene 1

[*A room in the governor's residence in Aydın. The buzz of the* CROWD *is heard outside. Now and then a voice is heard over this hum. From the balcony,* MEHMET EFE *addresses the* CROWD. CRAZY YANİ *and* TURNA ALİ *are inside.*]

MEHMET: Friends! You said, come. I came. I saw your condition. Your condition is heartbreaking. I am no orator, but my hand gets things done. I shall get to work at once. First of all, in accordance with your wish and support, I assume the office of governor of Aydın.

VOICES: [*From outside.*] Long live our Mehmet Efe of Atça!

CRAZY YANİ: [*Apparently disturbed, looks at* TURNA ALİ.] This boy's making a mistake again, a mistake. To get stuck in the great swamp that they call the big city . . . no intelligent person would do that.

MEHMET: [*Calls out from the balcony.*] My door will be open day or night, at any hour of the day. Whoever has any trouble, any need, should come to me.

VOICES: [*From outside.*] Long live our protector Mehmet Efe!

CRAZY YANİ: [*As though grumbling to himself.*] Idiot! Thinks the people will bring him only their troubles, their needs. He doesn't know that if you give encouragement to the people, they will bring their greediness, their impudence, their impertinence.

MEHMET: I ask you to go to bed with your doors open tonight. I'll give a cauldron to whoever loses a pot, but when I catch the one who stole that pot, I'll show him. Understand that.

VOICES: [*From outside.*] Long live our Mehmet Efe, Commander of the Mountains.

CRAZY YANİ: [*With a bitter laugh.*] If the governor's residence is not filled tomorrow with those who've lost their pots and pans, I know nothing about human nature. Plus, everyone will come with the name of the thief who stole from him.

TURNA ALİ: With the name of the thief who stole from him?

CRAZY YANİ: Sure. That is, with the name of his neighbor if there has been any little tiff between them beforehand.

MEHMET: I'm going to write to the sultan immediately. I'll report your plight.

VOICES: [*From outside.*] Long live our Mehmet Efe, the dread of the tyrant's heart!

[*Enter* MEHMET *while the noise outside gets louder and louder.*]

CRAZY YANİ: You're going to write again?

MEHMET: [*Suddenly bewildered.*] Write . . . what?

CRAZY YANİ: How many times have you written?

MEHMET: What else can I do?

CRAZY YANİ: Take action. Use the sword where a sword is needed, the Book where the Book is needed, a speech where a speech is needed.

MEHMET: You don't understand me. I don't want to go against our sultan.

CRAZY YANİ: Well, what's this you're doing?

MEHMET: Ah, if only my voice was heard by him . . . if only I could tell him . . . if only I could convince him.

CRAZY YANİ: You couldn't get your voice heard by him . . . if you got it heard, you couldn't make it clear; if you made it clear, you couldn't convince; if you convinced him, you couldn't make him move because he too has things he wants to explain, to argue, to put into motion. The government is a wheel that runs very, very slowly. During one of our campaigns, I asked a French captain in the harbor of Alexandria . . . a French captain who could speak Greek, "What crime did your king commit that you had to chop off his head?" He said that the king wasn't at all a bad man; he just moved slowly, very slowly. Do you see what he meant?

MEHMET: Evil is everywhere. To catch up with it all is not possible.

CRAZY YANİ: You clear away as much as you can, show how it can be cleaned up, show the way, and others will emerge and do what you're doing.

MEHMET: Me, by myself?

CRAZY YANİ: Action . . . one should take action. When you act rapidly, there will be more of you. What is it you want? That taxes should be collected fairly? You'll do that. It will become a system. That military service should be regulated according to definite principles? You'll do that . . . no one will do otherwise. Equality before the law? You'll instill fear in the hearts of murderers, thieves, and rapists . . . it will be a law.

MEHMET: There is so much.

CRAZY YANI: You'll get much faster. Life is short, Son; what you want to do can't fit into a single lifetime.

MEHMET: I know.

CRAZY YANI: You'll do as much as you can.

MEHMET: And then?

CRAZY YANI: Then they'll corner you somewhere and make mincemeat out of you.

MEHMET: [*With a bitter laugh.*] So that's it?

CRAZY YANI: No. Actually you start there. Like a seed . . . a single seed that turns into a thousand. The wind disperses you, the birds disperse you; with or without wings everything that moves on earth disperses you. Thoughts disperse you, writings disperse you. It's something very, very great to be the first.

[*Deep in thought,* MEHMET, *paying no attention, goes to the governor's chair and sits down.* CRAZY YANI *lunges forward, grabs* MEHMET *by the arm and pulls him the other way.*] Get up at once, at once!

MEHMET: [*Gets up unwillingly.*] Why?

CRAZY YANI: Because once you sit there, your ass will get stuck.

[*Just then a* JEWISH SEAL ENGRAVER *brings in* MEHMET*'s seal.*]

JEW: [*Grinning.*] I've brought the seal you've ordered, Efe.

CRAZY YANI: [*Looks with bewilderment at the* JEW, *then at* MEHMET.] Seal? What seal?

MEHMET: It's needed for the correspondence. They said so.

CRAZY YANI: The correspondence, huh? [*Turns to the* JEW.] What's written on it?

JEW: [*Reads the engraving on the seal.*] Governor of the Province, Servant of the State, Descendant of the Prophet, Mehmet of Atça.

CRAZY YANI: Eh, that's just what was missing. We've played and danced to every tune but this one.

MEHMET: In order for our correspondence to reach the sultan's quarters, we've got to use big titles, so they said.

CRAZY YANI: [*Grabs the seal, pulls it away from the* JEW*'s hand, and reads it, stressing each syllable.*] Gov-er-nor of the Prov-ince, Ser-vant of the State, De-scen-dant of the Proph-et, Meh-met of At-ça. [*Turns to* MEHMET.] Since when are you a descendant of the Prophet?

MEHMET: [*Nervous, turns to the* JEW.] Take out "Descendant of the Prophet." Write "Governor of the Province, Servant of the State, Bald Mehmet of Atça." [*Says the word* bald *like a slap in the face.*]

JEW: But, sir . . .

MEHMET: Yes. Write "Bald Mehmet of Atça." Do you understand? [*Turns to* CRAZY YANİ.] Well, are you happy now?

CRAZY YANİ: [*To irritate him.*] What about that "Governor of the Province"? Do you really intend something of the sort?

MEHMET: [*Harshly.*] Do you think I don't deserve it?

CRAZY YANİ: [*Lays his hands on* MEHMET's *shoulders.*] Look, Son, it's not that you don't deserve to be governor, but governorship is not for you. It's too little for you. You are a cyclone fit for mountaintops. This chair, this room, this residence, this town will be too small for you.

MEHMET: The people want me for this office.

CRAZY YANİ: Then the people are doing the greatest injustice to you. There atop the mountains you had no site, no shape, no dimension. What about here?

MEHMET: Now the day has come to appear in flesh and blood . . . as a human being.

CRAZY YANİ: They'll be taken aback however you appear. Even if you were as beautiful as the prophet Joseph, they'd find you strange. They'd see your hand, your foot; they'd see your toes; they'd say, "He is a man like us." However, while you were there in the distance, everything about you had turned into a myth. Even . . . even . . .

MEHMET: Say "even your baldness." Don't be afraid. Say "even your baldness."

CRAZY YANİ: Even your baldness.

MEHMET: We should mix in with people, or else how can we find the remedy for these people's troubles?

CRAZY YANİ: [*Sighs.*] If a person yields that way to his own hypocrisy . . .

MEHMET: [*Sharply.*] Did you say "hypocrisy"?

CRAZY YANİ: Yes, hypocrisy. When we got to Aydın, our stated aim was to rescue our Turna Ali, for whom Wrestler Bekir had set a trap and put into the Aydın prison. Our present cause is to find solutions for these people's problems. But I know that the real cause is very different.

MEHMET: What do you mean?

CRAZY YANİ: Şerif Hüseyin would try to find a far-off place to hide his daughter from the chief bandit Bald Mehmet of Atça, who wanders idly about the mountains, but he would offer her with his own hands to Mehmet Efe, the governor of Aydın, in her bridal gown and veil . . . and that is the real reason.

MEHMET: [*As though a sore wound has been touched.*] Look, you Greek! I've a festering wound. Even if a friend's hand were to touch it, I would probably react the wrong way. Stop right there!

CRAZY YANİ: I will, but then what difference remains between you and the others? They also would slap my mouth to shut me up when I went too far.

MEHMET: [*Trying to defuse the situation.*] Today you're an out and out tyrant.

CRAZY YANİ: [*Snaps back.*] And you're every inch a moron. [*Exits.*]

MEHMET: [*His face twitching nervously, he remains silent for an instant, breathes heavily several times, and then turns suddenly to* TURNA ALİ.] What about you?

TURNA ALİ: [*With his typical sweet smile.*] You're not justified, Efe. You're not justified in your anger. Leaving his sharp tongue aside, Crazy Yani wants to make you see the truth. We live in danger here. This big town is a huge, ominous trap . . . it's not clear when it will close on us.

MEHMET: How do you know?

TURNA ALİ: While coming with Yani, we saw that people were gathering. We can't tell friend from foe. They stopped talking as we passed by.

MEHMET: I've promised those men.

TURNA ALİ: Those men can be helped in a different way, in an even better way.

MEHMET: I've promised, I'm bound.

TURNA ALİ: There in the wilderness our words are valued more.

MEHMET: I can't go back on my word.

TURNA ALİ: To be the fear in the heart of the villain and the hope in the heart of the oppressed is better for you than to be governor of Aydın.

MEHMET: [*Hesitantly.*] I have also made a promise to Fatma. "Wherever you are, I'll find you and I'll marry you," I told her. She's here, Ali.

TURNA ALİ: I know. We'll take her, and we'll go together.

MEHMET: Where to? To the mountains? What can a woman do in the mountains? I've chosen my way, Ali. I don't want to hold anyone here. Whoever wants to can stay with me; whoever prefers to go can go.

TURNA ALİ: I'll stay since you've chosen to stay.

[ŞERİF HÜSEYİN *appears at the doorstep.*]

ŞERİF HÜSEYİN: [*At the door.*] I've come because I heard you said your door is open anytime to anyone. May I come in?

MEHMET: [*Shocked.*] You?

ŞERİF HÜSEYİN: [*Enters.*] I've been very wrong toward you, very guilty, very unfair. I intend neither to deny it, nor to look for an excuse. I'm not going to say, "I've done you wrong, forgive me," either. It's enough of a disgrace to come to you; however, I deserve that.

MEHMET: What do you want?

ŞERİF HÜSEYİN: I've been sent by the town notables. After all, we've been acquaintances for a long time. They have sent me so that you can first try on me what you're going to do to them.

MEHMET: [*Grits his teeth.*] There's a pledge I've made concerning you.

ŞERİF HÜSEYİN: [*Smiles sardonically.*] Then I'll tell them that the *efe* has made a pledge concerning me.

MEHMET: Them . . . [*Gnashes his teeth.*] They should never get caught by me.

ŞERİF HÜSEYİN: Tchk tchk tchk! That doesn't conform to your sense of justice.

MEHMET: You! You! You are protected by an angel, but they . . .

ŞERİF HÜSEYİN: They do things the way people did before them, so do I.

MEHMET: Goddamn it! I promised I'd forgive you. During a moment of madness when I felt overjoyed, I promised to release you.

ŞERİF HÜSEYİN: [*Still mocking.*] Because they don't have lovely daughters . . .

MEHMET: [*Fighting himself.*] I promised to forgive not only what you have done, but also what you will do.

ŞERİF HÜSEYİN: Because they don't have their own Fatmas . . .

MEHMET: How easy it was to promise at that instant, how very simple. It was even necessary in a way; it was essential.

ŞERİF HÜSEYİN: [*Teases slyly.*] It was easy, wasn't it? It is. It's always easy to make a promise. Do you understand me now? Do you see now how I was unable in any way to live up to my word?

MEHMET: But I haven't promised the others. Don't let them appear before me.

ŞERİF HÜSEYİN: But you have . . . the promise you made about me saves them as well. You can't condemn them for the same crime for which you forgive me. It would be the greatest injustice.

MEHMET: Are you the Devil, you? Where have you come from? What for?

ŞERİF HÜSEYİN: I'm going, I'm going. Only, now that I'm here, let me remind you. I've made a promise, you know, to the hero who would defeat the wrestler of the bey of Arpaz. I'll keep that promise. If you like, we can start the preparations for the wedding. [*Exits.*]

MEHMET: My God! Even at the first step! Even at the first step! [*Without paying attention, goes and sits down in the governor's chair.*]

Scene 2

[*Two months later. A room in* MEHMET OF ATÇA's *mansion in Aydın. A door on the right leads to the bedroom. Dawn is breaking in crimson outside the windows. In the semi-darkness,* MEHMET *is seen sitting by the window. His pipe looks like an ember moving from his hand to his mouth and back.*]

FATMA: [*Comes out of the bedroom with a lamp in her hand.*] You woke up early again. [MEH-MET *does not reply, just smokes his pipe.*] You're very nervous these days. [*Again* MEH-MET *does not reply, smokes his pipe.*] Have I done something to hurt you? [MEHMET *shakes his head no.* FATMA *approaches* MEHMET, *strokes his head.*] What's the trouble? [MEHMET *is silent, smokes his pipe.*] Won't you even tell me?

MEHMET: [*Sighs.*] Have you ever had that feeling?

FATMA: What feeling?

MEHMET: As if you've flown down an abyss with no bottom . . . a never-ending abyss. When you reach the bottom, you'll be shattered to pieces, but the abyss is fathomless. It never ends.

FATMA: I'd like you to dream much sweeter dreams when you're with me.

MEHMET: [*Nervously embraces his wife; presses his head to her belly.*] I've got no time, Fatma, got no time. No time for sweet dreams, no time to love you. Each instant takes me a little farther away from you. [*Strokes his wife's belly.*] I haven't got the time to wait for nine months. See to it that I have my son in my lap as soon as possible.

FATMA: [*Smiling.*] Are you sure it's going to be a boy?

MEHMET: [*Still nervous.*] It will be a boy. It's got to be a boy . . . I want it to be. Plus, I want it right away, very quickly, tomorrow. I want it today.

FATMA: [*Strokes her husband.*] You're so impatient!

MEHMET: No one gives me a chance, Fatma. A merciless hunter is chasing me. Maybe I'll have no tomorrow.

FATMA: [*Startled.*] Why are you talking nonsense?

MEHMET: I want to see my son at least once before I die. [*A shudder goes through his body.*]

FATMA: I've never seen you like this, you're shivering.

MEHMET: It's not fear of death, Fatma; it's fear of going, leaving all my deeds half done. I married you, I couldn't love you enough to get satisfied. My son keeps growing in your belly, and how slowly. I knocked down many things, but I haven't had the time to put up new ones, to remove the debris. I look at those who started out with me. Their troubles, their problems, grow by the day. You think I can't find time for you because of them. They suppose that I can't take myself away from you to devote any time to them. And I know that danger is close by, perhaps behind that crimson dawn.

FATMA: [*Frightened.*] What are you saying?

MEHMET: Danger is so close, it has cast a spell on me with its snake eyes. I can't move.

FATMA: Is there something you know, then?

MEHMET: The sultan has appointed İbrahim Pasha, the former governor of Aleppo, as the governor of the subdivisions Hamit and Teke.

FATMA: What's that to you?

MEHMET: A renowned vizier such as İbrahim Pasha would not be sent there for no reason.

FATMA: But you haven't done anything against the sultan. You wear yourself out everyday from morning till evening to protect the rights of both him and his people.

MEHMET: I have appointed myself as the governor of Aydın, haven't I? That's called treason in the sultan's terms. No matter what I do in any way whatsoever, I can't absolve myself. It's true that I send to His Majesty what I collect to the penny from the people in accordance with the law. However, in this way we have ignored another of his rights, the right to appoint whomever he likes to any office.

FATMA: Would he find anybody fairer than you for this office?

MEHMET: According to what's being said, İbrahim Pasha's coming as if he's conducting a campaign, picking up soldiers on the way, and even bringing a new tax officer with him.

FATMA: A new tax officer?

MEHMET: Yes, for Aydın. In my place.

FATMA: In your place, eh?

MEHMET: İlyas Ağa, son of İlyas. With imperial rescript.

FATMA: What will happen now?

MEHMET: I hear that the governor of Saruhan, Karaosmanoğlu Hacı Mehmet Ağa,[7] prepares his nephew Yetim Ahmet Ağa on the side. Down at Menteşe, Osman Ağa of Tavas is also agitating.

FATMA: Any hope?

MEHMET: None, because I can't trust the people. They would betray me at the first opportunity.

FATMA: Aren't they the people who met you with open arms? Who embraced you with joy? Treated you with great respect and love?

MEHMET: These same people are now getting ready to meet the newcomers with open arms.

FATMA: Is it not for these people that you incurred the fury of the sultan upon yourself . . . that you came up against him?

MEHMET: [*Worried.*] No, in fact I deceived these people.

FATMA: You deceived them? You?

MEHMET: Yes, me. I could not apply here the law that I practiced everywhere else.

FATMA: Why?

MEHMET: [*Looks at his wife painfully.*] Don't you see why? Have you forgotten? I promised you that I'd forgive your father . . . that I'd forgive your father not only for the things he had done, but also for the things he would do.

FATMA: [*Has understood. Covers her face with her hands.*] My God, so that's why.

MEHMET: I did not realize how that comment of mine would be binding. [FATMA *sobs.* MEHMET *absentmindedly.*] Yani is right. There atop the mountains I was a cyclone that tore down and tossed about anything it hit. I had no base. Mine was a command that was always obeyed. [FATMA *sobs.*] The biggest injustices begin with a minor injustice . . . that I've learned. [FATMA *sobs.*] The expectation of these people who met me with open arms . . . you see, don't you, why those men are right? Why I can't trust them? Why I can't turn my back on them? Because I've abused their trust. I've made their greatest enemy a relative of mine.

FATMA: [*Almost moaning.*] And his cruelty he doubled by becoming your father-in-law. [*A moment of tense silence. Then with the same weak moan.*] Isn't there any hope then?

7. *Ağa:* In this case, a high official in the administrative system.

MEHMET: There is—the mountains . . . to gather my men and go to the mountains . . . to become a whirlwind with no base, nowhere to stop, no weight again. Once I lean my back against the mountains, then I will have no fear. Mountains know no betrayal. My unfairness did not affect the mountains.

FATMA: [*Straightens up with hope.*] Then what are you waiting for? [MEHMET *remains quiet, his eyes on his wife's imperceptibly swollen belly.* FATMA *unconsciously moves her hand to her belly and, moaning, collapses next to* MEHMET.]

[*All of a sudden, nervous and agitated blows strike the door.*]

TURNA ALİ: [*Calls from outside.*] Open, Efe! It's me, Turna Ali.

[MEHMET *sends* FATMA *away with a sign; lets in* TURNA ALİ.]

[*Steps inside.*] Everything's finished, everything's ruined. Yetim Ahmet Ağa raided Turgutlu, left no one alive, and now comes against us with the same speed.

MEHMET: [*Getting dressed in a hurry.*] What are you saying? Where did you get the news?

TURNA ALİ: Çakmakoğlu Şecereli brought the news, together with the few who ran away and saved their lives.

MEHMET: What about Çakmakoğlu Mehmet?

TURNA ALİ: He was among the fallen.

MEHMET: Those who barely save their lives from a calamity think that what they've left behind is the Flood. Couldn't this be the case now?

TURNA ALİ: They say two cannons incessantly bombard the city. Not differentiating between men and women or children or the elderly. Not differentiating between the guilty and the innocent.

MEHMET: [*Meanwhile getting dressed.*] Let's go. [*They exit.*]

[*The stage remains empty for an instant.* ŞERİF HÜSEYİN's *head soon emerges through the door where they left.*]

ŞERİF HÜSEYİN: [*Calls.*] Fatma! [FATMA *enters, her face very pale, her eyes red.*] You've heard, haven't you? [FATMA *nods yes.*] I'd gone down to wash, and I unintentionally heard their talk. Afterward I saw them go out and leave.

FATMA: We're ruined.

ŞERİF HÜSEYİN: First, there's chaos; you can't see anything at all. The thing to do is not to be seen in that commotion. Later the tumult will quiet down. It will become clear who's who. Until then we'll find a place to take shelter.

FATMA: What about Mehmet? Are we to leave him in the lurch?

ŞERİF HÜSEYİN: Where can we possibly put him—with that gang of bandits? He'd give up his own head, but not the rebels'.

FATMA: Would you expect him to leave them?

ŞERİF HÜSEYİN: A high mountain is never clear of mist or snow, my girl. He was always to big for any place. He thought a man becomes great by striking and crushing. He'll always draw lightning.

FATMA: That's not the way you talked yesterday.

ŞERİF HÜSEYİN: But I thought like that. I didn't think otherwise even for one moment. The world wasn't left to Sultan Süleyman . . . so should it be left to a bald rascal from Atça?

FATMA: You forget, Father, that he's still my husband. We have been tied to one another with your consent and by God's command.

ŞERİF HÜSEYİN: Heaven forbid! I didn't turn my daughter over to that fellow of Atça by my own free will and consent! I had to. I shall make that clear in my petition.

FATMA: Petition? What petition?

ŞERİF HÜSEYİN: In the petition I'll write immediately and leave with Osman Bey. I'll explain in detail under what conditions I had to give my beloved daughter to that bald villain of Atça. The fellow came, appointed himself by force as the governor of Aydın, called for me, and said, "If you're going to give your daughter, give her; if you don't, then I won't be responsible for what happens."

FATMA: [*Rebelliously.*] Shame, Father, shame! If he had signaled just once, I'd have run to him. He knew that, yet he would have thought that signal a disgrace. You, me, we, it's going to be people like us who'll cause his death. He used to know that, he did, but still he wasn't able to save himself from us.

ŞERİF HÜSEYİN: [*Sternly.*] Shut up!

FATMA: [*Grows impatient.*] If it's necessary, I'll tell this to the sultan. I'll say we are the blackest writing on his forehead. I'll say that if there's any stain on his life, it's because he's touched us.

ŞERİF HÜSEYİN: [*Slaps her.*] Shut up, harlot!

FATMA: [*Remains quiet for an instant, then in a calm tone.*] I'm not coming with you, Father. I'm not going to leave my husband. It's God-given matrimony. I'm his not only for his better days, but for his black days as well.

ŞERİF HÜSEYİN: You know the end that awaits him, don't you?

FATMA: I do.

ŞERİF HÜSEYİN: He asked for that.

FATMA: [*Rebelliously.*] Now that's a lie. They called for him, saying, "Come save us from these bandits." The ones they called bandits . . . the ones they called bandits . . . [*Stops, her eyes on her* FATHER.]

ŞERİF HÜSEYİN: [*Grabs her by the arm.*] Come on! You're coming with me while the roads are still open.

FATMA: [*Shakes her arm free.*] No use, Father. I'm closer to him than to you. I'm not only his wife, but also the mother of his child.

ŞERİF HÜSEYİN: [*Frozen on the spot for a moment.*] His child?

FATMA: Yes, his child. His son. If I live after him, I shall live for that because he ordered it. I'll raise the child like a storm, too; I shall send him to the mountains like his father . . . like a cyclone.

ŞERİF HÜSEYİN: [*Holds his daughter by the arm and pulls her.*] You fool! They'll tear that bastard out of your belly with a bayonet. Come with me!

FATMA: No! You go now and write your petition. Speak as ill of my Mehmet as you please. Say he was a scoundrel . . . say he was a drunkard, a bully, a bloodsucker, a rapist. Say, "I was scared, that's why I gave my daughter to him." Say, "I knelt before him and implored him to forgive me." Say anything you like. Only leave me alone so I can grieve for my brave husband.

ŞERİF HÜSEYİN: [*Drags her.*] If it's necessary, I'll take you by force.

FATMA: [*Shakes free of her* FATHER's *hand, reaches the door with one leap.*] You won't be able to, Father. I'm going to him right now. I give you ten minutes. After ten minutes, I won't hold him to his oath. You have only ten minutes, not a minute more. [ŞERİF HÜSEYİN *rushes forth to catch* FATMA, *but she flees through the door like a wild gazelle.*]

ŞERİF HÜSEYİN: [*Hurriedly looks for pen and paper and settles down to write.*]

To our Lord, the Sultan, the Refuge of the Universe:

I, having been subjected to the wickedness of the evil man named Bald Mehmet of Atça, of unknown parentage, apostate of God and the Prophet, belonging to a set of drunkards and hooligans, and thereby was forced to marry my beloved child, my daughter Fatma, to him. Your servant Şerif Hüseyin, born in Atça and the former headman of Atça . . . casting myself at your feet imploring, I declare that . . .

Scene 3

[*The governor's mansion in Aydın. A small council has assembled.* MEHMET, ÇAKMAKOĞLU ŞECERELİ, CRAZY YANİ, TURNA ALİ, *and* PALABIYIKOĞLU *are standing.*]

ÇAKMAKOĞLU ŞECERELİ: [*Speaks excitedly.*] Why are we standing still? What are we waiting for? What is it we're expecting? Yetim Ahmet Ağa crushed Mehmet in one blow. My brother was not to be crushed easily, but he got crushed. What are we waiting for, then? [*There is a moment of tense silence. All eyes turn to* MEHMET *at once, but he is sullen and silent.*]

CRAZY YANİ: Şecereli is right. We must make a decision right now. I see two options before us. The first is to get out of town to confront those approaching. That means to die fighting. The second is to take to the mountains. The mountains will safeguard us. Until we gain strength, I say, let's take the second.

TURNA ALİ: I agree with Crazy Yani. We got trapped in this goddamn Aydın and made a great many enemies. We can't turn our backs to these men. And those who are coming are the sultan's soldiers, with artillery and rifles and all that.

ÇAKMAKOĞLU ŞECERELİ: [*Angrily.*] So my brother died in vain; he died unjustly. I thought so. He wasn't my brother only; he was your brother, too. Having thought so himself, he remembered all of you even while dying. He sent his bravest men to inform you. Could it be that your friendship turns back at the doorstep of death?

PALABIYIKOĞLU: We're faced with two roads. Crazy Yani and Turna Ali point to this road . . . but Çakmakoğlu Şecereli to that other road. What does our *efe* think, let's hear what he has to say. [MEHMET *is silent. At that moment he is like a sleepwalker. It is not clear whether he understands what is being said. They wait tensely for a while.*]

ÇAKMAKOĞLU ŞECERELİ: I thought the news of death that I brought you would make you go out of your minds, but I see that everyone is more sensible than usual. As far as I'm concerned, for me the nicest death isn't that which comes the latest; it's the one that lifts a mountain off my back. Excuse me. I won't be patient like you. As soon as I get out of here, I'm going to gather my men, and I'm going to attack the first troops that come along.

CRAZY YANİ: True, our minds don't listen to our hearts. But your heart doesn't listen to your mind. What good will this death serve?

ÇAKMAKOĞLU ŞECERELİ: [*Places his hand over his heart.*] To still the ache here. To me, you're killing time for nothing. You take care of your own affairs. [*Walks to* MEHMET, *is about to grab his hand.*] With your permission, Efe! [MEHMET *says nothing, but holds* ŞECERELİ's *temples with both his hands, bends him down, and kisses his forehead.* ŞECERELİ *stops right in front of the door, walks back, and addresses everyone.*] Don't forget me, good-bye now. [*Turns suddenly and exits with brisk steps.*]

PALABIYIKOĞLU: [*Behind him, regretfully.*] We couldn't stop him, too bad.

TURNA ALİ: We couldn't have.

CRAZY YANİ: He has enough venom in him to poison a whole mountain.

PALABIYIKOĞLU: Let's go over the situation once more now. İbrahim Pasha and İlyas Ağa came from the north, from the direction of Saruhan and Turgutlu . . . Osman Ağa of Tavas from the east, from Denizli . . . Turgutlu, Bayındır, and Ödemiş are out of our hands. Tire was vacated by Çakmakoğlu Şecereli. On this side Nazilli, Köşk, and Kuyucak are still in our possession. If only Yörük Ahmet could last until we get there.

TURNA ALİ: [*Affectionately.*] Yörük Ahmet will hold out.

PALABIYIKOĞLU: In that case, we must act right away. We must hold onto Kuyucak before Osman Ağa of Tavas gets there.

TURNA ALİ: We'll take Yörük and from there take to the Madran Mountains [*Turns to* MEHMET.] What d'you say, Efe? [FATMA *enters just at that instant.*]

FATMA: [*Pale as a corpse.*] My father . . .

MEHMET: He ran away? He ran away the moment he smelled danger? [FATMA *nods yes.*] He must have tried to force you, too, as he was fleeing . . . so that you would run away with him. [FATMA *nods yes.*] Are you sick? You look very pale.

FATMA: I'm scared. If they kill you, what do I do?

MEHMET: [*Turns to* TURNA ALİ *at once.*] What were you saying just now?

TURNA ALİ: I was saying that if we get going right away, we'll reach Kuyucak before Osman Ağa of Tavas, take Yörük with us, and then take to the Madran Mountains.

MEHMET: [*Calm and decisive.*] I say let's scatter right away, here and now. Let's not appear together. [*Turns to* TURNA ALİ.] You take the word to Yörük. Whenever Osman feels himself secure and strong, he'll begin to relax.

CRAZY YANİ: [*Furiously.*] Are you crazy? Do you want to dissolve all your power like a bar of soap?

MEHMET: I don't think it suits me to hem and haw. I'll speak very openly. I'm not in a situation to engage in combat right now. [*Moves his eyes to his wife's barely swollen belly.*]

CRAZY YANİ: [*Harshly.*] For all this time, you've used us. You've shoved us into death, you've pushed us into fire. Wherever you've pushed us, we've closed our eyes, we've gone. Now the day has come for us to push you into the fire.

TURNA ALİ: [*On his face the soft look of the love he feels for* MEHMET.] Efe is about to become a father, Yani. He wants to gain time so that he can leave his wife and child in trustworthy hands.

CRAZY YANİ: When a man has reached your rank, he must be able to leave his personal troubles behind . . . he must be able to rise above love, love for child, sorrow for a brother, favor for a friend, all of those things. Otherwise, he'll commit a terrible error.

MEHMET: [*To everyone.*] I know I've taken a very heavy responsibility upon myself. Maybe you think I don't feel the weight of the load I carry.

CRAZY YANİ: What did I tell you during our first meeting at Kuyucak, do you recall? "You're the one who does the things I wanted to do, but couldn't." Then you asked me, "Are you alone?" Why did you ask that question?

MEHMET: It's very difficult to be alone. Only God can endure it.

CRAZY YANİ: You also have to endure it; you have to.

MEHMET: It's easy to talk that way in your position.

CRAZY YANİ: [*Having softened a bit.*] The love felt for a beautiful woman was an excuse, Son. What was real was not the love itself; it was its impossibility. The real reasons were those that made you rebel against that impossibility. It was the fate that set apart men as rich or poor, noble or common, prosperous or destitute. The real thing was the villain's whip. In order to open your eyes, to make you see what kind of a world you live in, to fill up your heart with that sacred fury, to lead you here and there like a storm, God used a small, beautiful woman as an excuse.

MEHMET: I wasn't even hoping for this much. [*His eyes on* FATMA.] To be able to see her without being seen, to be able to say her name without letting her hear, to be able to live in her shadow, in her darkness, that was the happiness I could dream of, only that much. Then I happened to find myself in a whirlwind. I drove men to death; it's my turn now, I know. What I'm doing is not putting off my turn, believe me.

CRAZY YANİ: The way a blacksmith takes a piece of molten metal and, pounding, makes it into the shape he chooses, so God has turned you into live fury. That's the real thing.

MEHMET: I disappointed you. Forgive me.

CRAZY YANİ: History does not forgive. Nor does it accept your excuse. History looks at the result. If you're the winner, whether you're right or wrong, fair or unfair, treacherous or honest, whatever you may be, it will reserve its most glorious pages for you. If you are the loser, it will pay no heed to those human feelings you bear in your heart and will say, "The Bald Hound of Atça was crushed."

[FATMA, *having controlled herself with difficulty until then, sobs.*]

MEHMET: [*Pulls her to him.*] I'm staying with you. I have but one life to give to the empire, and I'll pay that when the time comes, but not now. Not before making sure you and my son are safe. [*Addresses everyone.*] Nobody should be offended; I can't do otherwise.

CRAZY YANİ: History will forgive neither Şecereli's impatience nor your delay. I can't be part of such stupidity any longer.

MEHMET: [*Turns to* TURNA ALİ *and* PALABIYIKOĞLU.] What about you? Do you also think like Yani? [TURNA ALİ *looks at him with his kind and friendly eyes and smiles.* PALABIYIKOĞLU *frowns, bows his head, and remains silent.*]

CRAZY YANİ: They can't abandon you because they're bound to you not through their reason, but through their hearts.

MEHMET: And you? What was it that tied you to me, Greek?

CRAZY YANİ: My hope was far greater than theirs. I used to dream we would set out to discover a new world with you. I used to tell you of the beauty of that world, remember?

MEHMET: [*Absentmindedly.*] How can I not remember? A world where people are equal, where they're friends, they're brothers. Yet there's no such world.

CRAZY YANİ: There is such a world, there must be. If it doesn't exist, it must be created!

[*The sound of two cannon shots.*]

MEHMET: [*Suddenly assumes his* BALD MEHMET OF ATÇA *appearance, extends his pistol to* FATMA.] Take this; give it to my son! [FATMA *sobs.*] Hush! Don't cry! Tell him . . . tell my son I did not give it to him to keep as a souvenir. If he is going to follow me, he should step more carefully where I've stumbled. Well, good-bye. Now, into the heart of the fire! [*Rushes out. The others follow him.* FATMA *sobs.*]

[*Sounds of cannon shots rumble across the stage.*]

CURTAIN

◆ ◆ ◆

Old Photographs

DİNÇER SÜMER

Translated by Talat S. Halman

An Editor's Note

Major Turkish awards have traditionally tended to bypass plays that are not easily comprehensible. Dinçer Sümer's *Eski Fotoğraflar (Old Photographs)*, whose subtleties and sudden veerings baffle audiences, stands as an exception: it won the coveted prize for best play from the Turkish Language Society within a year of its premier by the State Theater in 1976 and before its publication in book form by the Ministry of Culture in 1978.

The play, full of inexplicable twists and characters in transformation, made its appearance as a Turkish response to the theater of the absurd. On the Turkish scene, the 1960s and the first half of the ensuing decade saw productions and publications featuring the work of Eugene Ionesco, Samuel Beckett, Edward Albee, Harold Pinter, and others. The *mysterium* of the absurdist vein fascinated some of Turkey's playwrights and large segments of theatergoers. Dinçer Sümer (b. 1938), as a burgeoning talent, tried his hand at this new mode and came up with a considerably successful and stimulating specimen. His two characters undergo surprising metamorphoses in the course of the play. Their identities, diverging from their old photographs, seem to be caught in flux. *Old Photographs* is thus a drama of often perplexing transmutation. The two protagonists are pitted against each other because of the breakdown in human communication and the animus born of empathy subverted.

Sümer ranks as one of Turkey's notable living playwrights. He holds a degree from the drama department of the State Conservatory in Ankara. For four decades, he was an actor and director with the State Theater. He also served as chief cultural advisor to the president of Turkey.

Author of film scripts and radiophonic plays, Sümer received many prizes for his work in both genres. Among his awards are one for a short story and one for a children's play (from the Arts Board of the Turkish National Parliament). Sümer has also published four volumes of poetry, two novels, and two collections of short stories. In this first decade of the twenty-first century, he has been conducting long weekly television interviews with Turkey's well-known cultural figures.

Some of Sümer's major plays, including *Old Photographs*, have been produced extensively in Turkey and in some cities abroad, especially in Germany.

The translation is by Talat S. Halman, whose biography appears on pp. 369–70.—TSH

Characters

WOMAN

MAN

ACT I

Scene 1

[*A hotel room. Entrance at center stage, door to the toilet on the left. An old iron bedstead, a dressing table, a chest of drawers, a wooden table, a flowerpot with a carnation on the table, a chair, and an open suitcase on the floor. Multicolored, beaded costumes with sequins are haphazardly thrown on the bedstead, on the back of the chair, and on nails in the wall. Transistor radio, telephone, photographs stuck in the edges of the mirror, bottles of medication and alcohol, tubes of lipstick, boxes and jars of face powder and face cream, illustrated magazines, novels, a dazzling wig, and shoes are scattered about. On the wall hangs a variety-show poster with the name "Sevtap" on it. The naked bulb hanging from the ceiling casts a deadly pallid light over all these objects.*

There is nobody on stage. On the radio, the song of a popular female singer who has a ruined and ponderous voice. A knock on the door.]

WOMAN: [*Off stage.*] Is that you, Seyit?

MAN: [*Off stage.*] It's me, Sister.

WOMAN: [*Off stage.*] Door's open.

[*The* MAN *enters. He is twenty-two years old, thin, and pale. He is wearing a busboy's outfit—black pants and white jacket.*]

MAN: [*Looks around.*] Sevtap, Sister, where are you?

WOMAN: [*Off stage.*] In the john.

[*The* MAN *sits down, making gestures that show a familiar pattern, and waits. With his hands on his knees, head bowed, he quietly listens to the radio. The toilet is flushed with a racket, then the* WOMAN *enters. She is old and burned out. She is wearing an old housecoat, and her hair is disheveled.*]

I got diarrhea—up here and down there. I'm in awful shape.

MAN: Well, you don't seem to be ready.

WOMAN: Let those pimps wait.

MAN: Veli Bey said you should go there at once. The nightclub is jam-packed tonight. Full of cotton farmers.

WOMAN: [*Sits in front of the mirror.*] All right, all right. See, I'm getting plastered. Uggh! Look at that face; it's like a festering sore.

MAN: The waiters are dead tired running back and forth carrying drinks and hors d'oeuvres.

WOMAN: [*Wearily.*] Good. [*Takes a cigarette from the small table.*] Light it up for me.

MAN: [*Jumps up, lights the cigarette.*] Veli Bey said: "Have her come at once."

WOMAN: Stop that or I'm going to curse the hell out of Veli Bey. [*Coughs as if she is about to choke.*] Give me a bit of something to drink. Seyit, hurry . . .

MAN: [*Rushes, pours water into a glass.*] Here, Sister, drink.

WOMAN: Not water . . . [*Points to the bottle of brandy on the table.*] Give me some of that. A bit of brandy . . . [*Cannot speak because of the cough.*] Like two little fingers . . .

MAN: [*Walks toward the toilet.*] I'd better get rid of this.

WOMAN: [*Doubled up and coughing.*] Pour it on the carnation. Into the flowerpot.

MAN: [*Turns back, pours the water into the flowerpot, and puts brandy in the snifter.*] Here, take it, Sis.

WOMAN: [*Gulps it down; she is out of breath.*] There's a lump right here over my heart. Like a piece of rock. It'll take me away with a bang some day.

MAN: [*Sincerely alarmed.*] God forbid.

WOMAN: Who cares—forbid, morbid! [*Puts a touch of lipstick on her lips.*] That ought to do it. [*Rises.*] As soon as I put that wig on my head, I'm done. [*Puts the wig on. Takes her nightgown off.*] Turn round.

MAN: Sister, if you like, I'll wait outside.

WOMAN: What a cheat you are!

MAN: What do you mean?

WOMAN: [*Laughs.*] Turn your back!

MAN: [*Turns his back.*] Why're you laughing?

WOMAN: [*Puts on her show costume.*] Nothing.

MAN: [*Uneasily.*] What do you mean "nothing"?

WOMAN: Stop bullshitting and come out with it! Why do you think Veli Bey slapped you across the face?

MAN: [*Stammers.*] I mean . . . I . . .

WOMAN: Attaboy . . . Now you're talkin'.

MAN: [*Perplexed.*] What has that got to do with this?

WOMAN: Well, you were doing some fancy footwork there for a while, saying things like "I better go out" and stuff like that. As if you couldn't care less about all that.

MAN: About what?

WOMAN: Like adjusting the mirror in order to peek.

MAN: [*Looks away from the mirror.*] Nothing of the sort.

WOMAN: [*Laughs.*] Look here, baby, I wasn't born yesterday!

MAN: So?

WOMAN: [*Laughs.*] Never mind. If the Devil were here, even he couldn't hoodwink me. Come over and fasten this.

MAN: [*Shyly tries to fasten the bra.*] You're like an older sister to me, you know.

WOMAN: How about Hicran? The songwriter?

MAN: [*Caught red-handed.*] Sister, I swear on everything sacred to me . . .

WOMAN: You said to her, "I yearn for you, I burn for you." You said, "I sigh for you, I die for you."

MAN: I never said that.

WOMAN: You did. You camped at her door and screamed, "I want you, I need you."

MAN: That's a lie.

WOMAN: She told us herself. Then she said she complained to Veli Bey about you. And Veli Bey . . .

MAN: [*Astonished.*] She told you, huh? That's what she told you, is it?

WOMAN: [*Looks for one of her shoes.*] Where's that shoe?

MAN: [*Sulks.*] That's not the way it happened.

WOMAN: [*Looks under the bed.*] Seyit, come and look for it, too.

MAN: Uh?

WOMAN: [*Points to the shoe on her foot.*] I mean, look for the other shoe. Come on, look around.

[*As both of them look for the shoe, only the radio is heard.*]

RADIO: Here's our news update. Representatives of the major states express optimism about the initiatives for permanent world peace. It has been disclosed that the United States used a million and a half tons of napalm bombs in the Vietnam War. Deaths due to cholera in South Asia and famine in Central Africa are rising every day. Weather forecast: plenty of sunshine all over the country. And now for your listening pleasure: light music.

[*Light music on the radio.*]

WOMAN: That's it. Over there . . . under the bed, all the way down.

MAN: Step back, Sister, I'll pick it up.

WOMAN: [*Straightens up, shakes the dust off her hands.*] Uggh! This place is covered with dust two inches thick. [*Coughs.*] This is no hotel. It's a breeding ground for spiders. [*Coughs as if she is choking, staggers, and collapses on the bed, face down.*] Seyit, give me a swig of brandy.

MAN: [*Gets up with the shoe in his hand.*] Sevtap, what's the matter, Sister?

WOMAN: [*Exhausted and panting, she points to the bottle of brandy.*] Give me that . . . quick . . . [*Writhing.*] I'm dying . . . I got something right here . . . [*Takes the bottle that Seyit holds out and drinks.*] Oohh, my God. God, how marvelous!

MAN: Sister, if you like, I'll go get you a doctor.

WOMAN: I don't want a doctor. I'm OK. It'll be gone in a minute. [*The phone rings.*] Would you get that?

MAN: [*Answers the phone.*] Hello? . . . Yes, sir. . . . She's here. . . . It's me, Veli Bey. . . . We're on our way. We were about to leave . . . when suddenly Sevtap became . . . I mean . . . [*Turns to the* WOMAN.] He wants you.

WOMAN: Give it to me. [*Takes the receiver.*] Hello? . . . Hi. Lower you voice. Don't shout . . . good . . . I'll be there in five minutes. . . . All right, I got that. You don't have to holler. Hey, look here, it's OK, I got it. [*Puts the receiver down.*] Just because I'm a few minutes late, that pimp's in a dither. Sure, the patrons keep asking about Sevtap. Sure, they're anxious to have me. [*Takes a cigarette.*] Light this, will you?

MAN: Sister, let's go, what do you say? He cursed bad on the phone.

WOMAN: [*Suddenly feels important.*] Light it!

MAN: [*Lights the cigarette.*] He was swearing real bad. He swore at my mother.

WOMAN: I know all about that dog. I've known him so many years, damn it. He knows that if I get mad and split, he's going to be in bad shape; he knows that for sure. If I leave, his nightclub will go to the dogs. I have my own clients there; there are those who are head over heels in love with me, ready to die for me. I am Sevtap, after all! Sevtap with the almond-shaped eyes! If I want to, you know, I can get them to sell their land, divorce their wives. I can douse the fire of their family hearth. Aah, if I want to, I can have them shoot other men dead. In my day, I made so many lords and gentlemen kneel before me. You saw how he panicked just because I'm a few minutes late. [*Pleased with herself, she sips her brandy.*] Oohh, my . . . if I wanted to . . .

MAN: [*Skeptical and restless.*] Sevtap, Sister, finish your cigarette . . .

WOMAN: Sit down, you! You're a leech. Stop grumbling! What's your duty supposed to be? To take Sevtap from the hotel to the nightclub and return her to the hotel. To carry her suitcase, to hold her coat.

MAN: [*With a vague anger.*] He swore at my dead mother.

WOMAN: Well, if you let him slap you across the face yesterday, he is sure to cuss your mother today.

MAN: I didn't do anything to him.

WOMAN: [*Laughs.*] Sure you did, and how! You were playing footsie with the new girl, weren't you? What's her name? Hicran or something?

MAN: I wasn't playing footsie!

WOMAN: You're all the same—dragged from the same gutter! [*Drinks brandy.*] You think I don't know it, huh? Look here, they don't call me "Sevtap" for nothing! When I do my number, I look around: damn it, not one man looks into Sevtap's eyes, into those almond-shaped eyes. The whole bunch of them are glued to my belly and hips. [*Drinks.*] You know what happened once right here in this room? A man who used to be the director of . . . whatchamacallit sat in that chair and cried his eyes out. You know what he was begging for? [*Breaks into laughter.*] Nooo, not for that. That lunatic was maybe a hundred years old. He was crying and begging me to give him my worn panties as a gift.

MAN: [*Frozen.*] Sevtap, let's get going, Sister.

WOMAN: And one day a blond boy who had drunk a bit of cheap booze dashed into my room brandishing a knife. "Heeeeyy," he was shouting, "I'm going to stab the hell out of you." He was a good-looking kid, real nice looking. I could tell he was a greenhorn. The way he kept crowing and crowing, I broke into laughter. I said to him, "Shit," I said, "you milksop, is this what you're after? OK, take it!" I got undressed and stood there naked from top to toe. Whaddya know, his eyes became like two saucers. He stood there stunned; he couldn't move his hands or feet. "Come," I said, "come on!" That mollycoddled boy was shaking like a leaf. I took a few steps toward him. He dropped the knife and ran out. [*Laughter.*] That's it, that's the way it happened! [*Takes the knife from the top of the dressing table.*] See, I've been keeping it right here since that day. [*Puts the knife down and picks up the snifter.*] So, Seyit, my boy, you think it's easy being Sevtap? My life is a novel, damn it. [*Sighs.*] Ooooh! Ah! [*Screams at Seyit, who is absentmindedly mauling the carnation.*] Take your hands off my carnation!

MAN: [*Pulls his hand away.*] Sevtap, we ought to get going.

WOMAN: [*Gets up.*] Let's go. [*Looks in the mirror.*] There, that's Veli Bey for you—that clown. Just because I'm a bit late, he goes bananas. The pimp! [*Drunk, cheerful.*] Sure thing, I'm the queen of that nightclub, damn it. Hey, wait. Tonight I'll put on more makeup. [*Puts rouge on her cheeks.*] And I'm gonna put on eye shadow. I'm the woman who's had directors, military police commanders, and cotton kings as her slaves. I'm not like the other girls at the nightclub. They're all half-baked. They're like tin. The new girls are all ninnies and nincompoops. Neslihan and İnci and the others. All they do is giggle, as if a spring up here has gotten loose . . . hee-hee-hee, hee-hee-hee. And they rub against the customers' legs under the table. [*Angrily.*] I'm the only woman who has never let a customer lay a hand on her during drinks. But I know how to make conversation, and I know the soul of a man. The new girls gulp two glasses of Scotch—and blop, like jello, they fall on the johns' laps—ready to fly!

MAN: [*Tense.*] Sister, let's go.

WOMAN: I could have done the same thing—go around in taxicabs, sleep in nice hotels. But nooo, there are some birds you can't eat. [*Gets angrier.*] I might not be a paragon of virtue, but I am a brave woman . . . well, I'm my own person . . . [*Convulses, presses her hands on her chest, writhes with pain.*] Aaah. There . . . again . . .

MAN: [*Runs over and holds her.*] Sister! Sevtap!

WOMAN: It's like the tip of a dagger goes in and comes out right here.

MAN: Your face turned white—white as a sheet of paper.

WOMAN: [*Panting.*] Right here. I got something in here. Lay me down on the bed for a minute.

MAN: [*Puts her on the bed, reaches out to turn the radio off.*] I better shut this off.

WOMAN: [*As if frightened.*] Don't turn the radio off! Keep it on!

MAN: [*Puzzled.*] We're not listening anyway.

WOMAN: Never mind. It's a voice, it's a sound—some sound in the room.

MAN: [*Curls up his lips incredulously.*] OK, then play on!

[*Pause. Only the music on the radio is heard.*]

WOMAN: I'm chilly. Cover me with that coat, will you?

MAN: [*Puts the coat over her.*] Sevtap, Sister, if you're sick . . .

WOMAN: [*Resists, as if she is holding out against something.*] No, I'm not sick. I suddenly got this chill, that's all. It'll go in a second. This isn't a hotel: it's an icebox. I could have slept in fancy hotels with central heating. I could have jumped into bed with that Erol who sells PX goods . . . then I would have been able to go around in a fur coat.

[*Pause. Music is heard.*]

MAN: [*Fearful.*] You know he might swear at my dead mother again . . .

WOMAN: Be a real man, and don't let him! [*Shivers, bundles up.*] I've got the chills again.

MAN: We're awfully late.

WOMAN: No, we're not. The stage is mine at quarter to one.

MAN: There are lots of customers tonight. All cotton farmers.

WOMAN: Never fear, Sevtap's here. I'll talk to Veli Bey.

MAN: I just don't want to get into a fight with anyone. I'm not going to stick around, anyway.

WOMAN: You're not?

MAN: I filed my petition to work in Germany.

WOMAN: Everybody is crazy about working in Germany! What sort of shit have they got there?

MAN: [*Apologetically.*] I'll go there.

WOMAN: [*Stares at him for a while.*] Seyit.

MAN: [*Snaps out of his thoughts.*] Yes?

WOMAN: Where are you from?

MAN: From Alacabel. About two hours from here.

WOMAN: Why did you come here? Because it's the big city?

MAN: No.

WOMAN: Why, then?

MAN: [*Nervously looks away.*] No reason.

WOMAN: Don't you have anyone?

MAN: I have an older brother.

WOMAN: Sooo?

MAN: I'll go to Germany first—then I'll bring my brother over.

WOMAN: Has your hometown dried up?

MAN: [*Tense.*] Dried up. [*Looks her straight in the eye.*] Dried up.

WOMAN: [*Thoughtful for a while.*] Oh, God . . .

MAN: What?

WOMAN: [*Irritated.*] Something just occurred to me.

MAN: What's that?

WOMAN: [*Frees herself from her thoughts.*] Nothing, nothing. [*Laughs.*] That's good, good. There you can lift yourself up by your bootstraps. You can get yourself a German girl, too. Like Hicran, a blondie! Boy oh boy! [*Straightens up, rises.*] Why're you opening your eyes wide like that? Isn't that the truth? If you had the field to yourself, you would have given it to her real good! Come on, put the coat on my shoulders! Why're you sulking?

MAN: That's not how the story goes.

WOMAN: [*Not believing him, she laughs.*] To hell with it. Hold my coat, OK?

MAN: [*Crushed; agonizing over being misunderstood.*] Sevtap, I swear on everything that's sacred to me . . . it isn't like that.

WOMAN: [*Turns around, picks up her handbag.*] How is it, then?

MAN: I didn't make passes at her. Or at anyone.

WOMAN: You mean she's lying?

MAN: I don't know.

WOMAN: You mean to tell me that out of the clear blue she made up all those stories to slander you? Don't tell me Veli Bey beat you up because of a tall tale?

MAN: I said to Hicran . . .

WOMAN: I get the picture. Never mind. Hold my coat. Let's go.

MAN: [*Saddened.*] Sevtap, Sister . . .

WOMAN: Shit on your Sister Sevtap!

MAN: I said to Hicran . . . I said, "Let's go away."

WOMAN: Where to?

MAN: [*Finds it difficult to answer.*] Wherever . . .

WOMAN: Then?

MAN: Look, Sevtap . . . Veli Bey is going to sell her . . . to the cotton growers . . . to the PX man. He'll sell her, I know it.

WOMAN: So why does that bother you?

MAN: Sister . . . [*Writhes.*] I . . . It's been only four days since Hicran came here—Tuesday, Wednesday, Thursday, Friday.

WOMAN: [*With interest.*] Don't talk as if you're crying. OK?

MAN: The night she came—she got drunk. She threw up. She was covered with puke all over. Veli Bey said to me: "Take her to her hotel and put her to bed." I did. I cleaned her up, washed her hands and face. I put her to bed. Just as I was leaving, she started to cry. "Esen," she kept saying, "don't leave me, Esen, hold my hand!" I said: "Miss Hicran, I'm not Esen." She kept weeping and mumbling. She was tossing and turning in her bed. Tears were rolling down her cheeks. "Kill me and then go," she was saying. "Esen, shoot me before you go!" If I were to leave her alone, I knew she would bang her head against the wall or the iron bedstead. I got so flustered. Leaving her alone would be the wrong thing, I thought. I held her hands, or else she would have flung her body all over the place. She put her arms around me and kissed me. Kept kissing. Finally, she was exhausted, spent. She passed out. I sat beside her and watched for a while. I felt pity and pain. It was a weird feeling. Sevtap, she was so beautiful. The way she slept, you'd think she was a baby or an angel. Wednesday and Thursday went by, but I just couldn't drive her image out of my mind. Her lovely face kept staring at me. I was unable to sleep. Last night I went to her hotel to get her. I had bought her a gift— a belt—and I had written a letter to her. I held out my hand to give her the belt and the letter. And I tried to tell her about my problem. My tongue and throat were dry, like parched soil. I just couldn't tell her. She opened the package, looked at the belt. "What's this?" she said. "For you," I said. She suddenly began to scream: "Fuck you, fag!" That's what she said. She cussed me up and down. Later, it turns out, she went and complained to Veli Bey. And then Veli Bey . . .

WOMAN: [*Touched, feeling sorry.*] Seyit, you were asking for it, goddamn it. Man, you're a real gonner . . . head over heels in love.

MAN: [*Bows his head.*] I don't know.

WOMAN: Damn destiny. I spit on its face.

MAN: Veli Bey's going to sell the girl. I know it, he's going to sell her.

WOMAN: [*Crushed, dejected.*] He's already sold her.

MAN: [*Devastated.*] Whaaat?

WOMAN: You have my sympathy, Seyit! In this game, you gotta make sure that your skirt doesn't get caught in the machine. I just hope it will turn out all right.

MAN: [*Moans.*] Oh, damn! My, my, my . . .

WOMAN: All right, get the things, let's go.

MAN: [*Mumbling.*] Her face was like a rose. She looked immaculate as she slept. She was like an angel, so lovely.

WOMAN: Oh, Seyit, I used to be lovely, too. I was a beauty myself. [*Pulls some of the photographs out of the edge of the mirror.*] Look at these! Is that me in these old photos? Take a good look! Just look at this one here. [*Holds out one of the photos.*] The one with the blond hair—that's me. My hair was long and vibrant; it flowed all the way down to my waist. I was that girl with the glittering eyes.

MAN: Who's the other one?

WOMAN: My older sister.

MAN: And who's that man? Why are his eyes gone in the picture?

WOMAN: [*With a vengeance.*] My sister's husband. I held a quilting needle into the fire and then stuck it through his eyes.

MAN: [*Bewildered, looks at another photo.*] Sevtap, who's this?

WOMAN: Satılmış. [*Gets angrier.*] Bedri is the guy in this photo. [*Shows another photo.*] This is Numan Bey. [*Holds out another.*] And that's Erol.

MAN: [*Taken aback.*] That's fine . . . but all of their eyes . . .

WOMAN: [*With a bizarre rigidity.*] I drilled holes into all of them! One day, all the demons inside me made me do it. I went berserk; I grabbed a quilting needle. I held it over the flame of the gas range until it was red hot. I spread the photos over the floor . . . [*Seems delirious.*] I pierced their eyes one by one! [*Clutches her chest.*] All those eyes . . . aaa-aah, that pain again! [*Writhes, staggers.*] Right in here! Like the tip of a knife. [*Retches.*] Aaagggh . . .

MAN: [*Drops the photos.*] Sister! Sevtap!

WOMAN: [*Retching, she runs to the toilet.*] Aagggh!

[*As the* MAN, *stunned, bends toward the photographs scattered all over the floor, the telephone rings. Frightened and helpless, he picks it up.*]

MAN: Hello? . . . Yes? . . . Who did you say is calling? . . . From Istanbul? [*Turns toward the bathroom.*] Sevtap, telephone! Istanbul. [*Into the receiver.*] Hello? [*Shouts.*] Say that again? . . . Who? . . . Miss Sevtap? Yes, she's here. Who's calling? . . . Who did you say? . . . Suna? Who? You're her daughter? Miss Sevtap's daughter? You mean, she's your mother? Just one moment. [*Puts the receiver down and walks toward the bathroom.*] Sevtap, telephone . . . from Istanbul . . . she says she's your daughter!

[*Waits for a short while, picks up one of the photos, and looks at it.*]

Scene 2

[*The home of the older sister and her husband. The living room of the ground floor of an old wooden house in a poor neighborhood on the outskirts of a major city. On the right, a door that opens onto the street; on the left, the bedroom door. A window in the center. Two wooden chairs, a table, a sofa with a calico cover, a chest of drawers with a mirror, a bulky old-fashioned radio set. A summer night.*]

The WOMAN *is ironing on her knees and singing along with the folk song on the radio. She is seventeen years old and beautiful, with long blond hair and a fully developed, lively body.*]

WOMAN:

You're my cinnamon, my clover;
Why are you so full of fury?
You're my tall and handsome lover:
You're just right for me, made for me.

[*The* MAN *enters. He is twenty-five years old and unemployed. He is the nervous type. He seems a little drunk. Although he has a devil-may-care attitude, from time to time he has fits of anger or becomes tense or explosive.*]

MAN: [*Pinches the girl's cheek.*] How about a nice pinch for your brother-in-law?

WOMAN: [*Pushes his hand away.*] Stop that!

MAN: Look here, Sis, you'll make me give you a piece of my mind!

WOMAN: You haven't got much of a mind to give.

MAN: Did that bastard show up?

WOMAN: He did. He wants two hundred more.

MAN: Cash?

WOMAN: [*Tries to look elsewhere. Evasively.*] I don't know.

MAN: [*Walks over to the bedroom door, opens it, and shouts into the bedroom.*] What's with you, Wifey? [*Gets mad when there is no answer.*] Why're you staring like a sheep, damn it? [*Turns to the* WOMAN.] Just look at her. Just look, huh? The way she's staring. [*To the bedroom.*] Hey, you bitch, I ought to cut your damn head off with a buzz saw!

WOMAN: [*Tries to calm him down.*] Calm down, will you!

MAN: [*Closes the bedroom door; angrily paces the floor.*] You know there's a demon in me that says go ahead, crush all the flowers, dump all the rags, send everything up in smoke!

WOMAN: Come on, what's eating you? There's no reason for all this. Let her do what's she's doing.

MAN: Damn it, that's no work, what she's doing! Making flower decorations for candy boxes!

WOMAN: They pay her half a buck for each one. That isn't bad. Besides, would it be better if she sat around doing nothing?

MAN: Yeah, that'd be better because this way, for every half a buck's worth of work she does, she brags a buck's worth. [*Shouts in the direction of the door.*] Bitch!

WOMAN: [*Fed up.*] Look, listen to me, enough is enough!

MAN: Someday I'm going to pack up and go. No, I'll just split! [*Looks for a cigarette.*] You got a cigarette around here?

WOMAN: No. [*Something occurs to her, and she gets up.*] Just a second. There should be cigarettes somewhere. [*Finds a pack in one of the chest drawers.*] Here you are.

MAN: [*As he takes the cigarette, he holds the girl's hand.*] If you weren't here, I swear to you, I wouldn't stay here one moment. If you weren't . . .

WOMAN: [*Brusquely pulls her hand back.*] Let go. Don't start up again.

MAN: Nurcan, look here, girl . . .

WOMAN: [*On the verge of an outburst.*] Goddamn . . . goddamn it.

[*The* WOMAN *goes back to her ironing. She is fuming. The* MAN *just stands there, his eyes transfixed on her. He puffs on his cigarette. On the radio: a slow melody played on a simple string instrument.*]

MAN: Oohh, my goodness! [*Pause.*] I went and spoke to the captain at the restaurant. [*Sneering.*] He says three hundred a week. Honest, I'm not gonna work for that! Damn it, am I anyone to work for a measly three hundred?

WOMAN: [*Belittling him.*] Then how much are you worth?

MAN: Careful, Sister . . .

WOMAN: Three hundred is nothing to sneer at. In a month, it adds up to—you know how much. Besides, it's a job—and you'd have regular hours. [*Points to the bedroom.*] That poor woman would be happy. She might even crack a smile.

MAN: I'd have to see it to believe it. All these years I've never seen her smile.

WOMAN: Well, after all, you ruined her happiness right from the start.

MAN: It was she who did that to me.

WOMAN: Don't say that. My sister loves you.

MAN: Too bad—I don't love her.

WOMAN: In that case, why did you marry her?

MAN: Of all the stupid things to do!

WOMAN: My God, what sort of a man are you?

MAN: This sort.

WOMAN: Listen to me, please. Can't you and I have an honest-to-goodness talk?

MAN: Let's do that, dear. Go ahead!

WOMAN: You, you've got to believe me. My sister is unhappy, very unhappy.

MAN: She's got no other skill. Every day she's unhappy three or four times and moans and weeps three or four times.

WOMAN: What's going to happen, then?

MAN: We'll go on as long as we can—and then when the time comes, it'll snap!

WOMAN: Why don't you sit down and have a nice friendly talk?

MAN: Oh, sure! Look, I can talk to this wall here, but it's impossible to talk to your sister.

WOMAN: What makes you the way you are? You never care about anything, never want to get along with anyone.

MAN: [*Rises.*] I'm going.

WOMAN: Stay a while. Let's talk.

MAN: I've got work to do.

WOMAN: No, you don't. I wish you had.

MAN: [*Feels cornered.*] I've got plans of my own.

WOMAN: No, you've got nothing. No plans, no projects. And that's why all hell breaks loose around here.

MAN: You'll see. Soon, you're gonna see. I'm gonna have such a great setup . . . you'll go bananas when you see it.

WOMAN: [*Smiles wearily.*] Oh, yeah, we know all about it. An artists agency.

MAN: I tell you: I'm gonna be the representative of the most beautiful singers, nightclub girls, and the like. I'm gonna sell packaged programs to nightclubs and casinos. I'm gonna have my own office with a walnut desk. I'll have armchairs. And my goons will stand guard at my door . . . the king of the agencies: Agent Cavid!

WOMAN: [*Upset.*] Stop!

MAN: Man, I'm gonna have real power! All those famous singers who get top billing will stand at attention in front of me. They'll move only when I say "Giddyap!" You're talking about money? I'm gonna make bags of money.

WOMAN: [*Restrains herself with difficulty.*] Yeah, you'll be riding in a Peugeot and smoking fancy cigarettes . . .

MAN: [*Lost in his dreams.*] My revolver in my hip pocket . . . I'll be wearing sunglasses. Heaven knows, I'll be king. The king!

WOMAN: Look, you're my brother-in-law . . .

MAN: [*Delighted, he begins to make a pass at her.*] My brother-in-law!

WOMAN: [*Steps back.*] You're incredible! My God, how can anyone let himself go this way? How can anyone have such flights of fancy?

MAN: I can fly. They don't call me "Cavid" for nothing. I'm waiting for the day I'll spit in the face of this world. [*Furious at something.*] You'll see, it won't be long now.

WOMAN: [*In the direction of the bedroom.*] Oh, my poor, unlucky sister.

MAN: There's anger in me. I want revenge. I've been slapped so hard that it hurts me more and more every day. I let them call me the pimp's bastard. I carried coats and suitcases for two years. Because of some good-for-nothing, I melted like wax. I was so bird-brained. But just you wait, as the world turns and turns . . .

WOMAN: [*Perplexed.*] What do you mean?

MAN: Heaven knows, I'm gonna make them pay me back the youth I squandered. I've got faith in God's justice. He'll give me the power to do it. Someday I'm gonna correct the error.

WOMAN: Error? What error?

MAN: My father's error, the Halil family's error, Veli Bey's error, Blond Hicran's error, Sister Sevtap's error . . . my own error . . . your error, your sister's error . . .

WOMAN: [*Seems frightened.*] Are you awfully drunk?

MAN: Things went wrong at the core. The root was rotten.

WOMAN: I just don't know what you're talking about.

MAN: It's the same with me, at least for now. I can't figure it out.

WOMAN: OK, then, who are the people you've mentioned? What have they got to do with us, with you, with my sister?

MAN: Let me tell you . . . the connection . . . everybody turns into a speck of dust and vanishes into thin air, but then falls into the bottom of the same pitch-dark well. After that, there's no holding on, no way of making it. You stammer, your sister moans, I use big words . . . on and on it goes.

WOMAN: It's my sister I'm worried about. She loves you.

MAN: There, that's the mistake: you love your sister, your sister loves me . . . and I love you.

WOMAN: You're talking nonsense.

MAN: [*Cornered; sincerely.*] I do love you. I swear on everything that's sacred to me. I'm in love. I love you.

WOMAN: Stop, I beg you, say no more. If my sister overhears . . .

MAN: [*Nonchalantly.*] So what?

WOMAN: Scandal . . .

MAN: [*Goes near her.*] Let's say she doesn't hear anything.

WOMAN: [*Doesn't get it at first; when she does, she snaps back at him.*] Damn you! What do you think I am? Do you take me for a . . .

MAN: A what?

WOMAN: [*Implores.*] I beg of you! I'm so sick of this, I could die!

MAN: Damn it, what can I do? I love you, that's all.

WOMAN: [*Sits on the sofa and sobs.*] One of these days, I'm gonna throw myself under a truck and rid myself of all this.

MAN: It'd be better if she, the one in there, would do that.

WOMAN: You're vile, you're . . .

MAN: Why's that? What use is she to anyone? Is she worth two bits?

WOMAN: She's your wife. Your wife.

MAN: [*Laughs.*] Did you ever see it with your own eyes?

WOMAN: How can you say things like that?

MAN: When your mother gave birth to her, your sister was stillborn. She was born dead. She's hard as a rock. Nothing.

WOMAN: Shame on you. You should be ashamed of what you're saying. It's sinful.

MAN: Is it her sin or mine?

WOMAN: I think I'm gonna pack up and leave this house.

MAN: I won't let you. You can't go anywhere so long as I'm here!

WOMAN: [*Cries.*] It's as if . . . I've got the feeling that all these things are happening because of me.

MAN: Well . . . in some ways.

WOMAN: Bald, blind, lame . . . no matter, I'll find someone to marry, and I'll go away at once.

MAN: I'll shoot the bastard.

WOMAN: Oh God, my God . . .

MAN: Don't pin your hopes on the man upstairs. He doesn't concern himself with such matters anymore. He says everyone's on his own.

WOMAN: Don't say things like that, or else God might strike you.

MAN: I've been struck enough, and I've become warped. Now I'm trying to get straightened out.

WOMAN: Look, this will lead us nowhere in the end.

MAN: It was no good in the beginning, either. It's best to dance to a new tune from now on. Best to blow a different whistle. Best to stop banging on the stupid kettledrums and to march to a different tune.

WOMAN: [*Determined.*] I am leaving this house. You'll see.

MAN: Where can you run away to?

WOMAN: [*Helpless.*] Eh? God is great.

MAN: [*Laughs.*] But the boat is small.

WOMAN: [*Stands before him, looks as if she has received an electric shock.*] You're very ugly, you're contemptible, you're vile . . . you're a dirty rat.

MAN: You're very beautiful, very warm like sunshine.

WOMAN: You're horrible, just horrible.

MAN: [*Puts his arms around her.*] I love you.

WOMAN: [*Struggles to free herself.*] Leave me alone. Your looks, your words, your face disgust me. Let go of me!

MAN: You're lying. You have a crush on me. You're in love with me.

WOMAN: [*Struggling.*] I wish to God you'd die. I hope you die soon. Drop dead.

MAN: [*Holds her tight.*] Why must you hide the truth? Why are you afraid of reality? If it weren't for her in there . . .

WOMAN: [*Cries.*] Please, for God's sake, leave me alone.

MAN: Let's call her out and have a talk. We'll tell her she can keep living here. Let her pick up her flowers and rags and come over to this room, to the sofa. You and I will move into the bedroom. We won't leave her high and dry or hungry.

WOMAN: You're out of your mind.

MAN: Everyone in his place. We could have a neat arrangement here.

WOMAN: Stop, I tell you. I beg you, let go. She hears us.

MAN: Sure she does. She's been hearing all along. Don't worry, she knows I'm in love with you. I've told her a thousand times. A thousand times. Why isn't she opening the door? Why does she turn her eyes away from this truth that's clear as day? Why is she scared of an easy arrangement?

WOMAN: [*Exhausted, weeps.*] Stop. Be quiet . . .

MAN: I want a woman who breathes, makes love, gives birth. A woman who has longings, who cuddles, who murmurs her love even in her sleep . . . a vibrant, lively, lustful, throbbing woman. And I want a bed that heartens you, a bed out of which you rise with vigor every morning. That's how my days would be bright with zest. That's how I would rise and come to grips with whatever work I must do. If I am a loveless, tired, jaded, bewildered, aimless person . . . if I am an ugly drunkard, is it all my fault? I have never had a chance to sit at a table with an immaculate white cloth, a table where bright, smiling people have their meals together. Whenever I saw two people hand in hand in parks, in cabs, on the seashore, my heart was filled with envy, anger, and fury. Because one thing was absent from my room, my hallway, my kitchen . . . something was missing. That thing was never there. [*Gently strokes the girl's hair.*] It was always missing. It was never there.

WOMAN: [*Lets herself go; sobs.*] Oh, my brother-in-law.

MAN: [*Softly.*] Now take a good look at me! Am I really awfully ugly? Am I disgusting? Horrible? Tell me.

[*The* WOMAN *collapses into the chair. She is exhausted. She covers her face with her hands and weeps quietly. The* MAN *walks over and opens the bedroom door.*]

[*Talks into the bedroom.*] That's the way it goes, my friend! Come on, you say something, too! Speak! [*When there is no answer from the bedroom, he walks up to center stage, weary and crushed.*] I wish I had never known that blond girl who cried in her sleep. I wish I had not let myself be dragged behind her. Maybe if I had been able to go to Germany. Who knows?

Scene 3

[*The waiting room of a train station in a southeastern city. Two wooden benches, a clock on the wall, and a timetable. A few city lights are seen through the window.*

The clock shows 4:30. Outside, occasionally torrential rain. A chilly night. The MAN *is asleep on one of the benches. He has a mustache and stubble. He is wearing a German-made trench coat and has a cap on his head. He looks about twenty-five.*

As the lights go on, the whistle of an approaching train is heard. Then the train grinds to a halt, although its huffing goes on.

The WOMAN *enters. She is pale, timid, and tired. She is holding a suitcase and wearing an old woolen jacket. On her head she has a kerchief. Bewildered, shivering, and scared, she sits on the edge of the other bench. She looks as if she is sitting on a bed of thorns.*

The sharp whistle of the train is heard as it pulls out. The MAN *jumps to his feet, grabs his suitcase, and begins to run out. Just then, he drops a revolver on the floor. The* WOMAN *reaches down and picks it up, and as she is on her way out, the train whistle is heard again. The* MAN *comes back. He is at the exit. The* WOMAN *hands him the revolver.*]

MAN: [*Stammers.*] This . . . revolver . . .

WOMAN: You dashed out . . . that's when you dropped it.

MAN: [*Takes the revolver.*] It wasn't the train I was waiting for. [*Puts the revolver in the pocket of his trench coat.*] I hadn't noticed you.

WOMAN: I've just arrived. On this train. You were asleep.

MAN: [*Takes out a pack of imported cigarettes, pulls one out; just as he is about to light it, he holds the pack out to the* WOMAN.] Would you like one?

WOMAN: I don't smoke.

MAN: [*Squeezes his cigarette, looks intently at the* WOMAN, *then . . .*] Where are you traveling to?

WOMAN: I've arrived . . . here.

MAN: Are you from here?

WOMAN: No.

MAN: Have you any relatives here?

WOMAN: None.

MAN: [*When he gets a negative answer.*] In that case, I beg your pardon.

WOMAN: Excuse me?

MAN: I know there was no reason to ask. Forgive me.

WOMAN: [*Nervously.*] I mean . . . I . . .

MAN: Yes?

WOMAN: This is my first visit here. I've come to work.

MAN: To work?

WOMAN: That's right. [*Has difficulty coming out with it.*] I'm a singer.

MAN: [*Skeptical.*] Is that right?

WOMAN: I sing folk songs. [*Shivers, coughs, bundles up.*] I'm a beginner.

MAN: It's freezing here! Why don't you go to a hotel? So long as you're going to stay in this town . . . there's a new, fairly large hotel.

WOMAN: I don't know . . . I will soon . . . after daybreak . . .

MAN: [*Rises to his feet, points to a place out the window.*] It's only a few steps from here. There, you can see the lights. [*Pause.*] I'm saying that because I see you're shivering.

[*The* WOMAN *is restless and fidgety. She takes a pack of cheap cigarettes out of her handbag and lights one clumsily. The* MAN *watches her with interest.*]

I thought you said you didn't smoke? [*Pause.*] What's your name?

WOMAN: [*With a sudden outburst of anger.*] Why do you ask?

MAN: [*Stammers.*] Well . . . you said you're a performing artist . . . I just wanted to identify . . . I'm interested in singers and folk songs.

WOMAN: [*Trembling.*] No, I'm not a singer. I'm not. I lied.

MAN: [*Taken aback.*] No, I mean . . . I . . .

WOMAN: That's enough out of you!

MAN: [*Takes a step toward the* WOMAN.] Believe me, I meant well. I just asked casually.

WOMAN: [*Steps back and shrivels up.*] Don't come near me! Don't touch me! Go away from me, or I'm going to scream. Don't come near, or I'll holler at the top of my lungs.

MAN: [*Stunned and scared.*] Be quiet! Don't shout!

WOMAN: [*Agitated.*] Why do you ask? Why does it concern you? I'm not taking an interest in you, am I? Who are you, anyway? Why are you here? What's your name? And that revolver of yours? Tell me, have I asked you any questions about all that? Did you kill a man? Are you a fugitive? Are the cops after you? Do I ask you questions? Have I inquired about the gun?

MAN: [*Perturbed, he picks up his suitcase and heads for the exit.*] Please stop. Calm down, I beg you. If you want me to, I'll leave at once. Keep quiet, I'm leaving.

[*Holding her head with her hands, the* WOMAN *crouches and convulses as she weeps. The* MAN, *bewildered, becomes immobile.*]

WOMAN: [*Sobs for a while, coughs as if she is choking, then calms down.*] Please forgive me . . . I'm being silly . . . I'm so tired, so exhausted. My nerves are shattered. I've gone without sleep for two days.

MAN: [*After a pause.*] I'm not a fugitive.

WOMAN: [*Softly.*] It doesn't concern me, anyway. I've been indiscreet.

MAN: I've frightened you, haven't I? I mean . . . is my face very . . . ?

WOMAN: Very what?

MAN: Scary?

WOMAN: [*Looks like a child, then smiles.*] Nooo. [*Pause.*] What are you going to do with it?

MAN: Huh?

WOMAN: The gun?

MAN: [*Evasively.*] Oh, nothing.

WOMAN: Nothing? You mean you carry it as a decorative piece, for show?

MAN: I know what I'm going to use it for.

[*Thunderous music. Rain becomes torrential.*]

WOMAN: [*Extremely curious.*] For what? [*Waits.*] Why did you stop speaking? [*The* MAN *walks over to the window and looks out. The* WOMAN *searches for something in her handbag.*] Are you from here?

MAN: From a village two hours away.

WOMAN: [*Takes an envelope out of her handbag and hands it to him.*] Do you happen to know this man . . . and this casino?

MAN: [*Reads what is written on the envelope, then looks at her intently.*] What do you want this man for?

WOMAN: That's where I'm going to work. They told me to give this envelope to him.

MAN: Who are they?

WOMAN: They said to take this letter, hop on the train, go there, and start working at once.

MAN: [*Almost scornfully.*] Have you ever worked at such places?

WOMAN: No. This'll be my first time. They said, "You have a real nice voice, go there, start working."

MAN: [*As if he is about to spit.*] Is this what you call being a singer? I know that god-awful place.

WOMAN: [*Feels crushed, full of doubt.*] What sort of place is it?

MAN: Stop giving me that innocent-girl routine!

WOMAN: [*Doesn't get it.*] Excuse me?

MAN: [*Angered.*] Damn it . . . [*Throws the letter in her lap.*] Damn, what's it to me, anyway? Take your letter back!

WOMAN: But I . . . I mean, to you . . .

MAN: I know the likes of you. You girls are a dime a dozen. Do you know Blond Hicran?

WOMAN: Who's Blond Hicran?

MAN: A whore if ever I saw one!

[*The* MAN *goes back to the window. The* WOMAN *seems frozen and shriveled up, her head bowed and her eyes dead. She keeps twisting the envelope in her hands. Rain keeps coming down hard.*]

Where's that goddamn train? [*Looks at the* WOMAN; *is remorseful and jittery.*] What a blockhead I am. You're not my mother or my sister. What do I care? In this dog-eat-dog world, everyone should take care of himself. This shitty world! Everyone has his own problems. I'm making an ass of myself. [*Without looking at the* WOMAN, *he offers her a cigarette.*] Never mind, light a cigarette!

WOMAN: [*Takes the cigarette and sighs.*] Never you mind!

MAN: In muddy waters, everybody clings on to some bushes so they don't drown. Never mind.

WOMAN: I've never been able to cling.

MAN: [*Points to the envelope.*] That's what you're clinging on to.

WOMAN: I decided I'm not going there.

MAN: The heart is its own king: do whatever your heart tells you to.

WOMAN: I don't want to go there.

MAN: It's a shame. You're a beautiful woman. They've ruined you.

WOMAN: No one has done anything to me.

MAN: [*With pity and contempt.*] Never mind, I tell you.

WOMAN: I swear on the Koran . . .

MAN: Drive that worry out of your sweet mind. It just doesn't concern me.

WOMAN: I'm not talking about it because it concerns you. It's just so.

MAN: [*Points to the envelope and laughs.*] There, you're already on the right track!

WOMAN: [*Looks at the envelope.*] I want to go back.

MAN: [*Doesn't care.*] Go back. No one's stopping you!

[*The* WOMAN *tries to say something, but cannot. She feels helpless, stuck, besieged. The* MAN *goes over to the other bench and leans against it. He bites his fingernails. Pause.*]

[*Without looking at the* WOMAN.] Go back! Don't hesitate, go! Whatever it is—your father's armchair or your mother's lap—return to it. Don't give it another thought. At whatever point you turn back, you profit. Just like the way you came, hop on the train and go back! I know the place that bastard Veli Bey, who's name is on the envelope, operates. There, they sell female flesh for a few pennies a pound. They don't care if you're crying your eyes out; they still sell you. You'd be ruined altogether. That casino has reduced so many poor girls like you to nothing. Return to home and hearth! [*Looks at her.*] Are you twenty yet? Well, just about, huh? Go back, I tell you, go back to your hometown, to your family!

WOMAN: [*Icily.*] If I had a place to return to . . .

MAN: Have you no one?

WOMAN: No one.

MAN: Someone who'll give you shelter, some friend . . .

WOMAN: Not a soul.

MAN: Where were you living before?

WOMAN: With my older sister.

MAN: So why don't you go back to her?

WOMAN: I can't . . . I won't.

MAN: Did you have a falling out?

WOMAN: No.

MAN: So?

WOMAN: [*Overwhelmed.*] It's a long story . . . my brother-in-law . . .

MAN: He doesn't want you?

WOMAN: [*Shuts her eyes.*] He wants me!

> [*The* WOMAN *is unable to speak; she only looks and trembles. The* MAN *takes his trench coat off and puts it over her shoulders. They gaze at each other, eye to eye. She suddenly begins to sob. She cries as if she is choking. She uncontrollably drains herself. He stares at her intently. A train whistle is heard from afar. He goes to the exit and looks out. She has found the gun in the pocket of the trench coat, takes it out, and holds it to her throat.*]

MAN: [*Comes back, sees what she is doing, and screams as if he is out of his mind.*] Stop that! Drop it! Hand it to me!

WOMAN: I'm fed up . . . I want out!

MAN: Drop it, I say! You're out of your mind!

WOMAN: I want it to end. I want to fall into the bottom of that black well.

MAN: Stop! Don't do it! Drop that gun!

WOMAN: I want it to come to an end! What's the use of living? I'm all alone, sleepy, hungry. I have no hope, no confidence.

MAN: No! You're going to go back. Hand me that gun!

WOMAN: I can't . . . I have no place to return to. I don't have the strength to get on that train. I don't have a ticket.

MAN: Is that any reason to take your life? How can you give up and suffer defeat this way? You'll see, everything will get better. Drop that!

WOMAN: [*Determined.*] Don't come near me. Don't come close. Let this come to an end.

MAN: [*Scared.*] Stop! Don't touch that trigger! One bullet—and everyone will rush in here. I've got a lot of things to do. Don't make life difficult for me. I've got plans.

WOMAN: Plans?

MAN: [*In a frenzy.*] I implore you. Don't do it! Listen to me. You're a lovely girl, you're young. You had a bad time of it for a few days. You went hungry for a couple of days. You have no money . . . but all that is no reason to . . .

WOMAN: No. It's because I'm lonely, because I'm without love, without any strength, because I'm afraid of getting tossed out of a black well like a speck of dust.

MAN: Coward! It's easy to pull the trigger, but you've got to resist, fight, and win. You must topple and crush those who are shoving you and dragging you. Hand me that! Don't make the people out there crowd in here. What's dying, after all? To survive by putting up a fight is the best way to live. Give me my gun! I reached where I am now all the way from the farthest corner of Hell. Look, I've been on the road for ten days. I have plans, things to do. Give me the revolver!

WOMAN: [*Bewildered and skeptical.*] Are you going to carry out your plan with this? With a gun?

MAN: With a gun. I've been traveling ten days. I came here with my pain, my fury, my vengeance. In ten days, my blade was sharpened ten times. That's how I came here.

WOMAN: To kill?

MAN: I have my revenge to take. Give me the gun!

WOMAN: [*Mumbles.*] How strange . . . oh my God, how weird . . .

MAN: Weird?

WOMAN: Stand back! [*Aims at him.*] Sit down!

MAN: [*Stunned.*] Look here now, what are you saying? Are you out of your cotton-pickin' mind?

WOMAN: Sit there!

MAN: [*Sits.*] Soo, now what?

WOMAN: Speak up! Tell me!

MAN: What?

WOMAN: About your coming here to kill . . . and the reason for it . . .

MAN: Give me my gun.

WOMAN: Later. First tell me all about it. Speak!

MAN: [*Perplexed.*] I'm gonna kill . . .

WOMAN: Who are you gonna kill—and why?

[*Pause. Thunder. Lightning outside the window.*]

MAN: I had one older brother. To me he was like father, grandfather, everything. There's a blood feud in our village. They shot my father when I was still in the cradle. Nobody knows why. It's something that goes way back to my forefathers and to the ancestors of the Halil family. When a male gets married and a son is born to him, the father is killed that very night. But it's like a seesaw—first, one victim on our side, then one on their side. When I came back from military service, I had a fear in my heart. "This is wrong," I said; "it must not go on this way." I said, "This mistake ought to be corrected once and for all." I went to see the elders of the Halil family, I kissed their hands, I begged them. I pleaded with them to end this bloodthirstiness. I said, "Is there anything better than peace in the world?" They said, "It's our turn now. We'll exercise our right—then, we'll consider it." I said, "Look, I'm prostrating myself before you; I'm extending my hand to you." They didn't utter a sound. Only my older brother and I had survived. I said to my brother, let's run away and settle somewhere else. He said, "I won't abandon my father's grave, my father's land to others." I could see no other way out, so I decided to go to Germany to work there. I came to the big city and registered as a worker for Germany. At that time, I had a job for a short while at Veli Bey's casino. One night a blond girl in a hotel room . . . [*Pause.*]

WOMAN: Why did you stop?

MAN: Anyway . . . well, my number came up, and I went to Germany. I'll earn good money, I was saying, I'll become strong—and talk my older brother into coming to live with me in Germany. Last fall I got word that my brother was married. In that foreign country, I started having sleepless nights: I was gripped by unbearable anxiety. During the day, it was as if I was in a dungeon, at night in Hell. I wrote letters to the Halil family and other village elders. Hoping to put an end to this hatred, I donated money to the village school and a transistor radio to the village meeting room. I mailed everyone greeting cards for Islamic holidays and for New Year's. I rejoiced because I thought that the dead-wrong tradition had come to an end, thank God. "Hurray for brotherhood and harmony," I shouted. Last month I received a letter from my brother, who wrote: your nephew is about to arrive into the world; you'd better get a gold bracelet for your sister-in-law. I went out and bought the gift. I was convinced there was no more blood feud, but ten days ago another letter came. It was our family's turn, and on the night my nephew was born, Yunus from the Halil family shot my older brother. I headed here at once. My brother's grave beckoned me. Now give me my gun. I've told you everything.

WOMAN: [*Hands him the gun, picks up her suitcase, and rises to go.*] Pity . . .

MAN: Pity whom? Me?

WOMAN: I don't know . . . pity something or a lot of things. Just a while back, I had felt some strength in me for the first time—a light had begun to flutter in my heart. I said to myself, "Here at last is someone who speaks the truth and who upholds what is good and heroic. Someone unlike the others. Someone who has the power and the faith to live and let live." What a pity! I had for a moment found the hope that not all the branches we can cling to had dried up, that not all of the fireplaces that give us heat had gone out. Pity . . . [*Walks toward the exit.*] Pity . . .

MAN: Where are you going? It's cold out. It's raining, too.

WOMAN: To the new hotel. It's only a few steps away. Isn't that what you said?

MAN: But still . . .

WOMAN: I'll show the letter and say I've come to work at the casino.

MAN: Sit down. Wait until daybreak.

WOMAN: Would twilight be better?

MAN: Sit.

WOMAN: [*Weary.*] Just a couple of steps away. I'll shiver, close my eyes, and nearly freeze as I take those two steps . . . then I'll find myself in the middle of the fire. I'll have tea. I'll have them bring me breakfast—butter and honey and cheeses and toast and milk. I'm destined to be defeated, isn't that right? After taking a couple of steps, I'll accept defeat, that's all. If the beauty of struggling is only in words, I'll free myself by giving up.

MAN: [*Stands before her.*] Stop!

WOMAN: Yes?

MAN: Don't go!

WOMAN: I'm shivering here.

MAN: Sit!

WOMAN: [*Takes a step back.*] I've got plans.

MAN: [*Confused and angry.*] I won't let you go.

WOMAN: Why not?

MAN: I don't want you to go.

WOMAN: And then?

[*Dawn is seen through the window. The rain has stopped. A train whistle is heard. The* WOMAN *and the* MAN *stand immobile, looking each other in the eye. Train whistle again.*]

This is your train.

[*The* MAN *picks up his trench coat and suitcase, goes to the exit, but stops there. The train arrives and comes to a halt, as indicated by the sounds. Nearby a rooster crows for a long time. The* WOMAN *and the* MAN *are silent and frozen like rocks. The sounds indicate that the train starts to leave the station, gain speed, and hurtle along, blowing its whistle. Outside it is getting light. The* WOMAN *sits on the bench. The* MAN *comes over and sits beside her. For a while, they sit without looking at each other. The train's whistle is heard in the distance.*]

[*The* WOMAN *shivers, bundles up.*] It's cold.

MAN: [*Wraps his trench coat around her shoulders.*] Now?

WOMAN: Fine.

MAN: [*Following a pause.*] The sun's breaking through.

[*The* WOMAN*'s eyes are closed. Her head is bowed and rests on the* MAN*'s shoulder.*]

My name's Satılmış. Yours?

[*When the* MAN *gets no response from the* WOMAN*, he turns around and looks at her. Seeing that she has dozed off, he smiles. Outside, a sunny day is starting.*]

CURTAIN

ACT II

Scene 1

[*This scene is played in the dark. Light appears only a few times when the* WOMAN *and the* MAN *lying in bed strike matches and smoke cigarettes.*]

WOMAN: Kiss me . . . once more. Kiss me again . . . [*Silence.*] I love you so much, so . . .
MAN: [*After a pause.*] I want a cigarette.
WOMAN: There should be some over there.
MAN: Here they are. Matches?
WOMAN: Let me see . . .
MAN: Just a moment . . .
WOMAN: No, don't turn the lights on!
MAN: Can't find the matches.
WOMAN: Here you are!
MAN: Would you like a cigarette?
WOMAN: Yes.

[*A match is lighted; its flame moves about and goes out. Held away from one another, the two cigarettes flicker.*]

Say something.
MAN: [*His cigarette flickering.*] I'm thinking.
WOMAN: What about?
MAN: How wonderful it is to be with you . . .
WOMAN: [*The light of her cigarette moves near his.*] I'm happy. [*The two cigarettes flash together.*] Very . . .
MAN: You are so beautiful . . .
WOMAN: I love you. A thousand times, a million times.

MAN: You're so warm . . . so soft.

WOMAN: [*Laughs.*] I'll tell you something. It'll probably make you laugh. It's a certain feeling I have. I imagine myself in a forest. It's green, so green. I'm standing under the tall trees, maybe a thousand years old. I can hear the streams, the birds, the wind. They blend together, they become deliriously beautiful. They become a long, delightful silence. I stand stark naked in that forest, surrounded by songs. [*Laughs.*] Is what I'm telling you ridiculous?

MAN: No. Tell me more.

WOMAN: [*Her cigarette flickering.*] Take me in your arms. It's as if there's a spout inside me, and water keeps running out of it. Something that was tied down, held captive, felt dead is suddenly coming alive. Can you tell me what this is?

MAN: I can't tell. It's hard to explain it.

WOMAN: This thing that's surging inside me . . . I had felt it, this gush of cool water, once when I was a child, when I was very little. My father was slender, had white hair and a pale face.

[*The melody of an old song is played on a lute, with the pick slowly articulating each note.*]

My father's eyes were huge. They were blue, those eyes. He used to play the lute at night. I used to kneel on a cushion in front of him and listen. He would play the lute, sip his drink, and tell me about Ma. His hand that held the pick was very thin, with long fingers and purple veins. On winter nights, I often dozed off on the cushion. Then my father would put his scarf around his neck, pick up his lute, and go to work. Then my older sister would clear my father's table, clean out the ashes of the stove, sit down on the sofa, and embroider. When the room turned cold, I would wake up shivering. Between dozing off and waking up, I would miss my father. That's when, in my childhood, I sensed inside me that tumultuous stream. Those days when my father would leave on a small bus for other places, I would sit at the window and watch. Other musicians and some fat women with heavy makeup crammed into that old bus and went away to tour remote cities and towns. Many days later they would come back tired and messy. My father used to hug me, press me to his chest. He used to kiss me, kiss me. One day the bus came back as usual. The musicians with all that stubble and the fat women came off. But Father wasn't there. [*Sorrowfully and desperately.*] Put your arms around me, hold me tight. Don't ever go away.

MAN: I won't.

WOMAN: You were gone three days. It seemed like three years. Don't go again.

MAN: I had a lot of things to take care of. They're done now. I won't go again.

WOMAN: I saw some furniture at the market. Three armchairs, a couch. A machine-woven green rug. They weren't too expensive. Oh, I want some flowers, too. A carnation in a pot . . . these days, houses have no gardens. That's the way it goes, what can you do?

But a carnation on the window ledge . . . we have a nice place. From our window, we have a view of the sea in the distance.

MAN: The official said: "Your marriage papers will be processed at once."

WOMAN: Take me to a restaurant after the ceremony. [*Cheerful and flirty.*] Make me drink wine, just a little, OK?

MAN: OK.

WOMAN: Look!

[*A square-shaped vague light has fallen on the other side. The window is now visible in pale yellow light.*]

Moonlight.

MAN: Moonlight.

WOMAN: I love you very much.

MAN: I love you very much.

WOMAN: Kiss me . . . you have a stubble.

MAN: [*After a pause.*] Your hair's lovely.

WOMAN: Just my hair?

MAN: Your neck, your face . . .

WOMAN: Can you see my face?

MAN: No.

WOMAN: Be sure to shave tomorrow morning. I washed and ironed your shirt. So tomorrow take me by my arm, and let's go out together.

MAN: We'll check about our documents at the marriage license bureau, then we'll go to the movies.

WOMAN: Let's do that.

MAN: We'll also take a look at the furniture you saw.

WOMAN: Three armchairs and a sofa. And that green rug. I don't know if you'll like it . . .

MAN: Radio, carnations . . .

WOMAN: A few pots and pans, knives and forks, and drinking glasses . . . that should do it.

MAN: I'll buy you an overcoat, shoes, stockings, a woolen jacket . . .

WOMAN: [*Happy.*] Oh, thank you.

[*Lute heard in the background. Shadows move on the window.*]

MAN: Are you chilly?

WOMAN: No.

MAN: Why don't you get dressed?

WOMAN: Hold me in your arms. Hold me tight. Love me.

[*Silence. Then the windowpane is shattered noisily by a hard object. A flash as a gun goes off. The* WOMAN's *terrified screams keep echoing.*]

Scene 2

[After the preceding scene, which took place in the dark, the entire stage lights up.

Numan Bey's apartment building. A floor-through apartment furnished with dazzling, expensive furniture. Glittering red armchairs, rugs, lampshades, glass tripods and tables, a small cocktail cart. Night.

The WOMAN, *who is about twenty-five, with short black hair, wearing a chic dressing gown, is talking on the telephone. She has been drinking the Scotch on the cocktail cart and is drunk.]*

WOMAN: How wonderful to hear your voice after all these years. My dearest sister, I'm so happy to hear you're well. Why're you talking to me like that? Please don't hurt my feelings. All those things you heard, they're all lies, they're wrong. What's that? Lead a more decent life? Get a job? [*Drinks.*] God knows, I've thought of that. I've tried it, too. Whoever told you I didn't look for a job? Some of them just didn't care if I happened to be decent or not. Some asked me about that and wanted to see my diploma, too. Yes, they required typing and shorthand. Oh yes, I told everything. It was a shameful thing to do, and there were times I cried. It just won't do: to weep and at the same time to tell about yourself. I swear to you, Sister. Day in and day out, I went through the "Help Wanted" ads in the papers. Some were looking for people who could speak English or French, but no one seemed interested in applicants with long hair and honor. I once got a job at a store that sold knitwear. At closing time, the boss pulled down the shutters and slipped his hand down my shirt. I screamed, cried, bit him. He sacked me. Then I became a singer. Don't say things like that, Sister, you don't know. I couldn't have returned to the family. [*Drinks.*] How's my brother-in-law? No, don't swear like that. No bad-mouthing, huh? Look, it's my birthday today. I'm home all by myself. I bought myself a present. No, Numan Bey isn't like that. What sort of a man is he? I don't know. No, he's not the way you think at all. Every day he comes down here, asks me how I'm feeling, stays a little while, then goes back up again. He lives on the top floor. No, he has no one. He owns this building. I don't know what would have become of me without him, if he hadn't taken me and my child under his wing, if he hadn't given us food and clothing. [*Affectionately.*] My baby is in the other room. I put her to sleep a short while ago. [*Drinks.*] That night, they all came running in here—cops, the people who live in this apartment building, Numan Bey. [*Cries.*] No, I am not in love with him. He lied to me. He said to me: "I'll be gone on business for three days." He went and committed murder. And that night . . . apparently, they had been trailing him, and they waited until that night. And they unleashed their fire through the window. Later, I was happy he died. A man with such hatred in his heart. [*Drinks.*] After all that fury, all that vengefulness, I decided it's useless to live and love. Never mind. Numan Bey is a nice man. He's a kind person, he's so good. [*Groping for words.*] It's not easy to understand such kindness. No, I swear to God. [*Flustered.*] I wish he would touch me, caress me, ask to make love so that I can repay him. [*Laughs repeatedly.*] Of course I want it. Sometimes I become petrified—my hands, my feet . . . I burn all over—my breasts, my groin, my belly. My sleep is so troubled. In my dreams . . . in my dreams, I keep getting raped. I wake up, I shower under ice-cold water, I take pills. Why should I feel ashamed when I tell you about this? You're my older sister, after all. I swear, there's no one. I don't even leave home. It's been quite a while since I was with people. Numan Bey is the only one . . . and the young man with eyeglasses. When I go down to see the super or someone like that, sometimes I run into him. He says "Good morning." This morning I bumped into him again. He said hello and smiled. He's the tenant right across from me. He carries books by the armful. Loneliness has gotten to me, you know. I stopped and talked with him a little bit in front of the door. He's curious about him and the night he died. I told him. What could I say? I said he was my husband. This youngster works at a factory, it seems. He's going to school, too. I said to him: "It's my birthday." I said: "I cut my hair." He said nothing. [*Drinks.*] See, I cut my hair. I got bored with long hair. [*Nostalgically.*] If I could see you only once, Sister . . . just for a minute . . . I miss you so. Sister, say something, please . . .

[*Doorbell rings.*] Wait a minute. Somebody's at the door. It's gotta be Numan Bey. Don't hang up.

[*Puts the receiver down. A moment later she returns holding a pot with a carnation. She is happy like a child. She puts the flowerpot on the cocktail cart and picks up the phone.*]

Oh, Sister, a carnation. That young man who wears eyeglasses, he brought it for my birthday. I asked him in. He wouldn't come in. Sister, it's my birthday. My carnation is so lovely. I cut my hair today. [*Drinks.*] I bought myself a birthday gift. What did I buy? Well . . . [*Holding back her tears.*] I mean . . . here, I bought this . . . this telephone . . . a toy telephone. [*Gets up; the telephone cord swings back and forth.*] What I wanted . . . [*Weeps.*] I miss you. Sister, I miss you so much. So . . . [*Drops the phone.*] so much . . .

[*Kneels beside the flowerpot, covers her face with her hands, and weeps. Music is heard in the background. Doorbell rings. With anticipation and excitement, the* WOMAN *wipes off her tears, straightens her hair, and runs to the door. She comes back with the* MAN *(Numan Bey). She has lost her excitement. Numan Bey is an old, thin man with a bulging tummy and white hair. He is carrying a large package.*]

MAN: How are you?

WOMAN: Fine.

MAN: [*Holds out the package.*] Open it. See if you like it.

WOMAN: [*Standoffish.*] What's this?

MAN: For your birthday.

WOMAN: [*Crushed.*] Numan Bey . . . thank you so much, but . . .

MAN: Go on, open it!

WOMAN: [*Opens the package and takes out a white dress.*] Very beautiful.

MAN: I thought it would look great on you. I'd like to see it on you. How about putting it on?

WOMAN: [*Like a robot.*] All right.

[*The* WOMAN *takes the dress into the bedroom, leaving the door half open. The* MAN *sits in the armchair and checks the bottle of Scotch.*]

MAN: [*Calls out.*] You've been drinking again, haven't you? You never listen to me. I always want you to be healthy, good, and happy. And I want you to stay beautiful and lively like this. Why don't you answer me? Neslihan!

WOMAN: [*From the bedroom.*] Yes?

MAN: Aren't you listening to me? Don't you hear me?

WOMAN: [*From the bedroom.*] I'm getting dressed.

MAN: Look, I might decide to ban drinking. [*Apprehensive.*] What if you get sick? What if your face grows pale? Or if your voice becomes hoarse? No, no, no, you're not going to cause me any anxiety. I want you to promise me.

[*The* WOMAN *enters in the white dress. She looks very beautiful. She is attractive and cold like a mannequin in a shop window.*]

[*The* MAN *is breathless at the sight of her beauty.*] You're so . . . so beautiful. [*Approaches her, then steps back; walks around her.*] You're like an angel . . . like a nymph out of an ancient myth. Yes, yes, exactly like her. Take a few steps over here. [*The* WOMAN *takes three steps.*] You are graceful, pure, immaculate. You're so lovely. [*Taken by surprise, he becomes impetuous.*] Your hair? Your hair?

WOMAN: [*Icily.*] I cut it.

MAN: [*Writhing like a wounded animal.*] You can't do this. You shouldn't have. You had no right. I, after all, think only of your well-being, your beauty. You shouldn't have cut your hair, never.

WOMAN: [*Shuts her eyes.*] I got bored with long hair.

MAN: [*Sinks into the armchair.*] You should never have done this. I . . . your hair . . . you shouldn't have cut . . . I want your hair.

WOMAN: [*As if asking for pardon like a prisoner.*] I was terrified of my hair. I was afraid my hair might strangle me in my sleep.

MAN: Grow your hair long again! Your hair should grow long fast. I want it to be like before. Grow your hair.

WOMAN: [*Docile.*] All right.

MAN: [*Panting.*] Grow it! You should never have cut it off. Well, it's happened. I'm going to buy you a wig. Just like the hair you cut off. Who knows, maybe it'll look exactly the same as your real hair. Then maybe I can delude myself, console myself. [*Rises and holds the* WOMAN *by her shoulders as if he is afraid of breaking them.*] Sit in your armchair! [*Makes her sit down.*] Yes! Now cross your legs! [*Holds out a cigarette and lights it.*] Yes, there's your cigarette. That's it. Throw your head back! Greeaat. [*Sits in the armchair opposite the* WOMAN.] You are exquisite in white.

WOMAN: You keep getting me white things to wear.

MAN: Always white! Oh, if only your hair . . . anyway . . . first thing tomorrow morning, I'll make the rounds of stores that sell wigs.

WOMAN: [*Dejected.*] My hair weighed me down. Burned my head . . . my neck . . .

MAN: Don't say that! How about singing that song!

[*The* WOMAN *sings. Although she cannot carry the tune, she pronounces the lyrics clearly. The* MAN *listens with a pained expression, then joins her for the refrain.*]

WOMAN:

> My grieving heart, tell me again
> Whatever there is to speak of.
> Tell me, does anything remain—
> What is left of untasted love?

MAN and WOMAN:

> Tell me, does anything remain—
> What is left of untasted love?

WOMAN:

> Is it like laughing and crying?
> Is it like living and dying?
> Let me hear over and over
> Again the voice of my lover.

MAN and WOMAN:

> Let me hear over and over
> Again the voice of my lover.

WOMAN: [*Wearily.*] Should I take it from the top again?

MAN: Nooo, you're not singing with enthusiasm tonight.

WOMAN: [*Reaches for the drinking glass.*] I sang the way I sing every night.

MAN: Forget it!

WOMAN: [*Complaining.*] Numan Bey . . .

MAN: You're not going to drink!

WOMAN: Why not?

MAN: It affects your voice. The color of your face changes, too. Besides, you cut your hair. [*Takes the glass out of the* WOMAN's *hand, empties it out into the flowerpot.*] From now on, alcohol is forbidden to you.

WOMAN: [*Lunges forward.*] Heeey! What are you doing?

MAN: [*Taken aback.*] Huh?

WOMAN: My plant . . .

MAN: [*Notices the flowerpot for the first time.*] What's this?

WOMAN: A carnation plant.

MAN: Where did it come from?

WOMAN: He gave it to me. The guy with the eyeglasses.

MAN: Who?

WOMAN: The tenant in the apartment across . . .

MAN: [*Skeptical.*] Why?

WOMAN: Today is my birthday.

MAN: [*Jealous.*] I didn't know you got together with others.

WOMAN: We chatted once or twice. When we open our apartment doors at the same time, he says good morning to me.

MAN: And you?

WOMAN: I say good morning, too.

MAN: When did he come here?

WOMAN: He never set foot in here.

MAN: [*Points to the flowerpot.*] And that?

WOMAN: He handed it to me at the door.

MAN: [*Looks the* WOMAN *straight in the eye furiously for a while; then paces around, trying to take command of the situation.*] Your voice is changing. The color of your face, too. Your hair . . . [*Turns to her.*] Don't speak to him again! [*Points to the flowerpot.*] And throw that away!

WOMAN: Why?

MAN: Because you've become different.

WOMAN: [*Defiantly.*] I love my carnation.

MAN: [*After a pause, despondently.*] You are different.

WOMAN: [*As if she has a premonition.*] What do you mean "different"?

MAN: [*Evasively.*] Nothing.

WOMAN: Speak, speak up!

MAN: What do you want me to say?

WOMAN: Your secret.

MAN: [*Astonished.*] My secret? I don't understand.

WOMAN: [*Curtly.*] Me neither.

MAN: You're very strange tonight.

WOMAN: That's right, I am strange tonight.

MAN: It's because of the drinking . . . and your hair. Throw the plant away! And never speak to him!

WOMAN: No!

MAN: What took place between you and him?

WOMAN: [*Ruthlessly.*] What do you think might have happened?

MAN: [*Angrily.*] Tell me everything!

WOMAN: Stop shouting!

MAN: [*After a pause, he walks to the door, feeling defeated.*] I'm leaving. [*Turns back.*] Is there anything you want?

WOMAN: There is.

MAN: [*Stops and walks back to her.*] What?

WOMAN: To make love!

MAN: [*Shocked.*] Neslihan!

WOMAN: [*With a sudden fury.*] Who's Neslihan, damn it? Why did you give me this name? Why do you keep calling me "Neslihan"?

MAN: [*Backs up toward the door.*] Look, baby . . . sweetheart . . . tonight you're not feeling so good. We'll talk some other time.

WOMAN: We're going to talk now. Come here!

MAN: [*Exhausted.*] No, I don't feel well tonight. I'm sad.

WOMAN: Sit down!

MAN: [*Standing, he seems to sway.*] But why? What do you want from me?

WOMAN: To make love!

MAN: [*As if he is about to faint.*] No, no!

WOMAN: Come near me! Here are my lips! Look, my tongue, my teeth . . . my armpits, my breasts, my thighs. Come, make love to me! Let's make love!

MAN: You're out of your mind! You're mad!

WOMAN: Tonight we're going to settle our accounts. We're going to repay each other.

MAN: What do you mean "repay"?

WOMAN: Look, I am full of life, full of warmth. I am a woman. I am on fire. Damn it, love me, make love to me. Let's make love!

MAN: [*Shattered.*] I'm old—too old.

WOMAN: What's troubling you? What's the secret you're hiding? What's all this for, then? All this furniture, all the clothing?

MAN: Don't . . . I beg of you.

WOMAN: Tell me! What is it you're paying for with these things? Who am I?

MAN: I want to go up to my place. I want to go to sleep.

WOMAN: Who am I? Tell me! Am I your kept woman, your mistress, your prisoner? Who am I? Why have you been feeding me, giving me clothing?

MAN: You're drunk tonight.

WOMAN: If I'm your whore, then come on—take what you're entitled to.

MAN: I've always been good to you. Always thought of your beauty and well-being. Always protected you.

WOMAN: No. You rubbed off all my colors and painted me white.

MAN: I was hiding you, safeguarding you so that you wouldn't cry in your sleep.

WOMAN: Yes, you were hiding me away. You put me to sleep and kept me in mothballs. "Put your white dress on, sit in your armchair, cross your legs, light your cigarette, let your hair loose, sing me that song!" [*Sobs.*] Go away!

MAN: You can't treat me this way. You are everything to me. You are my one and only. I'm too old.

WOMAN: Go away! Leave me alone!

MAN: Everything I own . . . all I have is yours. I'll turn over to you the deed for this building. If you like, I'll adopt your daughter. You are my everything . . . my dreams, my remorse. Don't kick me out!

WOMAN: Tell me what your secret is. Reveal it. Who's in the photographs in your room?

MAN: [*Staggers.*] You saw them? You went upstairs and saw them?

WOMAN: I did. Today I got your key from the super and sneaked in. All over your walls . . . who is the woman in those photographs? The woman with long hair, dressed in white? [*Grabs the* MAN's *lapels and shakes him.*] Who is she? What's her name?

MAN: [*His eyes filled with tears.*] Others knew her as Hicran, but she was Neslihan. She was Neslihan.

Scene 3

[*A tea garden. A lovely, sunny day. Two tables with white tablecloths. Chairs around the tables. Trees in bloom.*

The WOMAN *is seated with her back to the audience. She is drinking tea. She has on a chic white raincoat and is wearing large sunglasses.*

Music is heard from the loudspeaker in the tea garden.]

WOMAN: [*Shouts to backstage.*] Sweetie, baby, stop running, you'll get drenched in sweat. [*Pause.*] Oooh, darling, don't maul the sand like that! Your lovely dress is getting ruined. [*Pause.*] Aah, be careful, you're going to fall! [*Pause.*] Come out of the sandbox at once. Didn't I tell you to play in the sun? That's it. Atta girl! Good for you, my honeybun. You'll keep away from the pool, right?

[*The* MAN, *Bedri, enters. He is a workman, about twenty-five years old, with a bright face and clean clothes. He walks to the other table, sits, and opens his newspaper.*]

[*The* WOMAN *rises.*] Heey, stop shoving my daughter around. How about playing nicely, huh? [*She is startled.*] Put down that piece of rock!

[*The* WOMAN *runs down the stage and disappears. It is then that the* MAN *notices the* WOMAN *and stares after her. The* WOMAN *comes back.*]

MAN: Good morning.

WOMAN: [*Glad.*] Good morning. [*Hesitates between going back to her own table or to the* MAN's *table.*] Children . . . why can't children play properly? I wonder why they always push and shove each other.

MAN: I guess they want to be like grown-ups. [*Laughs.*] Won't you take a seat?

WOMAN: [*Sits down.*] Lovely day, isn't it?

MAN: Lovely. How about tea?

WOMAN: [*Points to the other table.*] Actually, I've already had some.

MAN: Please have some more. [*Calls out.*] Two cups of tea for us!

WOMAN: I didn't get a chance to thank you—for the plant.

MAN: Oh, yes . . . you're welcome.

WOMAN: That night . . . I can't tell you how overjoyed I was with the carnation.

MAN: It occurred to me when I was on my way home. I thought of picking it up and bringing it to you. Remember, that morning you said . . .

WOMAN: Yes. I was so happy. Really. I'm taking good care of it. I water it every day. It's beginning to get buds.

MAN: Good.

WOMAN: [*Looks back.*] My kid . . . I keep thinking of her over there. There's a pool . . . and all that sand and dust.

MAN: [*Looks in the same direction.*] She doesn't mingle with the others.

WOMAN: No. Actually, she behaves well. [*Ebullient.*] You'd be surprised to see her drawings and her handwriting. She already knows her ABCs. It's only recently that I discovered this playground. I'll bring her here as often as I can . . . good for sunning and fresh air. [*Catches the* MAN's *eye.*] Were you saying something?

MAN: [*Averts his glances.*] Nooo, I wasn't. [*Takes out his pack of domestic cigarettes.*] Would you like one?

WOMAN: [*Looks at the cigarettes, then takes her American cigarettes out of her handbag.*] I better not switch brands.

MAN: [*Lights the cigarettes.*] Whatever you like.

WOMAN: [*After a pause.*] I'd like to tell you something. It's as if I know you from somewhere. You look awfully familiar . . . as though we had had many, many talks.

MAN: [*Looks down; then with assurance.*] No, I don't think so.

WOMAN: Weird. You look like someone I know, but I can't tell who it is.

MAN: I'm not from this town. I'm from a faraway place. I'm a villager.

WOMAN: But you don't look like a villager. The way you speak and act . . .

MAN: I've been working here for two years now, but I'm actually a villager.

WOMAN: [*Laughs.*] A villager wearing glasses!

MAN: [*Stares at her for a while.*] How are you related to that man?

WOMAN: Pardon?

MAN: The landlord?

WOMAN: Not related to him at all. I'm moving out soon, anyway.

MAN: Why?

WOMAN: [*Gropes for words.*] It's a bit too small for me.

MAN: It's only you and your daughter. Your apartment has two rooms and a living room.

WOMAN: [*Nervously.*] It's small—too small. It's beginning to get to me. I'm moving out.

MAN: [*Looks at her out of the corner of his eye.*] He doesn't seem like a bad guy.

WOMAN: Who?

MAN: I'm talking about Numan Bey.

WOMAN: I didn't say he was a bad guy.

MAN: They're saying a lot of things about him. The super, his wife, and the grocer . . . they say he worked in Germany many years, and when he returned, he sold the land he had inherited from his father and bought the apartment building. The super's wife says that the walls of Numan Bey's apartment are plastered with photographs.

WOMAN: [*Tense.*] It's none of my business.

MAN: The super's wife says that all the photos are of you.

WOMAN: No. She's mistaken.

MAN: Yes, maybe she's mistaken. She says she might be. But those photos are supposedly just like you. Exactly like you.

WOMAN: I'm going to move out of there. As soon as I find a job. Maybe even tomorrow morning. I talked to some people. They told me to drop by tomorrow. If I manage to get a job, I'll move out of that place at once.

MAN: What kind of a job is it?

WOMAN: [*Despondently.*] I'll become a model. Maybe I'll pose for those illustrated novels they serialize in newspapers. I have a good voice; I can become a singer if I want to. The president of a film company keeps insisting that I should be in the movies, but I haven't made up my mind yet. Why are you staring like that?

MAN: Forget it.

WOMAN: If I want to, I can get all sorts of jobs. For one thing, I'm young and attractive.

MAN: [*Subdued and pensive.*] There's bound to be some job suited to your youth and beauty, right?

WOMAN: Sure. What do the others have that I don't?

MAN: The others?

WOMAN: I mean those whose names are up on the marquees.

MAN: [*Uneasy.*] Yeah . . . yes.

WOMAN: Don't you believe that you can become a performer or something like that?

MAN: To tell you the truth, I don't know enough about it. I'm not up on these matters.

WOMAN: [*Tries to convince herself.*] If I want to, if I had wanted to, I could have become all those things. But I didn't want to.

MAN: Why didn't you?

WOMAN: [*Surprised.*] I don't know. I just didn't want to. My circle of friends, my background, pressure from people I know . . .

MAN: Are the circumstances different now? Aren't the people close to you exerting pressure?

WOMAN: People close to me? I have no one who's close to me. [*Tries to smile.*] From now on, this is the way it goes: "All I need is a bit of food—then nothing will make me brood." From now on, I'll live the way I want to live. I am sick and tired of the boss's bad breath. I won't wait with my head bowed. I'll get a job. I can take care of myself, of my daughter. [*As if she expects support.*] Can't I do it?

MAN: To tell you the truth, I'm astounded when I listen to you.

WOMAN: You find it hard to believe, huh?

MAN: Yes, I'm surprised. When you say all these things, I think you're out of your mind. But then I realize that you change, you come alive, you become truly beautiful.

WOMAN: Become beautiful? How do you mean?

MAN: Believe me, I have yet to figure out what sort of a person you are. When you were talking about marquees, about becoming a star of photo serials based on novels, you sounded so foolish, so timid, so weak. But you're so vibrant, honorable, and lovely when you rebel against living with one's head bowed, putting up with the boss's bad breath. Forgive me, but I'm trying to say what I really think.

WOMAN: [*Pleased.*] Tell me, tell me!

MAN: Your looks . . . yes, you are very beautiful, but sometimes I notice that your beauty goes hand in hand with an incredible inner emptiness and a limitless stupidity. You suddenly turn into a person who is loveless, servile, bloodless, unreliable, and annoying. When you're like that, I feel like making up an excuse to get up and leave.

WOMAN: [*Takes offense.*] Leave?

MAN: Wait, listen! I'm trying to tell you what my thoughts are. Yes, like right then, your eyes suddenly glitter. What a lovely sight that is. Something like passion flows out of you—when you are overjoyed about the carnation, when you talk about your child, when you make plans to get a job and earn a living. That's when you are really lovely—a beauty that has meaning, that defends life, that is vibrant. For a long time, I was so curious about you. That's why I kept eavesdropping when the supers and the grocers were gossiping. I was curious not because you happened to be my next-door neighbor or beautiful or a woman. Every time I ran into you, every time we said hello, there were two separate women there—one was melancholy, depressed, mortified. But the other one? She was agonized, full of passion, a person who savored even a hello, radiant and lively. A woman one wanted to see, yearned to speak to and be with.

WOMAN: [*Excited; tries to understand.*] Slow down. More . . . tell me in such a way that I can follow.

MAN: OK, I'll try. Now, look . . . I'm wiping out of my mind all the feelings and thoughts I used to have and those momentary encounters. Look, now we're sitting here, talking to each other. Right this minute, I'm trying to get to know you, to identify you.

WOMAN: Yes?

MAN: Who are you? What's your background? Where do you come from? Right now your earlier relations, sins, and good deeds have no significance. As far as I can tell, you have an urge for settling accounts, for an inevitable self-renewal. You say: "I'm going to move out." You become impetuous when you say: "I have nothing to do with those photographs." "I'm going to work," you say. Your boredom, your longing for change, your rebellion—these are what concern me now. I can clearly see your loneliness, your sense of responsibility, your striving to find your place, your bewilderment.

WOMAN: Tell me, tell me more!

MAN: It's this throbbing, desolate, emotional appearance of yours that matters. Yes, it's more important than your being lovely or having your name on the marquees. Now please forget your anger, your lack of love, the many injustices you may have suffered . . . forget the inequities of the world we live in. Don't give a thought to the fact that you've gone to waste, that you've been misused, that you've been reduced to nothing. Make this sunny day the dawn of a new age. Choose a new "you" for yourself!

WOMAN: How? Explain it to me.

MAN: If a person is capable of holding firm, and if with full faith he can move toward truth and light, then fears come to an end. Loneliness, despair, and lovelessness also end.

WOMAN: You mean . . . I mean, what should I do now?

MAN: You want to work, right?

WOMAN: I'm obliged to work.

MAN: Right. Would you like me to help you? I can get you a job.

WOMAN: [*Happily.*] What sort of a job?

MAN: A job unlike the ones you were talking about a short while ago. To tell you the truth, I don't believe a job of that type is in the offing for you. Remember, you said, "I can get movie roles, I can become a model," and things like that? I just can't see how.

WOMAN: [*Bows her head.*] Yes, maybe it isn't easy. But if I go out and talk to employers, I might be able to find something. I'm not unattractive.

MAN: The job I'm going to propose makes a person even more attractive. It gives you the joy of working with others, of engaging in the human struggle, of producing and creating. It teaches peace, the loveliest kind of tiredness, the meaning of the sweat of the brow. It ennobles the human being, gives happiness and prosperity.

WOMAN: [*Excited.*] You talk so beautifully.

MAN: Agreed? Will you start at once, tomorrow?

WOMAN: Sure. What do I do?

MAN: You'll be a worker.

WOMAN: [*Surprised.*] I don't get it.

MAN: A worker in a textile factory—or a battery factory.

WOMAN: [*Disappointed.*] You mean . . . an ordinary worker?

MAN: Yes. You'll be one of those who flow through the avenues early in the morning.

WOMAN: [*Tense.*] Nooo. You're putting me on. I'm sure this is a big joke.

MAN: Why should I be joking?

WOMAN: [*Nervous.*] I . . . I had assumed you would come up with something more suitable for me. Oh noo!

MAN: You don't think being a worker is suitable for you?

WOMAN: I . . . my hands . . . I have pure white hands. My fingernails are polished. Besides, I'm attractive. Yes, very beautiful.

MAN: [*Annoyed.*] My idea goes against your grain, is that it?

WOMAN: You've been mocking me.

MAN: Nothing of the sort. I never mock anyone.

WOMAN: You told me I'm attractive and intelligent—that my eyes glitter. You said you were curious about me. And then . . . noo, this won't do. You may doubt it, but if I want to . . . I'm tall, I have a good voice.

MAN: [*Realizes that he has wasted his breath.*] As you like. I tried to tell you about a new start, a new road, but I failed.

WOMAN: [*Nervous.*] No. You took an interest in me, you talked to me. You said very nice things that affected me. I thought you and I . . .

MAN: Yes?

WOMAN: You brought me the flowerpot. You told be about myself at length. Every so often you looked me straight in the eye. And once you held my hand.

MAN: [*Realizing what she had been thinking, he is surprised.*] And you thought that I . . . you . . . [*Laughs.*] Oh, come now, how could you think something like that?

WOMAN: [*Pathetically.*] Try to remember all the things you told me. If a man says such things to a woman, what does it mean?

MAN: It means . . . it means that he has something to tell.

WOMAN: What was it you wanted to tell me? Happiness, love, a sunny day, and things like that?

MAN: [*Losing hope.*] If you like, we can start from the beginning again. All over again. Would you like that?

WOMAN: The upshot of it all will be my getting a factory job.

MAN: Yes, that's what I'll try to tell you.

WOMAN: I don't want it! I hoped that you would tell me about me as a beautiful woman, about my loneliness. I hoped that you would understand me. [*Sobs.*] That you would love me, that you were in love with me.

MAN: You're a friend of mine, a good friend. As I told you at the beginning, it's not your beauty or your attractiveness that concerns me. Oh, God, I suppose I didn't manage to make myself clear. Look . . .

WOMAN: Don't waste your breath. It now dawns on me that you don't love me.

MAN: [*Finds himself in a difficult situation.*] Yes. My love is not like the love you are thinking of. But if we had been able to understand one another, we might have established a fine bond between us. You wouldn't have felt lonely any longer; you would have come out of that void. You would have become someone who gains strength among working people for whom toil and love go hand in hand.

WOMAN: Please stop! I don't want it! If you're going to tell me again about people streaming through the streets at the crack of dawn, you might as well not talk. I'm not one of those people.

MAN: [*Laughs with a pained expression.*] Yes, you are a lovely, tall woman with white hands.

WOMAN: Somebody advised me not to talk to you. I should have listened. It's a pity. If you were interested, I might have fallen in love with you.

MAN: [*Laughs.*] Don't ever do it! Besides, I love someone else, I'll have you know.

WOMAN: Is she beautiful at least?

MAN: Very . . . very beautiful. She's one of those people who stream through the streets at the crack of dawn.

WOMAN: [*Sneering.*] I shouldn't have expected anything less. [*Rises.*] Anyway, take care.

MAN: I thought we were going to have tea.

WOMAN: I don't want it. I won't have any. You'll see . . . my name will go up on the marquees . . . star billing, too. You're laughing, huh? Keep laughing. [*Takes an old envelope out of her handbag.*] All I have to do is present this letter! That'll do it!

MAN: [*Looks at the envelope; shattered and weary.*] That'll do it!

Scene 4

[*The same hotel room as in Act I, Scene 1. Music played in that scene continues on the small transistor radio.*

The MAN, *Seyit, stands frozen, holding photographs in his hands. This final scene will continue from where the play's opening scene ended.*

The MAN *looks alternately at the photos and his own face in the mirror. He seems stunned and terrified. The* WOMAN, *Sevtap, returns from the bathroom. She is exhausted and terribly pale.*]

WOMAN: What's suddenly come over me? I nearly passed out and died.

MAN: Hey, Sister, telephone.

WOMAN: Is it Veli Bey again, that stubborn oaf?

MAN: No, it's long distance—Istanbul.

WOMAN: [*Comes alive.*] Istanbul? [*Grabs the phone.*] Hello? Suna, my dearest. My beautiful child. . . . Yes, it's me, your mother. . . . I'm well, my darling. I'm very well, my love.

And you? . . . Oh, I'm so happy to hear that. . . . My voice is what? [*Tries to clear her throat; uses her voice with great care.*] No, no. I swear to you, I feel just fine. Maybe a slight irritation in my throat. How's school? [*Happily.*] You're my one and only . . . loveliest girl in the whole world. I wired you some money last Monday. Did you get it? . . . Right. That's good. . . . What's that? . . . Winter coat? You did the right thing. Wear it in good health. . . . What? Excuse me? . . . Me, too. [*Her eyes are filled with tears.*] I miss you, too, very much. . . . [*Cries.*] No, I'm not crying. It probably sounds like that on the phone. I'm feeling fine, just fine. I have my radio and my carnation. [*As if frightened.*] . . . No! Don't ever do anything like that! If you do, you'll get me mad. I'll come over there to see you. Maybe I'll take the plane, see you, and fly back. We'll have kebab somewhere, then we'll see a film. Just the two of us. . . . I didn't get that. Speak louder. Who? There's who? . . . Who loves whom? You—each other? . . . What? . . . What's that? . . . His name's Esen? [*Fearful.*] Did you say he's a nice boy? Sure . . . I understand, my child. His name's Esen, huh? Oh, yes, write to me. Write long letters. . . . You're sending me a snapshot? His picture? Of course. . . . Sure I love you. [*Weeps.*] You're my everything. . . . No, don't say that! Suna, I figured it out . . . five more months. Then, yes, I'll come to you. Permanently. Five months from now, when the house is all paid up. After that, we'll never live apart. Yes, the two of us, we'll go to kebab places. We'll walk by the seashore; we'll go to tea gardens. Hello? Suna! Hello? Operator, please don't cut us off. We can't hear each other. No. How many minutes? Please connect us again. [*Nervous.*] Hello, please! [*Taps on the telephone and shouts.*] Don't cut us off! Damn it, don't cut us off. Just one more minute. I was about to say something. One little moment . . . OK? Operator, you garbage—would your mother die if you let us talk one more minute? [*Hangs up.*] At least I heard her voice, her laughter. [*Seems to have come alive and become beautiful.*] See, that's the way it is, my boy Seyit. [*Rises, pours brandy into the snifter.*] That was my daughter I just talked to. [*Takes a sip.*] I haven't seen her for four and a half months now. Since the fall . . . she's a high school student. She's exactly seventeen. You ought to see her—she's one of the loveliest in the world. She has long hair and huge eyes. She's such a dear. She's my darling. [*Drinks.*] Let me see, what was it she said? [*A bit displeased.*] She's sending me some photographs, is that it? Did she say, "His name is Esen"? Well, something like that. I should be with her now. Damn destiny that separates mother and daughter. [*Drinks; comes eye to eye with Seyit.*] Hey, boy, what are you looking like that for? Put those photographs down! Heeyy, Seyit, I'm talking to you, damn you! Are you lost in dreams or what! Giddyap! Wake up!

MAN: [*Sheepishly.*] Sevtap, Sister, why did you punch holes in the eyes in these photos?

WOMAN: Haa!

MAN: [*Shows her the photographs.*] I'm saying, why are there holes here? The eyes?

WOMAN: Stop talking nonsense. Damn it, we're going to be late for work.

MAN: Sevtap, I said to Hicran . . .

WOMAN: [*Laughs.*] Poor boy, you are so obsessed with that girl, you're out of your mind.

MAN: All I wanted from her . . .

WOMAN: Was what your father wanted from your mother.

MAN: No . . . I . . .

WOMAN: [*Looks in the mirror.*] Tonight they're going to get a good view of Sevtap. They'll realize there's nobody like Sevtap. [*Puts makeup on.*] I am lovely. Damn it, I'm always beautiful. Tonight I'm going to present the variety show of my life. And then tomorrow once more. But five months later . . . [*Adjusts her wig.*] My Suna's hair comes all the way down to her waist. It flows, it glitters. [*Takes another sip.*] Tell me, Seyit my boy, am I not lovely?

MAN: You are lovely, Sister.

WOMAN: [*Takes a cigarette.*] Light this, then! Go ooon!

MAN: [*Lights her cigarette.*] Sevtap, can you sing the song: "Like laughing and crying, like living and dying"? The song that Hicran used to sing?

WOMAN: [*Drinks.*] Yeah. So what?

MAN: [*Stammers.*] Sister . . . if I go to Germany, if I manage to go . . . well, maybe I won't be able to. But I can't return to my village, either.

WOMAN: [*Tipsy.*] What're you talking about?

MAN: Maybe I'll stay here. I say, maybe I should tell Hicran.

WOMAN: [*Gives one laugh after another.*] Damn it, how did you get that nagging notion in your head?

MAN: [*Bows his head.*] I love her. I swear to God, I love her. If only she would love me, too.

WOMAN: [*Laughs cynically.*] Hah, haaa . . .

MAN: I'll work hard. I did finish junior high. Now I can attend high school at night.

WOMAN: [*Making fun of him.*] Yes, eventually you can become a doctor or a general!

MAN: No, that's not what I'm saying. Stop drinking and listen to me. If she'd love me, if she'd find me acceptable, I swear I wouldn't let anyone come near her. I'd hold her by the hand, put her on a train, and carry her off . . . to a faraway place . . . a place where no one can sell anyone or curse anybody's mother.

WOMAN: [*Rises, staggers.*] Oooh, I'm drunk as hell. I'm falling . . . hold me . . . [*Sings.*] "What is left of untasted love . . . "

MAN: [*Implores.*] Sevtap, Sister, look here . . . if I were to go away from this place . . . I know I can never forget her. Years from now, even when I'm very old . . . even if I'm dead . . .

WOMAN: Tonight they're going to watch Sevtap with the almond-shaped eyes. Let everyone see her. [*Dances and wiggles.*] Tralla la la, tralla la la . . .

MAN: Tell me the truth, Sister, did they really sell Hicran? Did they sell her, huh?

WOMAN: [*Dances.*] Tralla la, tralla la la . . .

MAN: Please tell me, please.

WOMAN: [*Drunk, laughs at the top of her voice.*] December, January, February, March, April! Everything will be fine in April! We're going to go through the marketplaces, parks, and restaurants. We're going to go on ships, my daughter and I. In April . . .

MAN: Oh, Sister, you drank too much.

WOMAN: It's wonderful. I'm drunk. I'm turning like the hands of a clock. Tonight those gentlemen, those fat cats, are going to get an eyeful of Sevtap with the almond-shaped eyes. I'm going to dance as I've never danced before. Follow me, we're going! You're going to carry my bag and my coat. March, you stupid bastard!

MAN: Stop. You're going to fall. You'll bang into something. [*Keeps an eye on the* WOMAN; *takes the bag.*] Let's go. [*As they walk toward the door, the phone rings.*]

WOMAN: [*Turns back.*] The phone . . .

MAN: Never mind, leave it alone. It must be Veli Bey. We're on our way.

WOMAN: Just wait. [*Walks over to the phone and picks it up.*] Hellooo? What're you hollering for, damn it? Shut up. Stop screaming! I know . . . I know it's you, Veli Bey. I'm on my way. I was about to leave. [*Laughs heartily.*] Tonight I'm numero uno. Tonight I am the queen. [*Freezes suddenly.*] What? Come again? Why? [*Turns pale, looks as if she is about to collapse.*] Giving me what? The boot? Look, Veli Bey, listen to me. Stop cussing and cursing. [*Phone is cut off.*] Motherfucker. [*Collapses onto the bed.*] He says, "Don't come to work anymore. I don't want you."

MAN: What's he saying?

WOMAN: [*Shattered and exhausted.*] "Your account has been closed," he says. He closed it.

MAN: But why? That's not right!

WOMAN: [*Drunk, on the verge of sobbing.*] "Bitch," he said. "You're all washed up. You're dead. I'm closing your book and throwing it at you." [*Covers her face with her hands.*] My account is closed.

MAN: [*Snuggles up to her.*] Sevtap, Sister, don't cry. Let's see . . .

WOMAN: [*Weeps; her makeup runs down her cheeks.*] I knew it. I knew this was going to happen, I knew it was going to end this way. I knew it—and feared it.

MAN: Sister, please don't cry. I beg you, don't cry.

WOMAN: I was scared stiff. Scared that I wasn't attractive—that I was old and ugly. [*Cries, nearly chokes.*] Finished. They won't let me dance again.

MAN: [*Holds her hands.*] You're beautiful—very beautiful.

WOMAN: [*Drunk, almost crazy.*] I was. No more. I'm finished. [*Coughs and weeps.*] I shall never be able to dance from now on.

MAN: You can dance somewhere else. Again. You're lovely.

WOMAN: [*Gets up, lifts her arms, and attempts to dance, but after a turn she collapses into the chair.*] No. I won't be able to go on. I'm finished. I'm through.

MAN: [*Tries to lift the* WOMAN.] Look, listen to me! Look, I want to tell you something.

WOMAN: [*Loses herself altogether.*] I don't want to. I want nothing. It's all over. No more Sevtap. Let go of me. Go away!

MAN: Sevtap, Sister, come to your senses. Believe me. I swear you are beautiful.

WOMAN: You're lying, damn it, you're a damn liar. [*Grabs his lapels and shouts.*] You have always lied to me! Always! Why didn't you love your sister? Why? Tell me!

MAN: [*Bewildered, he tries to free himself.*] Sevtap, Sister, Sevtap . . .

WOMAN: I tell you, there's no more Sevtap, damn you, you bastard. Was I Sevtap where I came from? Was I Sevtap before I cut my hair? Why did you go away for three days and kill? Why did you commit murder, why?

MAN: I . . . I don't get it . . . Sister, I am Seyit, Seyit!

WOMAN: Why didn't you love me, you bastard? Why those photos, those white dresses? Make love to me, damn you. Why don't you make love to me, you weakling?

MAN: Sister, are you crazy? I . . . I . . .

WOMAN: Why did you bring me the carnation that evening? Why didn't you tell me everything the right way? Why didn't you love me?

MAN: Sevtap, I beg you, come to your senses, Sister.

WOMAN: Damn it, I'm not Sevtap. Back home, I was Sevgi. My name was Sevgi. Why did you let me out of that sunny garden? Why didn't you tell me about everything real nice?

MAN: Oh, Sister, Sister.

WOMAN: Why? Tell me why, you fag! Why did you make me swallow that sleeping pill in the taxicab? And then you put more pills into my wine and stripped me naked when I dozed off. Didn't you have any pity or sympathy?

MAN: [*Scared.*] Let it go. Let go of me. Let my collar go.

WOMAN: I was a tiny little woman. Why did you sell me to gentlemen, to rich folk? Why did you force me to dance and dance and dance? And now, why? Why, why? I'll dance yet. Just a bit more. In April, by the seashore, at the kebab place, in the bazaar. I am beautiful! Lovely . . . I have long hair that goes all the way down to my waist. [*Cries, whirls, struggles to dance.*] I have to dance some more . . . I must dance. [*Whirls madly.*] I shall dance!

MAN: [*Moves around her like a madman.*] Sevtap, Sister . . .

WOMAN: It's "Sevgi," damn it, "Sevgi." I am Sevgi. [*Whirls in the same spot, sobs, dances.*] Back home, I used to be Sevgi. [*Holds her breasts, writhes.*] Right here . . . there is something right here. [*Stiffens for a moment, then collapses where she is standing.*]

MAN: [*Nearly out of his mind.*] Sevgi, listen to me. Look. Hear me. [*Shakes the* WOMAN.] Sevgi. Hey, Sevgi. [*Lunges forward and picks up the phone.*] Give me the nightclub. Quick, the nightclub . . . [*With his eyes transfixed on the* WOMAN, *he waits, frozen like stone.*] Hello, Veli Bey? She's dead. Sevgi died. She's dead. . . . What's that? Can't you hear me? I'm saying: "Sevgi . . . she's dead." Don't you understand? . . . Oh, yes, because of all that racket there . . . you can't hear because of the music. [*Shouts.*] Sevgi . . . is dead! [*Grabs the knife off the stool.*] She's dead, damn you! Sevgi's dead! How can you not hear, you damn fatso? She's dead—Sevgi!

[*The stage freezes. The music on the radio goes up and out.*]

RADIO: This is the end of our light music program. You will now hear the day's news highlights. The Conference for a Lasting Peace continues. The authorities assert that they are optimistic and that in the near future . . .

[*As the lights dim, a small light falls on the carnation in the pot.*]

CURTAIN

◆　　◆　　◆

The White Gods

GÜNGÖR DİLMEN

Translated by John D. Norton

An Editor's Note

Ancient mythology, especially of the Near and Middle East, fired the imagination of many accomplished Turkish playwrights from the mid-1950s onward. Foremost among them is Güngör Dilmen (b. 1930) who burst on the theatrical scene with his enchanting *Midas'ın Kulakları (The Ears of Midas)* in 1959. This play's English version (by Carolyn Graham) appeared in the volume *Modern Turkish Drama,* edited by Talat S. Halman (Bibliotheca Islamica, 1976). Dilmen later expanded it into a trilogy, including *Midas'ın Kördüğümü* (Midas's Gordian Knot) and *Midas'ın Altınları* (Midas's Gold), which remain untranslated. *The Ears of Midas* has become a perennial favorite and has enjoyed the distinction of serving as the libretto of Ferit Tüzün's opera of the same name.

Güngör Dilmen's powerful play entitled *Kurban* (the term *kurban* means "victim" and "sacrifice") treats the Medea theme in a Turkish village setting, and *Akad'ın Yayı* (Akkad's Bow) dramatizes an Akkadian myth.

With *Ak Tanrılar (The White Gods),* Dilmen entered a terra incognita for Turkish dramatic literature—Mexico and its colonial history. In a brief review of *Ak Tanrılar* published in 1976 in the American journal *Books Abroad,* Talat Halman noted:

> It stands as a culmination of the mounting Turkish interest in distant cultures and countries. A provocative historical drama, it deals with heroes and scoundrels, with the ravages wrought by "civilizing colonialists." Although the dramatic tensions are frequently striking, Dilmen's poetic language transforms the play into an elegy for a dead world. . . . Some of the finest passages evoke the feeling and imagery of Aztec poetry. The play is just as much a poetic experience as it is a dramatic experience. . . . *Ak Tanrılar* is in a league with *The Royal Hunt of the Sun.*[1]

According to the translator John D. Norton,

> Dilmen wrote this play after a long and detailed study of the sixteenth-century Spanish conquest of Mexico. Dramatic purposes have required some fusing of several characters

---

1. Talat S. Halman, review of Güngör Dilmen, *Ak Tanrılar, Books Abroad* 50 (1976), pp. 712–13; reprinted in Talat S. Halman, *The Turkish Muse: Views and Reviews, 1960s–1990s* (Syracuse, N.Y.: Syracuse University Press, 2006), p. 259.

into one and some departures from the strict historical record. For example, the real Malinali was not an Aztec but a Tabascon. Similarly, the use of a telescope in Act II, Scene 1 is a deliberate anachronism. Although the Turkish original is written in free verse it has been thought best to render this translation in prose.[2]

Norton is director of the Centre for Turkish Studies at the University of Durham, England. He studied Turkish at the School of Oriental and African Studies, London University, and served at the British embassy in Ankara. After leaving Turkey, he taught modern Turkish studies at Durham and served as director of the Centre for Middle Eastern and Islamic Studies. He first met Güngör Dilmen in 1971 when the playwright was teaching at the University of Durham.

Güngör Dilmen's biography appears in the short introductory essay about his play *I, Anatolia,* on p. 205 of this volume.—TSH

Characters

MEXICANS/INDIANS:

FALLING EAGLE, young commander

CITIZENS (Aztec men and women)

DREAMERS (including one OLD MAN and two WOMEN)

MONTEZUMA (Motecuhzoma), king of Mexico, age forty

MESSENGERS

SMOKING EAGLE, young commander

MALINALI (Malinche or Malintzin; later the Christian DOÑA MARINA)

MAGICIANS

EMISSARIES

CHIEF LEOPARD, collaborator

CHIEF JAGUAR, collaborator

THREE PRIESTS

MONTEZUMA'S SON

PLUMED SERPENT, the Aztec god Quetzalcoatl (the White God)

SMOKING MIRROR, the Aztec God of Night

AZTEC GIRL, sister of Smoking Mirror

SPANIARDS:

PEDRO DE ALVARADO, officer

CRISTÓBAL DE OLID, officer

FRIAR BARTOLOMÉ DE OLMEDO, a padre with the Spanish force

BERNAL DÍAZ

MARTÍN LÓPEZ

---

2. From an introductory note in Norton's unpublished manuscript of the translation.

HERNÁN CORTÉS, conqueror of Mexico

GONZALO DE SANDOVAL, officer

FOUR CONQUISTADORES (and other SOLDIERS)

JUAN ESCUDERO, Diego Velásquez's man

CRISTÓBAL DE TAPIA, Diego Velásquez's man

OFFICER with Tapia

DIEGO VELÁSQUEZ, governor of Cuba (does not make an appearance)

DON CARLOS (Charles V), king of Spain, emperor of the Holy Roman Empire (does not
    make an appearance)

ACT I

Scene 1

[*On the great pyramid in Tenochtitlán, the capital of Mexico. Upstage, the shrine of*
SMOKING MIRROR, *the God of Night. On one side a black drum.*

A windy night. FALLING EAGLE *greets the* AZTEC MEN *and* WOMEN *who have climbed,
puffing and panting, to the top of the pyramid.*]

FALLING EAGLE: And what brings you from your beds to the top of the pyramid before the
    break of day? What is it that you are seeking here?

DREAMERS: We have come to tell great Montezuma of our dreams.

FALLING EAGLE: What fears will you plant in our king's heart this time with your gloomy
    forebodings?

DREAMERS: The fears that the gods planted in our hearts as we dreamed.

FALLING EAGLE: Are you the only ones in the whole of this great land of Mexico to see these
    grim visions?

DREAMERS: Had others seen what we have seen, they too would be with us now; their feet
    would have carried them to the top of the sacred pyramid as well.

FALLING EAGLE: Go back to your homes at once! Keep your lunatic visions to yourselves.
    Montezuma has nothing to learn from you.

DREAMERS: Don't come between us and the king, brave Falling Eagle. He summoned us.
    Montezuma himself summoned the citizens who have seen in their dreams the doom
    that is drawing closer and closer to Mexico.

FALLING EAGLE: Will only death silence you? Go down, I say, at once! If you don't go down
    of your own accord, I'll hurl you down, and the people will gather your corpses from
    the base of the pyramid in the morning.

[MONTEZUMA *comes out of the shrine of* SMOKING MIRROR.]

MONTEZUMA: I hear the brave young Falling Eagle's angry voice. What's going on here? Who are you? [*Silence.*] I know why you've come.

DREAMERS: We've come to tell you our dreams, Montezuma.

MONTEZUMA: But my worthy commander Falling Eagle was trying to prevent you. [*Pointing to the sky.*] Doesn't this new visitor to the skies of Mexico tell him anything?

FALLING EAGLE: Is it just a comet that's robbed you of your reason? It's perfectly natural, and, what's more, it's not the first time we've seen one.

MONTEZUMA: Natural! Natural! That's the only word you seem to know. You call everything natural.

FALLING EAGLE: Your fear of that comet isn't natural.

DREAMERS: Montezuma, listen to us!

FALLING EAGLE: Don't listen to their nonsense! Send the poor wretches away; let them be gone.

MONTEZUMA: They are not poor wretches. Although the capital is now sleeping in the shadow of the Great Pyramid, these dreamers don't allow to fade and vanish the visions they have seen foretelling the fate of the land; they hold onto them. With their hearts purged of personal cares, they all become like one mirror reflecting the fearful future of the land. Speak, old man!

OLD MAN: I stood before Smoking Mirror, the God of Night. His stone lips moved, and midst smoke and sparks came forth these words: "My enemy, the White God from whom I took this land, the White God whom I sent into exile, is returning." Then he moaned your name, "Montezuma, Montezuma."

FIRST WOMAN: I saw the comet that casts its cold light upon Mexico. I saw it descend like a winged serpent. Then it burst into flames and set the capital ablaze.

SECOND WOMAN: And I saw its face. It smiled in triumph and said, "Mexico is mine."

FALLING EAGLE: All these happenings are repeating the same gloomy forebodings in different ways.

MONTEZUMA: It's not the dreams alone; other sinister happenings in the land tell the same story. Star Mountain has started to belch forth fire before it is time. Three times the lakes have grown so big that they threatened to drown the capital. In the country, the Aztec women are bringing forth such strange creatures that one would think they had mated with snakes.

DREAMERS: Montezuma, calm the rage of the god returning from exile by offering him sacrifices.

FALLING EAGLE: You yourselves could be those sacrifices.

DREAMERS: We have no fear of this, Falling Eagle. We are nothing other than the dreams we saw.

FALLING EAGLE: This is a form of sickness, a sickness of the mind. Don't seek reality in mystic dreams. Mexico has never been so strong. In lands hundreds of days' march from here, your name is respected in the hearts of the people. You are the Aztecs' most fortune-favored king. Under you, the country's star shines brighter than ever before.

MONTEZUMA: Falling Eagle, look without blinking at that comet that has come to our skies and now stays fixed there. These are nights when the secrets of the heavens are revealed. Doesn't it look to you like a flaming snake smiling at us from afar?

FALLING EAGLE: A fairy tale! Forget it!

MONTEZUMA: It's what I believe most truly.

DREAMERS: It is the White God, the Plumed Serpent, who, it is said, will come when the cycle of years is changing. These dreams we have had come from him.

MONTEZUMA: Once upon a time Mexico, Tlaxcala, Totonac, Maya, and Olmec were not separate countries, but all one kingdom of peace where heaven and earth were in harmony, and this meant immortality. The White God was the country's only god. His heart was a burning fire, he was the fount of virtue, and this meant immortality. His enemy, Smoking Mirror from the kingdom of the mortals, came to him stealthily and diverted him with mortal tastes and took his kingdom from him.

FALLING EAGLE: That's just an old wives' tale.

MONTEZUMA: Our White God went into exile and opened his bosom to the briny breeze. With the last spark that had not died in his heart, he consumed himself in fire and became a comet, then went to the worlds beyond. But while he was rising above the purple seas, he said, "I shall return!"

DREAMERS: And behold, he is returning.

FALLING EAGLE: Don't be a prisoner of dreams.

MONTEZUMA: This serpent of the skies has poisoned me. There's no sleep for Montezuma.

FALLING EAGLE: Look, the star that scared you has begun to fade. There's daylight on the water. Look at the capital reflected in the lakes. Listen to Mexico awakening.

MONTEZUMA: One day my capital may not awake; it may not awake with these sounds. Perhaps another city may awake in its place, but it will not be the heart of Mexico.

FALLING EAGLE: From the mouth of any other person those words would be treason.

MONTEZUMA: Look in that direction, Falling Eagle. What do you see?

FALLING EAGLE: It's misty. I can't see anything.

MONTEZUMA: Look straight in that direction.

FALLING EAGLE: If there were no mist, I could see Star Mountain, but I wouldn't be able to see beyond the mountain chain—even if there were no mist.

MONTEZUMA: But a king must be able to see. He must see beyond the mountain chain and the Purple Valleys and the Red Valleys, the Tall Grass Steppes, the Yellow Deserts, then his eyes must pass over the other mountain chains that divide us from neighboring lands, then across the land of the Totonacs, over the Rivers of the Sky and beyond to the Mountains of Purple Foam. The king must be able to see the whole of Mexico, whether or not there is mist. In time, he must know the land as he knows his own body. Otherwise he'll bring disaster to Mexico.

FALLING EAGLE: I think I understand what you say, but why are you telling me all this? You are the king; I am Falling Eagle, a commander to obey your orders. I see only the red side of my sword.

MONTEZUMA: [*Shaken.*] If only I knew why I have spoken like this. Perhaps I'm not sound in body. Perhaps I have some sickness that started long ago.

FALLING EAGLE: [*Takes* MONTEZUMA's *arm.*] Last night they found blood all over your bed again. You cut your arms and your chest.

MONTEZUMA: To open my inner eye. Right here a blood clot has formed. If I make myself bleed from a spot close to it, perhaps I'll get rid of it in the flow of blood.

FALLING EAGLE: For some time past, Montezuma, you have not been like the great king who led his armies straight from one victory to another and then to yet more. You talk like a priest striving to grasp meaning from signs of the unknown.

MONTEZUMA: When certain questions are asked, such currents and undercurrents begin to pass between our minds and our hearts that render us incapable of acting as we intend.

FALLING EAGLE: Tell me what those questions are.

MONTEZUMA: Those questions are not for young hearts. They are certainly not for raw warriors who see the safety we enjoy now and suppose that Mexico will be safe forever.

FALLING EAGLE: Well, in our legends this Plumed Serpent is a good god who bodes well. If he holds the future, you should be pleased.

MONTEZUMA: How do you know I'm not pleased? But I'm frightened even more so.

FALLING EAGLE: Now my mind is thoroughly confused.

MONTEZUMA: I'm pleased because he'll bring light. I'm afraid because this light may destroy us. He'll want to arrange everything anew, to change everything from top to bottom. This could mean annihilation for us.

FALLING EAGLE: Your fears are unfounded. Our fairy-tale White God will never come.

[*A* MESSENGER *enters panting and prostrates himself before* MONTEZUMA.]

MONTEZUMA: What's this? Have you too come to tell me the visions you have seen?

MESSENGER: What I have seen is real. White-skinned strangers who came from beyond the seas in floating houses with wings have set foot on our shores.

MONTEZUMA: What?

MESSENGER: We saw them right up close. They're higher beings than humans, and they have dark red beards. Their bodies are covered with clothes that make sparks fly when they're struck with a sword. Then two-headed, four-footed creatures the likes of which we have never seen until this day came upon us like a whirlwind. But I can't bring myself to speak of the most terrifying thing of all. We saw green land dragons that tore out huge trees by the roots and flung aside great boulders; their voices were more terrible than that black sacrificial drum.

[*The* MESSENGER *begins to strike the drum. As the lights dim, to the ominous beat of the drum is added the sound of cannon fire for Scene 2.*]

Scene 2

[*The Spanish encampment. In* CORTÉS's *tent. Downstage, a large sixteenth-century parchment map with drawings of boats, points of the compass, and wind-direction indicators. The map shows Spain, the Atlantic, Cuba, and the New World, with its coasts vaguely indicated.*

ALVARADO, *holding a pair of compasses and a ruler, is adding new places and other information to the map.*

Sounds of cannon fire, horses neighing, and general commotion.]

OLID: Our cavalry display had the desired effect on these natives. They'd never seen horses in their lives. The neighing, rearing, galloping Arab steeds had them all agape.

OLMEDO: Don't laugh. Try to put yourself in their place.

DÍAZ: I did just that, Padre. I put myself in the Indians' place. I couldn't tell rider from horse, and I was dumbstruck when these fearful creatures with four feet and two heads came at me.

OLMEDO: You don't seem very dumbstruck, Díaz.

OLID: The cannons drove the Indians completely out of their minds. Their eyes came out on stalks whenever the cannonballs tore down the trees or ripped into the rocks.

DÍAZ: Well, Alvarado, are there any new developments? Tell me, where are we now? It always gives me confidence to be in a place whose name I know. You've drawn the coasts in splendidly, but the interior is completely empty. That river you found—were you able to follow it to its source?

ALVARADO: It rises near a volcano.

DÍAZ: [*Reading the map.*] Alvarado River. Aha, you've already immortalized your own name. I wish you'd find a river for me. Even a small volcano would do—only let it be an active one.

LÓPEZ: Hmm, don't you think it would have been more appropriate to name it after our commander?

ALVARADO: I did suggest it to Cortés first of all. He just shrugged his shoulders and smiled indifferently.

LÓPEZ: Whatever the Velásquez clique may say, I'm fond of Cortés. He's a modest commander.

DÍAZ: You birdbrain! Cortés isn't a man to be content with one mountain and a river. That's why he seemed indifferent.

[CORTÉS, SANDOVAL, *and a few* CONQUISTADORES *enter.*]

CORTÉS: Let the cannons be silenced. That's enough for today. Let's not show all our tricks straight away. Now we can speak with the tribal chiefs. Meanwhile, we must keep them in awe of us.

SANDOVAL: And what about Velásquez's men? How are we going to bring them to heel? They began to grumble while the ships were still at sea. They're accusing you of making off with the fleet from Cuba.

DÍAZ: Let's sort out Velásquez's men. It's funny, you know, I was once a Velásquez man myself.

LÓPEZ: How many men shall we leave behind?

CORTÉS: It will be best to win them over. By the grace of God, these gentlemen will cease to be merchant seamen for Velásquez, the governor of Cuba, and will bring honor and renown to Spain.

DÍAZ: And how is that to be achieved?

CORTÉS: I don't want to say any more on that subject for the moment. Let the tribal chiefs come in.

[*Several* INDIANS *enter bearing gifts in baskets and on trays. They greet* CORTÉS *timidly.*]

INDIANS: May our pale-faced guests be pleased to accept these humble gifts.

ALVARADO: Is this all you've brought? You haven't come up to the standard of the Tabascons; they sent us their noblest and most beautiful young women and girls. Have you no gold?

CORTÉS: I'll talk to the natives, Alvarado.

[*To the* INDIANS.] Our hearts have a pitiless disease whose only remedy is gold.

INDIANS: The place for gold is Mexico. Mexico. That's where it comes from. From great Montezuma's kingdom.

CORTÉS: Who is this Montezuma whose name is so revered by all the tribes? Where is Mexico?

INDIANS: To reach Mexico you must cross the Mountains of the Coast, cross the Yellow Deserts, cross the Red Valleys, cross the Purple Valleys, and then you will find Mexico set amid three lakes.

Scene 3

FALLING EAGLE: Let's attack them without delay, or they'll find ways to incite the coastal tribes against us.

SMOKING EAGLE: Let's send them back where they came from. Don't let them spread their evil seed throughout Mexico.

FALLING EAGLE: The Tabascons have even begun to offer their women and girls to these strangers. Where will such growing friendship lead?

MONTEZUMA: Let's first think carefully, my bold children, of all the consequences of open war with them. If the White God or the children of the White God are coming, let us avoid any action that would lead our country to destruction. Let us see whether the strangers are enemies. Let us defeat them with cunning. I'll send my magicians against them with the most powerful spells.

FALLING EAGLE: Let's fight them openly, not with magic, whose effect and results are uncertain.

MONTEZUMA: If those who are coming are indeed enemies as you suppose, I'll send 150,000 of my warriors against them on the first day and another 150,000 the next day.

FALLING EAGLE: If you send a tenth of that number into action, the country will be secure.

SMOKING EAGLE: They're a mere handful of men. Our lookouts counted some 300 or 350 men, but they're not idle; the threat is growing.

FALLING EAGLE: Just give the word! I'll loose my bowmen against them.

MONTEZUMA: Falling Eagle, since when have you elected yourself counselor to Montezuma?

FALLING EAGLE: Since the day Montezuma made me privy to his fears.

MONTEZUMA: It seems that my fears have now passed on to you.

FALLING EAGLE: And you seem to have gained a strange confidence, as if the messengers brought you good news from the coasts.

MONTEZUMA: Fears can sometimes be harbingers of great joy. The White God is returning to his country after a long, long absence.

SMOKING EAGLE: They're not gods, these strangers. I've seen them with my own eyes. They're flesh, bone, and spirit, just like us.

MONTEZUMA: The gods take various forms. They of course don't appear in their true form before us. The closer they come to Mexico, the more they will look like us. What could be more obvious than that? All the omens show that it is the exiled god who is coming back. For days, he journeyed through storm and tempest; now, on reaching our shores, he has stripped off his heavenly form and become flesh and blood.

FALLING EAGLE: The gods should remain remote from us, like these stone statues. Talk between them and us should be from heart to heart, not with words that soon lose their meaning.

MONTEZUMA: The White God is coming from beyond the stormy seas.

FALLING EAGLE: When he comes, what will become of us?

MONTEZUMA: That is just the sort of question that adds fear to my joy. Perhaps he will judge us. But why should we fear that? We have done deeds of which we may be proud. Will he find Mexico as it was when he left it? Of course, he'll have changed, and we'll have changed. If we have made mistakes, he'll forgive us some of them, and we shall atone for some with our sacrifices.

FALLING EAGLE: This sacrifice might be the whole of Mexico.

MONTEZUMA: My blood runs cold whenever that thought comes to me.

FALLING EAGLE: The white-skinned strangers must go.

MONTEZUMA: [*Approvingly.*] They must go! Let my magicians set out at once!

FALLING EAGLE: Not the magicians, Montezuma, the army!

MONTEZUMA: Let my magicians go forth against the white gods. Let my magicians use their strong spells to make the white gods flee in terror. Let my magicians use their incense to give the white gods dreams filled with fear—dreams more dreadful than we have dreamed here. Let my magicians shower poisonous insects upon them while they sleep. Let my magicians cow the hearts of these white gods just as they have cowed our minds with the dragons that spew forth thunderbolts.

[*Exit* FALLING EAGLE *and* SMOKING EAGLE. *Enter* MALINALI, *young and beautiful.*]

Malinali, I am entrusting to you a task of great importance. I have complete faith in your love of your country and in your virtue, so I shall send you, after the magicians, like an offering to the White God. Get close to him. Win his trust and his love. Open his heart. Learn his secrets. Is he the true White God returning from exile, or is he a stranger who covets our land? The future of Mexico depends on your finding out the truth.

MALINALI: And if he's not a god, this uninvited stranger?

[MONTEZUMA *gives her an Aztec obsidian dagger.*]

Scene 4

[*The Spanish encampment. Night. Some of the* CONQUISTADORES *are sitting round a fire. One is playing a guitar.*]

FIRST CONQUISTADOR: Governor Velásquez is always unlucky with his fleet commanders.

SECOND CONQUISTADOR: Juan de Grijalva, who commanded the last expedition, was a religious maniac.

THIRD CONQUISTADOR: But at least he was loyal to the governor of Cuba; he didn't play dirty tricks on him like Cortés has.

FIRST CONQUISTADOR: He was loyal enough to go back to Cuba.

DÍAZ: Yes, he returned with the ships he couldn't sink.

FIRST CONQUISTADOR: He was the greatest fanatic on earth. All he thought about was converting every Indian he came across. He had no time either for war or for trade.

OLMEDO: It is one of our duties to add these pagan Indians to the flock of Christ.

DÍAZ: On condition that we take their gold! They have plenty of gold and no faith. With us, it's just the reverse. The problem lies in how to exchange one for the other in a way that will please the angels.

FIRST CONQUISTADOR: What's really needed is a commander as loyal to Velásquez as de Grijalva and at the same time as competent as Cortés, but it's hard to find those two virtues in the same person.

FOURTH CONQUISTADOR: Cortés is every inch a commander.

SECOND CONQUISTADOR: There's no one who doesn't know that he made a secret agreement with the governor's secretary and His Majesty's purser so that he could get this command.

THIRD CONQUISTADOR: They persuaded the governor that Cortés was the only person who could lead this expedition successfully.

DÍAZ: Velásquez likes to receive recommendations about people.

SECOND CONQUISTADOR: A large share of the booty will go to those gentlemen in return for their favors.

THIRD CONQUISTADOR: Didn't someone open Velásquez's eyes?

ESCUDERO: He stripped Cortés of command of the fleet that night.

SECOND CONQUISTADOR: But he was late, too late.

DÍAZ: We were already weighing anchor. When he learned that the fleet was slipping away, he sent after us the only vessel he had left, signaling time and again with flashing lights, "I order you to return." Until daybreak it kept on, "I order you to return," then, "I request you to return," then, "Please return."

FOURTH CONQUISTADOR: [*With guitar.*]
Our ships were running free,
Our ships were running free,
The wind blew from the north.

[*While the* CONQUISTADORES *are laughing,* CORTÉS *enters.*]

ESCUDERO: You can't just ignore an order to return, Cortés. Will you explain the situation to us, for heaven's sake? Are we to return to Cuba, or are we rebel sailors who have made off with the fleet?

SECOND CONQUISTADOR: Yes, tell us. We're on our own now. If we flout the order from Governor Velásquez, we are rebelling against the king.

THIRD CONQUISTADOR: We may be men who deserve the noose or the stake, but we do have some sense of what's right and wrong.

FIRST CONQUISTADOR: I've saved this neck from the noose three times, and I don't begrudge it, but at least we have the right to know the reason why, haven't we?

SECOND CONQUISTADOR: We have wives and families in Cuba.

CORTÉS: Those who want to can go back to the pigsties they left in Cuba.

FIRST CONQUISTADOR: There's no call for insulting language.

ESCUDERO: If you ask me, you're a commander who's been stripped of his authority.

SECOND CONQUISTADOR: Everyone's equal here.

DÍAZ: Pull yourselves together, men. Cortés is our commander.

CORTÉS: Drunkards! You loaded more wine than powder aboard the ships.

[CORTÉS *kicks a cask of wine.* ESCUDERO *sets upon him. While* ESCUDERO *and* CORTÉS *are fighting with swords,* MONTEZUMA'S MAGICIANS *suddenly appear, wearing brightly colored face masks, carrying baskets, and creating clouds of incense. They prostrate themselves before the* SPANIARDS *in salutation. They play flutes and endeavor to make their magic work.*]

DÍAZ: Oh, this was all we needed!

FIRST CONQUISTADOR: Where did this lot spring from?

DÍAZ: They're Montezuma's men.

SECOND CONQUISTADOR: They're casting spells. Let's hope they do us some good.

THIRD CONQUISTADOR: Do you suppose they're purifying us?

FOURTH CONQUISTADOR: What a blissful fragrance that incense has.

DÍAZ: I feel quite euphoric.

FIRST CONQUISTADOR: I'm beginning to feel dizzy.

SECOND CONQUISTADOR: I can see colors cascading before my eyes.

DÍAZ: How about joining them with your guitar?

THIRD CONQUISTADOR: What if they're up to no good?

FOURTH CONQUISTADOR: These devils want to put us to sleep.

SECOND CONQUISTADOR: They'll rob us of our religion and faith.

CORTÉS: Let's close our eyes and pretend we're asleep.

DÍAZ: Peer out through your eyelashes.

FIRST CONQUISTADOR: Farewell. I'm going to Cuba.

CORTÉS: I'm in Spain, before the king. We're dreaming while we're awake, and we know it's a dream. Ugh!

[*One of the* MAGICIANS, *holding a container, tries to make* CORTÉS *drink from it.*]

DÍAZ: Drink it, Cortés, it's a health-giving draft.

[*The other* MAGICIANS *open their baskets. Snakes and insects are revealed.* CORTÉS *shakes himself and leaps up. He forces the* INDIAN *offering him the drink to swallow it himself. The other* SPANIARDS *also throw themselves upon the* MAGICIANS *and drive them off. As the stage darkens,* CORTÉS *sees* MALINALI *under a single light. He grabs her by the arm.*]

CORTÉS: Who are you? Have you, too, come to bewitch us?

[MALINALI *smiles, showing no fear as she looks* CORTÉS *in the face.*]

Scene 5

MONTEZUMA: My magicians could not defeat the White God. He forced them to drink the poison. The stinging black and green insects stung my magicians. Those potions that were to rob him of his wits he has used to rob my magicians of theirs.

FALLING EAGLE: It was bound to happen.

MONTEZUMA: I'm not surprised at this outcome, either.

FALLING EAGLE: Command me to do what the magicians couldn't—drive all these strangers into the sea before they have time to take refuge in their floating houses.

MONTEZUMA: Who was relying on magicians alone? Malinali, I have faith in you.

[MONTEZUMA *and* FALLING EAGLE *remain motionless.* CORTÉS's *tent is illuminated.* CORTÉS *is sleeping, stripped to the waist.* MALINALI, *candle in hand, is gazing at him. It is apparent that they made love shortly before.* MALINALI, *with a strange smile on her face, brings the obsidian dagger closer and closer to* CORTÉS's *heart, but draws it back. Then an expression of fear appears on her face. She caresses* CORTÉS's *head lovingly. She walks upstage, addressing the night.*]

MALINALI: He is the one. He is the God of Mexico, the Plumed Serpent, returning to his true home from beyond the stormy seas. He is the White God. [*Hurls the dagger away. Lights dim.*]

MONTEZUMA: [*As if talking in his sleep.*] He is the White God, returning to his true home from beyond the stormy seas.

FALLING EAGLE: The girl, too, is betraying us.

MONTEZUMA: I shall show the White God and the children of the White God the might of Mexico in another way.

FALLING EAGLE: Is there any other way than war?

MONTEZUMA: With gifts. I shall satisfy his desires with great gifts. I shall send the heaviest pieces from my treasury to the White God—the sacred symbols that adorn the Great Shrine and the large Aztec sun beaten out of soft gold.

FALLING EAGLE: You're going to make your enemies a present of the country's treasure? Don't take leave of your senses, Montezuma! When they see all this gold, they'll go mad with wonder. If there were any who didn't want to move on to the capital before now, they certainly will after seeing the gold.

MONTEZUMA: They will perceive the might that lies behind these riches, and they will withdraw. White God, I am sending thee Mexico's gold sun. Be content with that. Come not to my capital. Turn and go away!

FALLING EAGLE: With this golden invitation, you'll bring ruin upon the country. Three hundred have come today. If we don't stop them, three hundred thousand will come tomorrow.

MONTEZUMA: If the White God really wants to come, who can stop him?

Scene 6

[*The Spanish encampment. A stifling day. Fatigue is evident on every face.*]

ESCUDERO: These damned flies will finish us off before the Indians get the opportunity.

FIRST CONQUISTADOR: The local tribes have stopped sending us food. They've withdrawn into the interior. And it's not only hunger, but fever too that we have to contend with. These cursed sands have now swallowed up thirty-five of us.

CORTÉS: Did I bring all these calamities upon you?

ESCUDERO: Maybe not, but since you insisted on having command, it's your job to get us out of here alive. Give the order to go back to Cuba.

CORTÉS: To go back to Cuba?

ESCUDERO: Don't think I don't know what's going through your mind. So let the soldiers know, too. Tell them we're not going back to Cuba. You're silent. This indecision of yours will cost us dearly, señor.

CORTÉS: The situation will improve soon.

ESCUDERO: You're certainly trying hard to improve it, spending the whole day in your tent with that Mexican beauty.

[*The* CONQUISTADORES *laugh.*]

How much longer do we have to be patient?

CORTÉS: That's the same question Caesar, Alexander, and Tariq ibn Ziyad were asked. Ah, it's a sign that my fortune will change.

ESCUDERO: Are you now comparing yourself to those great conquerors, señor Cortés? For heaven's sake, be realistic. We see gallows in our dreams. In Cuba, the governor has proclaimed us rebels. If the king confirms the proclamation, we shall be sailors in betrayal of our homeland.

FIRST CONQUISTADOR: Let's go back to Cuba!

CONQUISTADORES: Back to Cuba! Back to Cuba!

SECOND CONQUISTADOR: Let's elect another commander for ourselves.

THIRD CONQUISTADOR: Otherwise these sands will be our grave.

FOURTH CONQUISTADOR: Withdraw, Cortés. Let's sail away.

DÍAZ: [*Enters in a state of confusion.*] The ruler called Montezuma has sent us gifts—there's a solid gold sun as big as a cartwheel!

ESCUDERO: Did you say gold as big as a cartwheel?

DÍAZ: Yes, an enormous solid gold sun as big as the wheel of an oxcart.

CORTÉS: Are you sure you're not sunstruck?

SANDOVAL: [*Enters.*] It's true, Cortés. Díaz isn't exaggerating. It's a gigantic sun disk made of soft gold, and its face is decorated with various symbols.

DÍAZ: There it is, gleaming and glistening in front of the tents.

[CORTÉS *and the* CONQUISTADORES *run out. Shrieks of joy. The Mexican* EMISSARIES *enter.*]

EMISSARIES: Montezuma is giving the gold sun of Mexico to the Plumed Serpent. Malinali, we don't know if you are a trustworthy Indian girl. Great Montezuma hopes you will not betray this land that reared you. Do all that is in your power; make the White God turn and go. Don't let him reach our capital.

MALINALI: His command will be carried out.

[*Enter the* SPANIARDS.]

LÓPEZ: We have been more than recompensed for what we have been through.

DÍAZ: Even the fever victims tossing and turning in their beds recovered when they saw the gold.

FIRST CONQUISTADOR: The object of our expedition has been achieved in a day.

CORTÉS: [*Mumbles to himself.*] The object of our expedition?

SANDOVAL: We have a great opportunity, señor Cortés. Now we can make the soldiers do what we want. All that has to be done is to share the gold prudently.

CORTÉS: [*Thoughtfully.*] We shall share the gold prudently. Load great Montezuma's gifts onto the ship of our testy friend Escudero.

DÍAZ: [*Whispers to* CORTÉS.] Take care. As soon as he hoists sail, he'll be in Cuba at once.

CORTÉS: [*Jokingly.*] Come on, he wouldn't dare.

DÍAZ: If you ask me, Escudero is dying to get back to Cuba, anyway, so think what the temptation will be when the holds of his ship are crammed with gold.

CORTÉS: [*Firmly.*] Do what I say! Have the wine casks unloaded and let all the sailors enjoy themselves to the full to celebrate today.

EMISSARIES: May the White God and the children of the Plumed Serpent be satisfied with these gifts. Let them shut themselves up in their winged houses and go beyond the seas!

CORTÉS: Who is this Plumed Serpent, this White God, they speak of?

MALINALI: Montezuma's lost god. It was said that one day the White God would come again from beyond the stormy seas in winged houses and appear with a colored crest of quetzal feathers on his head. The White God, the Plumed Serpent—you yourself.

CORTÉS: In that case, let me don the deity's regalia.

[*Sounds of celebration.*]

Scene 7

EMISSARIES: We come back from the shores of the sea with good news. The danger has been repulsed. The strangers are turning around and going back, never to return to the kingdom of the sun.

MONTEZUMA: Going back? Won't they come to my capital?

EMISSARIES: Aren't you pleased?

MONTEZUMA: What depressing joy this is. Did he himself say that he would go?

EMISSARIES: His mistress, the Indian girl Malinali, trembled at your sacred name. "Montezuma's wish shall be carried out," she said.

MONTEZUMA: From where does she learn Montezuma's wishes, whereas I myself am a stranger to my own heart?

EMISSARIES: We also learned the thoughts of the men around him. They all want to load the gold into their winged houses and return to the land whence they came.

MONTEZUMA: It is sad that our sacred memorials have fallen into foreign hands. If he has agreed to go back, he's not the White God, he's just a cunning pirate who's plundering our deep blue bay.

Scene 8

CORTÉS: You know I always consult you, Díaz, before I make important decisions.

DÍAZ: Yes, I know. You asked my advice when you were having yourself appointed commander of the fleet. What's your question?

CORTÉS: What if you wrote a letter to the king?

DÍAZ: Me, write a letter to the king? What an honor! What shall I say?

CORTÉS: Something more than just a letter. A communiqué summarizing the expedition we have undertaken in the name of Spain in this new land.

DÍAZ: Why don't you write it?

CORTÉS: I don't want to come between you and the king. You and your friends put your heads together and write as you see fit. I don't want you to praise me, but state the facts. Give don Carlos the glad tidings that we are founding Spain's first great city in this new land.

DÍAZ: Which city are you referring to?

CORTÉS: The city we shall create on those hills yonder. Villa Rica de la Vera Cruz.

DÍAZ: Villa Liquor Flowing with Booze?

CORTÉS: Villa Rica de la Vera Cruz—the Rich City of the True Cross.

DÍAZ: You mean there is to be no return to Cuba? I guessed as much. "Díaz, my boy," I said, "We'll be staying here!"

CORTÉS: Look, I've scribbled out a rough draft here. There's no need to stick to it word for word.

DÍAZ: We'll write as we see fit, but give us the draft so that we don't forget anything. Let's not forget anything you want to say.

CORTÉS: Take a stroll round the tents, one by one, and choose me some responsible friends to take posts in the first government of Vera Cruz.

DÍAZ: Aha! So we're to set up a government, are we?

CORTÉS: If it should be proposed, I'd be willing to accept the post of chief justice. Now have Escudero brought in. I think they caught him trying to slip out of the harbor last night.

[*As* DÍAZ *leaves,* ALVARADO *enters, soon followed by* LÓPEZ *bringing in* ESCUDERO *with arms bound.*]

ALVARADO: The soldiers are getting restive. They want the gold shared out straight away. They're all like jackals that have caught the scent of blood.

CORTÉS: Let them keep licking it; that's all they'll get. This gold must shine not in their pockets, but in the darkness of their minds.

[CONQUISTADORES *stream in.*]

CONQUISTADORES: Let's share out the gold! Don't keep us waiting any longer! Divide the gold!

CORTÉS: One at a time, gentlemen, one at a time. First, let us give señor Escudero his due.

CONQUISTADORES: Let's divide the gold!

CORTÉS: At midnight last night, you were caught red-handed sailing your ship away from the harbor. Have you anything to say?

ESCUDERO: You stole a whole fleet away from Cuba. Am I to be held guilty for sailing a single ship away—my own ship, to boot?

ALVARADO: He sailed a whole fleet away from Cuba. OK, let's put it that way. You weren't able to sail a single ship away from here. That difference between you gives him the power to send you to the gallows.

CORTÉS: The ship was laden with gold. This friend of yours was caught trying to get away with your share of the gold.

CONQUISTADORES: Was he, by God? Taking our share, was he? Curse him! Damn him!

CORTÉS: As chief justice of Vera Cruz, I charge you with rebellion against our king, don Carlos.

ESCUDERO: You know you're the real rebel. By ignoring Velásquez's order, you yourself are in a state of insurrection against the king. It was right and proper that the gold should first be conveyed to Cuba.

CORTÉS: Velásquez would have taken the lion's share and distributed just a little largesse to these fellows. Isn't that so?

ESCUDERO: Are you totally ungrateful for all the favors you have been given, Cortés? Take out your orders. It says there that we must return to Cuba.

CORTÉS: It's true that I have received favors from Velásquez, the governor of Cuba. For years, I received his help and his consideration. He was like a father to me; he saw to it that I married well. I am indebted to him for a great many things. I hold him in high esteem. But if at a time when I could be achieving great things for the glory of Spain, my benefactor seeks to make me drag out my life on the sugar plantations of Cuba, then that's a different matter. My duty to Spain overrides my duty to Velásquez. [*Tears up the orders.*] Unfurl the standard! [*The unfurled standard bears the gold-embroidered arms of the Spanish king.*]

ESCUDERO: Governor Velásquez has no arms. This banner you have unfurled is the flag of insurrection.

CORTÉS: But it bears the arms of our king, don Carlos. From this day on, we bear allegiance directly to Spain. [*In front of the map.*] Between Vera Cruz and Spain there is no Cuba.

Between Cortés and don Carlos there is no Velásquez. [*Several people applaud.*] Take away this gentleman. Let us pray that this hapless fellow may be the last man I have to send to the gallows.

THIRD CONQUISTADOR: By however many persons our numbers are reduced, our share of the gold will increase in proportion.

CONQUISTADORES: The gold, Cortés, the gold!

SANDOVAL: Let's be rid of this gold before it becomes a curse to us.

CORTÉS: I ask you, what do you want to do? Go back to Cuba to serve your bloated governor? Or shall we march on to this Mexico that's full of gold?

SOME CONQUISTADORES: Let's go back to Cuba! Let's go back to Cuba!

OTHER CONQUISTADORES: Let's march on to Mexico!

CORTÉS: Let those who wish to bring new lands beneath the royal standard of Spain come with me.

DÍAZ: Friends, let's follow Cortés; let's follow the standard of don Carlos, our king.

SANDOVAL: Let's put an end to division between us. Discord spells disaster.

CONQUISTADORES: Let's divide the gold.

SANDOVAL: We got this gold without the loss of any blood.

FOURTH CONQUISTADOR: Well then, let's pack up and be gone from here without any mishaps.

SECOND CONQUISTADOR: While we have the locals terrified of us, let's raid the nearby villages and towns and carry off as much gold as we can find.

CORTÉS: I am promising you a greater glory.

SECOND CONQUISTADOR: Our bellies are full of promises. With my share of gold, I want to build a more glorious life for myself.

FOURTH CONQUISTADOR: It would be crazy to go farther into the interior. We have only a handful of men. When the Indians get over their first surprise and confusion, they will polish us off. Let's set sail for Cuba while we have the gold and the going's good.

SANDOVAL: You don't know these fellows.

CORTÉS: We shall know one another before long. I'll make this rabble into the finest fighting force under the flag of Spain. These men will cease to be merchant seamen for Velásquez; they'll become conquerors for Cortés.

CONQUISTADORES: Let's divide up the gold!

CORTÉS: Yes, yes, I'm going to share out the gold. First, though, the king's due.

CONQUISTADORES: The king's due?

SECOND CONQUISTADOR: One-fifth.

CONQUISTADORES: [*Impatiently.*] Long live the king!

CORTÉS: I'm delighted to see your loyalty to the king. It encourages me to say that I have no doubt all of you who have such deep affection for His Majesty will agree to what I'm going to propose to you now.

CONQUISTADORES: Tell us, Cortés, tell us what you propose.

CORTÉS: Let's not divide Montezuma's treasure. Let's not smash this golden sun disk. Let's send it whole to the king. Let this treasure be the one-fifth that is his due. Let us go to the source of all this gold and take our own share from there. Let this booty that we have obtained with so little effort be Spain's. Bigger spoils await us.

[*A sullen silence among the* CONQUISTADORES, *then grumblings.*]

Let those who do not accept my proposal, those who do not wholeheartedly support the sending of Montezuma's treasure to the king, sign this document. Of course, that is, if there's anyone among you who feels that way.

FOURTH CONQUISTADOR: I want to say a word about the procedure. Naturally I'm not opposed to all this gold being sent to the king, but we were told . . .

CORTÉS: I said, "Sign this document if you don't want all this gold sent to the king!" [*Silence.*] Very well, it is carried unanimously that we send all of Montezuma's gifts to the king. It was not for nothing that Escudero and his men went to the trouble of preparing their vessel for a voyage. The ship will sail, but for Spain, not Cuba.

DÍAZ: This gold will tell better tales than Velásquez's men.

CORTÉS: Set sail at once. We have no time to lose. Everything must be done with speed. Keep well clear of Cuba. As for the other vessels, if they lose heart and slip away in ones and twos, it may present a great threat to the unity of our force. What's your opinion on that?

DÍAZ: We must impose heavy penalties on those who want to make off. As we did to Escudero . . .

CORTÉS: We'll be in the interior. Won't it be somewhat absurd to try to punish them after they've gone? When the great conqueror Tariq set foot on our native Spain, he burned his boats.

DÍAZ: Why did Tariq burn his boats?

CORTÉS: [*Deep in thought.*] So that we shouldn't return to Cuba.

FIRST CONQUISTADOR: What job will there be for the sailors?

CORTÉS: Soldiering!

FIRST CONQUISTADOR: The ships must be burned!

CORTÉS: In Cuba, Velásquez proclaims us rebels. In Mexico, Montezuma greets us as gods.

SECOND CONQUISTADOR: What will the king say? We must consider that, too.

CORTÉS: Let's march beneath the king's standard. Awaiting us are more gold than we can carry away and glory such as falls to the lot of very few men. Let us gain these new lands for Spain. Conquerors, let us go forth and perform the task history has imposed upon us! Let us establish greater Spain!

SANDOVAL: Friends, let's follow Cortés! Let's follow this auspicious standard!

CONQUISTADORES: [*Shouting together.*]

We'll follow Cortés.

Long live Cortés!

Onward conquerors—to Mexico!

Let's set eyes on Montezuma.

Long live Cortés!

Long live Sandoval!

Long live Alvarado!

Down with Velásquez!

Forward conquerors!

[*Exit all but* CORTÉS.]

CORTÉS: Good-bye to all I have left behind.

[MALINALI *enters, in her hand a plume of colored feathers, symbol of the* PLUMED SER-PENT, QUETZALCOATL.]

It's not clear what the western longitudes have hidden: gunpowder, blood, fate.

[MALINALI *places the symbol of the deity on Cortés's head.*]

Tell me in detail, Malinali, about my forgotten past. Tell me the story of the lost god. I am the Plumed Serpent; in my eyes are dragons that melt gold. I have returned to my native land. I am marching to Mexico. My spirit will go on before me and will take the roads along which I shall pass. [*Lights dim while* CORTÉS *is kissing* MALINALI.]

Scene 9

EMISSARIES: The pale-faced foreigners are still marching on. They are about to reach the land of the Totonacs.

MONTEZUMA: Coming? What about the reports that they were content with our gifts and would go away?

EMISSARIES: That was what Malinali promised.

MONTEZUMA: After a time, they'll turn round and go back, that's for certain.

EMISSARIES: They've burned their boats.

MONTEZUMA: Where are they sheltering?

EMISSARIES: They've set up a place on the coast.

MONTEZUMA: That must be temporary quarters.

EMISSARIES: They are stone buildings with roots striking down into the soil.

MONTEZUMA: They're a long way away, a very long way away from Mexico.

EMISSARIES: The dragons they call horses go like the wind.

MONTEZUMA: They'll lose their way in the passes through the Mountains of Death.

EMISSARIES: They have a mysterious scorpion in a box that shows them the way.

MONTEZUMA: The roads are full of dangers.

EMISSARIES: They see ahead with a mirror.

MONTEZUMA: My heart yearns for the war cries of my early youth.

FALLING EAGLE: That's the talk I want to hear!

MONTEZUMA: Only the constant clash of sword upon sword can drive away the visions in my head.

FALLING EAGLE: I can't recall a single thing you didn't achieve once you'd set your heart on it.

MONTEZUMA: I used to be driven by rage.

FALLING EAGLE: And only victory could still that rage.

MONTEZUMA: Where was it you said the foreigners were?

FALLING EAGLE: In the country of the Totonacs. The warriors await your command.

MONTEZUMA: Send a messenger to the chief of the Totonacs.

FALLING EAGLE: Let's not leave this task to the chief of the Totonacs; he's not up to it.

MONTEZUMA: Tell him not to let the white gods set foot in his country.

EMISSARIES: The foreigners have seized the Totonacs.

FALLING EAGLE: Are we still going to delay?

MONTEZUMA: Send my warriors against the foreigners!

FALLING EAGLE: [*Exits enthusiastically.*] There speaks the true Montezuma.

> [*Right stage,* SPANIARDS *illuminated. Down stage, the imperial standard.* ALVARADO *points out the route of the advance on the map. From this point on, the scene continues on two separate parts of the stage: the Mexican* EMISSARIES *and* MONTEZUMA *are on one part; the* SPANIARDS, *who enter talking, are on the other.*]

CORTÉS: Let the Totonacs swear allegiance to me instead of to Montezuma. Montezuma is my friend.

MONTEZUMA: Friendship is between equals; if he is the White God . . .

CORTÉS: God is Montezuma's friend. Let him trust in me.

MONTEZUMA: [*Again shaken.*] I cancel the order to fight.

EMISSARIES: The warriors have sped down from the mountains.

MONTEZUMA: Tell Falling Eagle to halt the army!

EMISSARIES: Even if they had winged feet, the messengers could not catch Falling Eagle.

MONTEZUMA: It's night. The swiftest means are blazing torches from peak to peak.

EMISSARIES: Don't halt this avalanche. Leave it; let it do its work.

MONTEZUMA: I'll fight against them through others. I'll set the Tlaxcala tribe onto them.

> [*Marching* SPANIARDS *fire their muskets as if on a hunt. Sounds of fighting. An imposing portrait of don Carlos, holding the globe in his hand, descends right stage.* CORTÉS *addresses this picture, and* MONTEZUMA *addresses* CORTÉS.]

CORTÉS: 2 September 1519. Royal blood of Spain, great Catholic, king of kings, Charles V, I address you:

MONTEZUMA: [*On his own part of the stage.*] How should I address this god who has left the unknown and come here?

CORTÉS: We had our first major encounter in Tlaxcala—an unexpected attack—but with the local girl Malinali as our guide and through my troops' outstanding efforts, the danger was repulsed. Tlaxcala is the second stage of our expedition; Mexico is its real goal.

MONTEZUMA: Don't trust the Tlaxcala tribe.

CORTÉS: Don't believe the men Velásquez has sent to turn you against me.

MONTEZUMA: There are so many obstacles between us, preventing us from coming closer together.

CORTÉS: Grandson of Isabella the Great! Whenever I think of you, the shadow of Velásquez falls between us, and you grow dim.

[*Their voices intermingle.*]

MONTEZUMA: If only I could grasp his real intention.

CORTÉS: If only I knew what thoughts were passing through his mind.

MONTEZUMA: My fears would be stilled.

CORTÉS: My concerns would cease.

MONTEZUMA: Your being a god and our being free—how can both be?

CORTÉS: Say, "I acknowledge Cortés . . . "

MONTEZUMA: If only I knew—Mexico's roads are open.

CORTÉS: " . . . he is my commander in this new land. He will carry my standard. He will open up rich lands in my name!" A word from you will suffice. Let my foot tread firmly upon the ground because it is Spain that marches forward.

MONTEZUMA: This is the fate of all Mexico.

CORTÉS: They are accusing me of insurrection.

MONTEZUMA: The young men are reproaching me.

CORTÉS: Grant me a little time . . .

MONTEZUMA: They assume the god who is drawing near . . .

CORTÉS: Let me prove with deeds my loyalty to you.

MONTEZUMA: . . . to be an enemy who is coming to destroy us.

CORTÉS: Great Catholic, king of kings, don Carlos, we are continuing our march on Mexico.

MONTEZUMA: [*In fear.*] Let the foreigners turn and go away! Don't let them come near us!

EMISSARIES: [*On the Spanish part of the stage.*] Turn and go back to the place where the sun rises!

MONTEZUMA: Don't come to the capital.

EMISSARIES: Don't go to the capital.

CORTÉS: I am going to see Montezuma in his majestic capital.

EMISSARIES: [*On MONTEZUMA's part of the stage.*] They are drawing near to Cholula.

MONTEZUMA: They won't be able to get out of there alive.

CORTÉS: I'll talk with him face to face.

MONTEZUMA: I'm afraid I must forego that honor; the roads are full of dangers.

CORTÉS: No danger can divert us from our path.

MONTEZUMA: I'll still rule Mexico for many a year. My children will rule it for years after me. Let the White God go now and come again when the last child of my line is dying.

CORTÉS: I'm coming to Mexico in Montezuma's day.

MONTEZUMA: Enough, enough! What news from Cholula?

EMISSARIES: They lay in wait for the unarmed people and slit three thousand throats.

CORTÉS: The Cholula chiefs want to blame Montezuma for their sins. They say he gave the order to ambush the god's children.

[MONTEZUMA *remains silent and tense.*]

But I know that Montezuma, who loves and respects us, could not have given such an order.

MONTEZUMA: Don't let them come!

EMISSARIES: They've stayed on the other side of the fiery volcano. From that spot, they're going down to the Red Valleys and the Yellow Deserts.

MONTEZUMA: In the Yellow Deserts, death awaits them.

CORTÉS: Thank you for warning us, Montezuma, but we have no fear. We perceive well in advance the traps that are set for us.

EMISSARIES: They've left the Salt Lakes on their right. They've crossed the Blue Mountain Range and reached the High Plateau with Smoking Hill on the left.

MONTEZUMA: Let them halt there!

EMISSARIES: Do not come any farther!

CORTÉS: I am Montezuma's god. I am coming to Mexico to see him. I will talk to him about great matters, about existence and nonexistence.

MONTEZUMA: [*Enthusiastically now, his opposition having vanished.*] Come, White God, I await you in my capital!

CORTÉS: I am coming to add your name to mine.

MONTEZUMA: Like bats on the roof of a dark cave, my thoughts crowd in one upon another, moaning. Let the White God come and drive them all away. Let him bring light to us.

CURTAIN

ACT II

Scene 1

[*On the pyramid.* MONTEZUMA *is showing his guests the capital.* ALVARADO *and* OLID, *equipped with a telescope and surveying instruments, are furtively drawing a plan of the city.*]

MONTEZUMA: Behold Mexico, your country, spread out at your feet. We are now on top of the highest pyramid. Welcome, White God, to your true homeland. You have brought joy to Mexico. For many years, I have ruled this land in your name. Before me, countless numbers of my forefathers ruled in your name. Now you have come. How fortunate I am that you have come in my day. Without doubt, I am the happiest king of the land. As Falling Eagle said, I am a king my forefathers will envy. That's because you have come during my reign. My eyes aren't deceived by dizzying incense. I am not dreaming. For years, I have watched and waited for you, White God, to return from exile. You have come during my reign!

CORTÉS: Make a careful note, Alvarado, of the city's strategic points, the entry and exit roads, the system of defense, their shelters, their means of communication with the commercial regions. Yes, Montezuma, this view that is spread out here below us is the finest in the universe.

MONTEZUMA: Those causeways are the lifelines of the capital; they join us to three sister cities on the shores of the lakes. If need be, their bridges can be destroyed.

FALLING EAGLE: Why have the foreigners been drawing all this? [*Snatches the papers, pen, and pair of compasses from* ALVARADO.]

MONTEZUMA: Falling Eagle! When will you cease this disrespect toward our sacred guests?

FALLING EAGLE: You're ignoring their lack of respect.

MONTEZUMA: Give back those papers with the drawings! The White God and the White God's children want to get to know the changing fate of Mexico well. Now introduce yourself, fall on your face before them, kiss the earth they are standing on, and beg their pardon.

FALLING EAGLE: [*After a silent protest.*] My name is Falling Eagle. I am the chief of the Valleys of Falling Rocks.

MONTEZUMA: Falling Eagle! You are obeying my orders with disrespect.

CORTÉS: Arise Falling Eagle. You seem to be a noble young fellow.

FALLING EAGLE: [*Brushing aside* CORTÉS, *who was about to embrace him.*] Whoever you are, keep away from me, pale-faced stranger.

CORTÉS: Let's keep a close watch on this young fellow. Let's win over the leaders who can help us in our cause.

[*The* SPANIARDS *salute* CHIEF LEOPARD *and* CHIEF JAGUAR, *who are behind* MONTEZUMA.]

FALLING EAGLE: We are dragging the country to ruin.

CORTÉS: If we seize the key points, we'll rule millions of Indians like a flock of sheep.

MONTEZUMA: These pyramids were built for the glory of the god of light and civilization. No one can destroy Mexico.

CORTÉS: [*Sincerely.*] Let not Mexico and Tenochtitlán, the greatest city, be destroyed. Let its matchless splendor shimmer for all eternity on the sparkling waters of the Salt Lakes. Let not this land dedicated to me be destroyed.

FALLING EAGLE: If it changes hands from the bronze-skins to the pale strangers, it will be destroyed.

[*Sad music from a flute, a black drum, and cymbals. The* SPANIARDS *listen apprehensively.*]

ALVARADO: Who are these people approaching in ceremonial robes?

SANDOVAL: The splendor of the view has made us forget where we are.

DÍAZ: Obviously they didn't make these pyramids for wanderers like us or for romantic lovers who want to watch the sunset on the lakes.

ALVARADO: Look at those red stains on the black stones!

MONTEZUMA: Now you will see the Lord of the Lakes, the young man who is to be sacrificed to the White God.

OLMEDO: We don't want a sacrifice.

DÍAZ: Do not let an innocent young man's blood be shed.

MONTEZUMA: The Lord of the Lakes is a willing sacrifice. It is the highest honor for him.

OLMEDO: We must prevent this, señor Cortés.

CORTÉS: As the situation demands, Padre. For the moment, let no one make a move.

[*Three* PRIESTS *in black robes emerge from the inner temple.*]

MONTEZUMA: Has the sacrifice been brought?

PRIESTS: He is waiting beside the black stone—if he is to be sacrificed.

MONTEZUMA: What do you mean, "If he is to be sacrificed"?

PRIESTS: Perhaps when you see the sacrifice, your belief will waver and change.

MONTEZUMA: How will my belief change?

PRIESTS: He will say to you that these uninvited guests are not gods.

MONTEZUMA: Will the human sacrifice tell me that? [*They nod assent.*] You are priests of the God of Night. Of course, the return of the White God does not suit your purpose. But, see there, he has come. He is before us in human form; and with his coming, cruel Smoking Mirror's time has ended. Let the ceremony begin. Let the sacrifice be placed upon the black stone!

CORTÉS: I am forbidding human sacrifice in the land.

PRIESTS: The gods delight in sacrifice, but it's clear from their faces that these strangers are disgusted by it. They're not gods.

MONTEZUMA: Are we to show the priests of black magic to be right? Let the ceremony begin! Time is jealous and demands particular sacrifices on particular days in the land of the Aztecs. In the Month of the Flower, it yearns for the hearts of two lovers. In the Month of the Rains, so that the salt shall not go bad, it requires the heart of a young woman adorned like a goddess. Your coming, White God, demands the heart of the young, brave Lord of the Lakes. Now the heart of the Lord of the Lakes proudly leaps within him.

CORTÉS: You say he will be sacrificed willingly?

MONTEZUMA: [*Explaining.*] Prisoners of war are good enough to ward off common misfortunes, but to celebrate great occasions, willing sacrifices are chosen a year earlier. Throughout this year of waiting, the future victim is held in great respect throughout the land. He has Mexico's loveliest girls as his lovers and concubines—they fulfill his every wish. Approaching death gives a keen edge to every taste. The noble sacrifice that will now be offered to you had girls who loved him. They parted tearfully from him on the steps of the pyramid.

PRIESTS: [*Murmur.*] He had no one who loved him—other than his parents.

MONTEZUMA: Now he'll come out and do the Dance of the Plumed Serpent.

PRIESTS: He's still too green to do that dance; it's too demanding.

MONTEZUMA: A well-trained sacrifice has by now left all fear behind him. He will look with a smiling face upon the obsidian dagger. He knows this honor is the highest he can attain in this universe.

PRIESTS: He's not mature enough to look upon the knife without flinching.

MONTEZUMA: A willing sacrifice.

PRIESTS: It's not certain that he is willing.

MONTEZUMA: [*Angrily.*] Why do you keep interrupting and contradicting me?

PRIESTS: We are bringing another sacrifice in place of the Lord of the Lakes.

MONTEZUMA: Who?

PRIESTS: One who is dearer to you has been chosen for this honor.

MONTEZUMA: You don't mean Falling Eagle is willing to be the sacrifice?

PRIESTS: One who is even dearer to you than Falling Eagle.

MONTEZUMA: Who can be closer than Falling Eagle? [*The* PRIESTS *draw aside the cover of the shrine.* MONTEZUMA'S SON *is standing there, naked.*] My son!

PRIESTS: Your dearest one.

MONTEZUMA: Is this a joke? Take him away! Let the real sacrifice, the Lord of the Lakes, come forward.

PRIESTS: [*Insistently.*] This is the real sacrifice.

MONTEZUMA: Is not the young, brave Lord of the Lakes, whom I love, sufficient sacrifice?

PRIESTS: Instead of the Lord of the Lakes, toward whom you feel love, but against whom you harbor a grudge as well, we have chosen a more suitable sacrifice.

MONTEZUMA: [*Looks at the* CHIEFS.] Can this be so?

SMOKING EAGLE: For the first time, I am of the same mind as these black-robed priests.

FALLING EAGLE: On a subject that so vitally effects the existence of Mexico, give your irrevocable verdict not with a sick longing, but with a father's heart.

MONTEZUMA: What do you expect me to do?

SMOKING EAGLE: Strengthen your faith through the blood of your most dearly beloved.

PRIESTS: And become a priest; plunge the black flint dagger yourself into the bosom of your only son.

MONTEZUMA: You seem to have gone out of your minds.

FALLING EAGLE: I want to warn you for the last time. Despite all their successes that seem so supernatural, these strangers are not gods, and they are not the sons of gods. By letting them into the capital, you are plunging the land into danger.

MONTEZUMA: I said he is the White God.

FALLING EAGLE: I saw you wrestling with your doubts.

MONTEZUMA: Small doubts keep faith alive.

FALLING EAGLE: Do you still believe that he is the White God?

MONTEZUMA: Who else could he be?

PRIESTS: You don't have to make us believe. But with the rights conferred upon us by custom, we choose the sacrifice that is appropriate for the White God.

MONTEZUMA: If I had not believed he was the White God, I would long ago have flung his heart to Smoking Mirror, who moans in the dead of night.

PRIESTS: But if he really is the White God returning from exile, then even a beloved son whom you will sacrifice is scarcely enough.

MONTEZUMA: [*Softly.*] And if he is not the White God?

FALLING EAGLE: It will be for nothing that you smear your hands with your son's blood. Just test whether this man is the White God.

MONTEZUMA: How?

FALLING EAGLE: By the legend in the old inscriptions, for example, that the White God told while going into exile. He should know his own story better than anyone.

MONTEZUMA: [*Draws closer to* CORTÉS.] Show us new proof that you are the White God, then those like Falling Eagle who lack belief will see the truth, and the fire in my heart that flickers and cools will be fanned to life. We want to hear from your own mouth the story of the White God.

[MONTEZUMA *puts on the mask of the God of Night,* SMOKING MIRROR, *which the* PRIESTS *hand to him. He puts on a bloodstained dark robe like the priests' and picks up a dark mirror.* CORTÉS *assumes the identity of the* PLUMED SERPENT, QUETZALCOATL.]

SMOKING MIRROR: Who am I now?

PLUMED SERPENT: My enemy, Smoking Mirror, the sorcerer who took Mexico away from me.

SMOKING MIRROR: How did you lose your kingdom to me?

PLUMED SERPENT: [*As if racking his memory.*] Once upon a time, there was one Kingdom of Peace instead of these kingdoms of Mexico, Tlaxcala, Maya, and Olmec all warring with one another. Heaven and earth were in harmony, and this meant immortality. The sorcerer Smoking Mirror, the Lord of Darkness, came slinking up to me and held his dark mirror to my face.

SMOKING MIRROR: [*Holds up the mirror, which sends forth smoke.*] Look, look into my mirror, my dark mirror! See your true face there. Through living all alone, your eyelids are red and swollen, and your eyes are sunk in deep hollows.

PLUMED SERPENT: He told me I was seeing my face for the first time. I saw that I was ugly.

SMOKING MIRROR: Just taste a while the life of mortals. Listen to the dictates of the flesh. Share our couch tonight with my sister.

[*From the inner sanctuary, a young* AZTEC GIRL *emerges. She dances seductively around* PLUMED SERPENT *to the accompaniment of the same instruments that now play a lively tune. Then she offers him a drink from a goblet.*]

PLUMED SERPENT: [*Resists.*] First, I pushed away the fatal draft she offered me.

SMOKING MIRROR: Taste it with the tip of your tongue.

PLUMED SERPENT: [*Unable to resist.*] I drank the whole glass.

[*The drumming tempo quickens.* PLUMED SERPENT *and the* AZTEC GIRL *dance passionately. They embrace, fall to the ground together, and after more convulsive movements become still. The* GIRL *snaps and removes* PLUMED SERPENT's *symbols of godhead. She hands them to* SMOKING MIRROR. PLUMED SERPENT, *his energy spent, drags himself along the ground.*]

In the morning, I awoke filled with remorse, cold, and trembling. My eyes were two hollows from which dark waters flowed. My heart was weary, my desires were base. The King of the Dead ascended my throne: the cruel Smoking Mirror, whose face was the face of the night. I took a last look at my homeland and wept. Then, accepting my own exile, I opened my bosom to the salty winds and reached the great, stormy seas. There, with the last spark that remained in my heart, I set fire to myself and became a star and passed to the Great Beyond. But as I was rising over the infinite seas, I said, "I will return."

MONTEZUMA: [*Removes the mask from his face.*] He told the legend of his life as if he had lived through it.

PRIESTS: Shall the child be placed upon the stone? [MONTEZUMA *runs to his* SON's *side.*]

FALLING EAGLE: He could have heard the legend from an Indian.

MONTEZUMA: It's not enough. It's not enough! Show us further proof that you are the White God. Don't make me shed my son's blood in vain. If you are not the White God of Mexico, say so frankly, and I swear upon my honor that I will pardon you all and send you back laden with gifts. Just tell me you are not the White God. Don't make me pluck out my only son's heart.

CORTÉS: I am the true god of Mexico.

MONTEZUMA: Give us more powerful proof of your godhead. Make it as plain to my senses as this stone I am touching and the sound of that black drum.

[CORTÉS *offers his telescope to* MONTEZUMA.]

[*Amazed.*] Smoking Hill is but a few yards away; I feel I could touch its flowing lava. The White God's mirror brings the distant near.

CORTÉS: [*Turns the telescope the other way around.*] Now look through it this way!

MONTEZUMA: Now everything has gone far away, very far away. Is it the pyramid that has risen to the sky? The buildings in the capital are at the bottom of the precipices. The White God's mirror makes the near distant.

CORTÉS: The near and the distant are one within the other. I am the long-awaited White God. I was light. Now I am transformed to flesh and blood and have come down to my old homeland. Look at the sun!

MONTEZUMA: [*His eyes seared.*] I'm blinded!

[MONTEZUMA *blindfolds his* SON *and leads him by the hand to the inner sanctuary. The previous sad tune is heard again on flute and drum.*]

OLMEDO: Halt this satanic ceremony!

CORTÉS: No one is to move!

OLMEDO: Put your hand on your heart, Cortés!

CORTÉS: You too, Padre, pray for the soul of this young martyr.

OLMEDO: [*Murmurs.*] And the God of Abraham desired that he should sacrifice his only son.

DÍAZ: It's sad that this time no ram glowing with divine light will descend from Heaven.

ALVARADO: Montezuma's god is a pitiless god.

[*The actions of the sacrificial ceremony are apparent from the shadows falling on the veil of the inner sanctuary.* MONTEZUMA *plunges the knife into the bosom of his* SON, *laid out on the stone. He plucks out the heart, holds it for a time in his hands, and raises it to Heaven. The drumbeats grow louder and faster.* MONTEZUMA *emerges from the inner sanctuary, his hands covered in blood.*]

MONTEZUMA: I have no doubt; my faith is complete; he is the White God, and my son's blood is witness. [*Collapses in a heap at* CORTÉS's *feet.*]

Scene 2

[*With amazement, some* INDIANS *are watching the* SPANIARDS, *who have various instruments in their hands.* DÍAZ *has emerged, half-naked, from the bathhouse. An* INDIAN *is drying him.*]

FIRST CONQUISTADOR: [*To* DÍAZ.] You've got into some bad ways since you came to Mexico.

DÍAZ: I can recommend this to you, too. You feel as if you're walking on air when you come out.

SECOND CONQUISTADOR: Aren't you going about it the hard way? What's the use of washing? If you don't smell too sweet, just rub on some perfume—that gets rid of the smell.

THIRD CONQUISTADOR: [*Scratches himself.*] Like a good Christian, I took a dip in water once in my life—that was in church when I was baptized as a baby.

FOURTH CONQUISTADOR: And don't forget the time when the ship you were on capsized in a storm. But a God-fearing fellow shouldn't do more than that.

DÍAZ: I really like being clean—though not as much as being dirty. Those Indians were amazed by my skin, which had become hard and leathery through not washing. They stripped it off me in rolls with loofahs and special cloths. I've become so clean now that I can't bear the stench of your sweat. These Mexicans are fanatical about washing. They've built baths and wash places everywhere, with bubbling hot water flowing through them.

FIRST CONQUISTADOR: Devotion to their ablutions will not save them from the wrath of God.

SECOND CONQUISTADOR: They will be purified in the flames of Hell.

FOURTH CONQUISTADOR: But haven't we come here to save their souls?

THIRD CONQUISTADOR: [*Spits on the ground.*] Come off it! Who's bothered about anyone's soul? We've come here to save these bits of gold from falling into anyone else's hands.

DÍAZ: No, friends, we haven't come here for plunder; we have come to raise up these people, who are more backward than we are—in some respects. We shall teach them what we know. The truth gives happiness. [*The* CONQUISTADORES *applaud mockingly.*]

FIRST CONQUISTADOR: Yes, that's so. We're the gods of civilization, are we not?

SECOND CONQUISTADOR: We shall bring light and learning to the people of this land.

FOURTH CONQUISTADOR: Long live Díaz! The truth gives happiness.

THIRD CONQUISTADOR: So long as we take the gold in return.

SECOND CONQUISTADOR: Come on now, gods of civilization, let's show what we're made of.

FOURTH CONQUISTADOR: I've invented the wheel, and I'm making the first cart, see! Mine is the most useful invention.

DÍAZ: You know, it's astounding—they succeeded in casting gold in the size and shape of a cartwheel, but they don't know how to make and use a real cartwheel.

SECOND CONQUISTADOR: I'm inventing the compass.

THIRD CONQUISTADOR: And I'm inventing glass.

FIRST CONQUISTADOR: And I the sail.

FOURTH CONQUISTADOR: And I the windmill.

DÍAZ: They already know how to make use of wind power.

SECOND CONQUISTADOR: We'll teach them that the world is round.

FOURTH CONQUISTADOR: And we'll teach them some lessons they'll never forget.

FIRST CONQUISTADOR: That the sun stands still, and Mexico goes around it.

THIRD CONQUISTADOR: These things will leave them utterly bewildered.

DÍAZ: [*Murmurs distractedly.*] Nevertheless, in many ways they are not in the least behind us.

THIRD CONQUISTADOR: [*Scratches.*] You know, this beats everything! Here are we, Spain's craftiest adventurers—in our time we've been expelled from school, escaped from prison, and dodged the rope—but now we stand, gods of civilization, scratching our scabs.

DÍAZ: [*Continues his train of thought.*] In many ways, they're more advanced than we are. In personal relationships, they are so sincere, friendly, and honest that we might think of their behavior as stupidity. Are they more backward than we are in the arts? In sculpture? In architecture? They've built the most beautiful cities on earth. They're masters of massive constructions: these pyramids, the shrines, and houses set among lakes and gardens. Who can hold a candle to them as gold- and silversmiths?

FOURTH CONQUISTADOR: They're living in the Stone Age and the golden age at one and the same time.

FIRST CONQUISTADOR: They've skipped the Iron Age. They'll pay dearly for that.

SECOND CONQUISTADOR: Will there be a war?

DÍAZ: No, we are soldiers of peace.

FIRST CONQUISTADOR: [*Strokes his sword.*] The sparks that European steel will draw from Aztec flint will set alight the fires of the colonial age, which will demand many sacrifices.

FOURTH CONQUISTADOR: But human sacrifice has been prohibited in Mexico, or is that White God fairy tale to be believed?

FIRST CONQUISTADOR: One must beware of knowledge that would overshadow belief in the White God.

FOURTH CONQUISTADOR: And what about the rules of our religion?

FIRST CONQUISTADOR: Their turn will come, but Cortés's godhead must prevail a little longer.

[*Sound of a distant explosion.*]

SECOND CONQUISTADOR: What was that?

THIRD CONQUISTADOR: Is war breaking out?

DÍAZ: The White God is showing another of his miracles. He's blown up the statue of the God of Night on top of the great pyramid.

FIRST CONQUISTADOR: Come on now, Christ's elect, rack your tiny minds and reveal all your knowledge and skills. We're not just bringing syphilis and scabies; we're the bearers of Western civilization.

[*Applause. Sound of another explosion.*]

FOURTH CONQUISTADOR: There goes the statue of the Goddess of Flowers, too.

FIRST CONQUISTADOR: Show them all you know—but don't explain cannons and gunpowder, our military secrets.

Scene 3

CHIEF LEOPARD: [*To* FALLING EAGLE.] You see how ill-founded your fears were.

CHIEF JAGUAR: They have come to raise us up.

CHIEF LEOPARD: And they are proving that by their deeds.

SMOKING EAGLE: [*Hesitantly.*] They've taught us more than a few useful things.

CHIEF LEOPARD: I didn't care for these foreigners at first, but . . .

FALLING EAGLE: [*Mockingly.*] I wish you'd call them "gods."

CHIEF LEOPARD: No, I never believed they were gods.

CHIEF JAGUAR: They're only humans, made of flesh and blood like us.

CHIEF LEOPARD: They're superior humans, though, and they're educating us.

CHIEF JAGUAR: They're teaching us things we could never have discovered for ourselves. They're working hard to help us.

SMOKING EAGLE: Why do you suppose they're showing such concern for us?

CHIEF LEOPARD: Helping others is one of the things they believe in.

FALLING EAGLE: I don't think that's the reason.

CHIEF LEOPARD: You have a suspicious, envious heart.

CHIEF JAGUAR: You're always looking on the dark side.

CHIEF LEOPARD: Aren't we going to accept anyone as a friend?

FALLING EAGLE: The strangers raised you, Chief Leopard, right to the top rank in the army in one go.

CHIEF LEOPARD: I got there through my own ability.

FALLING EAGLE: It's interesting that it was the foreigners who brought out this ability of yours. You, Chief Jaguar, are running all of Mexico's mines for the foreigners.

CHIEF LEOPARD: I'm proud of what I'm doing. I've increased gold output. The foreigners know the value of our natural wealth better than we do. With their help, we are improving the country.

FALLING EAGLE: Thanks to the foreigners, you and a handful of able people have very quickly improved yourselves, not the country. Your new style of life is dazzling.

CHIEF LEOPARD: Come on, Chief Jaguar, you just can't talk to this fellow; enmity for foreigners has got into his very soul.

[*Exit* CHIEF LEOPARD *and* CHIEF JAGUAR.]

FALLING EAGLE: Go then! Go and tell on us to your new masters!

[*To* SMOKING EAGLE.] They're competing with one another to curry favor with the foreigners. The noble families of Mexico are offering their daughters to these plunderers because that sort of tie with the foreigners is now reckoned an honor. Diseases we never knew, never even heard of, with names like *gonorrhea* and *syphilis* are now the scourge of the land. Don't these outbreaks show who these "gods of civilization" really are?

[SMOKING EAGLE, *tense, remains silent.*]

Scene 4

[CORTÉS, *by candlelight, is writing a letter to the king. Upstage, five* SPANIARDS *with their backs to the audience recite the letter in chorus.*]

CORTÉS: When the soldiers saw the magnificent city standing above the lakes, they thought they were dreaming.

SPANIARDS: The waters reflected the city's red towers and white pyramids.

CORTÉS: This is the Mexico I present to my sovereign.

SPANIARDS: It has buildings unparalleled in Seville or Granada. Seventy thousand people a day trade in its markets. There are skins of tiger, leopard, jaguar, deer, snake, and iguana; scented plants; drugs to drink to make one feel euphoric or energetic; obsidian, volcanic glass, quartz sculptures, beaten gold vessels; brightly colored fruits, amber, cacao; balms for countless ailments, sweet perfumed oils that make the skin glisten; precious stones spread out on green rush matting, some known to us, some new—rubies, meteorites, crystal, sapphire, shining so bright they tire the eyes.

CORTÉS: This is the Mexico I present to you, don Carlos.

SPANIARDS: The unimagined beauty of the ever-fertile soil awaits its new owners.

CORTÉS: And the simple, childlike people, if handled skillfully, will provide the cheapest labor for this colony beyond the seas. The excellent services of Chief Leopard and Chief Jaguar are beyond praise.

SPANIARDS: The mountains that rumble with fire inside them, like salamanders, are rich with gold, silver, and copper.

CORTÉS: This is the Mexico I present as a gift to my king.

[DÍAZ *enters agitated, holding a carrier pigeon.*]

DÍAZ: This Mexican pigeon Montezuma gave us as a pet that we have taught to fly between the sea and the capital has brought us bad news. Smoking Eagle, commander of the eastern armies, has attacked and routed our coastal base.

SANDOVAL: The insurrection could spread to the capital tomorrow.

DÍAZ: Time is not on our side; our divinity has worn very thin.

SANDOVAL: Worse! They're openly debating whether they're superior to us.

ALVARADO: Our bronze cannons are no longer dragons spewing forth thunderbolts.

DÍAZ: Indians are riding on the backs of our horses.

SANDOVAL: The feel of gold has driven our soldiers mad. They're behaving scandalously in public.

DÍAZ: The initial wonder and fear have died down, and those feelings have now turned into hatred.

ALVARADO: Falling Eagle is inciting the people against us.

SANDOVAL: The only thing we can now rely on is Montezuma's belief in us.

ALVARADO: How much longer will that last?

SANDOVAL: Some important people such as Chief Leopard and Chief Jaguar are our men, too.

DÍAZ: But one can't place too much reliance on them. They're of no use to their own country.

SANDOVAL: They've cast their lot with us.

OLID: [*Bringing further news.*] Smoking Eagle has entered the city. The first thing he did was raze the bridges.

DÍAZ: We're trapped here.

ALVARADO: He'll go and tell Montezuma how clever he's been.

SANDOVAL: Those Eagle chiefs have come out openly against us.

OLID: What if they are able to open Montezuma's eyes?

DÍAZ: What are you thinking of, sir?

[CORTÉS *has from the outset been worriedly walking back and forth. Then he halts, having made up his mind.*]

CORTÉS: We shall make Montezuma a prisoner in his own country.

Scene 5

[SMOKING EAGLE *shows* MONTEZUMA *a Spaniard's head in a rush basket.*]

SMOKING EAGLE: See here with your own eyes, Montezuma, the end of the white-skinned foreigners that you call gods.

MONTEZUMA: Why did you do this?

SMOKING EAGLE: He will tell you better than anyone that he is not a god.

MONTEZUMA: I didn't order you to do that.

SMOKING EAGLE: You wanted to know whether or not the strangers were gods. How could I prove it to you without killing a few of them?

MONTEZUMA: I didn't want such proof.

SMOKING EAGLE: But I have brought it.

MONTEZUMA: So I see. Won't you speak to me with your purple lips, pale-faced stranger, and say to me, "We are mortals, too, like the Aztecs"? What was this poor wretch's crime?

SMOKING EAGLE: At their base on the coast, they were making Indians toil like slaves. They had taskmasters with whips. I attacked them with a handful of my warriors and routed them.

MONTEZUMA: [*Despite himself.*] They were men around the White God. The fact that they have died doesn't prove that he too is mortal.

SMOKING EAGLE: Just give the word. Let me bring you the head of Cortés, too—that cunning man who deceives you with his lies of godhead.

MONTEZUMA: [*Shaken.*] To whom did I sacrifice my son?

SMOKING EAGLE: To cold stones. The gift of the heart you offered did not reach any god.

MONTEZUMA: Hold your insolent tongue.

SMOKING EAGLE: Your anger shows that your eyes are opening. I'm glad about that.

MONTEZUMA: My son, I can still feel your heart beating in the palm of my hand.

SMOKING EAGLE: If you act now, your son's blood will not have been shed in vain. If you delay, you will sacrifice the whole of Mexico.

MONTEZUMA: O serpent! Serpent from the earth. Fear my revenge! News of the raid must not reach the foreigners in the capital.

SMOKING EAGLE: I came galloping all the way on a horse I captured, and as soon as I arrived, I had the bridges destroyed. It's not possible that any foreigner has reached the capital before me, unless he has wings.

[CORTÉS *and his men enter, armed.*]

CORTÉS: Good day, Montezuma.

MONTEZUMA: I haven't summoned you, Cortés.

CORTÉS: [*Mumbles.*] That's the first time you've called me "Cortés." [*Clearly.*] I've come of my own accord.

MONTEZUMA: You used not to let your men come into my palace so brazenly. And you're all armed, too.

CORTÉS: Our weapons are part and parcel of us.

MONTEZUMA: What is it you wish to say?

CORTÉS: I'm glad to see that our friend Smoking Eagle is here. This morning I looked at the coast with my magic mirror and saw that regrettable things were occurring at our base there.

MONTEZUMA: Your magic mirror will soon show you still worse things. [*At that same moment, the* SPANIARDS *seize and bind* SMOKING EAGLE.] Release him!

CORTÉS: I am your White God.

MONTEZUMA: My god is remote from me. [*Suddenly snatches from* CORTÉS's *head the symbols of the god* QUETZALCOATL, THE PLUMED SERPENT.] The Plumed Serpent's magnificent feathers have molted and revealed a deceiver's ugly, grinning face.

OLMEDO: Yes, señor Cortés, let's put an end to this deity game now; for days, we have been committing this sin. [*To* MONTEZUMA.] He is a mortal like you, and, far from being a god, he is only a commander at the bidding of a distant king. Indeed, his command has not even been confirmed.

MONTEZUMA: Guards! My guards, where are they?

SANDOVAL: The Spaniards are your guards.

MONTEZUMA: Are you going to arrest me?

CORTÉS: You'll be our guest for a while.

MONTEZUMA: Who is whose guest here?

CORTÉS: We are one another's guests.

ALVARADO: Our troops with heavy weapons have taken up positions on the right and left of the roads to pay their respects to Montezuma as he passes.

CORTÉS: Walk along smiling, Montezuma. Don't let the people think you are being taken by force.

[*Exit with forced appearances of happiness to the sounds of martial music.*]

Scene 6

[CHIEF LEOPARD *and* CHIEF JAGUAR *are calming down the people.*]

CHIEF LEOPARD: There's nothing to worry about, compatriots. Montezuma is going of his own accord to our white-skinned guests. There is a great deal we can learn from them.

CHIEF JAGUAR: Don't give way to the provocation by Falling Eagle, Smoking Eagle, and their kind. They're defeatists and traitors.

CHIEF LEOPARD: Show our special brand of hospitality to the foreigners, who want to make this place better and more beautiful.

Scene 7

[CORTÉS, DOÑA MARINA, OLMEDO, *and* OTHER SPANIARDS *are straightening up after praying before a large wooden crucifix. Sounds of the music ending the religious service are heard.* MONTEZUMA *and* SMOKING EAGLE, *who is bound, are watching the* SPANIARDS.]

CORTÉS: [*In his capacity as a judge, to* SMOKING EAGLE.] We can begin. Why did you raid our base on the coast?

SMOKING EAGLE: I wanted to open Montezuma's eyes. I proved to him how easily our enemies could be beaten.

CORTÉS: Did Montezuma ask you to do this?

SMOKING EAGLE: I did it of my own accord.

MONTEZUMA: [*Straightens up.*] I gave the order.

SMOKING EAGLE: He's saying that to save me.

CORTÉS: We don't believe that our friend Montezuma would have given such an order. So you admit your crime?

SMOKING EAGLE: My only crime was to fall so stupidly into your hands. Otherwise, it would be an honor for us to fight against the foreigners who have come creeping into our midst, abused our hospitality, and day after day have taken over more and more of our vital resources.

CORTÉS: Are you ready to take your punishment?

SMOKING EAGLE: But set free my braves that you have imprisoned in the courtyard. They were acting on my orders.

[ALVARADO *signals the number fifteen with his fingers.*]

CORTÉS: No. Fifteen of you shall be burned alive—on orders from Montezuma.

MONTEZUMA: On Montezuma's orders, you will be sacrificed on top of the pyramid.

CORTÉS: And as fuel for the flames, we shall use the javelins, arrows, and shields in all the arms depots.

MONTEZUMA: It is my command that all the chiefs position themselves at the head of their warriors. Let battle commence!

SMOKING EAGLE: I am going to be burned, Montezuma. If you can, give Falling Eagle this order you have delayed so long.

[As SMOKING EAGLE *leaves, he takes from his breast the red carnation he was wearing and places it in the nail wound in Christ's foot, while the* SPANIARDS *look on astonished.*]

MONTEZUMA: Is it this God of yours who commands you to destroy my people and trample my kingdom underfoot?

CORTÉS: We discovered this kingdom, Montezuma.

MONTEZUMA: And were we not here before you came?

DÍAZ: [*Mumbles.*] Well, yes, that's so.

CORTÉS: And now we are the conquerors.

MONTEZUMA: You mean to say you've come from across the sea to plunder?

CORTÉS: We are conquerors opening up new lands.

MONTEZUMA: Who gives you this right?

CORTÉS: Our swords.

MONTEZUMA: [*Inspecting the sword, mockingly.*] While we were using gold, you seem to have found tougher metals. The other day I saw one of your men fighting with an Aztec, and the steel was striking sparks from the Aztec flint.

CORTÉS: From these sparks, the great age of Spain will burn bright.

MONTEZUMA: Spain?

CORTÉS: The land we come from.

MONTEZUMA: Isn't your own country enough for you?

CORTÉS: We need Mexico's natural resources.

MONTEZUMA: We need our country's resources.

CORTÉS: Try to understand, Montezuma, the Western world is living in the age of great discoveries, inventions, conquests.

MONTEZUMA: What is this Western world you speak of?

CORTÉS: [*Pointing.*] Spain and its neighbors.

MONTEZUMA: Wouldn't it be more correct to call that the Eastern world?

DÍAZ: [*Laughs.*] True, everything depends on your point of view. We've become accustomed to think of ourselves as Western, but when you go west of west, the situation gets confused. Should one call this the extreme west or the extreme east? The two converge here, after all.

CORTÉS: [*Continues to expound his view.*] Such an age of awakening and exploration cannot be halted. The kings of Spain and neighboring countries are competing with one another to found new empires. And to found an empire you need to gain new colonies.

MONTEZUMA: Do you mean that as your era of empire begins, so our era as a colony begins?

CORTÉS: Well, of course the country that will grab the biggest part of the New World is Spain.

MONTEZUMA: [*To* OLMEDO.] I ask you, how can you reconcile this policy of yours with the commandments of your faith? This morning your revered priest was telling me about these commandments in order to win me over. Didn't he say, "Thou shalt not kill"?

CORTÉS: We've prohibited human sacrifice in Mexico.

MONTEZUMA: And lo and behold you are sacrificing my people. "Thou shalt not steal," he said. No doubt he meant, "Thou shalt not steal thy neighbor's money or poultry, but thou mayst steal his country." "Thou shalt not commit adultery," he said, but he should have added, "but thou mayst rape Aztec women and girls."

SANDOVAL: Are we going to let this fellow babble on anymore?

MONTEZUMA: [*Rushes to and fro, half-crazed.*] I command my braves to take to arms! I command it!

CORTÉS: Don't make me do something I don't want to do. [*With the help of two* SOLDIERS, *he puts* MONTEZUMA *in chains.*] Stand quietly, Montezuma. Don't resist!

MONTEZUMA: Set me free!

CORTÉS: This is only until they have been burned, and their ashes have been blown away by the wind. Look, how calmly Smoking Eagle and his braves stand in the middle of the square. I admire courage like that. Ah, see there, the pyre has been lit.

OLMEDO: That's how they burn the heretics in Spain, Montezuma.

OLID: It's a long time since we've seen such a good burning ceremony as this.

MONTEZUMA: Burn me with my brave Smoking Eagle and my fifteen Aztecs. Don't degrade just me in this way. Mexico no longer has a king.

LÓPEZ: Montezuma's order has been carried out.

CORTÉS: Don't leave him unattended. Doña Marina, don't let him do anything foolish.

[*Exit all* SPANIARDS *except two guards at the door.* DOÑA MARINA *prostrates herself at* MONTEZUMA's *feet. The light of the red flames strikes the darkening stage.*]

MONTEZUMA: You and I, Malinali, have betrayed this land in different ways. The faith of our forefathers led me astray. Now the land of those forefathers is under the foreigners' feet. But how do you ease your conscience as you hear the Aztecs' death cries?

DOÑA MARINA: Montezuma offered me to the white-skinned strangers. I had been taught that the greatest virtue for any woman was loyalty to her man. My man is the commander of the Spaniards. I have served him.

MONTEZUMA: You mean to say that you showed our enemy the way here because you were so true to your traditions? You don't even believe that yourself. You went to him with a duty to perform. You were going to let me know whether or not the one who was coming was a god.

DOÑA MARINA: I told you the answer.

MONTEZUMA: You said he was the true White God.

DOÑA MARINA: He worked his first miracle on me. He changed my name, and at the same time he changed my faith. He made a brand-new woman out of me. The sweet Aztec girl Malinali was no more, and in her place was the Christian doña Marina, whom all the Spaniards, from Cortés the conqueror down, treat like a queen.

MONTEZUMA: I can see the change your god has wrought in you. [*Stroking his chains.*] And this is the change he has wrought in me.

DOÑA MARINA: As I look at you, I can see the fate of all Mexico.

MONTEZUMA: Get away from me, don't touch me!

DOÑA MARINA: I showed them the way. I trampled my homeland underfoot, step by step.

MONTEZUMA: But in return they treat you like a queen.

DOÑA MARINA: I have attained a state of damnation more wretched than any other Indian woman will ever know.

Scene 8

CORTÉS: [*Addresses the king's picture.*] What anguish your persistent silence is causing me. Yet only one word from you would be enough. Just say, "I acknowledge Cortés as my servant, my slave. He is bearing my standard in the New World." [*Suddenly angry.*] Why doesn't don Carlos answer me? Why? Why? How many letters have I sent! How many emissaries have I dispatched! Falling Eagle may rise against us at any moment. Don Carlos should have given us support in these difficult days. And he the grandson of Isabella the Great and Philip, who made Spain what it is! Shame on him! I call him a king who can't look across the oceans.

OLMEDO: Show respect for the king's name.

CORTÉS: I'm gaining for him a country bigger and richer than Spain itself.

OLMEDO: The size of your gift may make the king think. The men Velásquez has sent to the palace are not idle; they're working on the king and saying, "Today this upstart adventurer does not acknowledge that he owes everything to the governor of Cuba;

tomorrow he may rebel against the Spanish Crown. Where will it all end if every commander whose head is turned by a success or two hoists the flag of rebellion? No one
who does not respect the order of the state should be protected."

CORTÉS: Do they think I'll disobey the king? If only don Carlos knew what was going on
in my heart.

OLMEDO: And if he knew what was going on in Velásquez's heart?

CORTÉS: I see you can relate the conversations between the king and my enemies as if you
had heard them with your own ears. Nevertheless, you don't have to be the White God
to know that such conversations take place. Very well, but what effect did our letter
and the gold we sent have on the king?

OLMEDO: They naturally carry a lot of weight. He apparently did give Velásquez a mild
rebuke, asking why he gave command of the fleet to a man he did not trust. But as a
judge in this case, don Carlos is in a tricky position. Perhaps he's made up his mind.

CORTÉS: You know a great deal, Padre.

OLMEDO: I was given the task of taking over the troops and removing you from your command, señor Cortés.

CORTÉS: [*Tries to joke.*] So the padre's been dabbling in politics. We had no idea.

OLMEDO: We've been in politics from the outset.

CORTÉS: Have you now? Who gave you this task? Velásquez?

OLMEDO: I'm afraid someone a hundred times more important—the king himself. Don
Carlos cannot allow two Spanish armies to fight over the spoils in the New World.

CORTÉS: Two Spanish armies?

OLMEDO: Velásquez has set out for Vera Cruz with a bigger fleet. He's marching on Mexico.

CORTÉS: [*Tries to hide his fear.*] Aha, Velásquez has suddenly grown in importance. How
strong is his army?

OLMEDO: Four times the size of ours—all Spaniards.

CORTÉS: That bird of prey, Falling Eagle, will beat the living daylights out of them.

OLMEDO: Velásquez's army is not coming to make war with Mexico. Its one aim is to take
its revenge on you. If need be, it will make an accommodation with Falling Eagle.

CORTÉS: They'll join forces with Falling Eagle and annihilate us here. Is that the plan?

OLMEDO: They hope our men will leave you and join the new army.

CORTÉS: Will my brothers who fought shoulder to shoulder with me betray me? You, for
example, didn't betray me.

OLMEDO: They will carry out the king's command. According to the decree that Velásquez
is said to hold, those who don't join the new army will be deemed in direct revolt
against the king.

CORTÉS: So he plans to isolate me from my fighting force?

OLMEDO: Just as we separated Montezuma from his people.

CORTÉS: Do you suppose Falling Eagle will stand idly by and watch this happen?

OLMEDO: I see you are now placing your trust in your mortal enemy.

CORTÉS: His desire for vengeance won't be assuaged with just one Cortés; he wants to rip out the heart of every Christian and squeeze it between his fingers. [OLMEDO *takes out a crucifix.*] And he's completely right. There's only one man who can handle these fierce Eagles, and that's me. If I'm not commander of the two armies, Falling Eagle will feed every Spaniard's heart to the dogs.

OLMEDO: Come, come, speak more realistically.

CORTÉS: Both Falling Eagle and I act realistically. Velásquez is coming to take my conquest from me.

OLMEDO: Personalities don't matter. The important thing is that another commander will take over where you leave off.

CORTÉS: On this subject we shall never agree.

OLMEDO: The aim is the triumph of Spain—and of Christ.

CORTÉS: The triumph of Spain and Christ is within Cortés's grasp. If my name is to be excluded from the Book of Spain, I'd better pledge my soul to the King of the Dead. On his forehead that the Spanish Crown has rendered immortal, the record of our conquests should be kept. What is victory, anyway, if it is not offered to a higher power?

OLMEDO: We have some new guests. [*Velásquez's representative,* TAPIA, *and another* OFFICER *enter.* DÍAZ *and* LÓPEZ *are with them.*]

CORTÉS: Who are you?

TAPIA: Velásquez's aides. We're looking for the rebel Cortés.

DÍAZ: Hold your insolent tongues. His title is "Commander in Chief Captain General Cortés."

TAPIA: We have come to take Cortés. Provided he does not resist, he will be given a fair trial in Cuba.

CORTÉS: And will be hanged fairly, too, will he not?

TAPIA: [*Attempting to open up the documents he is holding.*] I see, so you are Cortés. This is the king's decree that I am about to read to you.

CORTÉS: [*Preventing him.*] You've come a long way. You must be tired. First have something to eat and then rest.

TAPIA: Duty first. Let me read the decree in the presence of the military.

CORTÉS: Since he has come to take Cortés, he must be a top commander. Forgive me, I've been away from Spain for quite a long time, so I don't know the heroes who have won recent fame.

TAPIA: We have the task of taking you to Cuba.

CORTÉS: Fellow countrymen, whoever you may be, I salute you.

TAPIA: The king does not want two Spanish armies fighting each other in the New World.

CORTÉS: The padre was just saying the same thing. It would no doubt be a good thing if you told one of the two armies to surrender.

TAPIA: Only yours, Cortés. That is what the decree says.

CORTÉS: We haven't received the king's decree officially.

TAPIA: Let go of it and let me read it.

CORTÉS: If what you have in your hand is indeed such a decree, it should be read not in front of a mere handful of men, but with due ceremony before the whole army.

DÍAZ: [*Appeasingly.*] After all, we're fighting for the king, too, aren't we? It would never cross our minds to oppose him.

TAPIA: [*Boastingly.*] Be that as it may, we've come with a far mightier force than the one you slipped away from Cuba with.

CORTÉS: So we hear, and we're delighted to hear it. It must be that Velásquez has sent this army to reinforce us at this difficult time.

TAPIA: Don't make a joke of it, sir. We've come to take you in. It's up to you to prevent fighting between the two armies.

CORTÉS: That's true. A war of Spaniard against Spaniard must and shall be prevented. Take our esteemed guests inside and let them rest.

[*As* TAPIA *and the other* OFFICER *are on the point of leaving, they see* DÍAZ *and* LÓPEZ *starting to play dice.*]

TAPIA: Look at those rascals, gambling with gold ingots!

DÍAZ: [*Maintains the effect he has created.*] If you too join Cortés's army, even your horses will have gold saddles and stirrups. Here, take it and melt it down. Make a bracelet from it for your sweetheart in Cuba. Here, you have one, too. [*Tosses two pieces of gold to* TAPIA *and to the* OFFICER.] But if you follow green commanders who don't know how to humor the natives, you'll end up on the sacrificial altar, and your hearts will provide a feast for the dogs.

[*Exit* TAPIA *and the other* OFFICER *in confusion.*]

CORTÉS: These sleek beasts who've arrived from Cuba want to steal from us the conquest we have made and maintained for months with blood and fear. We are the ones who opened up Mexico. They are the ones who'll get the glory. Tonight this matter must be settled one way or the other: either Velásquez or me.

OLID: [*Worried.*] They're four times our strength in numbers, and they have heavy cannons and strong horses.

CORTÉS: Smoking Mirror, the God of Night, will aid us.

OLMEDO: You're talking like Montezuma.

CORTÉS: At this moment, I feel very close to him; he is my brother at heart! Díaz grasped the situation swiftly. Load up those two Spanish-speaking animals with gold and send them to Velásquez's new army. You go, too, Padre; soften them and bring them to heel with your religious admonitions.

SANDOVAL: What is it you've planned?

CORTÉS: We'll raid them at night and add their army to ours.

OLID: Isn't that sheer madness?

CORTÉS: If we have no other course, it can't be called madness.

Scene 9

FALLING EAGLE: [*Addresses the* AZTECS.] From now on, let no one talk to me of peace or the exalted nature of the white gods. Let's pluck them and their ilk out of our midst with our own hands. My bronze-skinned brothers, the country has fallen under the control of foreigners, and through Montezuma they are ordering the destruction of Mexico. Before the two enemy armies unite, let us, brother nations, unite. All the tribes—Aztec, Tlaxcala, Totonac, Tabasco alike—let us put aside our own petty interests, let us forget the cruel deeds we've done to one another in the past. Let us no longer remember that the Aztecs denied salt to the Tlaxcalans. Let us bury our old grudges we had as neighbors. Let us unite. We are the true owners of this piece of land. Let us unite against the common foe coming to destroy us all.

Scene 10

[SPANIARDS *enter in high spirits.*]

DÍAZ: [*Holds a guitar.*] We raided Velásquez's encampment tonight with Spanish songs on our lips and guitars in our hands. They thought we were coming to join them and didn't go for their weapons. Their commanders kept yelling, "Fire! Open fire!" but the reply they got was, "How can we fire, sir? These are our brothers who are coming." In the confusion, we seized the greenhorns and tied them up good and proper.

SANDOVAL: Just a little bit of gold and a few threats, and the whole new army has joined our side. We're four or five times stronger.

DÍAZ: What Cortés said has turned out to be true—our revered Governor Velásquez didn't send the fleet and the army to take revenge on us, but to help us in our hour of need!

[*The* SOLDIERS *laugh.*]

ALVARADO: Now Mexico won't stand a chance of recovering.

OLID: What about Falling Eagle?

SANDOVAL: His end is near, too.

[*Enter* LÓPEZ.]

LÓPEZ: When we sent a message saying Montezuma wanted to see them, the Lords of the Lakes, their men, and Spotted Deer, commander of the western Aztec armies, came, and we've taken them into custody.

ALVARADO: On Montezuma's orders.

CORTÉS: Not a very upright course of action, but in our situation the ends dictate the means.

LÓPEZ: We're sending men all over the place and getting people to do what we tell them because we say it's on Montezuma's orders.

ALVARADO: If we can just get our hands on Falling Eagle, we'll be able to breathe easily.

[*Noise of a commotion drawing nearer.*]

DÍAZ: Look at them!

OLID: The hour we dreaded has arrived, boys. Mexico is about to rebel.

SANDOVAL: Falling Eagle is leading them. They're coming this way.

CORTÉS: Man the guns!

OLID: They're coming in droves. How shall we cope with them?

SANDOVAL: If war breaks out, it will be tragic for Mexico.

DÍAZ: And it won't be all that healthy for us, either.

CORTÉS: Don't let a single Spaniard show himself on the balcony. These people are furious. Bring Montezuma; he's the only one who'll be able to calm this bunch of madmen.

DÍAZ: Has he calmed down, then?

ALVARADO: For days, he was bellowing like an ox from his pain. At one stage, he started to beat himself with his chains, and if the guards hadn't stopped him, he'd have killed himself.

SANDOVAL: He doesn't utter a sound now. He just stares all the time at the clouds, his face like a weeping rock.

[MONTEZUMA *is brought in.* CORTÉS *undoes his chains in a friendly, apologetic way.*]

CORTÉS: Forgive me for treating you like this, but it was for your own good.

MONTEZUMA: It's all right if you don't undo them; I've got used to them.

CORTÉS: You're free.

MONTEZUMA: You've only undone the chains on my hands and feet.

CORTÉS: Falling Eagle has raised a rebellion against you.

MONTEZUMA: Isn't it against you?

CORTÉS: Speak to your nation. Don't let war break out, or Mexico will be totally destroyed.

MONTEZUMA: I am no longer their king.

CORTÉS: Speak to them, you are still the king.

MONTEZUMA: Are you giving me back my kingship? It's not a power that can be taken away and then given back, you know.

CORTÉS: You are the only one who has any influence with them.

MONTEZUMA: I'm like a castrated beast; I've lost something that cannot be replaced.

CORTÉS: Don't let blood be shed for nothing.

MONTEZUMA: [*Murmurs.*] Don't let blood be shed for nothing.

CORTÉS: When they see you, they will calm down and return to their work.

MONTEZUMA: The skin is Montezuma's, but the will is the White God's.

CORTÉS: You and I should feel honored to serve our great king.

MONTEZUMA: [*As if he has again fallen under* CORTÉS's *influence.*] We should feel honored.

CORTÉS: *Let Mexico bow to me as the representative of our master the king. A happy future awaits the country.*

MONTEZUMA: *A happy future.*

CORTÉS: *Only you can make the mob that Falling Eagle has incited come to their senses.*

MONTEZUMA: *Only I can make them come to their senses.*

CORTÉS: *Come out onto the balcony and calm the people with some suitable words.*

MONTEZUMA: *[Decisively.] I will talk, señor Cortés, and my nation shall listen to me. [Picks up the chains that are on the ground.] I shall have Falling Eagle, who is rebelling against me, put in chains. Burned, too, like Smoking Eagle.*

CORTÉS: *Now you're showing the good sense that befits the king of Mexico.*

MONTEZUMA: *My warriors will understand me.*

[The rear of the stage is opened up. When it becomes visible, the sound from the crowd suddenly ceases. Still farther back, lights show FALLING EAGLE *and his* INDIANS.]

FIRST CONQUISTADOR: He has silenced them simply by appearing before them.

SECOND CONQUISTADOR: He's going to speak to them now.

THIRD CONQUISTADOR: The silence of death has descended on the city.

FIRST CONQUISTADOR: What is doña Marina saying?

*[*MONTEZUMA *quickly takes the chains in his hand, fixes one end to himself, winds the other around the balcony railings, and locks it. He stands there bolt upright. The* INDIANS *call out together in sorrow and anger.* FALLING EAGLE *is seen picking up a large stone from the ground. He throws it at* MONTEZUMA. *Amid increasing uproar, the people, too, start to stone* MONTEZUMA.]

SECOND CONQUISTADOR: Get back.

THIRD CONQUISTADOR: He's deceived us.

FIRST CONQUISTADOR: He's showing his people that he's a prisoner.

THIRD CONQUISTADOR: Take him inside.

SECOND CONQUISTADOR: Falling Eagle and the Indians are stoning Montezuma.

THIRD CONQUISTADOR: Save him.

FIRST CONQUISTADOR: The people have lost all control of themselves.

SECOND CONQUISTADOR: Don't let them see you, señor Cortés.

THIRD CONQUISTADOR: Blood is gushing out of Montezuma's forehead. *[Two* SPANIARDS *holding shields leap forward to drag* MONTEZUMA *off the balcony.]*

THIRD CONQUISTADOR: Our boys will be injured, too.

SECOND CONQUISTADOR: He's smiling affectionately at Falling Eagle. *[The* CONQUISTADORES *drag* MONTEZUMA *inside, seriously wounded.]*

DÍAZ: His end is very near.

SANDOVAL: He's trying to say something.

OLMEDO: Do you hear me, Montezuma? Save your soul before you die.

MONTEZUMA: [*Lightly pushes aside the crucifix that* OLMEDO *is holding.*] Who's casting the shadow of a cross upon me? You have opened up my kingdom. Are you now going to open up my heart? Save yourself the trouble. Your pale-faced god cannot save me. Nor do I want to be saved. Leave me alone with the spirits of my forefathers. They are perching like bloodthirsty birds of prey, waiting for me with sharp talons to judge and to punish. Behind them, the dead are arising, like a pale dawn, to greet the king who brought disaster to Mexico.

DOÑA MARINA: [*Consolingly.*] All is not lost. The situation may change. Do you hear the noise outside? The Aztecs are continuing the war.

MONTEZUMA: My Falling Eagle, my man; he was right all the time.

DÍAZ: [*To* DOÑA MARINA.] Can we give him anything to ease his pain?

MONTEZUMA: The stones my children threw landed soft as birds on my head and body.

DOÑA MARINA: Falling Eagle keeps on attacking.

MONTEZUMA: I held him back too long. I am the accursed of the country. How shall I cross the seven abysses? How shall I cross the seven deserts? How shall I cross the nine seas all alone? Not even a dog would make the journey with me.

OLMEDO: Take refuge in Christ, and you will be saved from these evil visions.

MONTEZUMA: Who wants to be saved from them? But whatever the punishment the judges mete out to me, it will be trifling beside the enormity of my crime.

CORTÉS: [*Consolingly.*] You will live, Montezuma.

MONTEZUMA: My Mexican days are over.

CORTÉS: You will live to see the generous forgiveness of our master, the king.

MONTEZUMA: May the gods preserve me from suffering anguish so deep. It's well that my son is dead. He will not keep my accursed name alive.

CORTÉS: I will keep it alive.

[*Outside, a wind instrument of some sort is heard, its sounds full of sadness.*]

MONTEZUMA: Tunes from the Land of the Dead have begun within me.

DOÑA MARINA: Falling Eagle is attacking again.

MONTEZUMA: Ashes of the stars are falling on my brow. Far away a world is clearly being torn asunder along with me.

CORTÉS: What's he saying?

DOÑA MARINA: [*Allowing herself to revert to her old beliefs.*] He is face to face with the ruler of the Kingdom of the Dead. [*Checks herself, takes out a crucifix, and closes* MONTEZUMA's *eyes.*]

OLMEDO: May God have mercy on this unbeliever's soul. He remained true to his devilish gods to the very end.

CORTÉS: Mexico is orphaned. We are alone. He should be taken away swiftly, but with due respect, as befits a king. Continue the battle. Fire the cannons!

[*Sounds of cannon fire as* MONTEZUMA's *corpse is borne out.*]

Scene 11

[SPANIARDS *enter the deserted stage, right; defeated and dejected male and female* IN-DIANS *enter, left.*]

INDIANS: They came at us again with cannons and guns, with their horses and naked swords—cold steel against our flint daggers. They came against us with all their barbaric cruelties, these gods of civilization.

SPANIARDS: With specially made boats, we struck at the city from within while we surrounded it on land.

INDIANS: They came to crush us, but the bitterest pill was to see Indians of brother tribes in the treacherous circle around us. The white-skinned foreigners got Indians to destroy Indians.

SPANIARDS: We got the Tlaxcalans and Totonacs to rebel against the Aztecs and join us.

INDIANS: We stood together on the last day, a life-and-death stand where the waters divide. We ate nothing. We had no food left.

SPANIARDS: We've destroyed the water pipes to the city. Let them drink the Salt Lakes now, let them drink brine, let these Aztecs taste the bitter waters that will torment their hearts.

INDIANS: We drank nothing. We had no water left.

SPANIARDS: They were broken by hunger and thirst, but that didn't make them any the less loyal to their young commanders.

INDIANS: Every time Falling Eagle gave the heartrending call to charge, there was movement in the piles of corpses, a few specters would straighten up, looking like bloodstained sculptures, to make a final charge with their javelins, to shout the name "Aztec" one last time, then to fall forever.

SPANIARDS: The siege lasted eighty days, then Mexico was destroyed to its foundations.

INDIANS: Not one stone was left upon another. As best we could, we scattered.

SPANIARDS: Falling Eagle must die. Falling Eagle and his ilk must die!

INDIANS: So said the White God.

SPANIARDS: That the New World may live.

INDIANS: When Falling Eagle fell, so did Mexico.

SPANIARDS: On 13 August 1521.

INDIANS: We scattered. In the year of the Three Houses, Mexico fell. In the Month of the Flower, on the Day of the Snake, the city fell and we scattered. For long nights, blood rained down upon us.

DÍAZ: The battle ended. A silence that raised up ghosts descended upon the whole area.

INDIANS: On the Day of the Snake, the city fell, houses were roofless and gutted, brains were splattered on the stones. We scattered.

SPANIARDS: [*Dreamily.*] The like of their great buildings was never seen in Seville or Granada.

INDIANS: The gods of civilization took all the men prisoner and drove them to the mines. They wiped out the old and the weak.

SPANIARDS: And the great Catholic, the king of kings, don Carlos, spake, "We recognize Cortés. He is our commander and carries our standard in our new colony."

INDIANS: The Aztecs fell like a body whose heart has been stolen. In the Month of the Flower, on the Day of the Snake, Mexico fell. We scattered.

CURTAIN

◆   ◆   ◆

Fehim Pasha's Mansion

TURGUT ÖZAKMAN

Translated by Refik Erduran

An Editor's Note

Turgut Özakman (b. 1930), a prominent playwright for more than five decades, became a national phenomenon as a docu-fiction writer in 2005 when his gripping story of the Turkish liberation struggle that culminated in the creation of the Republic of Turkey in 1923 exploded on the scene as a runaway best-seller. He gave it the powerful title *Şu Çılgın Türkler* (These Crazy Turks), which pays tribute to the desperate endeavor against imperialists and invaders. In a country where most novels sell a few thousand copies and even all-time best-sellers by Yaşar Kemal and Orhan Pamuk have seldom exceeded sales of a few hundred thousand, an unprecedented and unimaginable million copies of Özakman's hefty volume (747 pages) sold within two years. In addition to whopping royalties, the book brought Özakman immense fame, nationwide acclaim, honorary doctorates, and renewed interest in his plays.

Özakman achieved early recognition as a playwright, especially with the Istanbul City Theater's exciting production of his play *Pembe Evin Kaderi* (The Fate of the Pink House) in 1951. That same year brought him a law degree from Ankara University, after which he practiced law for some time. He later studied drama at the Cologne Theater Institute for a year. On his return to Ankara, he became a dramaturge at the State Theater. He then took a job with the Turkish Directorate of Press and Publications, later serving as an assistant to the press attaché in Bonn. Özakman had varied careers for the next thirty years: chief of documentary and drama programs for Radio Ankara, deputy director-general in charge of news and programming at the Turkish Radio and Television Administration, independent film producer and public-relations representative, teacher of theater arts in Izmir and Ankara, deputy director-general of the State Theater, member of the High Council of Radio and TV Administration, and member of the faculty in the theater department of Ankara University.

Özakman is the author of two dozen plays, some of which are among the most successful in Turkey's theatrical history. He has also written numerous documentary and film scripts, two major novels, and several studies of late Ottoman and early republican history. Since 1968, Özakman has received many of Turkey's top awards, including the Presidential Award for Culture and Arts (1999).

Fehim Paşa Konağı was produced in Ankara in the 1979–80 season and was published in 1980. When the Turkish Ministry of Culture published Refik Erduran's English version,

Fehim Pasha's Mansion, in book form in 2002, a short introductory statement included the following observation:

> Turgut Özakman's favorite subject material is the shaping of Turkish society in the last decades of the Ottoman Empire. . . . Fehim Pasha was the right-hand man of the despotic sultan in the early years of the twentieth century. He had a stable of professional bullies who served him and his master by intimidating all dissidents, and his mansion was a hotbed of intrigue. *Fehim Pasha's Mansion* is the story of a young man, son of a former famous street fighter in the service of the pasha, who rebels against the "might is right" philosophy and the decadent macho culture of the regime. In his defiance of the centuries-old order the emergence of a new humanism can be discerned. The play is not, however, didactic. Peopled by mostly comic characters, its story is told in a highly amusing and lighthearted manner.[1]

The play, which is enriched by music and dance, is a bittersweet depiction of a repressive era when intrigue and betrayal were the order of the day, but the free spirit of some brave individuals gave signs of better days to come.

The lyrics of songs in *Fehim Pasha's Mansion* are especially often intractable from the standpoint of translation. The translator, Refik Erduran, a creative writer himself, has wisely and imaginatively opted for adaptation. Erduran is also a distinguished playwright who is represented in this anthology by his play *My Lovely Scarf.* His biography appears in the brief introduction to that play on p. 345–46 of this volume.—TSH

Characters

NARRATOR

RASİM BABA,[2] former professional bully, now coffeehouse proprietor

PERTEV BEY[3]

AZİZ

ARİF

OSMAN

YUSUF, Rasim's son, actor

AYVAZ, footman in Fehim Pasha's mansion

NURİ BEY, Fehim Pasha's steward

FEHİM PASHA

SERGEANT ÖMER, professional bully in Fehim Pasha's employ

WIFE, Fehim Pasha's wife

MİHRİBAN, Fehim Pasha's daughter

---

1. Turgut Özakman, *Fehim Pasha's Mansion,* translated by Refik Erduran (Ankara: Ministry of Culture, 2002).

2. *Baba:* Literally "father," but often used to address an older man respectfully.

3. *Bey:* "Gentleman" or simply "Mr." (used after the first name).

SERVANT GIRLS

HADİ BEY, Suat Pasha's steward

SUAT PASHA (Mad Suat Pasha), Fehim Pasha's chief rival

VOICE, a single voice in the crowd

CROWD/VOICES

PARTY SPOKESMAN

TARÇIN BEY (does not make an appearance)

KAVUKLU (does not make an appearance)

ACT I

NARRATOR:

in the thirty-second year of his reign
Sultan Abdülhamid
lay on the hard bed of his power
reading a novel
his palace reeked
of *dolmas*[4] cooked in olive oil
of gillyflowers and rot
so in short all was right
the people of Istanbul
began to go out every night
to watch the moonlight

that's when something went wrong
in Resne[5] a Captain Niyazi climbed a mountain
to raise the flag of rebellion
his password
liberty or death
Sultan Abdülhamid was the first to understand
that coming days would be more exciting
than the novel he was reading
so to crush the "freedom lovers"
he sent Şemsi Pasha

---

4. *Dolma:* Literally "filled" or "stuffed"; here used to refer to vegetables such as zucchini, tomatoes, peppers, and grape leaves stuffed with rice and currants.

5. Resne: A small Balkan town where Captain Niyazi started his military push against the Ottoman government in 1908.

destination
the city of Monastir[6]

now it's the year nineteen hundred eight
the month July
we're in Istanbul
a little coffeehouse
on a narrow street
behind Fehim Pasha's mansion
so sit back and watch
let's see what happens in Istanbul

[*The coffeehouse.* RASİM BABA, *walking with a limp, brings coffee, holding the cup in his left hand.* PERTEV BEY *gets up.*]

PERTEV BEY: Oh, how kind of you.

RASİM BABA: Please don't get up. I zigzag more if I hurry.

PERTEV BEY: Relax. I was getting up for the coffee, not for you.

RASİM BABA: [*Laughs.*] Here, sir.

PERTEV BEY: Where's the boy? You're alone again today. [*Sits.*]

RASİM BABA: Yeah. I'm alone.

PERTEV BEY: What happened?

RASİM BABA: Fate played a dirty trick on me. Long story. Has to be told from the beginning to be understood.

PERTEV BEY: Tell me. I love stories.

RASİM BABA: When the midwife told me I had a son, I pulled my gun. Bang bang bang! The ceiling looked like a sieve. When the boy took his first step, I sacrificed a ram. The day he first said "Daddy," I bought clothes for forty needy people. When he was circumcised, I felt so happy, I drank so much, I mistook my mother-in-law for my wife, almost got into her bed. [PERTEV BEY *laughs.*] Ah, my friend, those were the days I was on top of the world. King of the jungle. Anyone tangled with me, his end was near. One slap, and he was out of the game. One day Fehim Pasha's majordomo came calling. "Pasha wishes to see you," he said. You know what happens when a guy like me begins to make a name for himself. Right away, Fehim Pasha's got to have him in his stable. Otherwise, God forbid, the new star might end up in the service of some other big shot. So I ended up in the pasha's service. Which meant I could strike fear into the heart of the whole town even more. Before long, word came again that the pasha wanted to see me. I went to pay my respects. He said, "Rasim, that Tanaş is getting on my nerves. Go teach him a lesson." Tanaş was a Greek toughie collecting protection money downtown.

6. Monastir: A Balkan town.

PERTEV BEY: Don't I know it!

RASIM BABA: But he was real tough. No run-of-the-mill hooligan. I sent word to him. "If he crosses my path," I said, "I'll crush him." From then on we both were on red alert, and one night we ran into each other in Madame Marika's house. Everybody took cover. The music stopped. So I drew my blade from under my arm and threw it in front of his feet.

PERTEV BEY: Whew.

RASIM BABA: That means . . .

PERTEV BEY: "My slap alone is more than enough for you."

RASIM BABA: Good man! So then he draws his blade and tosses it in front of me.

PERTEV BEY: Uh oh.

RASIM BABA: And that means . . .

PERTEV BEY: "Cut the bullshit. No one alive can stop me with a slap."

RASIM BABA: Right! I love telling fight stories to a man who knows the language of fights.

PERTEV BEY: I've been in the mansion so many times, I had to learn it.

RASIM BABA: Anyway, there I am, watching him like a hawk. Let him move a muscle, and I'll tear him to pieces. I'm tense, trembling all over.

PERTEV BEY: Hey, don't get excited.

RASIM BABA: Finally, I see he's about to make his move. So I pull back my right arm a little. [*Does so.*] Of course, he expects a slap from my right hand. But I turn like lightning and give him one with the back of my left. Like this. [*His bad knee hits the table.*] Ouch!

PERTEV BEY: What happened?

RASIM BABA: My knee. [*Sits and strokes his knee.*] Hell. Can't even tell a fight story anymore.

PERTEV BEY: Come on! So what happened next?

RASIM BABA: As God is my witness, one slap was enough. That big man just collapsed. His friends quickly took him away. It's an unwritten rule: a man who bites the dust like that drops out of the competition. That's what Tanaş did. He opened a pub, may he rest in peace. I used to drop in there every now and then. We used to have a few drinks together. When Fehim Pasha heard what happened, he gave me a revolver with a mother-of-pearl handle. But I used guns just for fun. Only cowards need those things.

PERTEV BEY: Right.

RASIM BABA: Anyway, my fame increased even more. I was really on top of the world. One night I had the stupid idea I wanted to drink and gamble a little. So I'm sitting in Çolak's den, playing cards, when these two young punks come and sit at the next table. I'd heard that some of Tanaş's Greek friends wanted to get back at me for what I did to him. I cut the game short and walked away.

PERTEV BEY: Good.

RASİM BABA: At the door, Çolak stops me. He asks why I'm leaving. "Did we do something wrong, sir?" he says. And he grabs my two hands.

PERTEV BEY: Uh oh.

RASİM BABA: I wanted to pull back, but the man looked so hurt, I couldn't do it. That's when I felt a knife go into my left leg, just behind the knee, and another into my right elbow. That was a turning point in my life. Everything's been downhill ever since.

PERTEV BEY: Pity. Pity.

RASİM BABA: When I left the hospital, my left leg was dead, my right hand gone. That meant curtains for me. I wasn't about to be a lame servant in the pasha's stable, so I went into hiding for ten years.

PERTEV BEY: Really? You never told me that.

RASİM BABA: Too embarrassing, I guess. But I must've lost all sense of shame in the end. Look how I'm singing about it like a nightingale.

PERTEV BEY: Ten years, eh?

RASİM BABA: It was obvious what they wanted. I'd be walking around like a lame duck, and they'd make a plaything of me. Huh! No such deal.

PERTEV BEY: How did Tanaş take this?

RASİM BABA: He stopped speaking to all his friends. I made prayer beads at home. He had them sold and sent me the money. You see, we were kind of family, all professional toughies.

PERTEV BEY: Ten years. Sounds too long to believe.

RASİM BABA: Oh, it wasn't so bad. My son was growing up. His mother died, so I'm doing the housework and training the boy—how to punch, how to slap, how to kick, when to hit, when to duck, the rules of the game, the slang, tactics, tricks, the works. I'm all excited about it 'cause the boy looks really promising. Strong, fast, rock hard. "They did in the father, but the son's even better." That's what I hope everyone will say. I may be out of the game, but my name will be up there like a flag. Right?

PERTEV BEY: Sure.

RASİM BABA: It's been a year now since we opened this coffeehouse. Business isn't bad. I thought my lionhearted son would take charge here. He'd be shouting orders right and left, beating the daylights out of anyone who glances at one of the neighborhood girls, breaking the arms and legs of any fool who didn't show proper respect to me. [*Demonstrates how arms and legs are broken properly.*] But that's not what happened. You've seen what the little idiot does when he stops by. He waters the flowers, or he sits reading something like a goddamned *molla*. I mean, if he's going to read, he could at least read a proper war novel. No, it's got to be some silly love story or other. He doesn't drink. He has no war cry. If he comes across a cockfight, he turns away. Watching him, I could weep like a woman. People used to call me "the Destroyer." Now the son of Rasim the Destroyer acts in plays, puts on shadow shows, plays the tambourine, sings, even dances with little bells in his hands. You're a wise man. Please tell me what I should do. Shall I die, or shall I kill him?

PERTEV BEY: My friend, the only wise thing to do now is take the young man to Fehim Pasha's mansion.

RASİM BABA: No, no, I can't do that. I'd die if the pasha saw me like this.

PERTEV BEY: You know I'm giving music lessons to his daughter. Want me to speak to him?

RASİM BABA: No, thanks. I've got to take care of this myself. But you see the fix I'm in. Fate is a great joker, isn't it?

[AZİZ *and* ARİF *can be heard calling.*]

AZİZ: [*From offstage.*] Rasim Baba!

ARİF: [*From offstage.*] Rasim Baba!

PERTEV BEY: Who's that?

RASİM BABA: It's Aziz the quilt maker and Arif the barber.

[AZİZ *and* ARİF *come running, panting.*]

AZİZ: God be . . .

ARİF: . . . with you.

PERTEV BEY: With you, too, friends.

RASİM BABA: What's up?

AZİZ: Er . . .

ARİF: Go on, Aziz. Tell him.

AZİZ: I will, Arif. I made two wedding quilts for the mansion. Today they paid me with a gold piece. So what does one do when one feels rich?

ARİF: We went to have a few drinks and hear some music.

AZİZ: So we find a back table and sit.

ARİF: Three men are drinking in the right-hand corner. They're Fehim Pasha's goons.

RASİM BABA: Just tell me—is there a fight in this story?

AZİZ: There sure is.

RASİM BABA: Then I want all the details.

ARİF: Tell him the details, Aziz.

AZİZ: I will, Arif. Just then three other men come in and sit in the left-hand corner. Then, when they see Fehim Pasha's men . . .

RASİM BABA: They almost faint, eh? Ha ha ha!

AZİZ: No, not at all. [RASİM BABA's *grin freezes.*] One of them tosses a coin to the musicians and yells, "Cut that racket out and play 'Sergeant'!"

PERTEV BEY: [*Laughs.*] "Sergeant," eh? Ho ho!

RASİM BABA: Wait a minute. What's all this about?

AZİZ: Sing it, Arif.

ARİF: [*Sings in a peculiar tone.*]

> *Oh Sergeant, Sergeant dear,*
> *In love you may be cool.*
> *But when it comes to blades,*
> *You're such a shaky fool—*
> *Can't even use your tool.*

RASİM BABA: Hey, stop. Whoever Sergeant is, they're making a monkey of him.

AZİZ: Sergeant is Fehim Pasha's new hit man.

ARİF: Name of Ömer. "Sergeant Ömer" they call him.

RASİM BABA: So, did he take this lying down?

AZİZ: No way.

RASİM BABA: 'Cause if he did, he'd be finished.

AZİZ: He tossed the musicians two coins.

RASİM BABA: That's more like it.

AZİZ: Sing it, Arif.

ARİF:

> *My friends, each one a hero,*
> *Are sitting on my right.*
> *But on my left there's only air.*
> *For you, dear Mister Zero,*
> *Are sitting there.*

RASİM BABA: Ha! How'd you like that, Pertev Bey?

PERTEV BEY: Good choice of song. Like a slap.

RASİM BABA: Sooo, what did the bastards do? Slip away quietly?

AZİZ: Not likely. [RASİM BABA's *broad grin freezes again.*] They tossed three coins. Go on, Arif. Sing it.

ARİF:

> *Ömer the foolish husband—*
> *He is the best thing in my life.*
> *He's got a lovely, leggy, willing wife.*

PERTEV BEY: Haven't heard that song for thirty years.

RASİM BABA: Never mind the song. If blood didn't flow right away, your Sergeant Ömer can go straight to Cowards' Paradise.

AZİZ: It flowed, it flowed.

RASİM BABA: Thank God.

AZİZ: Sergeant Ömer raised the roof with a war cry.

RASİM BABA: Good start.

AZİZ: People scattered.

RASİM BABA: They'd better. We need room. And the music?

AZİZ: Stopped.

RASİM BABA: Fine.

AZİZ: So Ömer jumps up, runs to the middle.

RASİM BABA: That's my boy.

AZİZ: One of the other men gets up, goes to stand in front of him.

RASİM BABA: He's pushing his luck.

AZİZ: The big knives are out. The men are circling each other. Slowly. [AZİZ *and* ARİF *are reenacting the scene.*] And insults are flying in the air.

RASİM BABA: What're they saying? Word for word.

ARİF: "Look here, Fehim Pasha's lapdog."

RASİM BABA: Watch your tongue!

ARİF: You said word for word, didn't you?

RASİM BABA: Sorry.

ARİF: "If that no-good Fehim Pasha is a man, then I'm a fucking eagle."

RASİM BABA: You son of a bitch! [*Begins to choke* ARİF.] Fehim Pasha's the best man in the country. He pays you in gold every time you cut his hair. Have you seen the likes of him, you ungrateful eagle? [PERTEV BEY *and* AZİZ *rescue* ARİF *from* RASİM BABA.]

PERTEV BEY: Easy! Don't get excited. He's only quoting. All right, guys. Go on.

AZİZ: Let's go on, Arif.

ARİF: OK, Aziz.

AZİZ: Here we go. "Who's your keeper, fucking eagle?"

ARİF: "Suat Pasha the Madman." [AZİZ *laughs sarcastically, imitating* SERGEANT ÖMER.] "Don't laugh, gutter rat. They call him that because he's brave. And he's no brownnose informer, like your pasha."

RASİM BABA: Let's stop this before I kill someone. What are you saying, "an informer"?

PERTEV BEY: Keep your shirt on. Please.

AZİZ: "What's your pasha's rank, anyway?"

ARİF: "My mad pasha gets his promotions on his own, not licking the sultan's ass."

AZİZ: "Hah! Everyone knows whose asses your pasha licks."

ARİF: "Yeah? Whose?"

AZİZ: "The godless 'freedom lovers.'" [PERTEV BEY *and* RASİM BABA *rush to clamp their hands over* AZİZ's *mouth.*]

PERTEV BEY: Hush! Idiot! He said "freedom."

RASİM BABA: Are you crazy, man?

PERTEV BEY: Did anyone hear?

RASİM BABA: God! I hope not!

ARİF: I'm really curious. Who are these people? The "freedom lovers"? [PERTEV BEY *and* RASİM BABA *leave* AZİZ *and rush to silence* ARİF.]

PERTEV BEY: Shut up, fool!

RASİM BABA: I'll wring your neck.

PERTEV BEY: What's with these guys?

RASIM BABA: If one doesn't get us in trouble, the other will.

PERTEV BEY: Look, Arif, we'll let go of you now. But you won't say a word, OK? [ARIF *nods.*] Lets go.

RASIM BABA: [*Pleads.*] Just tell us about the fight, you bastards!

AZIZ: Shall we, Arif?

ARIF: Yes, Aziz, let's.

AZIZ: OK. Here we go. [*Lets out what sounds like a high-pitched scream, runs out of breath.*]

RASIM BABA: What was that?

AZIZ: A war cry.

RASIM BABA: I thought you were passing a kidney stone. You mean someone challenged the other with a cry?

AZIZ: Right. Sergeant Ömer did.

RASIM BABA: That means he's about to attack.

ARIF: Yep. He did.

AZIZ: He made a feint.

ARIF: Then went in real low.

AZIZ: Stuck the blade in the groin.

ARIF: Pulled up, kind of crosswise.

AZIZ: Before you could say "ouch," everything was on the floor—blood, piss, shit.

ARIF: Ugh.

RASIM BABA: Ah, he meant business. It was no dance.

AZIZ: They wrapped the man in something and took him away. Sergeant Ömer and his friends let out some more war cries. Then they disappeared.

ARIF: The sun came up.

AZIZ: We ate some soup.

ARIF: And hurried here.

AZIZ: To tell you what happened.

RASIM BABA: Good for you. Ah, I know what it'll be like tonight in the mansion. Fehim Pasha will want to celebrate. He'll have Sergeant Ömer sitting on his right. Of course, he'll invite Ömer's father, too, if he's alive. The old man will see his son honored, and he'll be so proud, so proud. How I envy him! [*Pounds the table with his fist and hurts his hand.*] Owwwww!

PERTEV BEY: What happened?

RASIM BABA: Aw . . . nothing. [*Sits nursing his hand. A war cry is heard nearby. Jumps up, listens carefully.*]

PERTEV BEY: [*Looks worried.*] Who is it?

RASIM BABA: I know all the war cries in town like you know melodies. This is new. And there's something wrong with it. [AZIZ *and* ARIF *are anxious to go.*]

AZIZ: Well, so long.

ARIF: We'll be seeing you. [*They are on the way out when they come face to face with* OSMAN.]

OSMAN: Get back, jerks. Anyone blocks the way, I crush him. [AZİZ *and* ARİF *quickly retreat into the coffeehouse.* OSMAN *advances with a swagger, confronts the others.*] Just now I heard something like a cat's meow. Who was it, Pop?

PERTEV BEY: [*Pretends not to hear.*] What did you say, young man?

OSMAN: [*To* AZİZ.] OK. You tell me, jerk. [AZİZ *is too terrified to reply.*] Cat got your tongue, eh? [*To* ARİF.] You! The jerk that looks like an upright earthworm. Do you know?

ARİF: [*So nervous he can hardly speak.*] I . . . I . . . I . . . I . . . d-d-don't . . . don't . . .

OSMAN: Hey, what is this place? Some kind of home for the handicapped? You, old man, come here. Let's see what you look like.

RASİM BABA: Son, you look like a brave young man.

OSMAN: Cut out the sweet talk. Are you the owner here?

RASİM BABA: [*Looks devastated.*] Yes.

OSMAN: OK. The name's Osman. I'm the new cock of the walk, and I don't want to hear anybody else crowing around here. That's point number one. Point number two: I want my share of the earnings in this place. You're in clover, and a brave young man like me is going half hungry. That's not right, is it? So I'll stop by every week, and you'll hand me what it takes to set things right. Enough talk for now. See you soon. [*Thumps his chest by way of salute and swaggers off. A long silence.*]

PERTEV BEY: Rasim . . . [RASİM BABA *raises his hand, imploring for silence.* PERTEV BEY *stops talking.* RASİM BABA *sits, crushed.*]

AZİZ: I'd like to punch him in the mouth.

ARİF: Yeah, and k-k-kick his b-b-butt.

AZİZ: Flatten him.

ARİF: Jump on his b-b-back.

AZİZ: Harness him.

ARİF: Giddap!

AZİZ: Clop, clop, clop. Straight to the horse market.

ARİF: I'd love that.

AZİZ: Oh, how I wish we could be tough guys.

RASİM BABA: [*Gets up with sudden determination.*] Aziz, Arif, keep an eye on things around here. I'm going home.

AZİZ: Sure.

ARİF: Will do.

PERTEV BEY: If you're going into hiding for another ten years, let's say good-bye.

RASİM BABA: No, no. Wait here, Pertev Bey. I'll be right back.

NARRATOR:

so he rushed to his little house
opened the tiny door
with the huge key

tiptoed up
to one of the squeaky-clean rooms
what does he see there
but his lionhearted son
rehearsing for a play
it's not easy being other people
when one can hardly be oneself
I have no problem doing that
being very versatile
however
three's a crowd here
allow me to disappear

[RASİM BABA's *house.* RASİM BABA *enters, stands watching* YUSUF, *who is impersonating two characters of the* Orta oyunu.[7]]

YUSUF: [*Stands on the left, impersonating* TARÇIN BEY.] Don't you know me, sir? I'm Tarçın Bey. You used to say you admired my refinement. [*Walks to the right, impersonates* KA- VUKLU.] Of course I remember you. How are you, my boy? [*While playing the part of* KAVUKLU, *he demonstrates that he is deriding* TARÇIN BEY's *effeminate manner.*] How are you? Are you well? [*Walks left.*] I'm fine, sir. And you? [*Walks right.*] I'm fine, too, thank you. How is your dear father? [*As* KAVUKLU.] I'm afraid we've lost him. [*As* TAR- ÇIN BEY.] Goodness! Where did you lose that lovely man? [*As* KAVUKLU.] I mean he's no longer with us. [*As* TARÇIN BEY.] Oh. He moved? [*As* KAVUKLU.] Yeah. He moved in a box. [*As* TARÇIN BEY.] Really? Is that a new kind of carriage? [*As* KAVUKLU.] Dad is dead, man! Dead as a doornail.

RASİM BABA: [*Unable to contain himself any longer, bursts in.*] Not yet! Dad isn't dead yet. He even survived a deadly shock today. Nor am I going to die before I clear things up. Got it, Tarçın Bey?

YUSUF: Very well, Father. Let me get your slippers.

RASİM BABA: No, get your fez. We're going out.

YUSUF: To my theater?

RASİM BABA: To Fehim Pasha's mansion.

YUSUF: Oh no, Father. Please. I can't go there.

RASİM BABA: Why not?

YUSUF: Well, for one thing, those people wouldn't want me in their midst.

RASİM BABA: Look, after ten long years, I'll swallow my pride and go there to ask for a favor. The whole mansion will welcome me with open arms. "Ah," they'll say, "Rasim the Destroyer is back!" You'll see. Now let's not waste any more time.

---

7. *Orta oyunu:* An Ottoman-Turkish version of the *commedia dell'arte.*

YUSUF: Father, you know as well as I do that the mansion is not for me. I can't pick flowers because they're living things. I can't step on grass; I can't touch a bird for fear of hurting it. That mansion is full of men sporting guns and daggers. What would I do there?

RASİM BABA: There's a famous street fighter called Bekir in your plays. Just imitate him, OK? Come on, move!

NARRATOR: [*Enters dressed as* AYVAZ, *a footman.*] I told you I was versatile. Now I'm a footman in the mansion. First-class actors are modest, so I don't mind playing the part of a servant.

[NURİ BEY's *room in the mansion.*]

NURİ BEY: [*Has taken his seat; shouts to the* NARRATOR.] OK. Ready.

NARRATOR: Right. We're in Fehim Pasha's mansion. That's the room of Nuri Bey, his steward. I make my entrance. [*Does so as* AYVAZ.]

AYVAZ: Sir, someone's here to see you.

NURİ BEY: Who is it?

AYVAZ: A strange-looking man.

NURİ BEY: Doesn't he have a name, jackass?

AYVAZ: Yes, sir. He says he's called "Rasim."

NURİ BEY: Which Rasim?

AYVAZ: He told me, but I forgot.

NURİ BEY: Maybe it's Rasim the Naked from Kasımpaşa.[8]

AYVAZ: Nope.

NURİ BEY: Then it's Rasim from Üsküdar. They call him "the Muddy One."

AYVAZ: Nope.

NURİ BEY: Don't tell me it's Rasim the Camel from Eyüp.

AYVAZ: Nope.

NURİ BEY: There's no other Rasim. Except the Destroyer.

AYVAZ: That's it, sir! That's what he told me.

NURİ BEY: But he doesn't come here.

AYVAZ: It figures, sir. He acts like half of him came here, half stayed behind.

NURİ BEY: All right. Let me see him. [AYVAZ *leaves.* NURİ *takes a handgun from a drawer and puts it in his pocket.* RASİM BABA *and* YUSUF *enter.* YUSUF *stays in a corner.*] Is it really you, Rasim?

RASİM BABA: It's me all right.

NURİ BEY: Wouldn't know you. I've seen people go downhill, but you take the prize.

RASİM BABA: Correct.

NURİ BEY: You disappeared from view for so many years. What've you been doing?

---

8. Kasımpaşa: A section of Istanbul.

RASİM BABA: Trying to die. Couldn't even manage that.

NURİ BEY: So what is it you want now?

RASİM BABA: I'd like to see the pasha for a minute.

NURİ BEY: If it's money you want . . .

RASİM BABA: [*Draws himself up.*] You know me, Nuri Bey. I may have gone downhill, but I'll never reach the begging stage.

NURİ BEY: No offense, Rasim. Right now Sergeant Ömer is with him. They're talking about something that happened last night.

RASİM BABA: Just announce me, please. The pasha will be delighted.

NURİ BEY: Things have changed, Rasim. I'm not sure he'll remember you. Even if he does, what makes you think he'll want to see an acquaintance from way back?

RASİM BABA: [*Glances at his son.*] The pasha is very fond of me, Nuri Bey. [*Draws close to* NURİ BEY *and whispers.*] For God's sake, don't make me look bad in front of my son. If the pasha says no, please make up another reason.

AYVAZ: [*Enters.*] Sir! The pasha wants you.

NURİ BEY: [*Jumps up and buttons his coat.*] Coming. I'll do my best, Rasim. We'll see. [NURİ BEY *and* AYVAZ *go out.*]

YUSUF: Father.

RASİM BABA: [*Turns away from him.*] What?

YUSUF: You see how things are.

RASİM BABA: If you love me, shut up, or I'll take it out on you.

YUSUF: All right, Father. [*Lowers his head and keeps quiet.*]

NARRATOR: [*Appears, still dressed as a footman.*] Well, it's time you met Fehim Pasha. Many plays have been written about him. This won't be the last. He was the son of Sultan Abdülhamid's foster brother. The only man the sultan loved, other than himself. Heaven knows why. It's not easy to understand anything about the sultan, anyway. He has his defenders and detractors. Me, I'm a footman in this scene, too. So I'd better hold my tongue. Here's Fehim Pasha, and here's Sergeant Ömer. See you at the end of the scene.

[FEHİM PASHA's *room.* NURİ BEY *enters, waits respectfully.* FEHİM PASHA *is laughing at something* ÖMER *has just said.*]

FEHİM PASHA: Bravo, Ömer! That's hilarious. And you're getting to be number one.

ÖMER: Thanks to you, Pasha.

FEHİM PASHA: Come in, Nuri, come in. Ömer here taught a lesson to one of the punks of Mad Suat Pasha, and the man's friends made tracks—fast.

NURİ BEY: Congratulations, Ömer.

ÖMER: Thanks to you, sir.

FEHİM PASHA: Let's celebrate this tonight. Prepare a feast.

NURİ BEY: It's ready, Pasha.

FEHİM PASHA: That's what I like about this son of a bitch. Always ahead of me.

NURİ BEY: Thank you, Pasha. Who'll be invited?

FEHİM PASHA: No highfalutin pashas and such, right, Ömer? Just friends.

ÖMER: You're the greatest, Pasha.

FEHİM PASHA: I love these rough bastards, Nuri. I always have. They say that mad moron Suat Pasha loves the people. [*They all laugh.*] What a phony! If he loves the people, how come he never ever eats with a commoner? Eh? He has hordes of people serving him. Did he ever talk with any of them? Does he know the name of one? So tell me, for God's sake, who is the people's man? Him or me?

NURİ BEY: It's no contest, Pasha.

FEHİM PASHA: Who knows what's good for people, him or me?

NURİ BEY: You, of course. Right, Ömer?

ÖMER: No contest, no contest.

FEHİM PASHA: He says if we had a parliament, all the people's troubles would be over. What a bright idea! If we granted liberty to our poor people, what would they do with it? They'd hand over power on a platter to some rascal or other. Safest thing to do is to break all the platters.

ÖMER: You're so right, Pasha. If our present leaders didn't hold our hands, we couldn't walk from here to there.

FEHİM PASHA: [*Laughs with pleasure.*] Let's have music and dancing girls tonight.

NURİ: All done, Pasha.

FEHİM PASHA: Hey, you're too damned brilliant.

NURİ: We have a visitor. One of your old favorites.

FEHİM PASHA: Who?

NURİ: Rasim the Destroyer.

FEHİM PASHA: Doesn't ring a bell.

NURİ: He wants to see you.

FEHİM PASHA: No, no. Give him some money and get rid of him.

NURİ: As you wish, Pasha. [AYVAZ *enters.* NURİ BEY *whispers to him.*] What is it?

AYVAZ: [*Replies in a loud voice.*] The pasha's wife demands to see him in the harem right away.

NURİ BEY: Sshhh! Watch your language, stupid!

FEHİM PASHA: What's he saying?

NURİ BEY: Your lady entreats you to visit her at your earliest convenience.

AYVAZ: That's not what she said. She wants you to get there on the double.

FEHİM PASHA: What kind of talk is that, blockhead?

AYVAZ: How would I know? Go ask your wife.

FEHİM PASHA: What! You baboon! [FEHİM PASHA *jumps up.* AYVAZ *escapes.* FEHİM PASHA *runs out after him.*]

ÖMER: Hey! He's gonna kill him.

NURİ BEY: Relax. It's just an excuse to obey his wife without looking bad. He'll be in the harem in no time. [*They laugh.*]

NARRATOR: [*Appears as* AYVAZ.] I was right, wasn't I? It's not my fault if he's henpecked. Oooh! The harem scene is ready. I better get away . . . on the double.

[*The harem.* FEHİM PASHA's WIFE *and their daughter* MİHRİBAN *are chatting. Nearby, a* SERVANT GIRL *sits embroidering something.*]

MİHRİBAN: Mother, you're giving Dad a hard time.

WIFE: That's the only way to handle him. The more you say yes, the more he says no. Just watch—today I'll make him see reason.

SECOND SERVANT GIRL: [*Enters.*] Madam, the pasha's here. [MİHRİBAN *and the* FIRST SERVANT GIRL *rise.*]

WIFE: That's real speed, eh? [*The* GIRLS *giggle.*]

FEHİM PASHA: [*Enters.*] You summoned me, darling?

WIFE: I requested the pleasure of your company, darling.

FEHİM PASHA: What's up?

WIFE: I hear there's a big bash tonight.

FEHİM PASHA: A little dinner with some friends. Anything wrong with that?

WIFE: Of course not, dear. But if it's a little dinner, why the music? Why the dancing girls?

FEHİM PASHA: Music? Dancing girls? I ordered no such thing. Oh, I know; it's that busybody steward's doing.

WIFE: Darling, I'm the wife of His Majesty's head informer. Intelligence flows my way even when I don't ask for it. If you knew the things my little informers tell me about you . . . [FEHİM PASHA *coughs, indicating the* GIRLS.] Anyway, it looks like tonight you men will have your little dinner party with music and dancing girls, but we the women in your harem will, as usual, say our little prayers and retire to our little bedrooms. Right?

FEHİM PASHA: Yes, sure.

WIFE: Well, you're wrong.

FEHİM PASHA: What d'you mean?

WIFE: My beloved husband, you're an experienced administrator. Surely you know that when injustice reaches unbearable proportions, it leads to an explosion. Don't you think requiring us to sleep while you're enjoying your revelry is an injustice of that magnitude?

FEHİM PASHA: You summoned me here to discuss this nonsense? I was dealing with great matters of state.

WIFE: Well, it's time you dealt with our little matters, too. Your chief rival, whom stupid people call the Mad Pasha, entertains his women every night with music and storytellers.

FEHİM PASHA: So now that madman will undermine law and order in my own house!

WIFE: Here's the last word: either you do something for us this very day, or I swear I'll open a window, lean out, and shout at the top of my voice. D'you know what the shout will

be? "Long live freedom!" [*Little screams and gasps of horror from the* GIRLS.] I'm serious. I swear on my honor, I'll do it.

FEHİM PASHA: [*Yells at the* GIRLS.] Get lost! All of you! [*The* GIRLS *run out.*] Woman, are you
out of your mind, or are you seriously ill?

WIFE: I've never been healthier, thank heaven. I am, as they say, fit as a fiddle.

FEHİM PASHA: It's my job to suppress "freedom lovers," remember?

WIFE: Well, you're not going to suppress me.

FEHİM PASHA: God grant me patience! [*Heads for the door.*]

WIFE: Oh, we were having such a nice chat. Where are you going?

FEHİM PASHA: To the garden. To do some shooting, or I'll suffocate. [*Leaves.*]

WIFE: Shoot all you want, my pasha. It'll clear your mind. [*Laughs loudly and exits in the
opposite direction.*]

[*The scene changes to the garden.* NURİ BEY *and* RASİM BABA *are talking.* YUSUF *stands
aside.*]

NURİ BEY: The pasha was delighted when I told him you were here.

RASİM BABA: [*Glances at his son proudly.*] Yes, I told you he's fond of me.

NURİ BEY: He's very busy today. "Tell Rasim to excuse me," he said. He'll invite you when
he has the time.

RASİM BABA: I'm grateful.

NURİ BEY: God be with you, Rasim.

RASİM BABA: [*Draws close to* NURİ.] You're telling me the truth, aren't you?

NURİ BEY: Sure. The minute I mentioned the Destroyer, he remembered.

RASİM BABA: Fine, fine. I feel better now.

FEHİM PASHA: [*Bursts upon them furiously, followed by* ÖMER *and* AYVAZ.] Nuri, you're the
dumbest steward alive.

NURİ BEY: Why? What happened?

FEHİM PASHA: Anything we do, the next minute they hear about it in the harem. That's
what's happened, you stupid bastard. Who's this?

RASİM BABA: [*Approaches him respectfully.*] It's me, Pasha. And this is my son, your humble servant.

FEHİM PASHA: [*Whirls on* NURİ BEY *again.*] Didn't I tell you to get rid of them? Do I have
time for riffraff?

RASİM BABA: [*In terrible confusion, turns to* NURİ BEY.] What's this? What's this?

FEHİM PASHA: [*Waves him away.*] Go away, go away. [*Addresses* AYVAZ.] You! Stand there. Nuri,
give me your gun. Look, Ömer, we'll put a cigarette in this dumbbell's mouth, and I'll blow
it to hell with one shot. Nuri, give the dumbbell a cigarette. [NURİ *hands him his gun.*]

NURİ BEY: Pasha, this servant is new. God forbid, he might get nervous and move.

FEHİM PASHA: All right. You, Ömer! You take the cigarette and stand there.

ÖMER: Pasha, I'll die for you if necessary, but this isn't necessary. I mean, I might have the hiccups just when you shoot, or a bird might poop on your hand.

FEHİM PASHA: Cowards all. [*Shoots in the air.*]

RASİM BABA: [*Walks over to the spot* FEHİM *indicated and stands waiting.*] Go ahead, Pasha.

FEHİM PASHA: What did you say this character is called?

RASİM BABA: [*Without moving.*] Rasim the Destroyer. That's what he was called. He fought and maimed and killed for you. He later became this way thanks to you. So now don't worry about hiccups or bird shit. Go ahead and shoot. Rasim the Destroyer just died anyway. Give me that cigarette.

FEHİM PASHA: What the hell are you chattering about?

RASİM BABA: I was planning to leave my son with you. Thought he might turn into a fighting man, serving you. But I've changed my mind. He'd better keep doing what he likes. Let him put on shadow shows,[9] play the tambourine, sing, act in the *Orta oyunu*. . . . I said go ahead, Pasha. Shoot away and feel better.

FEHİM PASHA: This is your son?

RASİM BABA: Right, Pasha.

FEHİM PASHA: He puts on shadow shows?

RASİM BABA: [*Is terribly embarrassed.*] Yes, Pasha. There's nothing I can do about it.

FEHİM PASHA: [*With ever-increasing pleasure.*] Plays the tambourine? And sings?

RASİM BABA: Unfortunately, yes.

FEHİM PASHA: You said he acts in the *Orta oyunu*? Plays women's parts, too?

RASİM BABA: Please don't rub it in, Pasha. Yes, he does all that.

FEHİM PASHA: [*Motions* YUSUF *to approach him.*] Come, let's have a look at you. [YUSUF *cannot move.*]

NURİ BEY: Go ahead, Son.

[YUSUF *approaches* FEHİM *respectfully.*]

FEHİM PASHA: [*Grins with pleasure.*] Just what we need. Eh, Nuri?

RASİM BABA: With your permission, Pasha, we'll get going. Come, Yusuf.

FEHİM PASHA: Hold it, hold it! Your son has just been accepted into service here. He'll entertain the women of the harem every night with shadow plays and stories. Let him bring his gear to the mansion right away. You can drop in, too, anytime you want. Well, that's that, thank God. Come, Ömer, back to our business. [*Walks away;* ÖMER *runs after him.*]

NARRATOR: [*No longer playing the part of* AYVAZ, *addresses the audience.*] Poor Rasim was hoping the pasha would accept his son on the strength of his own past service as a fighter. Instead, he himself was accepted on the strength of the young man's future service as an actor. Of course, what Yusuf will make of this opportunity remains to

9. Shadow shows: Turkish shadow theater known as *Karagöz*.

be seen. Now, if I were given a break like that . . . well, never mind. We're back in the coffeehouse.

[*The coffeehouse.* RASIM BABA, PERTEV BEY, AZIZ, *and* ARIF.]

RASIM BABA: It happened so suddenly, I couldn't say no.

PERTEV BEY: Why should you say no?

AZIZ: Sooo, our Yusuf will entertain . . .

ARIF: Every night . . .

AZIZ: The pasha's wife . . .

ARIF: And daughter . . .

AZIZ: And servant girls . . .

ARIF: All those beauties!

AZIZ: Sounds like paradise.

ARIF: What man would say no to that?

PERTEV BEY: Whoa!

RASIM BABA: That's right. Whoa! Don't even think like that. In Fehim Pasha's mansion, if a man so much as looks askance at those women, he's as good as dead. Right, Pertev?

AZIZ: Still, those Circassian wenches . . .

ARIF: How they giggle!

AZIZ: Those Sudanese girls . . .

ARIF: How they trill!

AZIZ: Those Greek beauties . . .

ARIF: How they twitter!

AZIZ: You don't have to look.

ARIF: Hearing them is pure temptation.

RASIM BABA: You know perfectly well this doesn't apply to my son. If he were a man in the real sense, would he be acting women's parts in plays? There, I've said it. The pasha took one look and understood. Shall I tell you what I'm worried about? After hobnobbing with all those girls, my son might take up embroidery.

PERTEV BEY: I'm in the mansion all the time. I'll keep an eye on him.

YUSUF: [*Comes in with a basket.*] I'm ready, Father.

RASIM BABA: All right, let's go. See you in the morning, friends.

PERTEV BEY: Good luck.

[RASIM BABA *and* YUSUF *leave.*]

ARIF: I'm green with envy.

AZIZ: Oh, how I wish we could be shadow puppeteers.

NARRATOR:

Our stage is this historic screen

That's full of light for those
Who haven't only looked but seen.
We're in the harem!

[*The harem.* YUSUF *behind a Karagöz screen. The* PASHA's WIFE, MİHRİBAN, *and the* SERVANT GIRLS *seated in front, watching his shadow play, which is interspersed with traditional songs. As the comic love story unfolds, the women laugh and clap heartily.*]

NARRATOR: [*Enters and interrupts the performance.*] All right, girls. That's all for tonight. Off with you. [*The* SERVANT GIRLS *react with squeals of protest:* "Oh, please!" "It's too early!" "We were having such fun!" *and so on.*] Sorry about that. But the playwright says Fehim Pasha will converse with his wife and his daughter now. So move. You too, Yusuf. [*The* SERVANT GIRLS *giggle as* YUSUF *passes by them on his way out. Then they leave.*] All right, Pasha. Your scene. [*Withdraws as* FEHİM PASHA *enters.*]

FEHİM PASHA: So, how was he?

WIFE: Better than a barrel of monkeys.

MİHRİBAN: The girls loved it.

FEHİM PASHA: Behaves himself, does he?

WIFE: Oh, yes. Very polite.

MİHRİBAN: Like a girl.

WIFE: If he weren't like that, you wouldn't have picked him, would you, my dear pasha?

MİHRİBAN: His face is so pretty! Isn't it, Mother?

FEHİM PASHA: What! You want me to spank you?

MİHRİBAN: Why? What's the matter?

FEHİM PASHA: You call a man "pretty." In front of your father?

MİHRİBAN: Really! I could have said that about the new horse you bought. How can you think I'd regard that destitute puppeteer in any other way? You mistake me for a servant girl or a kitchen maid. Shame on you! [*Exits angrily.*]

WIFE: You hurt her feelings, my dear pasha.

FEHİM PASHA: She's right, of course. I spoke like she could take that two-bit actor seriously. It's because I'm upset, I guess.

WIFE: Anything wrong?

FEHİM PASHA: Another pasha has been shot . . . in the street.

WIFE: In a gunfight?

FEHİM PASHA: Don't talk nonsense. Pashas don't get into street fights.

WIFE: Sorry.

FEHİM PASHA: He was sent to put down an uprising. It's the work of those dirty "freedom lovers."

WIFE: I don't understand this. Why don't you give those people what they want and be done with it?

FEHİM PASHA: Do you know what their first act would be if we did that? They'd hang me from the nearest lamppost.

WIFE: Ah, we don't want that. But why? Are they crazy?

FEHİM PASHA: Of course they're crazy.

WIFE: That reminds me. Do you know what that mad pasha of yours bought for his wife? Three rows of Ceylon pearls—pink.

FEHİM PASHA: I'm going to rid the country of that nut before he bankrupts us all. Now call back the girls. And Yusuf. Let them have more fun. [*Goes.*]

[*The* SERVANT GIRLS *bring in the traditional Orta oyunu set.*]

NARRATOR:

in the Balkans

in the remaining lands of the empire

some people had fallen in love with liberty

just as the young man in the following playlet

loves his sweetheart

they rose against tyranny

killed and died

while in Fehim Pasha's mansion

his daughter played the young man

and Yusuf played the girl

this twist amused her mother greatly

watch

[*Exits.*]

[*The* SERVANT GIRLS, MİHRİBAN, *and* YUSUF *act in the* Orta oyunu. *At one point,* MİHRİBAN *extends her hand to* YUSUF. *He hesitates.*]

MİHRİBAN: [*Speaks in her normal voice.*] It's all right. Give me your hand. [*They hold hands and continue acting.* FEHİM PASHA *enters and watches, unseen.*] Nothing can come between us. We are free to love. And love is a mighty river that overflows all barriers. No one can keep me away from you. Not even your tyrant of a father.

FEHİM PASHA: What, what, what? You shameless jade! [*The* GIRLS *scream.*] Wife, what's going on here?

WIFE: It's just a play.

FEHİM PASHA: Just a play, huh? Get out, all of you! [*The* SERVANT GIRLS, MİHRİBAN, *and* YUSUF *run out.*] All awful things start out as "just a play." That's what we thought when this liberty fad was started by Midhat Pasha.[10] We thought he was playing around

10. Midhat Pasha (1822–84): Prominent Ottoman statesman who introduced major reforms; strangled to death in prison.

with these ideas, but look what happened. We're in deep trouble now. Countless rebels are going up into the mountains. The whole region is teeming with rebels.

WIFE: They annoy you, and you take it out on us.

FEHİM PASHA: Girls! [*The* SERVANT GIRLS *enter;* FEHİM PASHA *points at the* Orta oyunu *set.*] Get these things out of here. Take them away. [*The* SERVANT GIRLS *carry out the set.*] My feet hurt. I had to stand in the sultan's presence for three hours today. For some reason, he ignored me. Something is changing, but I don't know quite what. Come, give me a massage.

[FEHİM PASHA *and his* WIFE *leave. The scene changes to the coffeehouse.* RASİM BABA *and* PERTEV BEY *are there.*]

RASİM BABA: I went to the mansion this morning.

PERTEV BEY: I'll go tomorrow.

RASİM BABA: They didn't let me in.

PERTEV BEY: Really? Why not?

RASİM BABA: They said my boy left the mansion yesterday and didn't come back.

PERTEV BEY: Where can he be?

RASİM BABA: Maybe he's in the women's bath.

PERTEV BEY: God forbid.

RASİM BABA: Come close. I heard something.

PERTEV BEY: What? [*They whisper.*]

RASİM BABA: A young officer, Major Enver,[11] is leading the rebellion near Salonica. Very popular. They call him the leader already. He's making the rounds of all the villages. People flock to him and swear they'll fight for freedom.

PERTEV BEY: Ssshhh!

RASİM BABA: Looks like sooner or later he'll be coming here, too, don't you think?

PERTEV BEY: He can't come here. Fehim Pasha won't let him.

[AZİZ *and* ARİF *come running in, greatly excited.*]

AZİZ: Rasim Baba!

ARİF: Uncle Pertev!

AZİZ: You said he can't come.

ARİF: But he's here.

[RASİM BABA *and* PERTEV BEY *jump to their feet.*]

PERTEV BEY: Are people up in arms?

RASİM BABA: Have they started singing freedom songs?

AZİZ: Which song?

---

11. Major Enver (1881–1922): One of the leaders of the Union and Progress government, a military commander who served as minister of war.

PERTEV BEY: "The Freedom Anthem."

ARİF: Nooo.

AZİZ: What's coming isn't freedom or anything like that.

RASİM BABA: Who's coming?

ARİF: Flat-footed Osman.

AZİZ: He wants his share of the earnings.

RASİM BABA: Oh dear, oh dear. [OSMAN's *war cry is heard.*] Ah, Yusuf, Yusuf. I wanted a warrior son to defend my honor. Instead, I got an actress.

OSMAN: [*Swaggers in, gives his fighter's salute.*] Hello there, worms. Let me have my dough, and I'll be on my way.

RASİM BABA: Listen. I don't want to look bad in front of my friends here, so I'd give anything to send you on your way, but I'm broke.

OSMAN: You want a going over, eh?

RASİM BABA: Tell me, have you heard of Fehim Pasha?

OSMAN: Everybody's heard of Fehim Pasha.

RASİM BABA: Well, my son is in his service. One of his toughest men. Isn't that right, friends?

PERTEV BEY, AZİZ, and ARİF: [*Very feebly.*] Y-yes.

RASİM BABA: And if he heard somebody was treating his old man like this, wouldn't he tear him to pieces? Break his limbs one by one? Huh?

PERTEV BEY, AZİZ, and ARİF: Yes.

RASİM BABA: Wouldn't he pick that man up by the scruff of his neck, shake him like a dog shaking a cat, and leave him on the floor like a heap of dung?

PERTEV BEY, AZİZ, and ARİF: Yes.

OSMAN: Wait a minute. Now you've got me confused.

[*A loud war cry is heard nearby.*]

RASİM BABA: You'd better get lost fast. I think this is him. [*Stops to consider, turns to the others.*] Yes, it's him! It's him! I'm sure.

OSMAN: That changes things. I'll see you later. [*Tries to leave quickly, but is suddenly confronted by* YUSUF. *Jumps aside.*] Excuse me, sir. Didn't see you coming.

YUSUF: [*Extremely drunk, walks with difficulty, his jacket over his shoulder.*] You excuse me, Brother.

RASİM BABA: [*Rushes to greet him joyfully.*] That was your cry, right?

YUSUF: Sorry, Father, couldn't help myself.

RASİM BABA: Hooray! And you've been drinking?

YUSUF: [*Sadly.*] Couldn't help myself.

RASİM BABA: Didn't I tell all of you the mansion would make a man of him in no time? Don't hold back, Son. Do whatever you feel like doing.

[*From a corner,* OSMAN *is watching carefully.*]

YUSUF: [*Tries to let out another cry, but this time it is more like a whimper.*] Aaah.

RASIM BABA: Tell me . . . what happened to you? [YUSUF *tries to sing a love song, but is off key.*] You weren't in the mansion. Where were you?

YUSUF: I was on top of a cloud. [*Pretending to fly, collapses on a chair. They crowd around him.*]

AZIZ: Yusuf.

ARIF: Tell us, tell us.

AZIZ: What made you drink so much?

ARIF: Was it joy?

AZIZ: Or sorrow?

YUSUF: Love.

RASIM BABA: Ask him who the girl is.

AZIZ: A Circassian blonde?

YUSUF: Nope.

ARIF: One of those brown Sudanese beauties?

YUSUF: Nope.

AZIZ: I know. It's a Greek beauty with slanted eyes!

YUSUF: Nope.

ARIF: Who, then?

YUSUF: Mihriban.

[*Gasps of horror from* PERTEV BEY, AZIZ, *and* ARIF.]

RASIM BABA: Who the hell is Mihriban?

PERTEV BEY: Fehim Pasha's daughter.

RASIM BABA: Good God!

PERTEV BEY: Son, this is terrible.

RASIM BABA: They'll cut your throat.

AZIZ: Slash, slash.

ARIF: Just like that.

YUSUF: Let them.

RASIM BABA: They'll shoot you.

AZIZ: Bang, bang.

ARIF: Big fat bullets.

YUSUF: Let them. She held my hand. That's enough for me.

PERTEV BEY: Wait, wait. We've got to be careful. This is a serious condition. There's a name for it. I think they call it "obsession."

AZIZ and ARIF: Obsession!

OSMAN: [*Has been approaching stealthily and now suddenly descends on them with a war cry.*] Freeze! I'll make mincemeat of anyone who moves a finger. So, Pop, this is the champion fighter who'd tear me to pieces? This lovesick puppy would break my limbs? Turn me to dung?

RASİM BABA: Please, Son, come back later.

OSMAN: [*Stands above* YUSUF.] I can wipe the floor with you anytime.

YUSUF: Sure you can.

RASİM BABA: Oh, hell.

OSMAN: Pop, ever heard of a man called Rasim the Destroyer? He had a special left-hand slap. I know how to deliver it. Suppose I tried that out on this punk. You know what would happen?

RASİM BABA: [*Lowers his head.*] I do indeed.

OSMAN: Then hand over a gold piece.

RASİM BABA: Pertev, you got a gold piece?

PERTEV BEY: You must be joking.

RASİM BABA: Aziz?

AZİZ: Very funny.

[RASİM BABA *looks at* ARİF, *who is again too frightened to speak, but manages to turn out his pockets.*]

OSMAN: OK, cut the shit. [*Bends to grab* YUSUF. *In desperation,* RASİM BABA *lets out a war cry.* OSMAN *stops, turns to look.* RASİM BABA *draws back slightly, then delivers his famous slap.*]

AZİZ and ARİF: Oooooo!

[OSMAN *staggers, kneels, then falls on his face.*]

AZİZ: Ho ho ho.

ARİF: He's finished, the jerk.

RASİM BABA: [*Turns to* PERTEV BEY.] First things first. You were saying about this thing called "obsession." What is it?

PERTEV BEY: It's a condition. You can think of one thing only. And it consumes you.

RASİM BABA: So it's a kind of sickness.

PERTEV BEY: You could say that.

ARİF: Our neighbor's son had it. He walked around babbling in the streets. Show them what he did, Aziz.

AZİZ: OK, Arif. [*Walks around with uncertain steps, humming a strange tune.*] Boom boom! Boom billy billy booooom! Boom billy boom! Give me a big hand. I want a big hand.

RASİM BABA: Oh my God.

PERTEV BEY: Suppose Yusuf started doing this, boom billy booming in the streets. His father would die of shame.

AZİZ: We'd die of shame, too.

ARİF: So what can we do?

PERTEV BEY: There's only one cure for this sickness. Boy gets girl.

RASİM BABA: Yes, but how? We can't kidnap the pasha's daughter.

PERTEV BEY: Then we do the next best thing—ask for her hand.

RASİM BABA: And you think the pasha will say yes?

PERTEV BEY: He might.

AZİZ: We know him well. You've forgotten what kind of man he really is.

ARİF: He trusts me with his head every morning.

AZİZ: And me with his behind every night. [*The others look at him.*] I mean, I made his mattress.

ARİF: Remember, you told us—he acts tough, but he's the best man around.

AZİZ: He says he's a man of the people.

ARİF: Everybody around him sings his praises.

AZİZ: They say he's honest.

ARİF: Generous.

AZİZ: Modest.

ARİF: They're not lying, are they?

RASİM BABA: [*Is dubious, but cannot object.*] No, I guess not.

AZİZ: So why should a man like that refuse our Yusuf?

ARİF: Yusuf is a fine young man.

RASİM BABA: What do you say, Pertev?

PERTEV BEY: I need to collect my thoughts. Let's have some coffee.

RASİM BABA: Done. Osman!

OSMAN: [*Rouses himself.*] Yes, sir?

RASİM BABA: Get up and make coffee for us.

OSMAN: Yes, sir! [*Gets up with difficulty and staggers in the wrong direction.*]

RASİM BABA: This way, Son.

OSMAN: Yes, sir!

PERTEV BEY: What's wrong with him?

RASİM BABA: It's the famous slap. Has a long-lasting effect.

AZİZ: Some slap.

ARİF: God protect us.

YUSUF: [*Whimpers.*] Mihribaaaaaan . . .

RASİM BABA: Hey, we forgot about my son. Aziz, Arif, take him home. We'll stay here and make plans.

AZİZ: Right.

ARİF: Come on, Yusuf.

AZİZ: We're going home.

[AZİZ *and* ARİF *pull* YUSUF *up, try to drag him away. He suddenly draws himself up, lets out a war cry, and gets away from them.*]

RASİM BABA: Easy, Son.

YUSUF: You want me to go home, Dad?

RASİM BABA: Yes, you'd better.

YUSUF: Then I'll go home. [*Sings drunkenly.*]

> *Hey Pasha, Pasha,*
>
> *Call out your guard,*
>
> *Your flags unfurl.*
>
> *It is no use.*
>
> *Don't offer me*
>
> *A jewel or a pearl.*
>
> *It is no use.*
>
> *My eyes will pop,*
>
> *My toes will curl*
>
> *If I don't get*
>
> *The pasha's girl.*

[*Wanders out.*]

PERTEV BEY: Poor boy.

AZİZ and ARİF: His eyes will pop, his toes will curl . . .

RASİM BABA: That does it. You're right. Tomorrow we go to the mansion to ask for the hand of Fehim Pasha's daughter in marriage, or I'll lose my boy.

OSMAN: [*Brings coffee, distributing the cups skillfully.*] Coffee! Freshly made! Here you are. A cup for everyone.

NARRATOR: This is what happens if you put a green boy in a harem. Now these fools are going to the mansion to ask for the hand of Fehim Pasha's daughter in marriage. God help them! In the meantime, shall we have an intermission?

CURTAIN

ACT II

[FEHİM PASHA's *room.* NURİ BEY *enters, followed by* RASİM BABA *and* PERTEV BEY.]

NURİ BEY: Come this way. The pasha will be here in a minute. What's with your son, Rasim? They say he left without a word. Where's he now?

RASİM BABA: Home.

NURİ BEY: What's he doing? Rehearsing plays?

RASİM BABA: And how! He's rehearsing the parts of all the lovers known to man.

NURİ BEY: Good, good. I watched one of his shadow plays. He was imitating a famous street fighter.

RASİM BABA: Yeah, Bekir.

NURİ BEY: He let out such a war cry. We all thought it was the real thing and jumped to our feet. [AYVAZ *enters.*] What is it?

AYVAZ: The pasha's coming.

NURİ BEY: How's his mood?

AYVAZ: I only know my own mood. I'm OK.

[FEHİM PASHA *enters. They all greet him.*]

FEHİM PASHA: Rasim, did someone do something to annoy your son? Why did he quit like that? We all liked him. My wife and daughter are nagging me about him. . . . How are you, Pertev?

PERTEV BEY: I'm happy to be at your service, Pasha.

FEHİM PASHA: So what're we going to do about this boy? I'll give him whatever he wants. Every day I've got to deal with terrible problems. Spare me any trouble in the harem. What's bothering the boy? Tell me.

PERTEV BEY: Pasha, may I speak?

FEHİM PASHA: Ah, you'll be the mediator, eh? Go ahead.

PERTEV BEY: Frankly, I was worried when I got here today. But now I feel better, seeing our humble request will fall on friendly ears.

FEHİM PASHA: Sure. You're among friends, right, Nuri?

NURİ BEY: Certainly, Pasha.

PERTEV BEY: Our boy is young. But, as you know, he's quite talented.

FEHİM PASHA: He is. Isn't he, Nuri?

NURİ BEY: Very talented.

PERTEV BEY: His character is as attractive as his face.

FEHİM PASHA: I believe it.

NURİ BEY: So do I, Pasha.

PERTEV BEY: In time, with your gracious support, he may even become a good fighter.

FEHİM PASHA: Sure. Remember that war cry, Nuri?

NURİ BEY: Like a bomb explosion.

FEHİM PASHA: [*Laughs.*] That's right. So? Come to the point, Pertev.

NURİ BEY: If I'm not mistaken, your honorable wife and daughter also approve of our boy.

FEHİM PASHA: *Approve* is no word for it. For two days, they've been mourning because he's gone. I told you—they're nagging me about him.

PERTEV BEY: [*Gathers all his courage.*] So, to obey your command and come to the point . . . I'm like an uncle to the boy. In that capacity, I join his father here . . . [RASİM BABA *bows respectfully.*] in requesting . . . I mean, my friend would like to have . . . as his daughter-in-law . . . [*Takes a deep breath.*] your daughter, Mihriban.

FEHİM PASHA: [*Bellows like a bull.*] Whaaaaaaaaaat?

NURİ BEY: Have you gone mad?

FEHİM PASHA: You insolent dogs! This is going to kill me. You stupid bastards. Who d'you think you are to . . . I'm suffocating. How dare you mention my daughter? Just because I was fool enough to treat you like people, to feed you at my table . . . "We'll get to the point," they say.

So this is the point? [RASİM BABA *and* PERTEV BEY *are in full retreat.*] Get the hell out of here, you pigs! Nuri, hand me your gun. I'll shoot these creatures. [RASİM BABA *and* PERTEV BEY *disappear.*] A lame ex-fighter and a goddamned fiddler come here to ask for the hand of Fehim Pasha's daughter. Take me to my bedroom, Nuri. I'm dying.

NURİ BEY: [*Takes* FEHİM PASHA *by the arm.*] Don't give them another thought, Pasha.

FEHİM PASHA: No, forget about me. Run. Catch up with those morons. Tell them if they so much as pronounce my daughter's name again, I'll destroy their houses, I'll exterminate them and their families. Run!

NURİ BEY: Yes, Pasha. [*Runs out.*]

FEHİM PASHA: I don't believe it. I don't believe it. I don't believe it. [*Slowly walks away.*]

NARRATOR: I'm sure you could tell this was going to happen, couldn't you? But these morons can't think straight. What can we do? We're in the coffeehouse again. We'll be with those damned fools again, but it's not my fault.

[*The coffeehouse.* OSMAN, AZİZ, *and* ARİF.]

OSMAN: That one slap finished me. I thought it was the end. "Dying so young!" was what crossed my mind. Before that, what plans I had! I worked in another coffeehouse. I saved a little money and bought this tough guy outfit. I was going to live on protection money and make a name for myself as a toughie. With a little luck, I could join Fehim Pasha's crowd. The rest would be feasts and dancing girls every night. Then . . . what luck! First guy I hit turns out to be the inventor of the big slap. End of my dreams . . . of course, you told everyone how I was flattened?

AZİZ: Sure, I had to.

ARİF: We told everybody the way everything happened.

OSMAN: Right. Now order some more tea.

AZİZ: Oh, I've had enough.

ARİF: I'm full of tea.

AZİZ: How much do we owe you?

OSMAN: Twelve glasses' worth.

ARİF: We should've given this guy his gold piece. Would've been cheaper.

OSMAN: [*Shouts to an imaginary helper.*] Two glasses for the gentlemen! Make it real strong! [*Runs off.*]

AZİZ: Look at that. He keeps shouting his orders from here, then runs over there to take the orders.

ARİF: This kid is a moron, Aziz.

AZİZ: You're right, Arif. He's totally idiotic.

[RASİM BABA *and* PERTEV BEY *enter, red in the face and panting.*]

ARİF: They're here. [ARİF *and* AZİZ *rise to their feet.*]

RASİM BABA: Where's Yusuf?

AZİZ: In there.

ARİF: He's sleeping. Stewed is more like it.

RASİM BABA: Still shouting?

AZİZ: Regularly, every fifteen minutes. Like a cuckoo clock.

PERTEV BEY: [*Sits, wipes his brow.*] What's he saying?

ARİF: [*Shouts, imitating* YUSUF.] Mihribaaaaan!

RASİM BABA: Shut up!

PERTEV BEY: Idiot!

ARİF: Every time I open my mouth, I get slapped down.

PERTEV BEY: [*Points at the room;* RASİM BABA *rushes into it.*] First, ask what happened, then you can howl.

AZİZ: If it's bad news, break it to us slowly.

ARİF: We're so curious our tummies are bulging.

PERTEV BEY: That's what I tried to do—to tell the pasha slowly and gently. But it didn't work. He wouldn't permit his daughter to marry.

AZİZ and ARİF: [*Incredulously.*] Nooooo?

[OSMAN *comes quietly, distributes tea glasses, stands listening respectfully.*]

AZİZ: Did he say why?

ARİF: He doesn't like our boy?

PERTEV BEY: The pasha damned near shot us. We got away in the nick of time. The minute we mentioned the girl, he blew his top.

AZİZ: But the two would make a good couple.

ARİF: Yeah. What's so awful about it?

PERTEV BEY: That's what I thought on the way there, but on the way back, it hit me. The pasha's absolutely right. We're nobodies.

AZİZ: What did he say, exactly?

PERTEV BEY: He said, exactly, "You're nobodies." And, of course, it's true. To be somebody, you've got to have at least a house, a carriage, some gold, and a name people know. Do we have those things?

ARİF: Not quite.

AZİZ: Don't look at me.

PERTEV BEY: Then, from now on, nobody but nobody around here will say a word about that girl. Understood? The pasha has sworn to do away with all of us if she's mentioned.

ARİF: Uh oh.

AZİZ: This is awful.

PERTEV BEY: So that's that. End of story.

OSMAN: Just a minute, sir. I'm confused again. I used to work in a large coffeehouse with a lot of other boys.

PERTEV BEY: So?

OSMAN: There was a kind of rule there. If a customer acted mean to one of the boys, that boy would tell us, and then none of us would serve that man. He'd have to get up and go.

PERTEV BEY: What are you driving at?

OSMAN: I mean, if the pasha was mean to you, why don't we do that to him? Arif here won't go to the mansion to shave the pasha, and Aziz won't make any quilts and things for him. We can try to get all tradesmen and workers to act like that. Trash collectors, grocers, butchers, gardeners, milkmen, yogurt sellers, cobblers . . .

PERTEV BEY: You're crazy. There'd be big trouble.

OSMAN: Isn't there trouble anyway?

PERTEV BEY: Shut up. I do all the thinking around here.

OSMAN: Whatever you say. [*Draws back.*]

[YUSUF *can be heard shouting.*]

YUSUF: [*From offstage.*] Mihribaaaaan, my love!

ARİF: There he goes again.

AZİZ: Right on time.

PERTEV BEY: That boy will be the end of us. This town is full of informers. If one of them hears him, our goose is cooked.

ARİF: Still, I like Osman's idea. Let's get going, Aziz.

AZİZ: OK.

PERTEV BEY: Where are you going?

AZİZ: Where are we going, Arif?

ARİF: I'll speak to my friends among the tradespeople.

AZİZ: Me?

ARİF: You go ring bells. Talk to people you know.

AZİZ: What shall we tell them?

ARİF: What Osman said. I for one won't set foot in the mansion again.

AZİZ: Same here.

ARİF: Let's go, then.

AZİZ: Let's go.

[ARİF *and* AZİZ *run off.*]

PERTEV BEY: Damned if this obsession thing isn't contagious.

YUSUF: [*From the other room, offstage.*] I'm thirsting for your lips, Mihribaaaaan!

PERTEV BEY: Yes, our end is near. [*As he hurries to silence* YUSUF, *he sneers at* OSMAN.] Troublemaker! [*Goes.*]

OSMAN: Me, make trouble? [*As he too leaves, the* NARRATOR *approaches.*]

NARRATOR: I'm excited. This is my scene. You'll see, it's a turning point for me.

[NURİ BEY's *room.*]

NURİ BEY: Come in, Ayvaz.

AYVAZ: Yes, sir.

NURİ BEY: Those spoiled ladies are pecking at the pasha's head day and night.

AYVAZ: Like woodpeckers? [*Turns to the audience, gesticulating with pleasure as if saying,
"What do you think of that?"*]

NURİ BEY: Ha ha! Good for you, you bastard. That's a good figure of speech.

AYVAZ: I'm not so sure. I'd better take it back.

NURİ BEY: Why?

AYVAZ: Is the pasha's head wooden?

NURİ BEY: Look here, stupid, don't fool around with words. Are you good at telling stories?

AYVAZ: Nothing easier. In the village, that's all I do in winter.

NURİ BEY: Can you do imitations?

AYVAZ: Sure. Want to see how an Istanbul lady walks?

NURİ BEY: How? [AYVAZ *does an imitation of a snobbish lady walking.*] Enough. You'll tell
stories in the harem tonight.

AYVAZ: Me?

NURİ BEY: You'll keep your eyes on the floor, or you're dead.

AYVAZ: Eyes on the floor. OK.

NURİ BEY: Now go get ready. Move! [*Goes.*]

NARRATOR: Now watch me show my stuff in the harem. Quick! Change of scene.

[*The harem. The* PASHA's WIFE, MİHRİBAN, *and the* SERVANT GIRLS *listening to* AYVAZ
tell a story. The women are bored. MİHRİBAN *yawns. A passionate cry is heard outside.*]

YUSUF: [*Calling from offstage.*] I'm calling the greatest beauty in the world!

SERVANT GIRLS: [*Sotto voce.*] Aaaaah.

YUSUF: [*From offstage.*] The finest, brightest, loveliest girl!

AYVAZ: What's going on?

SERVANT GIRLS: [*Sotto voce.*] Ooooooooo.

YUSUF: [*From offstage.*] Mihribaaaaan!

WIFE: What on earth . . . ?

[*The* GIRLS *rush to the windows.*]

FIRST SERVANT GIRL: Oh!

OTHER GIRLS: What? What? What?

FIRST SERVANT GIRL: I see him.

MİHRİBAN: Where?

FIRST SERVANT GIRL: There. Under the lamp.

OTHER GIRLS: Ooooooooooo!

SECOND SERVANT GIRL: That's Yusuf!

MİHRİBAN: So it is. Unspeakable fool.

WIFE: What's happened? A revolution? How dare he!

SECOND SERVANT GIRL: Madam, it's love.

MİHRİBAN: If my father hears this . . .

SECOND SERVANT GIRL: He'll have him shot.

MİHRİBAN: Of course he will. This guttersnipe, shouting my name in the street. Open the
window. Quick.

YUSUF: [*From offstage.*] Mihribaaaaan!

MİHRİBAN: Open it, open it. [*Leans out.*] Yusuf, look up. Here. Come closer.

YUSUF: Our fathers don't know any good love stories, but we do. Right, Mihriban?

MİHRİBAN: Listen. Those stories take place between equals. You're a street dog. Go find
yourself a bitch to fit your station. [*Draws back. The* SERVANT GIRLS *sigh with disap-
pointment. To the* GIRLS.] What are you moaning about? Am I wrong?

FEHİM PASHA: [*Comes in wearing his nightshirt and nightcap.*] What the hell's going on
here? I was sleeping. Did I hear someone shout "Mihriban"?

MİHRİBAN: Yes, you did. Come see who it is. There. Yusuf.

FEHİM PASHA: What the . . . ! This is a direct challenge to me. Somebody get me a gun. A
gun, a gun. Quick. [*Turns and sees* AYVAZ.] What're you doing in the harem this time
of night? You want me to shoot you, too?

AYVAZ: I was telling a story, Pasha.

FEHİM PASHA: Get the hell out!

AYVAZ: [*Ingenuously.*] You mean, before I finish the story?

FEHİM PASHA: I'll finish you, fathead! Go tell Nuri to get here on the double. [AYVAZ *runs.
In order to save the situation, he feels like saying something to the audience, pauses for
a moment, then starts speaking, but is interrupted.*] I'm telling you, get going! [AYVAZ
flies.] Girls, to bed! [*The* SERVANT GIRLS *leave. To* MİHRİBAN.] Daughter, don't worry.
This thing will be solved once and for all first thing in the morning.

MİHRİBAN: Thanks, Daddy. He dishonored me. [*Goes out.*]

FEHİM PASHA: I'll eat him alive.

WIFE: What I don't understand is, how can that mild-looking, shy young man do this? He
must have gone mad suddenly. Suppose Mad Suat Pasha hears about it. We'll be the
laughingstock of the empire. [*Looks out the window.*] Ah, he's gone. So he's a coward
to boot.

NURİ BEY: [*From offstage.*] Pasha, may I come in?

FEHİM PASHA: Go to bed, darling. Leave us alone. [*His* WIFE *leaves.*] Come in, Nuri.

NURİ BEY: [*Enters. He, too, is in his nightshirt and cap, and is terribly embarrassed.*] Forgive
me, Pasha. I didn't want to waste time getting dressed.

FEHİM PASHA: Never mind. Now listen. Go find Sergeant Ömer, this minute. Wake him up if he's asleep. Got it?

NURİ BEY: I'll go find Ömer, wake him up. This minute.

FEHİM PASHA: Tell him to get rid of Yusuf . . . first thing in the morning.

NURİ BEY: Get rid of Yusuf. First thing.

FEHİM PASHA: Let him lie low for a few days. Then he can come here.

NURİ BEY: Lie low. Come here.

FEHİM PASHA: That's all.

NURİ BEY: Sorry your sleep has been disturbed, Pasha.

FEHİM PASHA: And I'm expected in the palace early in the morning. Maybe I'll have to stay there tomorrow night. Things are going from bad to worse. The rebels want a parliament. The grand vizier is ready to give in. Even the palace is shilly-shallying. I'm worried, Nuri. What shall we do if this liberty thing comes upon us?

NURİ BEY: You'll find a way out, Pasha.

FEHİM PASHA: Let's hope so. Good night to you.

NURİ BEY: To you too, Pasha. [*They go out in different directions.*]

NARRATOR: Just my luck! I was telling such a good story. That accursed Yusuf spoiled everything. Now we're back in the damned coffeehouse.

[*Coffeehouse.* RASİM BABA *and* PERTEV BEY.]

PERTEV BEY: How's it going?

RASİM BABA: Not too good. The boy got away from me last night.

PERTEV BEY: You don't say.

RASİM BABA: I've no idea where he went. He came back in the morning, weeping.

PERTEV BEY: Weeping? Nothing we can do about it.

RASİM BABA: Like a street dog, he kept barking and growling, wagging his tail and standing on his hind legs. Then he passed out. I guess he was trying to tell me something, but I didn't get it. So what else is going on?

PERTEV BEY: Aziz and Arif are busy. The idiots are talking to everybody, stirring up trouble. They kept moving their arms up and down, like shadow-play figures. They kept chattering. First Aziz, then Arif; then Aziz again, then Arif. Chattering, they awakened the whole neighborhood. I tried to make them see reason, but they wouldn't listen to me. And the strange thing is, I wonder what the people of the neighborhood found in all this gibberish to make them furious. Honest to God, I couldn't figure it out, but in the end Fehim Pasha was reduced to nothing in one night. They used to shake in their boots when they heard Fehim Pasha's name. Now they're openly grumbling about him. No one will serve him. The families who have men in service at the mansion, they'll talk to them this morning. Cooks, gardeners, grooms—they'll all be quitting. The pasha's without help. I mean, what're things coming to?

OSMAN: [*Tiptoes away from the stove; speaks in a low voice.*] Yusuf's awake.

PERTEV BEY: Hope he doesn't start shouting again. If the pasha hears, God knows what might happen. Go and keep him quiet.

OSMAN: OK.

[AZİZ *and* ARİF *come running. They are panic-stricken.*]

AZİZ: Pertev Baba!

ARİF: Uncle Rasim!

AZİZ: He's coming this way.

ARİF: Sergeant Ömer.

PERTEV BEY: I told you, didn't I? The pasha's heard what you two have been doing. Now he's going to get back at you. Let's see how you get out of this one.

AZİZ: He saw us.

ARİF: Didn't even look at us.

AZİZ: He's headed straight this way.

PERTEV BEY: [*Apprehensively.*] This way? Uh oh. Sounds like bad news.

RASİM BABA: [*Optimistically.*] How do you know? Maybe he's bringing good news. Let's sit down and wait. [*They all sit.* AYVAZ *and* ÖMER *appear.* AYVAZ *points to the others and keeps his distance.* ÖMER *approaches them. They rise.*]

ÖMER: Uncle Rasim.

RASİM BABA: Yes, Ömer?

ÖMER: Where's Yusuf?

RASİM BABA: What's up?

ÖMER: Something's up all right.

RASİM BABA: Tell me.

ÖMER: I said, where's Yusuf?

YUSUF: [*Comes out from behind the stove.*] I'm here. What can I do for you?

ÖMER: Come this way. We're going to fight.

OTHERS: Aaaaaaah!

RASİM BABA: No, you're not.

ÖMER: Uncle Rasim, you know how it is. I'm sure you've done these things in your time. This is the pasha's decision, and there's nothing we can do about it. So let's get it over with. I didn't jump on him suddenly. The other night you and I ate at the same table, so I'm giving your son a fair chance. Who knows, he might give me a sound beating and save his skin.

RASİM BABA: Ömer Bey, Sergeant Ömer, I know you're going to strike if the pasha has ordered you to. I did that, too, in my time. But just look at my son. Wouldn't your heart cringe to strike this boy? Can you really find it in yourself to bloody his shirt? When he first walked, I sacrificed a ram. When he first said "Daddy," I distributed clothes to forty paupers. I even put him to sleep with lullabies. How can I bear to watch you finish him off now? If you must take someone's life, take mine. I won't even put up a fight.

ÖMER: Too much talk. Come on, Yusuf.

OSMAN: [*Pushes* YUSUF *aside.*] Wait a minute. Uncle Rasim, please, please, give me a break. It's all or nothing for me. If I'm beaten, it won't make any difference. I was born beaten. But if I manage to beat a champ like Ömer, it'll be the break of my life. See, I've got my knife ready. A big one. So please let me fight him. Ömer, please say yes.

YUSUF: Ha! Most everyone around here seems to think you're easy prey, Ömer.

ÖMER: I'm sick of this gab. Come and fight.

YUSUF: [*Steps forward.*] Coming, Ömer. I kept quiet just to see what sort of man you are.

RASİM BABA: Yusuf! Don't, Son.

YUSUF: Don't you worry, Dad. Just watch. You'll love this.

ÖMER: Osman, give him your knife. You're all wasting my time.

OSMAN: Here, Yusuf. [*Hands his knife to* YUSUF, *who suddenly lets out a war cry and advances on his opponent.*]

YUSUF: Heeey! All bow before me! The Angel of Death—he's my best friend, my buddy, my partner. On Saturdays I spill guts; on Sundays I cut off hands. Mondays, I'm a hangman. Tuesdays, it's throat-slitting time. On Wednesdays I gouge out eyes. Thursdays, I drink blood. I'll have your skin in no time, make a drum with your hide. Come on, make a move. You look scared, champ. Ready to faint, eh?

RASİM BABA: [*Raises his hands to the sky.*] God is great!

AZİZ and ARİF: [*Watching with mounting excitement, start to sing.*]
> Ömer the foolish husband—
> He is the best thing in my life.
> He's got a lovely, leggy, willing wife.

[*The fighters are slowly and carefully circling each other.*]

YUSUF: What's the matter? Run out of steam? Come on, I thought you wanted to fight.

ÖMER: I'll strike to kill, punk.

YUSUF: Sorry, but I don't think you're up to it. If you can't spill my guts, I'll do it for you. There's this girl. I'd give my life for her. I've never, never hurt anyone, insulted anyone, lied to anyone. What I did was fall in love. Is that a crime? What harm's in it? My love would've saved her from all the filth in that mansion. But I don't love her anymore. When you get back, tell her. She may have a pasha for a father, but I have something better—the glory of my heart.

[ÖMER *makes his move.*]

RASİM BABA: Watch out! [YUSUF *wards off the attack.*]

ÖMER: Ah, shit.

AZİZ: You're the shit.

ARİF: Lapdog of the brownnose informer.

AZİZ: If your Fehim Pasha is a man . . .

ARİF: . . . then we're fucking eagles.

RASİM BABA: [*Shouts without taking his eyes off the fighters.*] Go on, boys! Go on! Tease him!

AZİZ: Don't laugh, gutter rat.

ARİF: He's not laughing, Aziz.

AZİZ: You're right, Arif. Wrong quotation.

RASİM BABA: Yusuf! Listen! Remember what I taught you about the pirate? This guy's fighting just like him. Sideways.

YUSUF: Got it, Dad.

RASİM BABA: Don't bend so low!

YUSUF: Right, Dad. [*Takes the knife in his left hand. Seizing the chance,* ÖMER *lets out his war cry and attacks again.*]

RASİM BABA: Now!

[*With the edge of his right hand,* YUSUF *delivers a terrible blow to* ÖMER's *right arm.* ÖMER *cries out in pain and drops his knife.*]

ÖMER: Damn you, Yusuf.

YUSUF: I'm sorry, Ömer.

PERTEV BEY: What happened?

RASİM BABA: That blow is called "the cruncher." Arm's broken.

[AZİZ, ARİF, *and* OSMAN *hug* YUSUF. *Holding his right arm,* ÖMER *sneaks away.*]

PERTEV BEY: We've got to celebrate this!

RASİM BABA: Of course! Osman!

OSMAN: Sir?

RASİM BABA: Prepare a feast for tonight. We'll eat and sing. Yusuf will sit on my right. Heeey! We're on top now! We're on top!

AZİZ, ARİF, and OSMAN: Heeey!

NARRATOR: All right, then. Feast scene. [*The others quickly set the table.*] How can I compete with this Yusuf? Now he's the man who beat the champ. Word's gotten around like wildfire. The whole town is celebrating. God knows where all this will lead. Let's watch.

[RASİM BABA's *house. All seated.* PERTEV BEY *plays music. They sing.* OSMAN *occasionally gets up to bring more food. There is a knock on the door.*]

RASİM BABA: What's that?

OSMAN: Someone's at the door.

RASİM BABA: Go look. [OSMAN *runs off.*]

PERTEV BEY: You don't think . . . ?

RASİM BABA: Quit worrying. You're always worrying.

PERTEV BEY: Didn't you hear? The worst has happened at the mansion. The help has left. The cook uses salt where sugar is called for, and vice versa. The pasha must be furious. He's sure to strike back.

OSMAN: [*Returns.*] Gentleman by the name of Hadi wants to see Yusuf.

RASİM BABA: Show him in.

OSMAN: Come in, sir. [HADİ BEY *enters.* YUSUF, AZİZ, *and* ARİF *rise and remain standing.*]

HADİ BEY: I'm very sorry to be disturbing you at this time of night. Please forgive me.

RASİM BABA: It's all right. Please take a seat.

HADİ BEY: If I'm not mistaken, you're Yusuf Bey's father.

RASİM BABA: That's right.

PERTEV BEY: Widely known as Rasim the Destroyer.

HADİ BEY: Oh, I know, I know. Until only recently it was the best-known name in town. Looks like your son will now take Istanbul by storm. I don't want to waste your time. May I speak with him? [*Looks at the others.*] Is he away?

RASİM BABA: First, tell me what you want with him.

HADİ BEY: All present are friends, correct?

RASİM BABA: Correct. Feel free.

HADİ BEY: We understand your son had an encounter with Ömer this morning. I'm sure you know that he is Fehim Pasha's number one bully. We're told your son broke his arms and sent him packing. What's more, he's reported to have said, "In my heart, there's a glorious ideal that's stronger than your pasha." Of course, anyone can guess what he meant by that—the ideal of liberty. Nowadays it takes real courage to utter those words. My pasha said, "Go find that young man." That's why I rushed here.

PERTEV BEY: May one ask who your pasha is?

HADİ BEY: The one known as Mad Suat Pasha. [*The others exchange glances.*]

RASİM BABA: Yusuf, greet the gentleman.

[HADİ BEY *jumps up with a great show of respect.* RASİM BABA *and* PERTEV BEY *also rise.*]

HADİ BEY: Oh, you mean he's here? Ah, what a fine-looking man! And so young. Yusuf Bey, you contributed a great deal to our cause by getting rid of that brute. Our many friends who were his victims have been avenged, thanks to you. Pasha sends you his greetings, along with a little present. Be kind enough to accept it. [*On a signal from* RASİM BABA, YUSUF *takes the bundle.*] We're sure you'll make good use of it. You're invited to our mansion tomorrow. Shall I send the carriage for you in the afternoon?

RASİM BABA: Please do.

HADİ BEY: Then I'll take my leave now. Good night. Our respects to you, Yusuf Bey. We feel certain that this is the beginning of a mutually beneficial relationship.

RASİM BABA: Osman, see the gentleman off.

OSMAN: Yes, sir.

[OSMAN *and* HADİ BEY *go out.*]

AZİZ and ARİF: [*Begin to dance with joy.*] Great day! Great day! Great day!

RASİM BABA: Cut it out.

AZİZ: Yes, sir.

ARİF: Aye, aye, sir.

PERTEV BEY: So what's the pasha's present?

RASİM BABA: [YUSUF *hands the bundle to* RASİM BABA, *who opens it.*] A revolver with a mother-of-pearl handle. Just like the one I had.

YUSUF: This is what I'm supposed to put to good use?

RASİM BABA: Actually, this will stay in your pocket. What you'll mainly use is your brain. But your star is shining bright, my boy. You know what this means, don't you? You're somebody now. You'll be honored everywhere. So will your old father with his broken wings. Don't you drag your feet, or I'll be angry.

YUSUF: But, Father, is this pasha any different? He sends me a gun . . .

RASİM BABA: What should he send to a fierce fighter like you? Candy? Anyway, you know what people say—he's a "freedom lover." By the way, Pertev, what does that mean exactly? "Freedom lover"?

PERTEV BEY: Well, when freedom arrives someplace, people fill the streets, sing marching songs, recite poems. So I guess "freedom lover" means a refined person who's fond of music, outdoors, and poetry.

RASİM BABA: Just the kind of man you like, Yusuf.

AZİZ: Refined persons, eh?

ARİF: Oh, how I wish we were "freedom lovers"!

[*They all freeze.*]

NARRATOR: [*Enters in his* HADİ *costume.*] Servant in one mansion, steward in another. Looks funny, but what can we do? I'm the only player in this troupe with that kind of range. All right, the freeze is over. [*The others come to life. Scene change.*] It's time you met Mad Suat Pasha. I present him to you now. No, no, I take that back. It's the reverse. I present you commoners to Mad Suat Pasha.

[SUAT PASHA's *room. He is seated in his armchair.*]

HADİ BEY: [*Enters and bows low in respect.*] Yusuf Bey is here, Pasha.

SUAT PASHA: Quick, quick, quick, show him in right away.

HADİ BEY: [*Does so.*] Please come in, sir. Our pasha's expecting you. [YUSUF *enters.*]

SUAT PASHA: Ah, here you are, my lionhearted young man! Look, I'm getting up for you. I don't get up even for cabinet ministers. But the really brave are different. Come close.

Here, kiss my hand. Now sit by me, Sonny. I said sit, Brother. [YUSUF *sits.*] What d'you say, Hadi? Just like we expected, eh?

HADİ BEY: Yes, Pasha.

SUAT PASHA: Sharp looking, isn't he? Like a knife. Now tell me. How did that mad dog cross your path? What did you say to him? How did the fight start? How did it go? Right, Hadi? We should hear it all from Yusuf himself.

HADİ BEY: Right, Pasha.

SUAT PASHA: Of course, you won't want to tell us all that. The really brave don't like to brag. But I'm different. With me, you can open up. I love fight stories. I was a lively lad myself in my youth. Fighting all the time. Now I just get others to fight, then listen to the stories. That's what that stupid Fehim Pasha does, too, but does he understand what he hears? The listener to the story must be as sharp as the teller. Isn't that so, Hadi?

HADİ BEY: Absolutely, Pasha.

SUAT PASHA: A man says "knife," our Fehim Pasha thinks he heard "wife." Ha ha. But, frankly, there are quite a few fools on our side, too. Some write delicate poetry, others purple prose. Most of them talk a lot. Idiots! What do our poor ignorant people have to do with poetry and such? Can stuff like that get them to move their asses? They have no idea what's good for them, anyway. That's something we know. Right, Hadi?

HADİ BEY: No doubt about it, Pasha.

SUAT PASHA: What's needed is a leader who will lead them. Anyone who crosses his path must be crushed like an insect. Period. Now, we'll celebrate tonight. Won't we, Hadi?

HADİ BEY: We certainly will, Pasha.

SUAT PASHA: With music, dancing girls, the lot.

HADİ BEY: Naturally, Pasha.

SUAT PASHA: Those friends who're writing subversive stuff on the sly—get a few of them here tonight. Let them see what the really brave are like. Maybe they can wake up from their hibernation. Hey, that's an apt word, isn't it? You like it, Yusuf?

YUSUF: Yes, Pasha.

SUAT PASHA: [*Slaps* YUSUF *on the back.*] Hey, I like the way you talk. Good fighter, good conversationalist. I like everything about you. Your father's alive, isn't he?

YUSUF: Yes, Pasha.

SUAT PASHA: Good. Hadi, invite him, too. Let's have fun together. And do something to keep the peace in the harem. Send them storytellers and things. They keep nagging me about the shadow plays in Fehim Pasha's harem. Now let's go out in the garden to do some shooting. It's good for the appetite. You have your gun with you?

YUSUF: No, Pasha.

SUAT PASHA: Never mind. We've got lots of 'em.

[SUAT PASHA *and* YUSUF *go out.*]

NARRATOR: [*As* HADİ BEY.] These two Ottoman pashas enjoy arranging human clashes like cockfights—it's not easy serving both of them at the same time. Now I've got to be a servant again, but I have a hunch I'll find my true calling before this play is over.

[FEHİM PASHA's *room. He is seated, looking tired and flabbergasted.* NURİ BEY *stands before him.*]

FEHİM PASHA: Are you joking?

NURİ BEY: No, Pasha. He beat him soundly in the street. Everybody saw it.

FEHİM PASHA: He beat our number one, Sergeant Ömer the champ?

NURİ BEY: The same. Then he said, "Tell your pasha that I'm a pasha, too."

FEHİM PASHA: What on earth does he mean by that?

NURİ BEY: It's not for me to think about these things, but this is what occurs to me. If these wicked "freedom lovers," God forbid, come to power, they will of course hand out titles and honors to each other. Maybe they made a promise along these lines to Yusuf.

FEHİM PASHA: Go on! He's nothing but a lowly actor.

NURİ BEY: Yes, but these members of the Union and Progress Party,[12] these Young Turks— they're slippery devils. They'll do anything.

FEHİM PASHA: The palace is topsy-turvy, too. The sultan made a new pasha grand vizier. I know who it is. He'll consider, consult, read reports, hold meetings. Forever. By the time he reaches a decision, it'll be too late. Anyway, the important thing is not to lose our grip on Istanbul. This foxy capital will find a way out of any fix. Where's Ömer now?

NURİ BEY: He's outside, waiting. I thought you might want to console him.

FEHİM PASHA: Show the blockhead in. [NURİ BEY *goes out.*] Console him? Hah! I want winners around me. You lose, you're out.

ÖMER: [*Shown in by* NURİ BEY. *His arm is in a sling. Obviously in pain, he tries to bow low to greet* FEHİM PASHA, *who jumps up from his seat.*] Pasha . . .

FEHİM PASHA: Have you no shame? You picked a fine time to humiliate me. Like I don't have enough troubles. I feed and clothe and entertain all of you. What for? So you'll be some damned use when I need you. What d'you think this place is—a home for the down-and-out?

ÖMER: Please, Pasha . . .

FEHİM PASHA: You should've figured out how to please me. All you people are good for is fighting. If you can't do that properly, get your gear and clear out!

ÖMER: Yes, Pasha. God be with you. [*Moves backward and leaves.*]

FEHİM PASHA: Let's have a few drinks, or I'll go berserk. Invite Hasan, too. He'll be our new chief bully.

NURİ BEY: Very well, Pasha.

---

12. Union and Progress Party: The dominant political force in the Ottoman Empire from the revolution of 1908 until the end of World War I.

FEHİM PASHA: Table's set, isn't it? Let's go. [*Begins to leave.*]

NURİ BEY: The table is set, but . . . I don't know how to tell you this . . . there's no food.

FEHİM PASHA: What d'you mean, there's no food?

NURİ BEY: The kitchen has come to a standstill.

FEHİM PASHA: Are you feeling all right? Anything can come to a standstill, but not our kitchen.

NURİ BEY: That's what I thought, but it's stopped.

FEHİM PASHA: Calm down. Tell me what happened.

NURİ BEY: I tried to keep this from you. Yesterday I managed somehow. But today I've had to close the kitchen.

FEHİM PASHA: I think I'm losing my mind. What's our kitchen—a damned shop? Take a deep breath, Nuri. Don't panic. Your pasha can fight his way out of any trap. If worst comes to worst, we can sneak to some little town and lie low till it blows over. Then we can come back here, stronger than ever. So now I'm asking again. Answer me calmly. The table is set, no?

NURİ BEY: It's set, Pasha.

FEHİM PASHA: Excellent. Now another bit of information, please. What're we having for dinner?

NURİ BEY: Boiled eggs, pickles, cheese, onions . . .

FEHİM PASHA: You don't say! Where in hell is the cook? Where are his helpers?

NURİ BEY: They're all gone. No one's here except me and the new servant.

FEHİM PASHA: Are you trying to make another mad pasha of me? What's behind all this? Someone organizing a rebellion under my nose?

NURİ BEY: Let me fetch the new servant, Pasha. I think he knows what's behind this. It seems there are strange goings-on in the neighborhood.

FEHİM PASHA: Where is he?

NURİ BEY: I don't know anymore. He should be nearby—unless he's left, too.

FEHİM PASHA: [*Runs out, comes back quickly, dragging* AYVAZ *by the ear.*] What's going on, dunce? Tell me the truth, or I'll crush you. [*Lets go of* AYVAZ's *ear.*] Speak!

AYVAZ: You want the naked truth, do you?

FEHİM PASHA: Yes!

AYVAZ: All right, then. It'll make me feel better, too. Your ship of state is sinking, Pasha. Want the details?

FEHİM PASHA: No, I don't need the details. You're the only one around here who tells the truth. I'm going to the harem, Nuri. Let's see how the women are doing. [FEHİM PASHA *goes out.* NURİ BEY *follows.*]

NARRATOR: If the scene is the harem, I shouldn't be there. I'm making my escape.

[*The harem. The* PASHA's WIFE, MİHRİBAN, *and the* SERVANT GIRLS *are singing and dancing.* FEHİM PASHA *enters, stands watching, astounded. When the women see him, they stop. All rise.*]

FEHİM PASHA: Another madhouse! What's going on here?

WIFE: What a nice surprise, darling! I thought you'd be staying at the palace tonight.

FEHİM PASHA: And I thought you'd all be in misery. Are you having a collective fit?

WIFE: You mean because the help quit? At first, we were lost. None of us can cook anything. Then we managed to boil some eggs. We found pickles, onions, cheese. So we had a kind of picnic indoors. It was great fun.

FEHİM PASHA: Darling, I'm afraid the fun won't last. We're in for rough times.

WIFE: You exaggerate, dear. Nuri will soon find a new cook and new helpers. Everything will be better than before.

FEHİM PASHA: My love, it's not that simple.

WIFE: You're pessimistic because you're overly suspicious, like our beloved sultan. So the people are mad at us because we didn't let that Yusuf have our daughter. The people! They're stupid and enjoy these sad stories of romance for a while. Then they forget them. Stop worrying.

FEHİM PASHA: You're right. That's how it was at the beginning. But forest fires can start with a spark. Now the people are lovesick—for something, whatever it is. They, not Yusuf, will be yelling under our window, and the shout won't be "Mihribaaan!" It'll be "Down with tyranny!" Pretty soon they'll be asking for my head.

WIFE: Oh, I didn't know all that. If I'd known, I'd have said, "Give them the girl."

MİHRİBAN: Mother!

WIFE: Didn't you hear what your father said? I'm not brave enough for these things.

MİHRİBAN: Really, Mother . . .

FEHİM PASHA: Stop talking nonsense. I'd die before I give my girl to that bastard. I hear he's joined Mad Suat Pasha's crowd.

WIFE: What! You mean he's in that man's harem, entertaining his ugly wife? Yusuf will never have our daughter!

FEHİM PASHA: Who said anything about entertaining? He's the top fighter there.

WIFE: That wimp?

FEHİM PASHA: Yesterday that wimp beat the shit out of our champion Ömer. He broke all his limbs.

[*The* SECOND SERVANT GIRL *cannot contain a delighted giggle. Then she puts her hand over her mouth.*]

Is he a "freedom lover," a Young Turk, or some other kind of subversive? We can't tell. But I wouldn't be surprised if they made him a pasha soon. Now get me something to eat, girls. I'll join your picnic.

WIFE: Get going, girls. [*The* GIRLS *run off.*]

FEHİM PASHA: Come with me, Wife. Help me undress.

WIFE: Of course, dear. Anything you say. [*They leave.*]

NARRATOR:

in his mansion

the new grand vizier sat

with a wool coat on his back

and a nightcap on his head

taking snuff

trying to figure out

how to save the ship of state

then to deepen his thought

he look a deep sniff of snuff

little did he know

at that moment

all of European Turkey was awake

and getting ready to proclaim

a constitution

while Istanbul slept

Now we're in the mansion of Mad Suat Pasha.

[MAD SUAT PASHA's *room. He enters with* HADİ BEY *and* YUSUF *in tow.* YUSUF *is in his new tough guy outfit and looks confused.*]

SUAT PASHA: Yusuf, my lionhearted boy, you've saved my future and the honor of this city! [HADİ BEY *looks at* YUSUF *with pride.* YUSUF *looks surprised.*] My friends, you know I've come straight from the palace. Let me share with you what I've heard. This morning the Union and Progress Party has proclaimed a constitution. [HADİ *extends his hand toward* YUSUF *in joy.*] Long live freedom! Long live the new regime! But . . . there's a "but" here . . . all this time I've been battling tyranny and its representative Fehim Pasha right here in the capital, these other "freedom lovers" just climb a mountain, enjoy the fresh air for a while, then proclaim a constitution. Suddenly they're set to have all the power. Is this fair? Fortunately, we now have the advantage in the court of public opinion. It's what this wonder boy of mine did. Do you know what he did, Hadi? [YUSUF, *too, listens inquisitively.*]

HADİ BEY: No, Pasha, he didn't tell me anything.

SUAT PASHA: Of course not, fool. He didn't even tell me anything. Which is as it should be. Real "freedom lovers" never divulge their secrets. Even when volcanoes are erupting inside them, they'll manage to look unknowing and confused. Like him. [*Points at* YUSUF, *who is looking more and more puzzled.*] Can you do that?

HADİ BEY: No way, Pasha.

SUAT PASHA: That's right. No way. Savor the moment, Hadi. You're in the presence of one of the most important personages of the new era. Yusuf, when historians interview you, do tell them about me. Say that Suat Pasha was an ardent and sincere defender of the Constitution . . . of freedom. What else? There were other things, Hadi. What were they?

HADI BEY: Justice.

SUAT PASHA: Yes, justice.

HADI BEY: Equality.

SUAT PASHA: Equality, too.

HADI BEY: That's all.

SUAT PASHA: Yes, defender of all ideals. For heaven's sake, what does that mean? [*Laughs.*] Even speaking of freedom disorients you. Just imagine if freedom itself comes. Right, Hadi?

HADI BEY: You were speaking about what our Yusuf did.

SUAT PASHA: Ah, yes. Thanks for reminding me. While all those around him were paralyzed with fear, this wonder boy dared organize a kind of strike right inside Fehim Pasha's mansion. So that son of a bitch is all alone now. This was being discussed even in the palace today. The sultan heard about it and sent word to Fehim not to come to the palace anymore. This means that from now on all of Istanbul is in the palm of our hands.

HADI BEY: Thanks to you, dear Yusuf.

YUSUF: [*Lowers his head.*] Thanks to you, too.

SUAT PASHA: Tell us. How did you organize such a difficult maneuver?

YUSUF: Pasha, I know nothing about these things.

SUAT PASHA: You're right, of course. These things should not be told. Let historians unearth them. Come on, let's go do some shooting. If you refuse once more, I'll be hurt. Don't worry about outshooting me and wounding my pride. I'm not foolish enough to think I can compete against the likes of you. [*Goes.*]

HADI BEY: [*Draws back to let* YUSUF *pass.*] After you.

YUSUF: No, no. Please.

HADI BEY: I insist. And if in your conversations with historians you care to mention the services of your humble servant, I shall be eternally grateful.

[YUSUF *flees.*]

NARRATOR: [*Comes forward as* HADI BEY.]
while in the mansion of Mad Suat Pasha at night
heroes and poets and other riffraff
happily drank to toast freedom
Sultan Abdülhamid paced his little room
in great excitement
reading the memo of the government
this time his palace reeked
of eggplant dishes

flowers and rot
finally he affixed his seal of approval
to the paper
and said yes to parliament
this meant that
with seventy-seven telegrams and one bullet
his regime had been sent packing
the news was in the papers next morning
and drove Istanbul's people mad with joy

And now we're back in Fehim Pasha's mansion.

[*A room with a bay window.* FEHIM PASHA, *his* WIFE, MIHRIBAN, NURI BEY, *and the* SERVANT GIRLS *stare out of the window with fear and anxiety.* FEHIM PASHA *has a gun in his hand. A* VOICE *and the roar of a* CROWD *are heard.*]

VOICE: [*From offstage.*] Long live freedom!

CROWD: [*From offstage.*] Long live freedom!

VOICE: Down with tyranny!

CROWD: Down with tyranny!

VOICE: Long live the Constitution!

CROWD: Long live the Constitution!

VOICE: Down with Fehim Pasha!

CROWD: Down with him! Down with him!

WIFE: [*Moves away from the window.*] I can't look anymore.

FEHIM PASHA: [*Takes aim at someone in the street.*] I'll shoot you down like a dog, you ungrateful wretch!

NURI BEY: Pasha, please. We'll all be torn to pieces.

FEHIM PASHA: [*Lowers his gun.*] What do you suggest we do?

VOICE: Long live the Constitution!

CROWD: Long live! Long live!

FEHIM PASHA: Why did our number one guard run away?

NURI BEY: I have no idea, Pasha.

VOICE: Down with Fehim Pasha!

CROWD: Down with him! Down with him!

FEHIM PASHA: They've got me on the brain.

GIRLS: Ooooooooh.

WIFE: What's going on? Won't someone tell me?

MIHRIBAN: [*Panic-stricken.*] They're breaking down the garden gate.

WIFE: How very rude of them.

VOICE: [*Offstage.*] Friends, stop! Don't!

CROWD: [*Offstage.*] Down with him!

FEHİM PASHA: If only we had one friend among these "freedom lovers"! But all our acquaintances who thought that way have been shot or exiled. Now there's no one who can help us.

VOICE: Don't, friends! No! Stop!

GIRLS: Oooooooooh!

WIFE: What's happening? Oh, I'd better look. [*Goes to the window.*] Hey! How can they enter someone else's garden without permission? Look at that one. He's swinging on our swing!

NURİ BEY: Pasha, looks like they'll try to break down the back door.

FEHİM PASHA: Come, let's go there. [FEHİM PASHA *and* NURİ BEY *go out quickly.*]

WIFE: Those two are running away. We'll be left alone here. Run! Don't let them get away!

[*The* WOMEN *run off, screaming. Outside, a marching song is heard.*]

[*The coffeehouse. Flags everywhere.* RASİM BABA, PERTEV BEY, YUSUF, *and* OSMAN *are listening to* ÖMER, *whose arm is still in the sling.*]

ÖMER: When I heard what was happening, I rushed to see the great pasha. I mean Mad Suat Pasha, of course. I said I'd always been a secret "freedom lover" myself. "But that awful Fehim Pasha," I said, "he wouldn't even let us say the word." Then I told him how I feel about freedom now. I mean, who doesn't love it? Best thing in the world—that's how I feel. Anyway, Suat Pasha says, "Go kiss Yusuf's hand. If he forgives you, I'll have you in my service." So Yusuf, my dear brother, how could I guess you were a hero of the great struggle? Now let me kiss your hand.

YUSUF: No, Ömer, you're my older brother.

ÖMER: Please, please, let me! It's an honor. [*Tries to grab* YUSUF's *hand.* OSMAN *restrains him.*] Let go! Don't hold me back. It's a free country now. Long live freedom!

PERTEV BEY: This is weird.

RASİM BABA: Look here, Ömer.

ÖMER: Yes, sir?

RASİM BABA: Sit down.

ÖMER: Of course, sir. [*Sits.*]

RASİM BABA: Osman, tea for Ömer.

ÖMER: [*Jumps to his feet.*] Oh, no! Please, no! Osman, my brother, for God's sake, you sit down. How can I let a great freedom fighter like you serve me? [*Runs inside.* OSMAN *is too astonished to move.*]

PERTEV BEY: Look at Osman. He's frozen.

OSMAN: Uncle Pertev, I'm a freedom fighter now, right?

PERTEV BEY: [*Laughs.*] Right.

OSMAN: [*Lets out a war cry.*] Let the people know. Anyone says a word against me or the Constitution, I'll wring his neck!

RASİM BABA: Shut up.

OSMAN: Yes, sir.

PERTEV BEY: Yusuf, my son, why aren't you with your pasha on a day like this?

YUSUF: I can't stand all this nonsense, Uncle Pertev. I was afraid of Fehim Pasha, the tyrant. Suat Pasha the "freedom lover" is worse. They're both bloodthirsty. Anyway, the good news is that leaders of the Union and Progress Party are coming to Istanbul. When they form the new government, they'll do away with all these pashas and things. Everything will be OK, and I'll go back to my shadow plays.

RASİM BABA: Shadow plays! You're the one who's talking nonsense. Son, you can't do as you please anymore. You're a hero of the great struggle!

YUSUF: I'm nothing of the sort, Dad, and you know it.

ÖMER: Yusuf, my brother, how can you say that? When everybody was shaking in his boots, one night you stood before the mansion by yourself. You challenged the tyrant single-handed. I heard you with my own ears. You were shouting, "Down with Fehim! Down, down, down!"

RASİM BABA: Really? I never knew that. Oh my brave, brave son!

YUSUF: Dad, I wasn't shouting "Down, down, down!" I was hollering "Mihribaaan!" Then she opened the window and called me a street dog.

OSMAN: Whaaat?

YUSUF: I'm glad she did. Brought me to my senses. I growled and barked all night, but I got rid of my stupid love for her.

RASİM BABA: Come to your senses now, Son. Please don't ruin everything.

OSMAN: Yes, Brother. Please forget about shadow plays. Now things are different for the likes of you and me. Freedom fighters can't be shadow puppeteers, can they?

ÖMER: And please don't forget me, Brother. When it comes to fighting for freedom, I'll be second to none. I'll cut off as many heads as it takes. Right, Rasim Baba?

RASİM BABA: I envy all of you.

[AZİZ *and* ARİF *come running.*]

AZİZ: Did you hear? Did you hear?

ARİF: The pee-pee-people . . .

AZİZ: . . . they stormed the mansion.

ARİF: Br-br-broke down the d-d-doors.

[*The others rise.*]

AZİZ: Fehim Pasha sent word.

ARİF: W-w-with us.

AZİZ: Says he'll surrender only to Yusuf.

ARİF: Everybody's w-waiting.

AZİZ: They're waiting for you, Yusuf.

ARİF: H-hurry up. [*Pause.*]

RASİM BABA: Let's go, Son.

YUSUF: Yes, Father. [RASİM BABA *and* YUSUF *go off.*]

PERTEV BEY: All together, boys.

ÖMER: Me too! Don't leave me alone anywhere. People don't know I've been a secret freedom fighter. They'd finish me off in a jiffy.

[*They leave.* ÖMER *runs after them.*]

NARRATOR: [*Appears dressed as a freedom fighter (riding boots; special coat, unbuttoned).*]
When they reached the mansion, the crowd parted with great respect for their hero, Yusuf
Bey, and let them go through. The harem was of course considered off limits even to the
most rabid crowd, so Fehim Pasha had taken refuge there. Yusuf was let in. Thus, he found
himself in that harem once again, but now it was the family's turn to entertain him.

[*The harem.* NURİ BEY *shows* YUSUF *in.* FEHİM PASHA, *seated at the far end, rises. His*
WIFE, MİHRİBAN, *and the* SERVANT GIRLS *stand behind a partition of straw matting.*]

NURİ BEY: Sir, the pasha is willing to surrender to you and you only. We're all in a terrible
state. [*Adds in a very low voice.*] I was for freedom, too, of course. But this devil kept
us under constant watch.

YUSUF: Where's the pasha?

FEHİM PASHA: I'm here. [*Comes forward, looking exhausted.* YUSUF *approaches him. They
stand staring at each other.*]

YUSUF: Pasha.

FEHİM PASHA: Sir.

YUSUF: Let me kiss your hand.

FEHİM PASHA: Certainly not. Please don't embarrass me any more than necessary. Of course,
I had absolutely no idea who or what you were, or I wouldn't have done all those asinine
things. I realize it's too late now. But, for what it's worth, I beg your forgiveness.

YUSUF: Pasha, I've eaten and slept in your house. One night you watched a shadow play I
put on.

FEHİM PASHA: Did I?

YUSUF: Yes. You liked it and gave me a gold piece. With it, I bought more gear for the
plays, including a party whistle. You know, the kind that grows long when you blow.
I love it, carry it with me always. Also, I got a nice tambourine with little silver bells
for my father. I wanted him to like music and get away from his murderous past. You
let me into your harem, which was a rare privilege. I'm only a man of dumb impulses,
an actor, the insolent son of a lame coffeehouse keeper. I have no other title or power.
You sent for me. Here I am, at your service. I'll do anything I can for you.

FEHİM PASHA: Nuri, leave us alone.

NURİ BEY: Yes, Pasha. [*Goes.*]

FEHİM PASHA: Sir, there's no need to keep up this pretense. I know who you are. The mad crowd outside came to a dead stop the second they heard your name. Why?

YUSUF: It's because I've never hurt any of them, never insulted anyone, never destroyed people's lives.

FEHİM PASHA: Look, Yusuf, I'm staring death in the face. I'll speak my mind. Whips and chains failed to control the senseless horde you call "the people." You think you can do it with love? Now quit fooling and listen to me. Here's my offer. You wanted my daughter. She's yours. You'll live in this mansion. With you here, the help will come back right away. You'll have all the money you need, lead the life of a pasha. In return, I want just one thing: get me out of here. Is it a deal? Eh? What do you say? . . . Wait. Don't speak. Mihriban! Come here.

YUSUF: [*Trembling.*] Pasha, please . . .

FEHİM PASHA: Keep quiet.

[*The* WIFE *and* MİHRİBAN *come out from behind the partition.*]

WIFE: Oh, Yusuf, I brought you your beautiful ladylove. Go on, Mihriban. Say hello to our gracious guest. [YUSUF *and* MİHRİBAN *exchange glances.*]

MİHRİBAN: [*Self-assuredly.*] Hello, sir.

YUSUF: Hello, madam.

WIFE: Darling, these two will make an admirable couple. May God protect them from the evil eye of envy! Thanks to Yusuf Bey, we'll go back to happy times. Isn't that so, Mihriban? [*Draws close to* YUSUF.] Why don't you say something? Look, we're all waiting for a kind word from you, wagging our tails like dogs. Pasha, you should have seen this young man when he was pretending to be a performer. He was full of wondrous words. Remember how charmed you were, Mihriban?

FEHİM PASHA: So what do you say, Yusuf?

YUSUF: I don't know what to say, Pasha, but if you'd permit me, I can perform a bit of a play the ladies used to enjoy.

WIFE: Go ahead, dear. Do whatever you like.

YUSUF: [*Slips into the part of the young lover in the traditional play that he had put on for them previously.*] "O proud and beautiful lady, how you shine in your usual finery! Lovely dress, lovely jewels, lovely perfume. And, wonder of wonders, you deign to look at me today. And you're smiling sweetly! Why the miracle, lady?"

[*Speaks in his own voice.*] Tonight I'll smuggle you out of here, Pasha. [*Leaves. Silence. Then the* SECOND SERVANT GIRL *begins to laugh.*]

WIFE: Don't laugh, you! I said stop, or you'll be sorry!

SECOND SERVANT GIRL: [*Continues to laugh.*] Yes, madam. Certainly, madam. Anything you say, madam.

[MİHRİBAN *suddenly runs out.*]

FEHİM PASHA: [*To his* WIFE.] There. We are reaping what we have sown. [*They, too, leave slowly.*]

NARRATOR: [*His jacket is buttoned, his head bare.*] Historians haven't recorded this, but I'll give it to you straight. Yusuf did smuggle Fehim Pasha out of his mansion that night. The new government expropriated all the pasha's possessions. His mansion became a center of the Union and Progress Party. As his wife, his daughter, the girls, and the footman were leaving the mansion, the opening ceremony for the center was being held. Now, people are expecting an important representative of the Union and Progress Party to make the opening speech. Let's see who shows up.

[*Withdraws. A huge flag is illuminated in the background. Colorful bunting all around* SUAT PASHA, RASİM BABA, PERTEV BEY, *and* YUSUF. AZİZ, ARİF, OSMAN, *and* ÖMER *are waiting in a row.* NURİ BEY *appears and very respectfully shows in the* PARTY SPOKESMAN, *resplendent in the "leaders' outfit" of the time (fur cap, riding boots, riding whip in hand, two revolvers in view).*]

PARTY SPOKESMAN: [*With abrupt motion, he walks center stage.* NURİ BEY *starts to applaud. The others join him.*] Thank you. I am İhsan, previously an employee at the Edirne Post Office. Now I'm the representative of the Central Committee of the Union and Progress Party. I heartily greet all of you. [*Applause.*] Thank you. Soldier and civilian, woman and man, young and old, we all are hand in hand and heart to heart. We all are brothers and sisters.

NURİ BEY: How true!

PARTY SPOKESMAN: The times of disunity and strife are over. [*Applause.*]

NURİ BEY: Yes, sir!

PARTY SPOKESMAN: We'll live in peace forever and ever. [*Applause.*]

NURİ BEY: We're all with you.

PARTY SPOKESMAN: Thank you. However, there are those among us who still do not understand this change. Skulls too thick to hear reason, hearts too hardened to accept sacrifice, tongues too slippery to praise the positive. I tell you frankly, here and now, that those skulls will be broken, those hearts torn out, those tongues silenced with whatever means necessary. [*Applause. Only* YUSUF *has stopped applauding.*]

NURİ BEY: You're right, sir!

PARTY SPOKESMAN: Thank you. I hereby open this first social center of the Union and Progress Party. May it be the scene of many happy events.

NURİ BEY: Amen.

PARTY SPOKESMAN: Long live union, long live progress! [*Applause.*]

SUAT PASHA: Sir, you spoke well. I liked your speech. We have with us here a popular hero of the struggle. He defeated that rascal Fehim Pasha single-handedly. [*Applause.*] May I suggest . . .

PARTY SPOKESMAN: [*Interrupts.*] May I suggest you tell me your name first.

SUAT PASHA: You mean you don't know me? I guess that's because you're not a native of Istanbul. I'm Suat Pasha, alias the Madman.

PARTY SPOKESMAN: Oh yes. Today you were appointed something or other in Yemen.

SUAT PASHA: Where?

PARTY SPOKESMAN: Yemen.

SUAT PASHA: I know I'm mad, but are you mad, too? I've rendered a great deal of service to the cause of freedom. I've had dozens of people killed for the cause.

PARTY SPOKESMAN: If you have objections, apply to the Central Committee. Who's the hero you were talking about?

AZİZ: Here he is.

ARİF: Right here.

PERTEV BEY: Name's Yusuf.

OSMAN: My brother Yusuf.

ÖMER: Famous freedom fighter.

RASİM BABA: And my son.

PARTY SPOKESMAN: I've heard of you, Yusuf Bey. Delighted to meet you in person. We urgently need brave fighters like yourself. Brave young men who know how to use a fist or a knife or a gun. Let me embrace you.

RASİM BABA: [*Pushes* YUSUF *toward the* PARTY SPOKESMAN.] Go, Son, go.

PARTY SPOKESMAN: [YUSUF *steps forward. The* PARTY SPOKESMAN *greets him with a bear hug.*] Please stick around after the ceremony. We'll go to headquarters together. Friends, I now give you your hero. He'll speak about his exploits in the service of the cause. [NURİ BEY *applauds enthusiastically, and the others join him.*]

SUAT PASHA: Yusuf, for God's sake, tell them about my services, too.

RASİM BABA: I'm so proud of you, Son!

AZİZ: Our own hero!

ARİF: Hero, hero!

[ÖMER *salutes* YUSUF *with a bloodcurdling war cry.* YUSUF *moves forward. Applause stops. Mounting excitement.* YUSUF *takes the party whistle out of his pocket and blows it. General shock.*]

RASİM BABA: Yusuf!

PERTEV BEY: What're you doing?

[YUSUF *blows again.*]

PARTY SPOKESMAN: Sir, this is not a circus.

[YUSUF *blows the whistle in his face. General consternation.*]

SUAT PASHA: Come to your senses, Yusuf! Tell everybody about our exploits.

ALL: Yes, tell us!

[YUSUF *salutes* SUAT PASHA *with a long, long blow.*]

RASİM BABA: He's off his rocker again. Grab him.

[RASİM BABA, AZİZ, ARİF, *and* OSMAN *rush to grab* YUSUF. *They drag him away.*]

YUSUF: [*On the way out, shouts merrily.*] Boom boom! Boom billy billy booooom! Boom billy boom!

PARTY SPOKESMAN: What's the meaning of this?

NURİ BEY: I don't know, sir. I really don't.

PERTEV BEY: Let's go, Ömer.

ÖMER: Yes, sir.

[*All leave.*]

NARRATOR: [*Comes forward.*] Every time I get a good thing going, this crazy Yusuf steps in and spoils it. But no longer. I sent headquarters a detailed report about the incident. This is the end of Yusuf as far as they are concerned. And, of course, the end of Yusuf means the end of the play. For the very last scene, we're in the coffeehouse once more.

[*The coffeehouse.* RASİM BABA, PERTEV BEY, AZİZ, ARİF, OSMAN, SUAT PASHA, NURİ BEY, ÖMER, *and* YUSUF.]

RASİM BABA: [*Has grabbed* YUSUF *by the collar.*] Tell us, wise guy! Savvy showman! Dandy! Actress! Tell us why you pulled this stunt. Made a monkey of yourself.

SUAT PASHA: You blew it for all of us.

NURİ BEY: Everything was going our way.

ÖMER: Bastard. You've shamed all us fighters.

YUSUF: Dad, I will speak—if you take your hands off my throat.

RASİM BABA: Speak, fucking eagle. Sparrow is more like it. [*Lets go.*] Go on.

YUSUF: You know I had great hopes for the Union and Progress crowd. But they're looking for murderers, too. Hearing that dashed all my hopes. I'm bored with these fight stories. You hear? Just plain bored. No one's talking about really exciting things—like passion, hazel eyes, lovely faces, flowers, and butterflies. We only scream, strike, break, hit, cut, loot, shoot, plunge a knife, take a life—that's all we're after. They say they want to make people happy, but the way they go about it makes everybody unhappy. Can there be lilies in a pool of blood? Can you keep a lawn green if you water it with tears only? Real tough men don't like to step on a single ant. To me, the strongest hand is the one that strokes the most people. Brave hearts have room for everybody. That's what I . . .

SUAT PASHA: Enough of your nonsense. These ungrateful Union and Progress bastards will start to oppress people soon enough. Then how're you going to stop them? With talk of birds and flowers? Come, Ömer. I'm tired of this clown. Let's go get ready for the good fight.

NURİ BEY: Pasha, may your humble servant go with you?

SUAT PASHA: What do you do? [NURİ BEY *whispers in his ear.*] Ah, good. Very good. Come along. Let's go, boys.

ÖMER: Right, Pasha.

[SUAT PASHA *leaves with* ÖMER *and* NURİ BEY. *Silence.* RASİM BABA *sits.*]

YUSUF: Please don't worry, Father. The phony hero made a monkey of himself, not me. Your wise dandy, actress son Yusuf is doing fine. We can make a good living without hiring ourselves out as murderers. I promise you, lots of people will rush here to see the heroic freedom fighter, crazy Yusuf. Osman will make tea. Won't you, Brother?

OSMAN: Glad to, Brother.

YUSUF: I'll entertain. It'll be much more exciting than fight stories. I'll tell sexy stories, read poetry, put on shows, play music, sing. Here I go.

[YUSUF *begins to sing.* ARİF *and* AZİZ *join him joyfully.* PERTEV BEY *picks up his instrument and accompanies him.* FEHİM PASHA's WIFE, MİHRİBAN, *and the* SERVANT GIRLS *go by with bundles and baskets in their hands. The* SECOND SERVANT GIRL *is last. When she sees* YUSUF, *she slows down, stops, stares at him.*]

MİHRİBAN: Come along, you!

SECOND SERVANT GIRL: Yes, miss.

[*The women go off.* YUSUF *gets up to gaze after the* SECOND SERVANT GIRL. *His song ends.*]

NARRATOR: Now this is history: Fehim Pasha tried to escape from Bursa to another town. People recognized, caught, and lynched him on the spot. As for me, I'm a respected member of the party establishment. Living off Istanbul quite nicely, thank you. In the end, I may even be the husband of the beautiful Mihriban.

[OSMAN *brings the tambourine with the little silver bells and hands it to* RASİM BABA.]

I don't know if it will please you or not, ladies and gentlemen, but this is where the play ends.

AZİZ: You know, I could do better.

ARİF: Yeah, I wish we were writers.

[RASİM BABA *is surprised, looks at* YUSUF, *and strikes the tambourine. They start a new song.*]

CURTAIN

◆　　◆　　◆

I, Anatolia

A Play for One Actress

GÜNGÖR DİLMEN

Translated by Talat S. Halman

An Editor's Note

Güngör Dilmen (b. 1930) is one of Turkey's foremost living playwrights. In a career that spanned half a century, he made a strong impact on his country's theatrical life with his lyrical plays, most of which have dealt with mythic and historical subjects.

Dilmen studied at the British High School of Istanbul and later earned a degree in classical philology at Istanbul University. After brief stays in Tel Aviv and Athens doing theater research, he spent nearly three years in the United States, studying dramatic writing and theatrical production at Yale and the University of Washington (Seattle). After his return to Turkey, he worked as dramaturge and deputy chief stage director for the City Theater of Istanbul and as radiophonic play consultant for Radio Istanbul. For many years, he taught courses, mainly in mythology, at the State Conservatory of Istanbul University and the Drama School of the Anatolian University in Eskişehir.

Dilmen's plays earned many of Turkey's major awards. *Ben, Anadolu (I, Anatolia)* came in first at the Best Play Contest organized by the International Industry and Commerce Bank in 1984 and received the Ulvi Uraz Theater Award in 1986.

Many of Dilmen's translations from ancient Greek, including plays by Aeschylus and Sophocles, were published and produced. He also translated August Strindberg's *Ghost Sonata* and attracted attention with his two children's books.

I, Anatolia was Turkey's most successful play of the 1980s, at home and abroad. In that period, this captivating one-woman play, mainly in free verse, about Anatolian women from time immemorial to the early twentieth century featured the legendary artistry of Yıldız Kenter, the greatest Turkish actress ever, who performed it hundreds of times in Turkish and dozens of times in English in many countries. Her tours took her to England (where she presented it at London's Queen Elizabeth Hall), the Soviet Union (at Moscow's Art Theater), Denmark, Sweden, Germany, Canada, the Netherlands, and the United States (New York at Lincoln Center, Washington, D.C., at the Kennedy Center, Atlanta, Miami, Philadelphia, Raleigh, and Ann Arbor).

In the late 1990s, Nergis Arı, a young actress, performed the play a few times in Turkey. The play had a new production in New York City (Off-Broadway) when fifteen of its mythological and historical characters were portrayed by four Turkish American actresses and one American, Jessica Winter.

The translation is by Talat S. Halman, whose biography appears on pp. 369–70.—TSH

Characters

CYBELE, the mother goddess of Anatolia and a symbol of fertility, worshipped by most ancient civilizations of the Near East and Mediterranean. As the leitmotif of the play, she represents in her various reincarnations the indomitable spirit of the women of Anatolia. All the other characters are in a way her children. In the opening scene, she appears at the downfall of the Hittite state. She subsequently marries a peasant, Gordius (father of King Midas), and the Phrygian civilization is born. Throughout the play, she tries to regain her status as a goddess among the newcomers to Anatolia.

PUDUHEPA (thirteenth century B.C.), queen of the Hittite king Hattusili III. The Hittites ruled one of the great empires of the ancient Near East from their capital Hattusha in eastern Anatolia. Puduhepa often dealt as an equal with other powers. In the play, she negotiates a political marriage treaty between her unwilling daughter and Pharaoh Ramses II of Egypt.

LAMASSI (nineteenth century B.C.), merchant, smuggler, and temple prostitute. She writes about her recent dealings to her Assyrian merchant husband stationed in the Anatolian trade colony at Kanesh.

MIDAS'S BARBER, first shares and then divulges Midas's secret. Midas was a king of the Phrygians, whose empire dominated central western Anatolia in the eighth century B.C. When in a musical contest he preferred the pipes of Pan to the lyre of Apollo, the offended god punished him by transforming his ears into those of a donkey. He kept this transformation a secret from all but his barber.

ANDROMACHE, wife of Hector. She inspired her husband to defend Troy against the Greeks in the Trojan War (usually dated to the twelfth century B.C.) and lost her son in the process.

NIOBE, a figure of mythology who boasted that having numerous children made her superior to the goddess Leto, her girlhood friend, who had only two. She was cruelly punished for her arrogance by seeing her children killed by Leto's children, Apollo and Artemis. After the children were killed, they remained unburied for nine days because Zeus had turned the populace to stone; the gods themselves buried the children on the tenth day. Niobe, worn out with grief, was then transformed into a rock on Mt. Sipylus in western Anatolia, where water flows over her face like eternal tears.

THE AMAZON, a member of the mythical race of female hunters and warriors frequently associated with northwest Anatolia. Amazons are sometimes thought to have formed the world's first and only society that practiced feminism to perfection. The Amazon in this play has committed the crime of falling in love with her prisoner of war. She is trying to defend herself in the presence of her queen, who hands down an unusual decision.

LYDIA (seventh century B.C.), wife of Candaules, king of the Lydians, whose empire succeeded that of the Phrygians. He was so proud of his wife's beauty that he urged

Gyges, his friend and commander, to peep at her naked body while she undressed in the royal bedchamber. The results were fatal when she avenged her honor by having Gyges murder the king and take the throne in 670 B.C.

ADA (fourth century B.C.), queen of Caria who was deposed by her brother Pixodarus. When Alexander the Great campaigned in Anatolia, Ada schemed with the conqueror and aided the Macedonian army in the siege of Halicarnassus (334 B.C.), the capital of Caria. Alexander reinstated her as ruler of the satrapy of Caria. He used to call her "my queen," which made Ada, a middle-aged woman, cherish more romantic feelings than the young conqueror intended.

ARTEMIS OF EPHESUS, the many-breasted fertility goddess worshipped during Hellenistic and Roman times in the ancient city of Ephesus. She was already a synthesis of two goddesses: Anatolian Cybele and Ionian Artemis or Diana. Yet another syncretism would take place as the rise of Christianity gradually transformed her cult into the veneration of the Virgin Mary, thus bringing an end to the pagan era in Anatolia. The Bible (John 19:25–27) says that Jesus entrusted his mother into the care of St. John, "and from that hour the disciple took her to his own home." It is known that John lived in Ephesus.

THEODORA (A.D. ca. 497–548), daughter of a bear tamer, who became the greatest empress of the Byzantines, who ruled Anatolia for a thousand years. She proves her strength of character at the most critical moment of the Nika Revolt (A.D. 532) in the Hippodrome in Constantinople, saving the empire single-handedly for her husband, Justinian, who was proposing to flee the uprising. Once Justinian was securely on the throne, she carried out many reforms for the benefit of women.

ANNA COMNENA (A.D. 1083–ca. 1150), Byzantine princess who failed in her attempt to gain power by plotting against her brother, John Comnenus, in order to bring her husband Nicephorus to power. The play depicts John commuting her death sentence to confinement in a nunnery, where she was to complete her great work, *The Alexiad,* the chronicle of her father Alexius's reign, which encompassed the decline of the Byzantine Empire, the coming of the Crusaders to Constantinople, and the rise of the Turks in Anatolia. Thus, many recognize her as the world's first woman historian.

NILÜFER HATUN, daughter of a Byzantine lord defending the frontier against the rapidly advancing Turks in the late thirteenth century. She was captured by the Turkish chieftain Osman Bey, founder of the Ottoman Empire, and married his son Orhan. In the play, Nilüfer Hatun tells her son, Murad I, about how the Byzantine bride Holophyra was kidnapped; became Nilüfer, the wife of Orhan Gazi; and mothered the Ottoman dynasty that ruled Turkey until 1922.

NASRETTİN HOCA'S WIFE, married to the thirteenth-century semilegendary humorist and teller of innumerable amusing stories that are still popular. Nasrettin Hoca was famous for his folk wisdom. His honest and simple wife is frequently depicted in humorous dialogues with the *hoca*.

AYŞE SULTAN, daughter of the Ottoman sultan Ahmed I (reigned 1603–17). In the play, she tells about her rather strange record of successive marriages and her husbands' fates.

NAKŞİDİL, stepmother of the Ottoman sultan Mahmud II (reigned 1808–39), who tried to restore the declining fortunes of the empire through a series of reforms. As a girl, Nakşidil was captured from her native Martinique by Barbary pirates and taken to the sultan's harem. Her cousin Josephine did equally well: she became Napoleon's empress. In the play, Nakşidil makes her last request of the sultan—she wants to die as a Christian.

NİGÂR HANIM THE POET (1862–1918), a distinguished Ottoman female literary figure who relates the chaotic times leading up to the collapse of the empire. Her education spanned both the Western and the Turkish traditions.

HALİDE EDİP (1882–1964), novelist, professor of literature, and member of Parliament in the newly formed Turkish Republic. In 1922, the year chronicled in the play, she is serving at the front as an interpreter during the last days of the Turkish War of Independence. Just as Cybele witnessed the fall of the Hittites and the emergence of the Phrygians in Anatolia, Halide Edip sees the fall of the Ottoman Empire and the rebirth of a nation from its own ashes.

ACT I

CYBELE:

I am Cybele, Goddess Cybele,
Anatolia's Mother Goddess.
I am Anatolia.

Huge rock monuments and statues were erected in my honor.
My chariot was pulled by lions with manes flaming like the sun.
I ultimately became a Hittite goddess,
But a terrible war burned down and ravaged the Hittite state
—And I was left in the middle of nowhere.
Now I am a goddess without a temple,
Like a queen bee that has lost its hive.
I must do something. The Hittite lands have not been deserted:
Other tribes are moving in. They need a goddess of their own.
I shall merge them with the Hittites and mold them into one.

But, before anything else, I have to get some food

And find a suitable husband.

Here in Anatolia, in our community,

An ambitious woman—goddess or not—

Must latch onto a powerful husband to get anything done.

She can harness him to her chariot

And steer him around without giving him the slightest inkling.

Hey, brother, can you spare a little something to eat?

[*Some food is thrown to her; she catches it.*]

What's your name? Gordius? Hello.

Oh, oh! You're on your way to the bazaar in Ankara—

If there is an Ankara left.

Good luck to you!

And who am I? Don't ask. Nooo, don't touch! I'm not like that.

Well, it's true I've fallen on bad times.

I've tumbled from a fairly high place. But what you have in mind—no sirree!

Keep your hands off me, I say, hands off! I am Goddess Cybele.

Yes, Cybele. Mother Goddess. Goddess of fertility and abundance.

And yet I look like I've been living through a famine, right?

"Look like" is no description for it. Real famine.

An eagle! That's an eagle hovering above us.

Go away! There, it swoops down again. Gordius,

This mad eagle is hell-bent to perch on your head.

There, it has alighted! Don't make a move. Don't utter a sound.

Its feathers are so shiny, its wings so wide.

A brave savage bird, with eyes plunging like an abyss.

This might be a heavenly voice

Or an omen.

This eagle has something to tell us.

Give me your hand, Gordius.

Yes, that's it! I'm not mistaken.

I'll tell you all about it. If you marry me,

I'll go along with anything you want: just say yes, that's all.

Good for you! There you are: now you have me.

Gordius, my love, this eagle that clings to your head

Is a harbinger of good fortune, the bluebird of happiness.

These callused hands of yours goading the ox
Should get ready to hold a golden scepter
And to caress a goddess.

Well, that's the way we got married, peasant Gordius and I.

Over there, on the other slope of the hill,
Some terribly confused people are caught in a debate:
They're all clamoring to create
A brave new country out of the rubble and ashes of the Hittite state.

"We've seen so many raids, so many migrations," they say.
"Now we are like a herd without a shepherd.
Someone should step forward to put us in array.
We must select a leader."

"But who? Who should it be?"
"There's no one really."
"Me! How about me? Me!"
I go over to them discreetly.
"Anatolians," I say to them, "My dear compatriots,
Let us hold a democratic election."
Oh well—*democracy* is a magic word:
It conquers everyone's heart.

"This morning," I say, "whoever is first to come down that slope in his oxcart,
We should take that as a good omen
And make him our king."

And then, from that hilltop, I let my beloved Gordius loose:
He comes down, his cart and oxen kicking up a storm of dust.

"Long live our king! All hail, Mighty King!"

Gordius is stunned:
"I'm poor Gordius, a nobody. How can I be your king?
You damn fools. How can you make the first man who comes along your king?"
I nudge him with my elbow. He changes his tune:
"What if it wasn't I who came first down that hill?" he says.
"You're lucky I was the one: that way you found a ready-made king
As brave and capable as Gordius. And this is my wife,"
He says, dragging me forward: "None other than Goddess Cybele!"
I address them: "Dear Phrygians!"

—because that's what most of these people call themselves—
"The Phrygian civilization is now replacing the Hittite.
Let us now go down to the plains
And build Gordium, the city of Gordius."
A surging spirit heralded the brave new age:
Sculptors made marble beam with a smile;
Ironsmiths flattened the sun on their anvils.
Thus was Gordium created.

The leaven is swelling, the ferment is on.
My children ask me:
"What are you kneading, Mother Cybele?"
—"A new civilization, my loves."
"What is civilization?"
—"Ferment in the community."
"What is the dough?"
—"Nature and the creative mind."
"What is the salt?"
—"Tears."
"And this trough?"
—"All of Anatolia
And beyond it the whole world."

The children of this land
Have come to know me
As Sacred Woman, Mother Earth, Great Beloved.
They spoke in many different tongues,
But I never set them apart.

They sang burning songs for me:
> *Cybele, Mother Goddess*
> *Don't let us go hungry:*
> *Feed our bodies and our hearts.*

If only they would learn to live together,
All my children would be abundantly fed
By my generous breasts.

◆   ◆   ◆

And now my images, my ever-changing sights . . .
Here in this lovely Anatolian land . . .

[*Hittite tablets are thrown on the stage.*]

What's going on? Ah! They're stoning me! If they don't like me, why don't they show their dislike some other way? Stop! Stop throwing those rocks!

[*Picks up a tablet.*]

Haa, Kubaba Anna, *Sal lugal kururu Hatti, uru Hattusha, ishami titia titiamanti.* Now it dawns on me. But you don't get it, do you? *Atavannai atavanti atanti, taranta salli sallanti!* I thought they were stoning me. It turns out I was mistaken. It's a mild reproach—that's all. These Hittite tablets are asking: "Didn't we live on this soil earlier than the Phrygians?" They are right: Hittites were here earlier. So were the Trojans. How could I ever forget you, my beloved Hittites?

Well, then, let us first greet the Hittites, those sculptors of the world's most glorious lions.

PUDUHEPA: I tell you, you are going to marry him! You will marry! You'd better come to your senses! What do you mean "I won't marry an old enemy"? In this blessed world of ours, is there anyone who isn't somebody's one-time enemy? Forget the old enemy! We are friends now—that's what matters! Can't get married unless you're in love, huh? Come off it! In this day and age? It was in primitive societies that people got married for love. Stop being such a reactionary!

Besides, you don't expect the mighty pharaoh to come here all the way from Egypt to serenade you under your window so that you'll like him. Who do you think you are—the living end?

In order for peace to prevail in our country, Anatolia has to be wed to Egypt. There's a price attached to being born a king's daughter, you know. Whether you'll be happy, I can't say. True, compared to you, he is well advanced in age. But this is the sacrifice you have to make for the sake of peace.

Listen. He writes so beautifully:

"I, Ramses, the son of God Amon, the sun's beloved."
—Why on earth is he "the son of God"? Well, let him be. There, he is the beloved of the sun!

"I hereby declare to Puduhepa, the mighty Queen of the Hittites . . . "
—See what a polite boy he is!

"I, your brother, am well. Since the ominous battle of Kadesh, I have been able to put my country back in order."
—Well, does any battle ever bear a good omen?

"So I, your brother, am well. My houses are well, too. So are my sons and grandsons, my horses and chariots."

—Ooh, his horses and chariots are in good shape. That's good to know! Look at the way he mentions his sons and grandsons in passing. Does it matter? It's much better than lying.

"I hope, sister Puduhepa, you too are well . . . "
—Hah!

"With God Amon's leave and River Nile's consent . . . "
—This is where he brings up his proposal. Nooo, my daughter, you're putting up this resistance in vain. That's enough now! Stop crying and sniveling! If I say you are going to get married, you are going to get married! You may laugh or cry—but that is what you are going to do.

Pick up the brass pen, my daughter, and write on soft clay. Once the clay is baked, we'll send it to the Egyptian land.

> Ramses, the son of the Sun, I am sending you my one and only daughter as your bride. Hereafter, let the heroes of the Egyptian land be friends with the braves of the Hittite land so that they shall eat and drink together, and their boys and girls shall love each other. Let them bring peace to our lands, to the whole world, so that we may cherish the blessings of peace together. I want peace—peace, the flowerbed of civilizations . . .

Stop, girl. Don't cry!
You are going to get married!
I'm ordering you to get married.
You will marry for the sake of peace!
For the happiness of our country.
Just as the Treaty of Kadesh was the world's first peace treaty,
This will be the first political marriage in history.

◆　　◆　　◆

An Assyrian woman, LAMASSI, writes to her merchant husband stationed in Anatolia.
LAMASSI: My beloved husband. I put the letter to you in the kiln and baked it—now I am sending it to you piping hot. Enjoy it.

> When you send me money, be sure to hide it securely inside the yarn. People have become just terrible lately. Although we are doing all the work, it's the customs officials who keep filling their own coffers. What sort of system is this? But it's you I'm worried about. I'm afraid you might once again be thrown into

the Kanesh dungeon. You do certain things with such fearlessness that I really can't understand you. Was it necessary to smuggle those huge quantities of goods across the border all in a single day? After all, these Hittites are no fools! Open your eyes and hold your tongue. Don't let your right eye trust your left eye. Be suspicious of everyone. People have become so mean recently. Last month I sent you half a donkey load of tin. Now, if you're smart, you can turn it into two donkey loads of gold.

By the way, did you get the latest shipments? You know which ones I mean. Open your eyes wide. And the money you make on them—send it to me as soon as you can. Don't pay the customs men a damn penny.

Those rumors that they started about me . . . they're all lies! Don't believe a single word. It's all untrue.

I am so snowed under, I have barely enough time to perform my sacred duties as a prostitute at the temple on religious holidays.

Our daughter, Ahaha, has bloomed into womanhood. I can't begin to tell you how lovely she is now.

The other day, what do you think she asked me? "Mommy, what does *Nin Dingir* mean?" How do you answer a question like that?

"Baby," I said, "it's like this, it's like that . . .

"*Nin*," I said, "means 'lady.' *Dingir*, as everyone knows, is 'god'; so 'god's lady'— and that means a duty performed by select noblewomen.

"To hell with that—it's 'prostitution'! That is done—it goes without saying—only on certain days: at feasts and festivities, at weddings and ceremonies. But, then, there seems to be no end to these celebrations of ours."

When the girl heard this, what do you think she said? "I want to become a *Nin Dingir* too!" "Oh, please, baby, don't ever do anything like that." But she ran straight to the temple.

I saw the priest petting her on the cheeks:
   "What is your name, child?"
   —"Ahaha."

I thought he would say to her: "You are too young to be a *Nin Dingir*." Oh, no!
   "Ah, huh . . . Ah, huh, huh. . . . A-ha-ha . . . Just the right age to gear yourself up to be a *Nin Dingir*."

I kept trying desperately:

"My dear priest, she is only a *shuppishara*, an innocent little girl!"

The priest kept kissing the girl:

"*Shuppishara.*"

The girl was saying:

"Ah, huh? Huh?"

And the priest said:

"Ah, huh, huh . . ."

And he kept going:

"*Shuppishara, sharashuppi, shappare shuppuru, shuppuru shappara!*"

Those priests in the temple are surely sharp with all that *shappuru shappara* they do in god's name!

I can't take it anymore. It's too much!

Life here is the same as ever.

We miss you a lot.

Listen to me, be sure to hide the money securely inside the yarn. People have turned vicious lately. Trouble is, we do all the work; customs officials make all the money! They're calling me from the temple again: I have to leave now for my *Nin Dingir*ing. Be well.

Your loving wife, Lamassi.

◆　　◆　　◆

Now after goddesses *moddesses*, queens *mueens*, prostitutes *mostitutes*, let's come to simpler people *meople*. Oh, excuse me, you don't get every second word *mord*, do you? No, it's not my mispronunciation, which I have been committing from the very start. In our language, we have an Mth dimension for every word *mord*. What is it exactly? Easier said than defined. When I say *goddesses*, you understand, but *moddesses* you don't understand. Queens you know, *mueens* you don't. People throughout the world speak of democracy, but speaking is one thing, living is another. Instead of democracy, we sometimes have to settle for *me-mock-racy. Memockracy* is . . . well . . . something like democracy, but not quite. So: theater *meater*, play *mlay*, actress *mactress*, audience *maudience*. Barber *marber*.

Oh, yes . . . Now, in this lovely Phrygian land

We are living the age of Midas.

Midas? A sixth-generation descendant

Of the peasant king Gordius.

Midas with the golden touch.

And now I turn into his private barber, *marber.*

I don't know how things are here, but in Anatolia throughout the ages barbers have been known as a talkative lot, chatterboxes. The most difficult customers are those who are fed up with their own faces. It is part of our trade to reconcile, by the sheer magic of scissors and words, our customers with their faces. We sort of barber them into the person they are yearning to be. But King Midas seems to be beyond any help from his barber.

MIDAS'S BARBER:

It all happened that day

When two gods had a contest before Midas—

Apollo with his lyre, Pan with his flute.

Who is the maestro, who is mightier?

And the garland of victory

Fell upon the goat-shaped god Pan.

But since that day

Something strange has come over Midas.

He now wears a red cap night and day,

Avoiding everybody, especially me.

Oh, my! Here he comes!

Good morning, my beloved king!

I didn't laugh. I didn't. Oh, Midas, why should I laugh at you?

When we see you, my lord,

We just don't know what to do with our faces.

If we laugh, that's a crime. If we frown, that too.

Do you know what you need, Midas?

You need a haircut.

What did I say? Did I say something wrong?

I don't understand why you are so furious.

Are you going to punish me? What did I do wrong?

Disclose the king's secret?

What secret? What is there to reveal? Why are you looking at my feet?

[*Falls down writhing in painful laughter.*]

Stop it! Let go of me!

Aaghh . . . the goats! Drive these goats away!

Oh, help! They're licking my soles. They're tickling me! Hey, stop that!

It tickles! I don't want to laugh this way! Midas, I beg of you,
Send these goats away! This is torture! Oh, God, I can't take it anymore!
I beg of you, Midas! Aagghh . . .

Oh, it was awful, Midas, I don't want your secret. Keep it to yourself. He is punish-
ing me because he's afraid I might spill his secret—a secret I know nothing about. I
don't want it, I don't want your secret. Oh, God! I wonder what his secret is.

Midas, what's your secret supposed to be?
He's taking off the cap.

Donkey's ears . . .
I get the whole story now, Midas:
These are god Apollo's gift to you.
In the contest, you ruled in favor of Pan, that's why.
Midas, how deep does this change go? Into your mind, too?
Oh, then, you are like that only with your ears.
Midas, would I ever tell anyone?
No, I saw nothing, I heard nothing.
My tongue . . . I'll hold my tongue . . . I will.
I salute you, my king!
So what's going to happen now? Am I dreaming?
What dream? I'll be damned: I saw with my own eyes, I touched with my own hands.
Those were real ears, firmly entrenched.
The ears of Midas—oh, those ears.
What can I do now? Nothing. I'll do nothing—that's the best way out.
I'll keep quiet. I'll forget it all.
Would I ever squeal? Huh—what do I care?
Uh huh, the ears of Midas, the ears of Midas . . .
I'm the only one under the sun to have seen them—
I touched them, only I have held them in my hands.
I wish I could go into Gordium's most crowded square
And shout at the top of my voice: "You, Phrygians,
Listen to me. Come, gather around me,
Open your ears . . . no! No ears."

[*Lapse of time.*]

But I can't bear it anymore.
Oh, if only I could tell it to somebody
And he could tell nobody,

And he in turn could tell nobody,
And nobody tells anybody,
Then nobody would know.
He'd kill me, he'd surely kill me.

[*Sees a well.*]

There, this well should take care of it.
Ooooooooo, ooooooo, oiiiiiii.
This well echoes so well. It is alive: it can hear me.
It's a huge ear, this well. Ooooo, ooooiii! This well echoes so well.

Hear me, then, big well . . . echo and echo and hear all the way, into the seven depths of Hell. "The ears of Midas are donkey's ears! Midas's asses' ears! Asses' ears are Midas's ears!"

ANDROMACHE: Is there, anywhere in the world, any woman whose dreams of her youthful years aren't at least slightly bruised after she marries? In the past, I would have said: "Yes, there is: I, Andromache." But where are those happy days now?

Gods have created me in order to unfurl the horrors of war before all eyes.

Achilles, the spoiled hero of the Achaeans, destroyed and burned down all the towns and villages. He massacred my defenseless old father, my seven brothers, then my grief-stricken mother. And now . . . oh gods, I cannot find . . . oh gods, I cannot find my son, my heart and soul, the only keepsake my Hector left behind.

Achaeans, take pity on this mother. Please return my son to me. Don't let him get crushed in the tumult. Did they take him to Achilles? Did they take him up to the tower in the fortress? Achilles will bring him back to me, won't he? All his fury was against Hector—and now Hector is no more.

But now where is he, my son? Where is he? Please bring him back to me. Please return Hector's beloved keepsake, my one and only son.

Noo! Noo! Don't do that, I beg you! Please don't do it! Gods, mortals, gods! Look, Achilles, I am imploring you. Let all your torment crush me . . . but please spare me this.

Noo, nooo! Don't do it . . . No!

NIOBE:
There is a weeping rock on Mt. Sipylus:
That rock cries. It weeps, that rock. Why?

I, Niobe, was a mother like any other.
One day, half jokingly, I bragged about my fertility,
And Goddess Leto, my girlhood friend, was annoyed with me.
"I have exactly twelve children—
Six boys, six girls. All she has is two."
My whole crime was to say this.
Her anger turned to envy, and her envy to cruelty.
"So, is that it, Niobe?" she said with a smile that chilled my heart:
"You are claiming superiority over a goddess, eh?"
And treacherous Leto had her children kill
All of my children, boys and girls, all.

Now my womb is torn apart with shrieks.
To help me endure the pain,
Turn me into stone, gods,
And yet let me shed eternal tears.

◆   ◆   ◆

[*Warlike music, clashes of sword and shield.*]

THE AMAZON: So we chose the radical solution. We ousted men from among us, created our ideal society of women.

We use male prisoners of war for breeding purposes only. Wish nature had done a good deed to enable us to get pregnant without the aid of men and to give birth to female babies only.

Having a child without loving a man. This is our principle. It's on that issue that I got screwed up and brought upon myself the queen's anger.

I accept my sin, Your Majesty. I fell in love with that handsome prisoner of war whom I pushed into my tent, dragged into my bed, and took into my embrace.

I confess. An Amazon never tells a lie. Such emotions as love for the opposite sex are signs of a degenerate ideology. Yet I committed the crime of falling in love with my prisoner. Why? I wish I knew that! It just happened. Nature played its trick on me.

Believe me, I fought against those sickly feelings with every single Amazonian principle, but I failed. I mustered all my hatred against him, but it was of no use! Amazonian principles were pulling me in one direction, my forbidden instincts in another. Of course, the Amazonian principles should be correct.

Oh please, my queen, you can't rule over everything. There's nature too! No, I take back my words. There's no such a thing as nature. Only the indomitable will and the indisputable rights of the Amazons can exist if the Amazon society is to survive. Wave the Amazon banner high!

Fine, but life doesn't go on with slogans. Haven't we gone a little too far in creating an ideal society? Haven't we imitated men in trying to prove our equality? Now we have the burden and drudgery that men had voluntarily undertaken before. What's the sense of wandering around with a spear and shield every single day?

I know you're going to accuse me of being a revisionist and a reactionary. I admit I loved that young man. If you ask me, these . . . what we call weaknesses are in fact our most beautiful powers. No, I won't tell where my forbidden husband is. Kill me, but I won't tell!

[*Her weapons are pulled away from her.*]

I'm being thrown out of the Amazon society. Is that it? Oh please don't do it, my queen. I'd rather die than give up my weapons! It's as if we were born with them. I beg you, my queen, at least spare my spear!

[*Beautiful clothes, embroideries, necklaces, perfumes, and so on come down on her. She tries them on with affected scorn, but also great delight.*]

As if taking away my weapons isn't enough, you're now humiliating me, insulting me with these.

◆　　◆　　◆

How on earth did a jealous husband like the Lydian king Candaules do this? How did he do what? Herodotus of Halicarnassus, the great historian, writes the following about the king of Lydia:

> King Candaules was madly in love with his wife. He was convinced that his wife was the most beautiful creature in the world. Among his officers, there was one he was especially fond of—Gyges.

> King Candaules trusted Gyges with all of his important assignments. And to Gyges he often bragged about his wife's extraordinary beauty. Finally, one day he tempted fate with inevitable calamity. The king said: "Gyges, you don't seem to believe me when I tell you how lovely my wife is. That is because ears cannot prove the truth the way eyes can. You must see her naked."

LYDIA:

Tell me, Gyges,
Where were you last night?

Ah, your face has turned red: it has spoken before your tongue.

But I still want to hear it.

It seems that what he whispered into your ear wasn't enough for him—

He had to bare his hidden treasure to a stranger's eyes,

To boast about my naked body.

Maybe you had to do it out of loyalty to Candaules,

But you still did it!

Whatever the reason, you committed this crime.

The queen's bedroom accommodates two.

One pair of eyes caressing my nakedness was one pair too many.

I had always addressed you as "My brother Gyges,"

Yet last night

You were other than brother to me, closer than husband.

I cannot remain between the two.

I first felt that sultry breath on my neck,

And I shivered from top to toe.

Shame, anger, fear—this was like a rape.

I surrendered myself to the plunder of your eyes:

I felt your eyes ravishing my nakedness—

And, believe me, with a strange delight

That sprouted beyond my shame and fury,

I too joined in this triangle of adultery.

I kept quiet. Not a sound.

The glitter in my husband's squinting eyes

Revealed to me that he had brewed this plot.

When you committed this sin, you had no choice, I understand that,

But now you have the choice to make amends, Gyges.

Either you or Candaules.

I am Lydia. I cannot be divided or shared.

Either remove yourself

Or . . .

Take hold of me and the Lydian throne.

Fine!

In that case, tonight I shall be watching you;

Come into our room again as our secret guest,

And bring Lydia's Age of Candaules to its end!

ADA: Come, come, my beloved Alexander the Great.

Look, everything turned out just as I had expected: victory for both of us.

Your advance units entered the city and once again they placed me on the Carian throne—the throne that my brother usurped from me when my husband died.

I owe this to you, Alexander, my savior, my beloved.

Your troops are protecting me in my own palace against my own Carian people. That is very sad.

Come, my beloved, come, defend me against their allegations, too. Guards, where is our emperor? You said he entered Halicarnassus. The sun has risen to the height of two lances.

Dear Carians, my countrymen, don't look at me that way: in your eyes, there's a fury that you don't put into words. You are accusing me of treason—of providing help to the enemy from within. I did help, yes, I won't conceal that, but I did it for the benefit of my country. If you had listened to me, Caria would not have perished.

It was madness to oppose Alexander the Great's superior might. You fought, you defended Caria desperately. Countless people died. Pity, pity, pity.

Yet Alexander the Great promised: "If you open up the border and the gates, if you don't put up any resistance to the Macedonian army, I shall not harm Caria and your beautiful Halicarnassus." My beloved Carians are staring at me with a quiet scorn.

Alexander, my love, you will be arriving soon, which means everything will improve.

Together we shall heal Caria's wounds; together we shall rebuild Halicarnassus, the darling of the seas, the city of sages and poets.

The more I read those four words, the more I yearn to read them: "My beloved Queen Ada."

We shall lay eyes on each other for the first time. I wonder if you will like me? I've heard that you are much younger than I, but I shall close the gap with my love.

Guards, welcome our emperor in a manner that befits him. Maids of honor, find as many flowers as you can and sprinkle them all over his path. You are coming, my love, you are arriving. Incredibly, my dreams are becoming real now. Darling, Caria is kneeling before you. What's that? You're accepting me as your mother? I'm becoming your spiritual mother, is that it? Gods, oh gods! How awful that neither have I been able to save Halicarnassus from destruction, nor has my heart's fondest hope come true.

What a great honor! Just when I was saying "My darling," I now must say "My son Alexander."

ARTEMIS OF EPHESUS:

> I, Mother Cybele,
> At Ephesus am now "Artemis of Ephesus":
> Among all the goddesses, I have the most abundant breasts.
> There is a big rush on my statues and pictures:
> Likenesses of Artemis of Ephesus, in all sizes and shapes,
> Adorn all the temples and houses.

But, it seems, we are on the eve of a new age in Anatolia. Jesus, who declared, "I am the Son of God," has recently been crucified. And another Jew, Paul, from our Tarsus—he too is a child of mine—has come to be known as "Saint." This Paul is spreading the new faith. According to the Scriptures, one of Saint Paul's proclamations is that nothing carved by the human hand is a god or goddess.

The people are incensed and enraged! They applaud me and curse him! I say, "I am proud of my people—the way they defend their own goddess." But deep down I feel sad. I know from experience that each new faith is a heresy for the former faith.

Applause for me and a curse on him! Yet the sermons of this upstart Saint Paul have a greater impact on me: I come to realize that we are on the eve of a new Anatolian age.

I turn into Virgin Mary, carrying the infant Jesus in my arms. Yes, the child Jesus grew up. With divine inspiration in his heart, he dedicated himself to the love of humanity. He celebrated peace and brotherhood. In God's name, he established ethical precepts for a better world. And for the sake of humanity, he was crucified.

◆　◆　◆

Six centuries go by. Now, we are in Anatolia's age of the Byzantine Empire. These years are Byzantium's most resplendent—the reign of Justinian the Great. Oh, excuse me, Justinian has not yet become "Justinian the Great." His fate depends on how he can cope with imminent adversity. At the Hippodrome in Constantinople, the Nika Revolt, a popular uprising unprecedented in Byzantine history—Justinian's wife Theodora saves the throne and catapults him to great power.

THEODORA:

> Theo-dora: the Gift of God. Claim your name.
> Such a crowd gave me this name in this same Hippodrome.
> I was a little girl who had barely begun to speak,
> Dark and skinny like a she-goat.
> Fearlessly I walked
> Into the cage of a python brought from Abyssinia.
> I vaguely remember how the monster's body turned and twisted,

How I stroked it.

The crowd stood still with bated breath

And then shouted: Theodora, Theodora . . . !

Thus chanting in unison, the people gave me my name.

The Gift of God: I, Theodora . . .

I have risen from the lower depths:

Daughter of Accachias, who earned his bread making bears dance,

Teenage whore,

Then circus acrobat, actress, empress—

Now virtually on my way to becoming a goddess.

I have come out of this crowd that gave me my name.

I know the innards of that crowd,

I know its heart.

You, our honorable commander Belisarius, Byzantium's young genius,

There is a pink surprise on your face.

You never faced such an enemy,

Which is your own people this time.

You will do battle until the emperor and I

Save our necks by sailing away in our ships,

And then, like a real Roman,

You will impale yourself on your own sword to embrace death.

For you, this might be a fitting end,

But it doesn't suit me at all.

Your Majesty, Justinian, my beloved husband,

I shall make you Justinian the Great,

I shall deliver you into greatness.

And you, our chief architects, Anthemius and Isidorus,

Weren't you burning with the desire to create

St. Sophia as the world's miracle of art?

Now who will erect the mighty dome

Whose inner and outer proportions will dazzle God?

You, Honorable Tribunian, the greatest jurist,

Byzantium's best gift to humanity, will remain unfinished:

Roman Law and Justinian's Codes.

Aren't we, the great Romans,

Pledged to bury ourselves in our masterpieces?

Death should create the human form,

Not distort it.

I have taken over the flower of immortality

From that giant python.

Now I'm not going to give it away,

I'm not going to be intimidated by the hollow noise of the same crowd.

There is a law in this world, such as death,

But there is no law that states that the emperor

Must flee from his throne before he dies. There is no such law!

None! No such law! It is in your power to oppose it.

Come, let us assess the situation in a cold-blooded way:

At the Hippodrome, there is no room

To rub shoulders, let alone to wave arms.

It seems, honorable Belisarius, this is what frightens you—

And this is what gives me courage.

Look at that hesitant multitude caught in a squeeze:

All those in the rear rely on those in the front rows

For anything they can possibly do.

Are you brave enough to take on the front ranks?

The rest is easy.

In what two situations does a mass of people become a single body:

In attacking and in running away.

Observe that crowd, watch it:

Take a look at the peddlers—they're selling souvlaki,

Selling stuffed mussels, selling sherbet, selling wine, selling girls.

Riot is riot; business is business.

Listen to the tumult, to its tone:

It's not the sound of a crowd that has firmly made up its mind.

How is it that I can see this?

Because this crowd is mine, it is me;

I have never parted ways with it.

How can it now dare sever itself from me?

I am your empress,

The first, the only, the genuine empress to come from among you.

I am the one to give new direction to history.

Never take one step back,

Or else you will step outside of history

—and then, farewell, golden Byzantium,

Farewell, magnificence.

No, I cannot be, I will not be divested

Of these purple robes while I am still alive.

Purple, I'm madly in love with you, purple!
And like a master of the mosaic art,
I patiently create my image on eternity! Theodora!

Nika, Nika! You will conquer. The victory is yours!
Belisarius, let the ships sail away without passengers
And lie at anchor in front of the Golden Horn.
Let the people see that no one is fleeing Byzantium.
Hold your heads upright, don't throw up your hands in despair!
Take heart from my determination.
We are now going through the python's cage.

[*Raises a sword.*]

And now, ready—
Now is the time to attack, Belisarius.
Nika! You will conquer! Nika, the victory is yours!
You are triumphant, my beloved husband, Justinian the Great.

◆ ◆ ◆

Theodora's passion for purple was the hallmark of yet another Byzantine dynasty—the Comneni. This dynasty used a masterful policy in resisting the further expansion of the Turks following the Battle of Manzikert and in reestablishing the power of the Byzantine state. The family adopted the title "Porphyrogenitus," meaning "Born in Purple."

Anna Comnena, the eldest daughter, was the world's first woman historian. Yet this exceptionally talented young Byzantine woman was not content with writing a history book alone. She also authored the plot to have her brother John killed so that her husband, Nicephorus, could take over the Byzantine throne.

ANNA COMNENA: The plot failed. That is the reason, Your Majesty, why I now stand before you as a criminal. No, no, I'm not going to invoke the moral prerogative of an elder sister to beg your forgiveness. There can be no such right between the two of us. If I told you I felt any love for you as my brother even for one day, that would be a lie.

As far back as I can remember, I have always been carried on shoulders as the empress of the future. My entire education was designed to prepare me for that. I was to achieve the glory of Byzantium—from where my father had left off.

The day you were born, you stole my light. The crown prince of Byzantium had arrived. I was suddenly pushed aside. That day I understood what it means to be a woman.

God knows, it wasn't only my burning ambition for power that dragged me into this plot. It was a conviction that took root in my heart—that I alone could bring back the old grandeur to Byzantium. That was my belief since childhood. They wanted to marry me off—first to the Turkish sultan Melikşah, then to his son. I didn't object because I was offering myself, knowingly, as a sacrifice for the sake of Byzantium. Even if I were to become the queen of the Turks, I was determined to serve the cause of Byzantium's welfare. It's as simple as that.

It's wrong to speculate about the past. It goes against the grain of historical scholarship. There's no need, either.

Since the Battle of Manzikert, the Turks have been forging ahead and striking roots in Anatolia. They have been swaggering their way through Nicomedia, Scutari, and along the Bosphorus. Their Çaka Bey[1] created a powerful navy in the Aegean. It had to be stopped.

I decided to set Byzantine history on its proper course. That was the intent of my coup against you. Yes, you are right. There can be no such thing as the right or the wrong course of history. If I survive, I shall include this statement of yours in my history.

Destiny and history . . . the complex relationship between them is quite strange. With this sudden change of my fortune, I perceive history far more clearly. Yes, that's the way it is. I wanted to topple you and to have my husband, Nicephorus, accede to the throne so that I could rule Byzantium.

I planned everything down to the last detail. But I overlooked one thing: the cowardice in my husband's heart. Nicephorus the Afraidus. I had always thought of history as the art of shaping the future while recording the past. Earlier I talked of history as a science. It is neither art nor science. It's a mixture of the two.

I used to be proud of being the novice of history. Just look at its ploy against me: Theodora, who was the daughter of a bear tamer, emerged as the most glorious empress of Byzantine history. Whereas I, Anna Comnena, born in purple, trained from the outset for the throne, now stand before you as a criminal.

Death? I accept it. But there is this: the law says that "a pregnant woman may not be executed before she delivers her baby." My pregnancy was not caused by a man, but by Time. This book I press against my belly is my first and last pregnancy—*The Alexiad* . . . the history of our beloved father, Alexius, and his reign. This book is

---

1. Çaka Bey: Turkish naval commander.

my exquisite pregnancy. Only I can deliver our father Alexius and all of you to immortality.

I'll be confined to a nunnery? I had resigned myself to death. Instead, I'm being sent to a nunnery. I shall withdraw from Byzantium's political life—and devote myself to my book.

For the first time, John, my brother, I am addressing you in gratitude. I thank you.

◆   ◆   ◆

I, Goddess Cybele—as Anna Comnena,
A child of mine from the twelfth century, bears witness—
Now stand on the threshold of a new age:

A new civilization, a new compound,
A new power, a new convulsion.

I, the Mother of Anatolian civilizations, declare
That in some ways it is my children
Who transform me.

My mountains and my rivers
Have begun to speak Turkish.

Let's stop and take a breath,
And then bring my younger children onto the stage.

ACT II

One of Anatolia's most beautiful rivers, the Nilüfer, emanates from Uludağ, Mt. Olympus of olden days. This peerless river was named after Nilüfer Hatun, the first Ottoman queen.

NİLÜFER HATUN: My son, how could a mother not rejoice in the success of her children?

I hear you crossed the Dardanelles and captured Gallipoli. Congratulations. This means that the conquest of the Balkans is under way. Adrianople is next. And then comes the biggest prize of them all—Constantinople.

I am happy to hear it, Murad, certainly I am. Why do I look so subdued, then? My joy is tempered with some conflicting feelings. Look, Son, here are two coins—one Byzantine, the other Ottoman. Make them into one single coin: one side Byzantine, the other Ottoman. That's me!

Poor Byzantium: my childhood, my early youth! In my flesh and blood, in my entire body, I lived your becoming Ottoman day by day. When I was a young girl, my heart was Byzantine, but my womb gave birth to two Turcoman lions who are to finish off Byzantium: your older brother, Süleyman, and you, my Murad.

In my childhood, my name was Holophyra. I was the daughter of the prince of Yarhisar, and I was engaged to the son of the prince of Bilecik. I remember the heated conversation between my father and the prince of Bilecik:

> Those Turcomans, they are striking root in Anatolia. This is a grave danger for Byzantium. We used to look down on them as nomads and shepherds, but day by day they became settled communities. Osman Bey especially is a busy beaver who is uniting the scattered clans and tribes and usurping the Byzantines' land, waters, trees, and sun, weaving a Turcoman carpet. He's the most elusive of them all: no one can catch him, up in the mountains or down on the plains.

At the end, my father and the prince of Bilecik decided to invite Osman Bey to my wedding and lay an ambush to kill him.

But our mortal enemy, Osman Bey, your grandfather, the intended victim at my wedding, sensed the plot with an uncanny premonition and routed the wedding at Bilecik. I found myself on the back of the saddle of Orhan Gazi, the son of Osman Bey. My wedding gown was fluttering in the wind.

It turned out they had a wedding feast prepared for me at Söğüt. And, again, I was the bride. And Holophyra was changed to Nilüfer. There you go; you're laughing, aren't you, Murad? Because you only know about your mother Nilüfer. What I am telling you is just a nice little tale. Only I know what I suffered during those days.

I obeyed whatever those Turcoman ladies told me to do. But I was defiant. Even captivity, bitter as it is, has its own honor. I was taught how to milk sheep and cows. That wasn't enough, though: I had to learn how to brew mare's milk—that horrid drink. I had to spin wool, to make dye by boiling various roots and leaves, and to dye the wool in wooden vessels and bowls. That was my punishment. I had to endure it. But I kept holding my head high to spite the Turcomans.

As time went by, I realized something else, Murad: they weren't making me do all that as a punishment. That type of work was natural for them. A noble lady was expected to have all these skills. I also realized that, contrary to what I had thought at the beginning, they didn't mind that I was the daughter of a Byzantine ruler who had tried to ambush Osman Bey. Nobody confronted me with this fact; nobody said I bore any guilt. That is when, my beloved son, I felt I was in limbo. I said to myself: "What am I, who am I among these Turcomans?" This really frightened me, Murad. I said, "I accept captivity, but I am a Byzantine: I cannot become a Turcoman."

We ate from a huge tray on the ground. The first few days they used to laugh their heads off because I wasn't able to sit cross-legged. But they weren't ridiculing me. From sunrise to sunset, they laughed at children exactly the same way—fondly. These Turcomans are themselves like children.

At meals, they openly discussed in my presence when they planned to capture Yarhisar and Bursa and Nicaea. Osman Bey even consulted me. I nearly went out of my mind!

One night as we were having dinner and I was holding a glass of wine rather than mare's milk, I screamed: "I am a Byzantine! I am a Byzantine! I am your prisoner, so treat me like one. Kill me! Because if I manage to run away, you ought to know that I will inform Byzantium about everything you told me."

Your father's face turned red. Not out of anger. More like embarrassment. He tried to run away. But your grandfather Osman Bey listened with a smile.

Next morning, two horses were ready. I thought maybe we were just going for a ride. Some time later we came to a place that looked familiar. Orhan Gazi said: "There, that's Yarhisar. That's your father's fortress. If you want to go back to him, go. You have my best wishes."

I began to move in that direction. My horse wouldn't go. I dismounted, but my feet wouldn't go. I turned back and looked at Orhan. His eyes were moist. I felt a twinge in my heart and a lump in my throat. I realized that Holophyra had become Nilüfer. Weeping and laughing, we rode full-tilt back to Söğüt.

Now, dear Murad, my love, the son of my beloved Orhan, you keep telling me, all puffed up with such pride: "I shall conquer Byzantium." That Byzantium was your mother.

NASRETTİN HOCA'S WIFE: Can you figure out who I am? You ask, "How can you?" You may be right. But I am the wife of someone very famous among the Turks—also very popular in Balkan and Middle Eastern countries: Nasrettin Hoca, a small-town preacher who became Turkey's most beloved storyteller and humorist. If I tell you my name, it'll mean nothing to you.

The story goes that they asked my husband: "What's your wife's name?"

"I don't know," he replied.

They pursued the matter: "Come on, how can a husband not know what his wife's name is?"

He retorted: "Well, I never had any desire to have anything to do with her—so I never learned her name."

Well, that's what he's supposed to have said. But for some five or six hundred years now he and I have been getting along fine. He was never an easy man. He was very touchy.

One night in bed I happened to say: "Would you move away a little?"

Six months later I got a letter from him—all the way from Baghdad, asking me: "Is this far away enough, or shall I move farther away?"

Because of all the droll things he did and said, the neighbors started to laugh at him. His reputation as a funny man spread fast. It's amazing how many countries have been claiming and sharing my husband. I once saw his statue in Samarkand in the middle of distant Central Asia. The statue shows him riding his donkey backwards. I couldn't resist asking him, "Why backwards?" He said: "Woman, don't ask, because I don't know, either. I guess one day I did a foolish thing like that." Then I asked, "Well, in that case why did they make your statue like that?" "Never mind Samarkand," he said, "did you ever see anywhere in the world a statue of anyone riding a donkey even the right way?"

That's what it's like being a funny man's wife. Still curious about my name? Well, in our society, they treat us as if women have no names of their own—you are always So-and-so's wife. I mentioned this to my husband once—and, believe me, I didn't do it to blame or scold anyone. He was deeply touched and saddened. He said to me: "You are right, my dear wife. From now on, whenever they ask me what my name is, I'll say, 'I'm the husband of the wife of Nasrettin Hoca.'"

Here in Anatolia a clever and prudent woman follows in the footsteps of her husband and steers him around any way she likes.

AYŞE SULTAN: I am Princess Ayşe, favorite daughter of Sultan Ahmed I. I suppose I was about ten years old when my father the sultan married me off. God rest his soul, he loved weddings and festivities. There's a good reason for that. When he was a prince, they forgot to have him circumcised, which became a sore spot with him. As soon as he became sultan, he organized a massive circumcision festivity for himself. Soon after getting circumcised, he started taking on wives, and he became a father at age fourteen. I was born as the first daughter of my father the sultan.

Yes, at age ten I was married to Nasuh Pasha, the grand vizier. My father the sultan used to be very fond of his son-in-law, Nasuh Pasha. Together they even played the javelin game on horseback. But something went wrong. They say Nasuh Pasha lied or something . . . and my father used to hate lies.

They strangled my husband before my very eyes. I was shattered, grief-stricken. I was a widow at age thirteen.

After that, I was married off to Blackbrow Mehmed Pasha the Martyr. Of course, my husband was not known as "the martyr" at first. He was martyred later, and I was a widow again.

Just about that time, my father the sultan passed away. My brother Murad IV, who succeeded him, married me off to Hafız Ahmed Pasha, the *beylerbeyi*[2] of Van. What a marvelous voice he had.

No sooner had we gotten married than a Janissary revolt took my Ahmed Pasha away from me. Once again I was a widow.

Scarcely a month later, Murtaza Pasha, the governor of Diyarbakır, became my husband. The marriage vows were taken, but Murtaza Pasha was nowhere to be seen. In those days, you could get married in absentia, a long-distance marriage.

I waited and waited, but the pasha didn't show up. Well, by this time, I was no spring chicken, and I was dying to see my husband and to be with him. For three years, he played hard to get. Then, finally, he arrived. My God, he was old enough to be my grandfather.

If the problem happened to be just old age, I could have coped with that. There is an old proverb:

> *Marry a young man: you'll curse fate and tear your chest apart;*
> *Marry an old man: you'll be placed on the throne of the heart.*

Aagghh. I just disliked this husband. Thank goodness, he too was martyred, at the Battle of Revan.

Then Voynuk Ahmed Pasha . . . oh no, I beg your pardon, I got them wrong. He came later. It was the other Ahmed Pasha, the *beylerbeyi* of Aleppo and Damascus whom I married then. I never liked him. And this marriage lasted very long . . . I suffered five long years. Would you believe he died a natural death?

Although they were marrying me off all the time, I never had one proper husband. That's fate. But then suddenly four suitors.

I'm grateful to my brother for asking me which one I would prefer: Mustafa Pasha the Clarinetist, Mehmed Pasha the Flatfooted, Yakup Pasha the Hunchback, or Mehmed

2. *Beylerbeyi:* Governor-general.

Pasha the Crooked Necked? Tell me, Brother, is none of them without a physical defect? And there was an İbrahim Pasha the Esteemed. He became İbrahim Pasha the Assassinated.

My brother asked me, but he made the final decision himself—he married me off to Ahmed Pasha of Hazargrad. I loved this husband of mine. It seems his ambition was to become admiral of the fleet. So I told my brother, and my husband was appointed admiral.

Stupid me! My husband the admiral of the fleet succumbed to violent seasickness and arrived at Crete in a terrible condition, where he became a martyr. Which means I was a widow once again.

Meanwhile, a new era was upon us. My brother Sultan Murad took the path to the other world. He was succeeded by my other brother, İbrahim, but İbrahim was going to do me no favors. He had come to be known as İbrahim the Mad: his case was bloody awful . . . sad. My mother had him deposed and imprisoned. Not satisfied with that, she had him strangled to death. In his place, her young grandson Mehmed IV was placed on the throne.

In reality, it was my mother, Kösem, who came to power with the title of Majestic Mother! But she was so involved in intrigue that she had no interest in me. She didn't care about my being left without a husband. When her daughter-in-law started to put on airs, she attempted to do away with her grandson. That brought Kösem to her end after a rule of forty years: they strangled her with a curtain cord.

Be that as it may, with the help of my nephew, the child sultan, they married me off to İpşir Pasha, who was the leader of the brigands rebelling in Anatolia.

Who cared if he was a bandit or a brigand as long as he became my husband? They installed him as grand vizier. It was their hope that only a brigand could gain control over a state gripped by anarchy.

But I had to wait for him for a long time. It turned out that this bandit called İpşir was scared stiff. The bastard was afraid of being confronted with his criminal record, of getting hanged. Finally, I sent Mercan Ağa[3] to grab him and bring him to me.

I said to him: "Look here, İpşir Pasha. Now you are the mighty grand vizier and my husband and so handsome."

---

3. *Ağa:* As used in this context, a palace official.

I enjoyed him to my heart's content for four months. Then came another Janissary revolt. What he had feared happened: they put a greasy noose around his neck and hanged my pasha. That made me a widow again.

What luck, eh?
First: Ahmed Nasuh Pasha of Drama.
Second: Blackbrow Mehmed Pasha the Martyr.
Third: Koran-reciter Ahmed, the *beylerbeyi* of Van.
Then came the governor of Diyarbakır.
Ahmed of Damascus became the fifth.
Ahmed the Horse Groom was sixth,
And the seventh was İpşir Pasha the bandit.
Just think: all these husbands, but really, the unlucky daughter of Ahmed I, Ayşe Sultan, can't be said to have had any husband at all!

NAKŞİDİL: My dear son and my sultan. The time has come for me to make my appearance before God. There is no need to grieve. I am anxious to reveal to you the deepest secret of my heart and to give voice to my last wish. For this, I invoke a mother's prerogative, and I request my sultan's forbearance.

My greatest happiness in this palace, to which I came from the other end of the world, was mothering you.

I used to tell you the tales of a totally different climate. Your boyish eyes would pop out in amazement—as they do now. One day I showed you on the map the island of Martinique, where I was born. Your tiny finger touched that minuscule island floating in the map's ocean, and you asked: "Mother, I am going to be the sultan of your island, too, right?" Did I laugh at that? Tears were rolling down my cheeks.

I and my cousin Josephine were raised on the island of Martinique, which is a French colony. One morning we were running—our long white robes kept getting caught on the violet thorns. We were running to Eliama the fortune-teller on the other side of the hill.

Eliama first took my palm in her hand. At the beginning, she was indifferent. Suddenly she looked startled. "Someday," she said, "you will be a queen." Then she looked at my cousin Josephine's palm, and, trembling like a leaf, she said: "And you—you will become an empress." She couldn't speak anymore. We left Eliama's hut giggling. We said that she was making fun of us. But in a peculiar way, deep down, we believed her; we wanted to believe her.

Then Turkish pirates unexpectedly abducted me. I was bought and sold at slave markets. Yes! They sold me, my dear; you don't have to frown like that.

And later . . . in the Ottoman palace I became Nakşidil Sultan, the queen of Abdül-hamid I, the secret lover of Selim III, and the stepmother of our sultan and caliph Mahmud II.

Fortune-teller Eliama had been right about Josephine, too. She became Empress Josephine, the wife of Emperor Napoleon Bonaparte.

My flighty cousin Josephine. Her letters are just like her. She hasn't changed a bit.

> Dear Aimée [my Christian name used to be Aimée], I was beside myself with happiness to learn that you are alive. We all had assumed that the ship you took had sunk and that you were buried in the cold darkness of the ocean. We mourned you many days. Later, our grief became twofold when we learned that you were not drowned, but taken captive by the Turks. Oh, dearest Aimée, we said, it would have been better to drown in the ocean's cold darkness then to fall into the hands of the infidel Turks. Well, when we later heard that you had become a queen at the Ottoman palace, our grief subsided somewhat.
>
> As for me, dear Aimée, I have been struck with the same disaster. I am an empress, too.

My dear Mahmud, I became a widow when your father Abdülhamid I died at age sixty-four. I wasn't your mother. I took the place of your own mother, who died when you were very little. I became your mother. I fell madly in love with Selim III, who ascended the throne at age twenty-seven.

An exceedingly romantic love started between us. Selim III was the world's most gracious and sentimental man. He was an artist rather than a ruler. He was a great composer and a virtuoso reed-flute player.

In an effort to save this anachronistic empire, he started to bring in some of the values and techniques of the West, but he did some childish things, too. From France, he got a Montgolfier-type balloon and started to fly from minaret to minaret in Istanbul. We all opened our hands toward the sky and prayed for our sultan to have a safe landing.

I don't recall if it happened because of my suggestion, but he wrote rhapsodical letters to Napoleon Bonaparte, whom he admired immensely. I penned those letters. And Napoleon sent replies that expressed sentiments of friendship. But when our great friend Napoleon one day attacked our territories without any warning, you should have seen Selim's disillusionment. I was shattered, but Selim said nothing to me that might have been remotely reproachful. Amazingly, I realized during those days that everything French in me had melted away in my Ottoman persona. When my dear brother-in-law Napoleon got a good beating at the hands of our people at the fortress of Acre, I rejoiced so much that I felt in my heart of hearts that I had torn myself away from my distant past and had become totally Anatolian.

[*After a slight swoon.*]

It doesn't matter, I am already across the border, in the twilight zone between the two worlds. Listen, when they came in to kill Selim, he was playing this reed-flute. And with this he defended himself against the assassins' swords. Look, except for a notch over here, it has survived intact. I have been living in this palace for thirty-three years now. I was brought here as a concubine. Later I became the most respected woman of this great empire. It was Selim III's exemplary humanity that made me a woman of this soil from top to toe.

He taught me about the great mystics of Anatolia: Yunus Emre, Hacı Bektaş, Rumi. I especially like these lines of Rumi:

> Come, come again, whoever, whatever you may be, come:
> Heathen, fire-worshipper, sinner of idolatry, come.
> Come even if you have broken your vows a hundred times;
> Ours is not the portal of despair or misery, come.

Why do I mention these sages and poets? I'll tell you, my son, about my heart's great secret, its innermost yearning. Like these poets, who had faith in the unity of all religions, I too came to believe in God's unitary supreme being. I am convinced that even though the paths might be far apart, all beautiful roads will lead to Him. My son, I was born a Christian. As I am dying, can you take me back to my childhood and early youth? I would like to die a Christian.

[*Her face lights up.*]

When you said, "No one can step between God and his vassals," you became eternally great in my eyes. My son, my sovereign, I thank you.

NİGÂR HANIM THE POET: Dear Diary. I see that we are both near the end. These blank closing pages are like a destiny we share. You are my only true friend. I tore you out of my heart—and placed you right before me.

I am Nigâr. My poetic talent is a gift of nature. My father was enamored of music. In her days of sadness, my mother used to recite poem after poem. I take after my mother.

I am now opening you at random.

1887: I am twenty-five years old. My first book of poems is entitled *Alas*. It's strange that no one showed any interest initially, but there was a run on it when they found out that the poet was a woman.

My fame is only a reward for my grief and sorrow.

Cemil Bey the Lutanist has set one of my poems to music:

I scream, and with my outcry I am left helpless;
Alas, there is no one to free me from distress.

He composed it in one of the lilting classical modes.

Madame Leylâ Saz, too, composed one of my poems:

I fail to confess my sorry state because of shyness.
Enough! Stop hurting me. With you gone, I am in distress.

I have attained the fame I had hoped and yearned for, but why, my God, am I so lonely?

◆   ◆   ◆

14 December 1889: This morning I was at the courts. Oh, İhsan! I have never been able to understand why or how I could love my husband, İhsan. He poisoned my entire life.

Mehdi Effendi, the chief editorial writer of the newspaper *Ahter,* wrote a poem about me. Being appreciated is a joy. He says my poetic art adorns the horizons. Another famous poet, who shall be nameless, asks the following about me: "How can a woman be a poet?" I immediately took up my pen:

"There can be no woman poet," says our Master.
So poetry's measured by manhood, is it?
In that case, I say, "You are a eunuch, mister,
For your verses give no pleasure—not the least bit."

◆   ◆   ◆

15 December 1895: Today I went to Eyupsultan with Pierre Loti. You would think this man is a Muslim in disguise. With me, he kissed the window of the mausoleum. Then we walked all the way to the top of the hill and strolled in the cemetery for a while. The panorama of the Golden Horn is breathtaking. My dear colleague Pierre Loti is deeply fond of Istanbul and all things Turkish—just like me. His melancholy eyes disclose the profound stirrings in his soul.

His Majesty the Sultan, I am told, liked my last poem very much. I am in high heaven. Under the Code for Service to Literature, I am to be given a monthly stipend. It's so wonderful to be appreciated.

Rumors of war are afoot again.

◆　◆　◆

7 July 1908: Thank heaven, constitutional government has been declared in our country, too. This step forward made all people with a conscience happy. This means that our noble nation, for the smallest particle of which I would gladly sacrifice my life, can now take the road to progress.

I came by a copy of the "Proposals for the Constitution."

Listen to Article 42: "Women are coequal with men and free."
—I like this very much. Naturally, if the he-lion is a lion, why isn't the she-lion a lion? But look at the following paradox: it accords the right to elect and to be elected only to men. What sort of equality is this?

Take Article 43: "In Turkey, there was no aristocracy in the past, nor is there one today."
—I cannot share this view. Only if there is an aristocracy in a country can the rare flower called art bloom. Isn't that the way it happened in Europe? Why do they refuse to understand this? If I had not come from an aristocratic family, if I had not grown up among upper-class people, could I have become a poet? I don't think so.

I say yes to equality between men and women, but no to equality among classes.

> To say that human nature can change is a lie;
> Your love has my heart as a nest in which to lie.

I hear Tevfik Fikret likes this poem of mine very much.

I feel deep admiration for my neighbor, the great poet Tevfik Fikret, but I don't share some of his ideas. He says: "The language of poetry should come closer to the people's colloquial speech." I say this would be the death of poetry.

◆　◆　◆

31 March 1909: There is a bloodbath in Istanbul. I locked the doors of the mansion and closed the shutters tight. I am told they want to strengthen theocracy. And the soldiers are objecting to the officers trained in military academies.

◆　◆　◆

7 April 1909: I am very sad today. Abdülhamid has been deposed. I wonder if the government might cut off the salary Abdülhamid was paying me?

◆　◆　◆

29 September 1911:

> *I loved you: that passion gave frenzy to my brain;*
> *Loving you made me taste nothing but bitter pain.*

I have turned forty-nine!

The Italians have declared war against us. Damn them all! Damn them all! I used to admire the Italians. They are an artistic nation. Even the Renaissance was one of their achievements. But why are they doing this to us? I just can't understand it.

♦   ♦   ♦

1915: We have won a great victory at the Dardanelles. They're all talking about a Mustafa Kemal. The Mustafa Kemal.

♦   ♦   ♦

October 1917: The czar's regime has crumbled in Russia. I am very happy to hear this. I hope a new government with no hostility against the Ottoman Empire will be established there. What's been happening to our people, my God? Wherever you go, you run into bedraggled, rude multitudes talking with a most atrocious rural accent. Where did they come from? I cannot bear my loneliness at home or all these crowds in the streets. I am often on the verge of tears. If it weren't for the opportunity of confiding in this diary, I would probably go mad.

Tonight I caught a bug on my neck. Disgusting creature. I was so scared. There is a typhus epidemic. I sent the bug to my doctor in a matchbox. He was nice enough to have it examined at the Children's Hospital. Thank God, it turned out not to be a carrier. But they sent it back in the same matchbox. That was all I needed.

♦   ♦   ♦

8 November 1917: We went up to Çamlıca Hill in the carriage that Prince Abdülmecid Effendi was kind enough to send. I had the honor of being complimented by His Highness. During those lovely hours, I forgot my sorrow.

♦   ♦   ♦

18 December 1917: I have been writhing in pain since this morning. I can't digest the ration bread. I don't know what to do. I have no flour, nor do I have a servant who can bake bread. My sickly body can take only so much of the ration bread, which contains broom corn, maize, straw, and God knows what else.

♦   ♦   ♦

17 February 1918: I am drifting in limbo. I keep staring at the rug beside my bed—and I think. Yes, what is the meaning of my existence? What is there for me to live for? I wish my life would suddenly end one night without my having to feel anything at all.

◆　　◆　　◆

19 March 1918: If there were any visitors during the day, I didn't hear them because, like everything else, the doorbell is broken.

Last night, as I was convulsing with high fever, I thought of the bedroom brazier that my dear father gave me as a gift many years ago. Only that warmed me up. And this way I paid one last tribute to my beloved father's memory.

The diaries of Nigâr Hanım the Poet, which fill eighteen notebooks, end with that sentence. Two weeks later she died of typhus. The question that once made her shudder—"Could insects carry a disease to me?"—found its answer beyond a mere foreboding.

◆　　◆　　◆

1922: Closing days of the War of Liberation in Anatolia. Now I am at the front, with the rank of corporal. I, Halide Edip, am interrogating the prisoners of war:

HALİDE EDİP: Your name, I say, your unit, place where you were taken prisoner? Next, please. And you? Your name, your unit? Please point out on the map the place where you fell captive. All right, next. You, and you, to the enlisted men's camp. Take that boy to the infirmary.

Please step this way, Captain. Your name? Your unit? Can you show me your ammunition supply routes? On the map, please.

Captain, were there any Anatolian Greeks in your unit? That is not an incomprehensible question. It's very simple. In your unit, did you have any people from this country?

Captain, the distinction is as follows: for us, you are the regular enemy . . . or, let's say you were, because the war has ended for you. You are our guest here. But how about those who fought against us although they were the children of this land? You know best what they should be called. Captain, are there among the prisoners any Greeks from this country? Maybe there are, but you don't know, you haven't seen any. All right, let's assume that. You may go. To the officers' camp.

[*Pours some tea from her flask.*]

Their condition is quite like the situation we were in at the beginning. Defeat and disorder. Complete chaos. We've heard that from Eskişehir on, they were driving the troops forward every day, promising them, "Ankara is right behind that hill over there." And yet there was no Ankara behind any hill they captured.

[*Sings a Greek song: "Samiotisa."*]

For me, Greek was a delightful language in which I sang songs in my childhood. A language of songs. It never occurred to me that someday I might use the same language to interrogate prisoners of war.

[*Looking through her binoculars.*]

War looks exciting when you look from afar. Offensive, counteroffensive; attack, counterattack. Advance and retreat. Turmoil.

It's like a festivity. But that kitchen where the dishes from the feast are piled up . . . that kitchen that is the hospital. It's horrifying. It's difficult for any heart to endure it.

Poor Turks . . . poor Greeks . . . poor world.

From here, Gordium, the Phrygian capital, is visible as an ancient ruin at the other end of the meadow. There, peasant Gordius, founder of Phrygia, tied the yoke of his oxcart to the pole so firmly that no one could untie the knot. The Gordian knot challenged the whole world. It was Alexander the Great who undid it, so to speak, by cutting it with his sword. But where is Alexander's world empire now?

In our time, it is women who drive the same oxcarts that Gordius and the Phrygians used to ride. These women might hearken back to the Hittites and the Phrygians, but they are dated by the loads that the oxcarts carry. Night and day they are delivering ammunition to the front. I marched with them to so many stations. I broke bread with them, shared their onions. Their children often turned blue in the bitter cold. Woe unto our times when the steel of the shells is more precious than the flesh of the babies.

But when night is the darkest and seems endless, daylight is closer than ever. Now, out of the ashes of the Ottoman Empire, a new nation is rising.

Back to work. Yes, step forward. Your unit? What was the final command you received? Where were the division concentrations? All right, carry on.

Next. You—yes, you. Step forward. Your unit? Where were you taken prisoner? Your country? I said, "your country," don't you understand? Your country, or let's say your village or town? What family do you belong to? Speak up! Why are you trembling like that? Speak up, don't mumble. What sort of Greek are you speaking? What dialect is that?

No, no, don't swear on your honor. Everything you're doing gives you away. You don't have to be afraid of me. Look how calm your comrades are. It is no crime to be taken captive in war. That is, of course, if you have committed no other offense. Your country?

Look, a seriously wounded Greek soldier gave me these letters and photographs just before he died. I promised him I would send them all to his family—village of Ligourion, Epidaurus, Peloponnesus. You, too, must have received such letters and pictures from your village, your family, and other relatives. Speak up, eh, *pedi mu*.

Halide, come to your senses! His life hangs on your two lips. That man is a traitor.

But remember those poor women and girls whose lives were wasted. Who took pity on them?

To send a young man to his death even if it happens on a battleground . . . beware that you might doom the innocent together with the guilty.

An Anatolian Greek is a child of this land! Because he took up arms against us, he is guilty . . . a traitor.

But, then, treason is sometimes a relative concept, isn't it?

I had promised those women and girls that they would be avenged. Vengeance against whom? Up to what point?

He is a traitor! The punishment . . . is death.

No, no, come to your senses! Novelist, nurse, interpreter . . .
And now are you turning into a judge, Halide?
Vengeance is an act of barren hearts.
Forgiveness . . . a commandment of the four holy books.
Forgiveness . . . the bounteous rain of the human soul—
Especially on the threshold of this new age.
Put him with the other prisoners. He's not from this country. He's not an Anatolian.
Adiosos. He's still a child.
What a lovely child. Like Apollo. Maybe Apollo himself.
A child of this land.

EPILOGUE

That's how the story goes . . . but how to end it?
A time span of thousands of years,
Our stage: all of Anatolia.
Whom can we squeeze into it, how, where?
If we give voice to forty people, the forty-first is mute;

If we play a hundred, the hundred and first is missing.
If we take up a thousand, what becomes of thousands of others?
I, I am an actress.
I can best endure as myself the more I change.

Deep in sleep, I ask myself,
"Who am I tonight?
In which age, where?"
My task is to give life to words,
To spin the yarn of passion,
To weave the human spirit, with its treasons and loves,
Into this narrow yet boundless frame.

Ours was a mere bird's flight through the ages,
We perched, flew away, then alighted again,
One at a time out of a myriad.

I, an actress,
Like the legendary phoenix
That catches new fire from its own ashes;
To catch fire once again
From the sparks that spring out of your hearts—
I bow before you.

CURTAIN

◆　　◆　　◆

Afife Jale

NEZİHE ARAZ

Translated by Nilüfer Mizanoğlu Reddy

An Editor's Note

Afife Jale (1902–41) holds a special place of honor in the history of Turkish theater: she became the first Muslim woman to appear on the stage in the closing years of the Ottoman Empire. Because of social and legal pressures and her family's severe objections, she suffered a great deal and fell victim to drug addiction.

Her tragic life is the subject matter of the eponymously titled play by Nezihe Araz (b. 1922), who ranks as one of the most versatile writers of her generation. During a career that spanned five decades, she achieved recognition as a journalist, biographer, playwright, columnist, poet, and writer of children's books. With degrees in psychology and philosophy from Ankara University, she pursued a diversified career as an encyclopedia editor and author of books ranging from a semifictional biography of Mevlana Celaleddin Rumi and portraits of Mustafa Kemal Atatürk and his estranged wife to a psychological portrayal of the Ottoman sultan Mehmed II, the conqueror of Istanbul.

Some of Araz's plays gained popularity when staged by the Turkish State Theater, Istanbul City Theater, and leading private theaters. Several among them won prizes, including the Ministry of Culture's Best Playwright Award for 1989. *Afife Jale*, produced in the 1988–89 season in Istanbul and published in 1994, received the prestigious Avni Dilligil Award in 1988. Konya University conferred an honorary doctorate on Araz, and the Turkish Republic named her a "State Artist."

Araz wrote two librettos, both of which were composed as operas by Okan Demiriş.

The translator of *Afife Jale*, Nilüfer Mizanoğlu Reddy (b. 1922), was one of the earliest translators of Nazım Hikmet's works into English (in the early 1950s). In 1988, she translated and edited a volume of stories entitled *Short Stories by Turkish Women Writers*. Her articles and critical essays appear in Turkish journals, and her translations of Turkish poems and short stories have been published in U.S. journals and anthologies.—TSH

Characters

AFİFE JALE
DR. SAİT PASHA, Afife's grandfather, Methiye's father
METHİYE, Afife's mother
BEHİYE, Afife's stepsister, three to four years her senior

247

SALÂH, Afife's older stepbrother

AUNT, Methiye's aunt

ZİYA, son of Afife's great-aunt

HİDAYET, Afife's father

SOFİ, nurse of Afife and others in the family

HOUSEKEEPER

CLERK

YOUNG WOMEN, including the next four individuals

BEHİRE, young woman who passed the entrance exam to the School of Dramatic Arts

REFİKA, young woman who passed the entrance exam to the School of Dramatic Arts

BEYZA, young woman who passed the entrance exam to the School of Dramatic Arts

MEMDUHA, young woman who passed the entrance exam to the School of Dramatic Arts

FIRST GIRL, Afife's friend

SECOND GIRL, Afife's friend

HÜSEYİN KEMAL, young actor

HÜSEYİN SUAT, playwright

KINAR, famous actress of Armenian origin

VASFİ RIZA, young actor

BEHZAT, young actor

JANITOR

ANAİS, famous actress of Armenian origin

CELÂL SAHİR, playwright

TAHSİN, chief of police

KONSTANTİN KAROPANA, president of the trolley company

MEHMET ALİ, minister of the interior

ACTOR

POLICEMEN

İBNÜRREFİK NURİ, playwright

FANCILY DRESSED WOMAN

KADIKÖY POLICE CHIEF

OFFICIAL

ELİZA BİNEMECİYAN, famous actress of Armenian origin

DRAMATIC ARTS THEATER EXECUTIVE BOARD MEMBERS

EXECUTIVE BOARD CHAIRMAN

DR. SUAT, Afife's doctor

BURHANETTİN TEPSİ, owner of a theater company

SENİYE, actress

FIRST WOMAN

SECOND WOMAN

MEN who accompany İbnürrefik Nuri

FUAT, governor of the province of Kastamonu, Afife's brother-in-law

SELÂHATTİN PINAR, musician and later Afife's husband

MESUT, Afife's nephew

DOCTOR

THE VOICE

ACT I

Scene 1

[*The stage is completely dark and seems to be empty, but there is a woman in the darkness. She is standing at the back of the stage on a platform, which is raised a couple of steps and is parallel to the audience. She is wearing a long, white gown with long sleeves that widen as they come down to her wrists and a high, round neckline. The gown is fitted around her waist and has a long train in the back that falls in folds. Her ankles are bare. Her arms are raised slightly above her shoulders and tied with ropes. Her head is tilted toward her left shoulder, but turned upward. This woman, who symbolizes struggle, determination, and awareness, gazes at the audience with piercing eyes for some time. She is silent, but sounds coming from a flute at this moment provide the accompaniment to express her loneliness and solitude. The quavering sounds of the flute announce to the audience the quavering of her inner world. Then the flute stops as though it has become fully drained and has nothing more to say.*]

AFİFE: Good evening, I am Afife Jale. You don't remember me, right? It's me, Afife. I am one of the first ones: like the one who lighted the first fire, who sang the first song, who told the first story, and who had the first love affair. I don't go too far back, only about half a century. But you still don't remember me. It's all right. I love people so much that I won't be cross. I have always loved. Now, meeting me like this, you'll get to know me and may remember me afterward, not in a pitying way, but in a thoughtful, loving, and embracing way. I hope you don't mind if I cannot embrace you; my arms are tied with ropes. I am in the closing years of my life now, kept in a mental asylum. The rules of the asylum require that I be tied up. At least, that's what they think. But their fetters cannot prevent the attachment of my own passions, my loves, and my feelings to this world. Aren't you a little curious? Who is this woman? Who is this beautiful woman in fetters? Well, I know only one language—one way of speaking to others. I know only one way that connects human beings. I know only one place that brings people together—that's this stage we're on now. In this play called *Afife Jale*, I'll speak to you as a woman who was a pioneer—a first, but also a victim. I am yours with all my heart.

Scene 2

[*The drawing room of an old Istanbul mansion that belongs to* DR. SAİT PASHA. *Sitting or standing there with him are* METHİYE, BEHİYE, SALÂH, *the* AUNT, ZİYA, *and* HİDAYET. *They are waiting for* AFİFE'*s arrival.* AFİFE *will come down wearing her first* çarşaf¹ *and show her respect to the grown-ups by kissing their hands.*]

DR. SAİT PASHA: Methiye, why doesn't the young lady come down?

METHİYE: Don't you know, dear father, your grandchild is clothes crazy . . . her primping is never finished?

SALÂH: I don't think she's primping herself. She's in a bad mood, she's petulant.

AUNT: Why is that? I saw the *çarşaf* in purple iridescent taffeta that Methiye had made for her. If you ask me, it is a bit too fancy. Too flashy.

HİDAYET: [*Irritably.*] My wife loves it.

BEHİYE: Grandfather, why don't the Parisian ladies wear *çarşafs*?

DR. SAİT PASHA: If they did, their men would be the first to tear them off their heads. What's the use of concealing from everybody's eyes the most beautiful creatures God created?

HİDAYET: But, Pasha, isn't covering up one of the fundamental rules of Islam?

DR. SAİT PASHA: My son, the meaning of "covering up" changes according to circumstances. A wise woman covers herself with her good manners, her virtue, and her intelligence. It's as simple as that.

SALÂH: [*Points to the nurse* SOFİ *and* AFİFE, *following in her new* çarşaf *with a cape.*] Lo and behold, look who's coming, look at the little lady. [AFİFE, *whose face is covered with a veil, stands in the middle of the room. She moves a bit, then she throws down her umbrella and handbag, starts crying, and puts her arms around her* GRANDFATHER's *neck.*]

AFİFE: Grandfather, I don't want to . . . I don't want to grow up . . . I don't want to wear all these things.

DR. SAİT PASHA: Ah, look at her! But, Afife, my dear, you can't help it, dear child. Come on, open your veil. You're right . . . if I were in your place, I would cry, too.

AUNT: Brother, please don't provoke her.

DR. SAİT PASHA: [*Takes out a little box from his vest pocket, lifts* AFİFE's *veil and dries her cheeks with his fingertips.*] This is your late grandmother's *çarşaf* pin. I hope you will be a wise, dear, and loving lady like her. [*Hands the pin to* AFİFE.]

AFİFE: Thank you very much, Grandfather. [*Turns to her* MOTHER.] Mother, where shall I put this?

METHİYE: [*Smiles, picks up the pin, and puts it on her head.*] Like this.

AFİFE: Can I take it off now? I feel miserable. [*First takes off the* çarşaf's *cape, then tries to kick off her high-heeled shoes.*]

---

1. *Çarşaf:* An outer garment that covers a woman from head to foot and is designed to hide her body from the view of men.

BEHİYE: Hey, young lady, you don't do that in front of people. There's something called manners.

ZİYA: Leave the child alone.

DR. SAİT PASHA: Let's go to the dining room. I don't know about you, but I'm starving. [*Walks as the others follow him.*]

Scene 3

[DR. SAİT PASHA's *study. There is a beautiful antique desk with carvings; its top is cluttered, and an elegant lamp stands on its left side.* AFİFE *enters dressed in her* çarşaf. ZİYA *is standing by the desk.*]

AFİFE: Grandfather, don't you think I look ridiculous? Your housekeeper stopped me in the hall and told me to put on my veil when I meet Ziya Bey.[2] She told me that now that I've started wearing the çarşaf, I have to cover myself. Grandfather, does this make sense?

DR. SAİT PASHA: Ah, it's nonsense. You grew up together, my God, you really did. You shouldn't have grown up so fast, my dear.

AFİFE: I came here to ask you a big favor. Are you really taking us to the Mınakyan Theater?

DR. SAİT PASHA: Did your father give you permission?

AFİFE: It seems he said, "Do whatever you want, and may God forgive Pasha's transgressions." [DR. SAİT PASHA *laughs heartily.*]

ZİYA: Can't you keep a secret?

AFİFE: Grandfather, I hear you have your private box in that theater.

DR. SAİT PASHA: Yes, it's true. Whoever pays at the beginning of the theater season can have a private box. Nothing extraordinary.

AFİFE: What is extraordinary is not the money you paid, but your interest in the theater. You're so nice, so different, Grandfather.

DR. SAİT PASHA: Ah, such beautiful compliments you pay me. [*Gets up.*] Ziya, I want to have a little stroll in the garden. You take care of this whirlwind of a girl. I need some fresh air, some oxygen.

AFİFE: I take offense! Do I pollute your air?

DR. SAİT PASHA: Oh, no, no, nothing like that. [*Exits.* AFİFE *and* ZİYA *glance at each other and smile.*]

AFİFE: We should have gone out, too, to feed the fish in the pond.

ZİYA: When you were five, you used to insist, "Let's go and feed the fish." Aren't you ever going to grow up?

AFİFE: You grew up! You're a big shot, a student in an elite high school. You grew up and forgot about me. My brother Salâh forgot about me, too. Now all he does is watch the girl on the balcony across from our house. Are there any girls around here that you watch?

2. *Bey:* "Gentleman" or simply "Mr." (used after the first name).

ZİYA: Afife, shame on you! Young ladies don't talk like that!

AFİFE: I hear a thousand times a day from my nanny Sofi about how young ladies are supposed to talk.

ZİYA: How are they supposed to talk?

AFİFE: Well, for instance, no matter how deeply I feel, I can't say to you, "I miss you." I'm not allowed.

ZİYA: I'm glad I don't have a nurse like Sofi because I miss you very much; I'll always miss you.

AFİFE: And you don't like me because I'm grown up now?

ZİYA: Why do you say that? Even if you become an old hag, I'll always love you, Afife. Be sure of that and never forget it.

AFİFE: [*Holds* ZİYA's *hands.*] Oh, it's so nice to hear that. If I didn't have my grandfather, my brother Salâh, and you, this world would be a terrible place for me, terrible.

HOUSEKEEPER: [*Enters. Seriously.*] Afife, dear, your grandfather wants to see you.

Scene 4

[DR. SAİT PASHA's *drawing room. It is after midnight.* DR. SAİT PASHA, METHİYE, BEHİYE, SALÂH, *and* ZİYA *are sitting and drinking tea. Only* AFİFE *is standing up, holding her teacup. They all are elegantly dressed. They have just returned from the theater.*]

METHİYE: Afife, enough is enough. Please stop talking for a while. You make me dizzy.

BEHİYE: Stop talking? How can she?

AFİFE: I feel dizzy, too, believe me. I don't know if I'm coming or going. Grandfather, it was a magnificent evening. Perhaps you prefer the comedies because you're always overworked, but I prefer the tragedies. Theater means tragedy.

SALÂH: [*Ironically.*] What do you mean?

ZİYA: What do you know about tragedy?

AFİFE: I'm afraid my secret is out. [*Smiles.*] Gentlemen, you're talking now to a lady who was just initiated into wearing her first *çarşaf*. Now, I'm going to confess. I secretly went to the theater without your permission, once with Behiye and Sofi and once with just Sofi.

BEHİYE: For heaven's sake! We weren't going to tell anybody.

AFİFE: What we saw were not magnificent like this company.

SALÂH: [*Jokingly.*] Grandfather, how are we going to handle this daredevil young lady?

DR. SAİT PASHA: Your mother, too, had her fling when she was young and secretly went to a picnic in Göksu. I remember well.

METHİYE: Father, please . . .

AFİFE: [*Takes a bow like an actress.*] One day if we're allowed to go on the stage . . . I, too, would like to enrich our theater with our beautiful Turkish language. I would like to be free to act. [*Again takes a bow.*]

DR. SAİT PASHA: Is this a threat?

AFİFE: [*Almost in a trance.*] Do you remember the applause? To be applauded like that! I wonder how one would feel after that? I feel as if I'm still hearing the audience's applause.

SALÂH: This girl is really crazy.

METHİYE: She frightens me.

ZİYA: Me, too.

Scene 5

[*The stage is empty except for a large door in the back. In front of this door, seven or eight* YOUNG WOMEN, *wearing* çarşafs, *are waiting. From their posture, it looks like they have been waiting there for a long time. The door opens slowly, and an elderly man (*CLERK) *appears wearing a fez and eyeglasses. He has a pencil behind his ear and holds an open sheet of paper in one hand. He looks at the floor. The women wearing* çarşafs *immediately lower their veils as soon as they see him and line up. It is obvious from their breathing that they are nervous and excited.*]

CLERK: Ladies, I'm going to read the names of the first Turkish girls who have been accepted as students at the School of Dramatic Arts after the examination given in October 1918. You are now free to attend the classes, provided that you are serious and remain within the rules of propriety. Our institution does not see anything objectionable to attending classes. However, when you are ready to perform the art you study, you will be able to act only in front of audiences consisting of women. [*The* YOUNG WOMEN *stir a little.*] Now, I'm going to read the names of those who passed the exam and have been accepted: Afife Hanım,[3] Behire Hanım, Memduha Hanım, Beyza Hanım, Refika Hanım. You have to apply to the theater administration with the appropriate documents, the photos, the stamps, etcetera. I wish you good luck. [*Goes inside without looking at the* YOUNG WOMEN *and closes the door. The* WOMEN *immediately lift their veils.*]

BEHİRE: What is this? We'll attend the drama school, but we'll play only in performances for women? What is the meaning of this?

REFİKA: What did you expect? Did you think they'd let us go on the stage without covering our heads?

BEYZA: You know the journalists asked the famous actor Muhsin Ertuğrul[4] the same question.

---

3. *Hanım:* A title meaning "Miss" or "Mrs."; in this instance, "Miss" (used after a first name).

4. Muhsin Ertuğrul (1892–1979): A prominent actor, stage director, and filmmaker who was a principal mentor of the modern Turkish theater. He served many years as the director of the Istanbul City Theater and the Turkish State Theater.

AFİFE: [*Animatedly.*] What was his answer?

BEYZA: He was very angry and said, "No, women will not go on the stage without head covers. We'll put a latticed screen in front of the stage, and behind that women will act wearing veils and *çarşaf*s."

AFİFE: Really?

BEYZA: "Of course without head covers," he yelled. "After so many tragic events, if we want to progress, we will have to accept the basic rules of civilized countries."

AFİFE: They don't even give you a chance to feel happy.

MEMDUHA: Why do you say that? They gave us permission. This is only a beginning.

AFİFE: Let's wait and see how it's going to end.

MEMDUHA: It'll be OK, and if not, this is not a life-and-death matter. We'll simply have to adjust.

AFİFE: [*Resolutely.*] I cannot adjust. I cannot live without the theater. This is my only hope in life.

BEYZA: She's crazy. She acts as if she was born in the theater.

AFİFE: It is not "as if"; it is absolutely so. I feel as though I've been acting since the days of ancient Greece. I feel this in my bones.

BEYZA: Girls, we've had enough babbling. What are we going to do now?

MEMDUHA: What shall we do? What devilish things are you up to?

BEYZA: Nothing devilish. Today there's a women's matinee at the cinema in Şehzadebaşı. The movie will start in an hour. It is *Tigre Reale* by Pina Menichelli. Let's go see it.

AFİFE: I've already seen it twice. If you go to the Rex, I'll join you. There they have the sisters Dorothy and Lillian Gish playing in *Orphans of the Storm*.

BEHİRE: Oh, I'm dying to see that movie. Mother said she was overwhelmed and cried her eyes out.

BEYZA: We'll be late.

BEHİRE: Weren't you the one who said a few minutes ago, "Let's go to the Şehzadebaşı cinema"?

BEYZA: Şehzadebaşı is quite a distance from Beyoğlu.

AFİFE: Come on, girls, let's get going. You talk too much. [*They exit.*]

Scene 6

[*A part of the dining room in* HİDAYET's *house. There is a dining table on the stage. This place is different in two respects from the elegant, Europeanized house of* DR. SAİT PASHA: *it is both more traditional and more modest in appearance.* HİDAYET, METHİYE, BEHİYE, AFİFE, *and* SALÂH *are sitting around the dining table having dinner.*]

HİDAYET: [*To* AFİFE.] I don't want to see you walk in the streets without your veil lowered. If I ever do, you can forget about your school. Remember that.

AFİFE: With the veil, I can't see where I'm going.

HİDAYET: How do all the other women see?

AFİFE: In fact, all the other women see nothing. They are like sheep; they do what they are told to do.

METHİYE: [*Worried.*] Afife!

HİDAYET: If you ever talk like this again, you'll be slapped. You can count on it.

AFİFE: [*Defiantly.*] You're going to slap me?

HİDAYET: You think I can't do it? You'll immediately go and complain to your grandfather, right?

METHİYE: [*Nervously.*] Please don't bring my father into this.

SALÂH: Please, let's eat our dinner in peace.

HİDAYET: [*Gets up.*] Eat your dinner in peace! My own daughter, more arrogant than my two stepchildren. [BEHİYE *gets up crying.*] Go ahead and eat.

BEHİYE: We love you as our own father.

HİDAYET: I can almost believe that when I see Afife's arrogant behavior.

METHİYE: Please, sit down and eat your dinner. Your stomach pains will start again.

HİDAYET: Hanım, every single day at this table my stomach acts up. It is because of your indulgence of your children and the way you educate them. How can one eat in peace in this house? [*Throws his napkin down and walks away.* AFİFE *quickly spoons something from the bowl in front of her.*]

BEHİYE: [*To* AFİFE.] It's all because of you. I am sick and tired of all this. Thank God our parents consented to my marrying that young man from the School of Political Science. I am rescued from this house, God willing.

Scene 7

[*The same part of* HİDAYET'*s house.* AFİFE *enters, holding a big curtain in her hand.* BEHİYE, SOFİ, *and two of* AFİFE'*s* FRIENDS *are there.*]

AFİFE: Both Mother and Auntie have left. Come on, let's hang this curtain. This is the backstage, this is the stage. Come on, help me. [SOFİ *is sitting on a wooden chair.* BEHİYE *is standing and looking disapprovingly at* AFİFE. *The two* FRIENDS *help her.* AFİFE *goes out and comes back with a big bundle of clothes. To the* FIRST GIRL.] Here's your dress for the song-and-dance number. [*Hands her a red dress.*] And this one is for the shepherdess tableau.

FIRST GIRL: Where did you find all these?

AFİFE: In the attic, of course! Come on, Sister, please pick up the zither. Please, please . . .

SECOND GIRL: How about you? What are you going to be?

AFİFE: [*Proudly.*] I'll be Madame Binemeciyan.

SECOND GIRL: Of course, nothing less would do.

AFİFE: I'll do a monologue. Neither Salâh nor Ziya wanted to act with me. We'll invite them when we're ready. Now wait for a minute. [*The* GIRLS *go inside.* SALÂH *and* ZİYA *enter from another door carrying their chairs and sit next to* SOFİ. *The* FIRST GIRL *appears and does a song-and-dance number. The* SECOND GIRL *accompanies her with the zither. Applause. Then* AFİFE *comes out from behind the curtain, dressed and behaving exactly like the actress* BİNEMECİYAN. *Excited,* ZİYA *gets up.* SALÂH *applauds wildly.*]

SALÂH: Bravoo . . . bravoo . . . [*Bows like Mınakyan⁵ in front of* AFİFE, *kisses her hand, and holds it; turns to the audience and imitates Mınakyan's accent.*] Our most honorable and splendid princess . . . the pride and the peerless embellishment of our stage . . . Eliza Binemeciyan!

AFİFE: [*Imitating* BİNEMECİYAN.] You are spoiling me . . . you are drowning me in your compliments. Ah, my dear . . . the delicate throbbings of my heart . . . my heart . . . [*In her own voice.*] I forgot what I was supposed to say. [*Stops; is upset.*]

SALÂH: Go on, go on, just improvise something.

SOFİ: Oh, I think it's the doorbell. [*Fans her face with her hand.*] Hurry, clean up the place. I'm afraid it's your father. [SOFİ *and the others straighten up the place in a hurry and take the props out of the room.*]

AFİFE: [*Trying to take the hat pin from her hat.*] Ah, how terrible . . . like all our best dreams, this too is unfinished. Isn't it always like this?

SALÂH: [*From the outside.*] Welcome home, sir. You're early today.

Scene 8

[*Either the library or the solarium in* DR. SAİT PASHA's *house.* ZİYA *is alone.* AFİFE *enters with a tray laden with fresh and dried fruits.* BEHİYE's *wedding party is taking place in the other parts of the house, and noises are heard.*]

AFİFE: I'm dying of starvation. I'm tired of the crowd and the noise.

ZİYA: Can't you live without complaining?

AFİFE: [*Restlessly paces the floor while* ZİYA *sits placid and resolute.*] I'm not complaining; I'm only relating what's going on.

ZİYA: Pretty soon you'll be going through the same thing. You're a big girl now.

AFİFE: Is that the reason why you and Salâh don't play with me anymore?

ZİYA: Isn't this a game, too?

AFİFE: Which one?

ZİYA: While people are having fun at the wedding party, you and I are alone here . . . just the two of us.

AFİFE: Are you bored to be alone with me?

---

5. Mardiros Mınakyan (1839–1920): A major producer-director of Armenian origin. His theater known as the Osmanlı Tiyatrosu (the Ottoman Theater) produced dramas or dramatized version of popular novels by such authors as Georges Ohnet, Xavier de Montepin, Octave Feuillet, Émile Richebourg, Victor Hugo, Alexandre Dumas fils, and Émile Zola, as well as by native playwrights.

ZİYA: You know I'm not . . . I always want to be with you. I'm tired of these secret get-togethers. I want to love you and caress you. I want to comb and braid your beautiful hair and put it up.

AFİFE: Me, too . . . I often think about these things.

ZİYA: I'm about to graduate from my school. We can get engaged anytime you want. Afife, do you know how much I love you?

AFİFE: And you, do you know how much I love you?

ZİYA: I don't know, but I feel it.

AFİFE: Maybe you're the one I love most in the whole world! Believe me.

ZİYA: Then you have to be mine. You must marry me.

AFİFE: [*Pauses to think.*] I'm not sure of that.

ZİYA: How come?

AFİFE: [*Talks deliberately with pauses.*] I really love you very much. You make me feel happy. I cannot tell anybody what I tell you. But there is something in me . . . something I haven't figured out yet.

ZİYA: [*With apprehension.*] What kind of a thing?

AFİFE: I wonder . . . I wonder if loving someone so deeply and so wholeheartedly is enough? I cannot explain.

ZİYA: We'll have children in the future. You'll love them as much as you love me. We'll have a home . . . later we'll have grandchildren.

AFİFE: [*As if talking to herself.*] To do something . . . to accomplish something . . . to take up something and to carry it along. I don't know . . . perhaps it's too early . . . too vague. I know that I love you . . . but . . .

ZİYA: You're not able to promise me!

AFİFE: I think you're right. I don't think I can.

ZİYA: I know how to wait—I even like to wait. Time ripens the fruit. I want to kiss you.

AFİFE: Im-pos-si-ble. [*Smiles.*] If grandfather sees, it would be improper. [*Laughs and moves away.*] Look . . . I want to tell you something. A secret! If one day I become an actress like Binemeciyan, would you marry me?

ZİYA: Are you crazy? They'll never allow Muslim Turkish women to go on stage.

AFİFE: Well . . . suppose they do?

ZİYA: If we live to see that day, we'll think about it then.

AFİFE: [*Laughs and naughtily flicks* ZİYA *on the chin.*] I see . . . you have already started thinking about it. [*Laughs again and exits laughing.*] Keep thinking, but maybe it's too late . . .

Scene 9

[*Evening at* HİDAYET's *house.* METHİYE *is sitting on a sofa by the window, crying and wiping her tears.* AFİFE *enters, sees her mother crying, and stops.*]

AFİFE: Mother, you're crying again. Please don't. You know Grandfather won't rest in peace otherwise.

METHİYE: I know.

AFİFE: Then stop crying, please. Believe me, I'm not able to cry myself because you're crying all the time.

METHİYE: Father . . . he was very important for me. He was my only support against the world and against my husband.

AFİFE: How about me? I can't explain it, but he had a special meaning for me, too.

METHİYE: [*Listening to voices offstage.*] I think your father just came in.

AFİFE: God knows what he'll find to roar about tonight! I'm tired of his bullying. You know, Mother, since Grandfather died, he has become more of a tyrant.

METHİYE: [*As* AFİFE *leaves.*] Watch your language, Afife! He is your father. [*Gets up to receive her husband.* HİDAYET *enters very agitated and holds a newspaper in his hand. Before he takes off his fez and his overcoat, he shoves the paper toward his* WIFE's *face.*]

HİDAYET: What's this scandal?

METHİYE: [*Fearfully.*] For heaven's sake, what's happened?

HİDAYET: Don't pretend you don't know! And if you don't know, just read about it. You've made me the laughingstock of the whole world!

METHİYE: [*Picks up the paper from the floor where* HİDAYET *had thrown it.*] Ohh . . .

HİDAYET: [*Grabs the paper from* METHİYE's *hand and hits it with the back of his hand.*] Isn't this Afife Hanım who is mentioned among the daughters of "good families" performing in the theater, our daughter?

METHİYE: Believe me, I didn't . . . know . . .

HİDAYET: You didn't know. What kind of a mother are you? You have a traitor in your midst, and you didn't know, is that it?

METHİYE: She is only a child. She hasn't done anything wrong yet. Let's see, maybe it's another Afife? Let's inquire and find out.

HİDAYET: You don't have to bother. I did inquire and found out. It is our daughter, but there must be something wrong. My daughter cannot be an actress, cannot be a whore, cannot be openly and officially labeled as a whore. Never, never, never. . . [*Keeps shouting and pounding the table with his fists. At that moment,* AFİFE *enters from the same door through which she exited; her head held high, she is determined and brave.*]

AFİFE: I'm sorry, please don't aggravate yourself. I will not become a whore!

HİDAYET: [*Terrified.*] So you want to be an actress?

AFİFE: Yes! And nobody can stop me.

HİDAYET: [*Walks toward her.*] I will! You impudent, shameless girl. [*Slaps her.*]

AFİFE: [*Startled, but keeping her head high.*] This slap has been the seal of approval for my acting profession, Father!

HİDAYET: Get out of here! Get out! Don't let me see you again because I will kill you, Afife. [*Again raises his hand.*]

METHİYE: [*Tries to hold* HİDAYET's *hand.*] You, too, will die. You'll have a stroke.

HİDAYET: [*Tries to free his hand from* METHİYE's.] You shut up! You stupid idiot! [*Slaps* METHİYE.]

AFİFE: Father, what are you doing?

HİDAYET: I don't want to see either of you again! Get out of here, get out. [AFİFE *exits.* METHİYE *sits on a chair and cries with her hands covering her face.* HİDAYET *paces the floor with his hands locked behind his back.*] O God, give me patience. Give me strength. [*At this moment,* AFİFE *reenters. She has her head covered, with her cape on her shoulders, and is carrying a bulky bag.*]

AFİFE: Mother, I'm leaving.

HİDAYET: [*Grabs* AFİFE *by the throat.*] Only your dead body will leave this house. [SOFİ *comes running.*]

SOFİ: Sir, you're going to kill her! What are you doing?

METHİYE: Leave her alone! Let her go!

HİDAYET: [*Lets her go.* AFİFE *falls down.* HİDAYET *pushes* METHİYE *and* SOFİ *with both of his hands.*] You'll turn me into a killer. Go away, go away.

METHİYE: She's only a little girl. My darling child.

AFİFE: [*Gets up slowly.*] Mother, I'm leaving.

METHİYE: I can't let her go alone. You asked for this! I'm leaving with her.

SOFİ: Madam, let's go to my house.

METHİYE: We have no place else to go at this late hour. [HİDAYET *collapses into a chair. The three women walk out.*]

Scene 10

[*The living room of* AFİFE's *new house. Although it appears to be shabby and worn, it still presents the painstakingly achieved aura of good taste of the former, more affluent days.* AFİFE *sits on a chaise longue covered with red velvet and reads a book. There are papers and magazines on the floor.* METHİYE *enters holding a tray with two demitasse cups and a* cezve, *a Turkish coffeepot. She sits on the armchair across from the chaise longue and pours the coffee into the cups.* AFİFE *pulls herself up.*]

METHİYE: Is your headache better now? The aspirin must have helped.

AFİFE: It's gone, Mother.

METHİYE: You read too much, without any rest. Your eyes give you a headache. God rest his soul, your grandfather the doctor used to say, "You are in charge of your organs; on Judgment Day your organs will complain and say, 'We did not receive proper care.'"

AFİFE: If my grandfather the doctor was still around, we would not have gotten into this mess. Father could not have thrown me out and treated you like this. I can't bear what you have to suffer because of me.

METHİYE: It's my own choice. He didn't do anything to me; he only said, "Either me or your daughter," and I chose you. Don't worry, dear, everything will be all right.

AFİFE: But, Mother, when, when? Look, a year has gone by. They pay me my small salary and tell me to wait patiently. To wait patiently so luck will appear at my door one day. You manage the house, but how can you live on such a pittance? I know you secretly sell some of your possessions here and there . . . but how long can this situation go on?

METHİYE: You mustn't worry about these things. Don't think about them.

AFİFE: Nobody has the courage to give me a role in a play. I didn't leave my home, my comfort, my well-being, my father, to sit around and wait. I want to go on stage, I want to act. Mother, you can't imagine how much I yearn for it. I ache for it. I feel it in my flesh and bones. Every night in my dreams I became Binemeciyan, Kınar, or Anais. I play their roles in my beautiful Turkish with my passion and my youth. I hear the applause, that beautiful applause that surrounds me. Mother, when I wake up and find myself all alone in my bed . . . I feel terrible.

METHİYE: You'll get sick. My dear, don't worry yourself to death. Remember what Kerem[6] said, "Black days don't last forever." Just a little more patience.

AFİFE: You know what, I almost miss Father . . . his voice, his calling me "Afife." When he yelled, "My daughter will not be a whore, will not go on stage and be a clown in front of everybody," the veins in his neck were purple, and they looked as if they were about to burst. I was so scared; I thought he was going to die.

METHİYE: Forget about these things. Your aunt said, "He's doing all right, nothing to worry about, think about yourself."

AFİFE: Shall I turn my coffee cup over? Will you read my fortune?

METHİYE: Of course. [*Gets up.*] Let me water this flower first. [*As she comes back with the water pitcher, the doorbell rings.*] My goodness! I wonder who that could be? [*Puts the pitcher on the table and goes to open the door.* AFİFE *straightens up and listens.* METHİYE *comes in with a visitor. The head cover that was on her shoulders is on her head now.*]

Scene 11

METHİYE: Come in, come in. She had a terrible headache, but she's better now.

AFİFE: [*Gets up to receive the visitor.*] Oh, welcome Hüseyin Kemal Bey. How are you?

HÜSEYİN KEMAL: I'm fine, thank you. How are you?

AFİFE: Thank you . . . a little tired of waiting, nervous because of waiting and sick because of nervousness. [*Laughs.*]

HÜSEYİN KEMAL: Afife Hanım, I believe you're not going to have to wait anymore.

---

6. Kerem: The legendary young lover in a popular Turkish epic entitled *Kerem ile Aslı* (Karem and Aslı).

AFİFE: [*Jumps up.*] What did you say? I don't believe it!

HÜSEYİN KEMAL: It's true. They're calling for you from the theater.

AFİFE: My God! I don't believe my ears! Mother, where are you? Mother, listen to this!
[METHİYE *walks in holding the coffee tray and offers coffee to the visitor.*]

METHİYE: What's going on, you crazy girl?

AFİFE: [*Puts her arms around* METHİYE's *neck.*] Mother, at last! At long last! They remembered me. They're calling for me. [*Jumps up.*] They're calling for me. They'll let me act.

HÜSEYİN KEMAL: It's in Hüseyin Suat's play *The Patches*. Madame Binemeciyan withdrew from the play at the last minute. It seems she's dying to go to Paris.

AFİFE: [*Claps her hands.*] Wonderful, wonderful . . .

HÜSEYİN KEMAL: Somebody has to act the part of Emel, and it's perfect for you. The theater board met, and after long discussions they decided to ask you first.

AFİFE: My God, I don't believe this! Mother, it's not a dream, is it?

HÜSEYİN KEMAL: But, of course, they are a little worried still. They're wondering if Afife Hanım will dare to do this.

AFİFE: What's the risk?

HÜSEYİN KEMAL: Up till now women who have gone on the Turkish stage have been Christians; you will be the first Muslim woman on stage. Have you any idea how they will receive you? How . . .

AFİFE: [*Interrupts him.*] I'll act very well. I'll put my whole being into it, and they will like me. I'll mesmerize the audience. That's how.

HÜSEYİN KEMAL: I don't doubt that you'll act very well.

AFİFE: I've read *The Patches* three times. If you have no doubts, then what's the problem?
[*Puts an arm around* HÜSEYİN KEMAL's *shoulders.*] Let's go. Ah, Kemal Bey, you were like an older brother to me, but now you have become my Gabriel, my messenger of good tidings. I'll remember you as long as I live. I thank you from the bottom of my heart. Come . . . I'll be ready in a minute. Let's go without delay . . . right away.

Scene 12

[*The dressing room of the Apollo Theater in Kadıköy. There are makeup tables, costumes, flowers, and so on. The Patches is about to end. There is excitement, agitation, and whispering backstage.*]

HÜSEYİN SUAT: It's all over, friends. Tonight this young girl finished Eliza Binemeciyan. From now on, there is no actress called Binemeciyan. May God protect Afife.

KINAR: You're right, Hüseyin Suat, God help her.

VASFİ RIZA: I don't feel very comfortable; I feel as if something is going to happen. An extraordinary event like this cannot end so peacefully. I have a premonition that we're going to have trouble. I hope they don't hurt Afife.

BEHZAT: Ssh! Vasfi Rıza! Ssh! Don't be a Cassandra. [*There is a sound of tumultuous applause. The sounds of "Bravo," "God save you," "Bravo" are heard backstage. Someone shouts, "Curtain." They repeat, "Open the curtain." There is commotion backstage. At that moment, the theater* JANITOR *enters. He grabs* HÜSEYİN KEMAL's *arm.*]

JANITOR: Sir, we're being raided!

HÜSEYİN KEMAL: What?

JANITOR: We're being raided, we're finished.

HÜSEYİN KEMAL: Hey, what's happening, what are you talking about?

JANITOR: They came, and they're waiting outside. They're waiting for Afife Hanım to come out. They are the men of Arnavut Tahsin Bey, the police chief.

ANAİS: Oh, what a disaster! What bad luck! How terrible for the young girl!

KINAR: Stop screaming! What's wrong with you?

VASFİ RIZA: Kınar Hanım, you take care of Afife. If necessary, get out by the fire escape. Anais Hanım, you find her *çarşaf* and her veil. God, the applause is still going on. [ANAİS *walks out.*]

BEHZAT: We can't even enjoy this.

CELÂL SAHİR: Gentlemen, keep cool. This was more or less to be expected. Hüseyin Suat Bey and I will go to the police chief and explain everything.

HÜSEYİN SUAT: Celâl Sahir is right. At least we can talk to the chief for a while and secure Afife's escape. We can keep him busy. Vasfi, Behzat, Kemal—see who's there and if it's possible divert their attention for a while. Don't let them come here. [ANAİS *enters, agitated.*]

ANAİS: Here's her *çarşaf,* her veil, and her pocketbook. Her mother was waiting for her, so I brought her in, too.

VASFİ RIZA: Good evening, madam. Congratulations. Anais, thank you. Now you must immediately leave and disappear.

METHİYE: What's going on? Is anything wrong?

VASFİ RIZA: Nothing's wrong, nothing to worry about.

ANAİS: Do I have to leave without congratulating Afife?

VASFİ RIZA: Never mind the congratulations now. [*Exits.* AFİFE *comes in running. She's very excited, in tears and gasping.*]

AFİFE: It happened! You see, it happened. My God, this will be my happiest opening night. [*Embraces* HÜSEYİN SUAT.] I don't know how to thank you! I'm so grateful to you. You wrote the play so beautifully. [*Embraces everybody one by one.*]

HÜSEYİN SUAT: You acted so beautifully.

AFİFE: Mother, dear. At last, at last . . .

METHİYE: Dear child . . . thank heavens, thanks, thanks.

CELÂL SAHİR: You were magnificent, Afife, I can't praise you enough.

HÜSEYİN SUAT: You were the first. We'll never forget this. You have begun beautifully! Beautifully . . .

VASFİ RIZA: You'll be the Joan of Arc of Turkey. God protect you from harm.

HÜSEYİN KEMAL: Congratulations, congratulations.

HÜSEYİN SUAT: Our stage needed a sacrifice like you for the dramatic arts. Afife, you volunteered for it. [*Kisses her on the forehead.*] May God protect you. Now go down with Kınar Hanım by the fire escape. We'll . . .

AFİFE: [*Coming to herself.*] What's the matter, what's going on?

HÜSEYİN SUAT: Let's find Tahsin Bey. [TAHSİN BEY *appears at the door.*]

TAHSİN: I'm here, you don't have to look for me. [*Everybody is startled and speechless.*] All of you please go out except for Afife Hanım and the playwright.

HÜSEYİN SUAT: [*Steps forward.*] I am . . . Hüseyin Suat.

TAHSİN: And you, Celâl Sahir Bey, you stay here with Afife Hanım, too. [*The rest exit.*] What do you think you're doing? Don't you know that a Muslim woman cannot go on stage—with her head uncovered, improperly dressed, moving around freely? Don't you know this is against the sacred laws of Islam? Don't you know you create trouble for the Ministry of the Interior, for the Office of Religious Affairs, for the municipality, and for the supreme head of religious affairs? There are so many non-Muslim women waiting at your door to go on stage, and you dare to do this! [*To* AFİFE.] You long-haired and short-brained woman! What makes you behave with such impudence and let yourself be debased like this?

AFİFE: But . . . sir . . .

TAHSİN: Shush, forget about "sir"! You apparently aren't ashamed to talk like this—and your head uncovered, too, like a man.

HÜSEYİN SUAT: Sir, if you permit me . . . this young lady did not commit any crime to arouse your anger. If anybody is to blame, it's me because I invited her to appear on stage.

TAHSİN: Sir, to act against the fundamental precepts of Islam is a crime, and if this crime is committed by a young woman, it is a double crime.

AFİFE: I did not behave against the fundamental precepts of Islam. I went on stage to perform the art of drama while preserving my honor and my dignity. I don't see anything wrong with that. You should have attended the performance and seen the people who applauded me with respect. [*Covers her face with her hands and begins to sob.*]

TAHSİN: [*Softens up a little.*] Why are you crying now?

AFİFE: [*Continues to cry.*] You're demeaning me. You're belittling me.

TAHSİN: No, it isn't me. It's the customs and the conventions that are threatening you. It's the backward and thickheaded fanatics who are making you feel debased. You tried to do something extraordinary without thinking about the price you would have to pay. [*Those present gather around* TAHSİN. *They can't believe what they are hearing.*] Gentlemen, as a human being, I, too, think like you.

MIXED VOICES: How is that? Is it really true? Oh, thank God, thank God.

TAHSİN: But I am the chief of police, and as the chief of police I cannot think like that. Look, Afife, after all this, do you still want to continue acting? What is your decision?

AFİFE: [*Holds her head high.*] Yes! No one can make me change my way, sir. This is a life-and-death matter for me. I sincerely believe that I'm not doing something dishonorable, and as long as you don't throw me off the stage by force, I will continue.

TAHSİN: You heard it. I really like a woman who can cry, but at the same time knows how to put her foot down resolutely. I, too, believe that Turkish women should go on stage provided that they remain within the rules of proper conduct. Fight on, Afife, my girl; I have no authority to give you official permission, but I can look the other way. Now stop crying, young lady.

AFİFE: I don't believe this. [*Runs to hold* TAHSİN'*s hands. He grasps hers in return.*] I am deeply grateful, sir. Thank you very much.

TAHSİN: I will give an order to the precinct chief of Kadıköy. You can continue performing . . . keep it up. [*Everybody shouts "Hurrah!" and embraces. Lights dim amidst joyful sounds.*]

Scene 13

[*The same room in* AFİFE'*s house as in Scene 10.* AFİFE *and* ZİYA *sit facing each other, holding their teacups.*]

ZİYA: You really don't listen to me.

AFİFE: I know what you're going to say. [*Gets up, imitating* ZİYA, *as if one hand is in a vest pocket and the other one in a side trouser pocket.*] "Well, you acted in your first play. You were marvelous. Even though you had to be smuggled out by Kınar Hanım through the boiler room, you were still marvelous. You charmed the chief of police, too. But it's over now. You had your satisfaction. Give up your ambition. Let's get married and have beautiful, healthy children. Be the mistress of your own home and the mother of your children."

ZİYA: [*Hurt.*] I have nothing to offer you . . . only myself. I don't think I'll even finish college and get my diploma.

AFİFE: I'm not thinking of that. Just love me, that's enough.

ZİYA: Afife, go slowly. Nobody can love you as much as I do.

AFİFE: Then try to understand me. Please, please. I have a blazing fire in me. You should be able to see that. Go against the grain, change something, go out of line, break a taboo, make the impossible possible only once . . . then you'll be able to understand me. My grandfather did.

ZİYA: So, then . . . I don't understand you at all!

AFİFE: But I love you, and I want you to understand me . . . at least understand me as a woman and allow me to live my life as a woman. You . . .

ZİYA: Aren't you afraid of anything?

AFİFE: Why? I love you!

ZİYA: I'm afraid. Will you continue living like this, listening to insults from the police chiefs and escaping through boiler rooms to get home every night?

AFİFE: [*Tersely.*] These moments, too, have their excitement.

ZİYA: You won't be able to stand them for long with your delicate constitution.

AFİFE: You don't know my inner strength. Theater is my life; I can't live without it.

ZİYA: [*Goes near her and caresses her hair.*] You had only one single performance, but you say, "I can't live without it." Tell me, can you live without me?

AFİFE: [*Puts her head on* ZİYA's *shoulder.*] Don't leave me.

ZİYA: Look, I had decided to tell you something after proposing to you again . . . no matter what your answer was. I want to tell you the decision I have made.

AFİFE: [*With trepidation.*] What decision?

ZİYA: I've decided to leave the College of Pharmacy for a while. I'm going to Anatolia to join the nationalist movement led by Mustafa Kemal Pasha.

AFİFE: Oh no.

ZİYA: Just as you say, "I'm doing my patriotic duty."

AFİFE: So . . . you're really going?

ZİYA: If my uncle were alive, he would have told me I was already late in joining the nationalist struggle.

AFİFE: He had given up all hope for the empire.

ZİYA: He was an enlightened, progressive, and militant nationalist.

AFİFE: I'm wondering if this rash decision has anything to do with running away from me.

ZİYA: Run away from you . . . are you crazy? Can one run away from one's hunchback? No, that sounded ugly. Can one run away from one's eyes, one's heart?

AFİFE: [*Sadly.*] A world without you? All empty . . . [*Hugs him.*] But you're right to go, but not right to leave me all alone.

ZİYA: I cannot give you up. You're willing to wait for me, aren't you?

AFİFE: Take everything with you before you go—my soul and everything I've kept for you.

ZİYA: Afife, my girl, you are so considerate. You are very precious to me. [*Holds* AFİFE's *arms and embraces her.*]

Scene 14

[*A part of the affluent house of a Levantine,* KONSTANTİN KAROPANA, *around 1920. The host prepares drinks, puts them in front of the guests,* MINISTER OF THE INTERIOR MEHMET ALİ, *and* AFİFE, *and raises his glass.*]

KONSTANTİN: I am raising my glass to His Excellency, the minister, whose presence honors my house. Welcome, sir. [*Glasses are raised again. To* AFİFE.] But I see your glass is empty.

AFİFE: It isn't, sir; I have a little white wine.

MINISTER: Don't you favor raki?

AFİFE: I don't like raki, and I'm not used to it.

MINISTER: But this evening, to celebrate this exceptional party and the magnificent table, permit me to put a little raki in your glass with my own hands. [*Pours.*] A little raki, a lot of water, and one ice cube. Konstantin Bey, are you by any chance related to Karopana Effendi, who started the first trolley company in Istanbul?

KONSTANTİN: Yes, sir, he was my grandfather, and I'm named after him. He started the trolley company in 1896, I believe. I followed in his footsteps and became the director.

MINISTER: Your grandfather was a close friend of my father's. Well, anyway, let's talk about how Afife Hanım is captivating the hearts of the people of Istanbul with her excellent performances. You've seen her acting, right?

KONSTANTİN: Yes, Your Excellency, she's wonderful.

AFİFE: You are very kind.

MINISTER: Please forgive my curiosity, but I'll take the liberty of asking you something because you came here alone. How is it that a beautiful, attractive, intelligent, and creative lady like yourself is alone?

AFİFE: [*Surprised and taken aback because she hadn't thought about this and hadn't felt alone.*] My brother is in Izmir, sir. And my fiancé . . . [*Stops, at a loss for words.*] . . . accepted another invitation a few days ago.

MINISTER: And he left you to us? What a stroke of good fortune. We are admirers of your art and your courage, too. I must confess, it's impossible to resist your charm when one gets to know you.

AFİFE: [*Coldly.*] You are very kind, thank you.

MINISTER: Madam, I believe the best brandy in Istanbul is served in this house.

KONSTANTİN: [*To* AFİFE.] What would you like to have? A Napoleon or a Courvoisier?

AFİFE: Thank you.

KONSTANTİN: Thank you "yes" or thank you "no"? Which one?

MINISTER: Of course she'll have some cognac. With your permission, let's drink it as we're having a private conversation with the lady about her work. Let's have our coffee and cognac together. [KONSTANTİN *pours the drinks and exits.*] Afife, my dear, cognac is a wonderful drink. [*Sniffs.*] Ah! [*Turning the glass between his palms.*] It's good to warm it up a little. To celebrate our meeting.

AFİFE: [*Takes a sip and coughs, making a face.*] I'm not at all accustomed to such exquisite pleasures. I have had no opportunity and no time to cultivate them. I have no desire for them.

MINISTER: But you can't live without these pleasures. Life has no meaning without them. I would like to initiate you. Come on, take another sip.

AFİFE: [*Picks up the glass and brings it to her lips, then puts it down.*] No, I will not do it.

MINISTER: A great actress must know about the pleasures of life and must get used to them. How are things going? Are you satisfied with your job at the theater?

AFIFE: Of course, it isn't easy. The problem is not the audience, but the higher authorities. Every night we perform with heavy hearts and worry about whether we're going to be raided.

MINISTER: If you wish, I can help you get rid of your worries.

AFIFE: [*Excited.*] How? Of course, I would like that. I am not asking for much; I only want to have the same rights to act as Kınar Hanım and Anais Hanım. That's all.

MINISTER: When I said "if you wish," I meant something different.

AFIFE: What do you mean, sir?

MINISTER: Being under the protection of the minister of the interior. This would mean a great deal to the higher authorities.

AFIFE: [*Now fully aware.*] What does "under the protection of" mean, sir?

MINISTER: It means you'll belong to me. You'll put an end to that story you told me about your fiancé going to another party and offer yourself to me. [*Holds her wrists and caresses them.*]

AFIFE: And is it the minister's special privilege to see every woman in sight as prey?

MINISTER: Don't you like me?

AFIFE: Not in the least . . . especially this attitude of yours.

MINISTER: Does all that riffraff you act with seem more appealing to you?

AFIFE: What have they got to do with this?

MINISTER: When the play is over, do you go home innocent? After all that provocation that happens on the stage? [*Moves his hands higher, gets closer, breathing heavily.*] Afife, don't try to act like an innocent and virtuous woman. I don't like innocent and virtuous women; I like the frivolous and naughty ones.

AFIFE: Please take your hands off me! I am not at all like the ones you like. I cannot be of any use to you. Leave me alone. I'm terribly upset.

MINISTER: But I'm the minister of the interior, and I know how important this is for you.

AFIFE: Leave me alone. Let me go. I don't care about your importance or whatever that means. I'm not the kind of woman who would say yes to the shameless proposal of a bully whom she meets for the first time.

MINISTER: But you're an actress! What's preventing you? Your place is well known anyway, so if not today, then maybe tomorrow you'll accept my proposal. [*Lets her go as* AFIFE *straightens her clothes.*]

AFIFE: You drank too much. Tomorrow morning you'll be ashamed of yourself. Please, let's forget this ugly incident.

MINISTER: But when you act these ugly scenes in the theater, aren't you ashamed?

AFIFE: That's an entirely different thing. You don't understand. It has nothing to do with my personal life.

MINISTER: OK, don't worry. I'll take you home; get ready.

AFİFE: Thank you, but my mother will be here soon to pick me up.

MINISTER: Oh, your mother! Is she also a participant in this game of virtue? Afife Hanım, who is your father?

AFİFE: Hidayet Bey. He's not important enough to be known by you, but he's an honest man. My grandfather, Dr. Sait Pasha . . .

MINISTER: Oh, Sait Pasha from Çamlıca?

AFİFE: Yes.

MINISTER: Oh, I see, but I don't really get it. How did they allow you to choose this profession?

AFİFE: I think you should not be concerned with any of this.

MINISTER: Yes, you're right. I'm interested only in you, and I always want to possess everything that interests me.

AFİFE: [*Sarcastically.*] Fine.

MINISTER: Today or tomorrow. [*Grabs* AFİFE's *arms with force and kisses her on the lips.*] The conquest has already started.

AFİFE: [*Very angrily.*] No, never!

MINISTER: This "never" will hurt you in the end, not me. [*Behind the door,* KONSTANTİN *coughs.*]

KONSTANTİN: Your mother is here. She didn't want to get out of the carriage. [*Embarrassed because he saw what went on earlier.*]

AFİFE: I'll be right down.

MINISTER: [*To* KONSTANTİN.] What a pity you've just missed a battle of words. [*To* AFİFE.] This way, madam. [*They walk toward the door.*]

Scene 15

[*Actors are performing the play* The Odalisque *on the stage. The audience will be presumed to be the audience of* The Odalisque. *On the stage are* AFİFE *and a male* ACTOR. *Some commotion takes place backstage and on the sides where the curtains are drawn. Sounds reach the audience, and the actors falter. Someone from the audience shouts, "What's going on?" On one side of the stage by the drawn curtain, an actor (could be* VASFİ RIZA*) waves his arms toward* AFİFE. *This movement should provoke the audience as much as it provokes the actors. Some people should get up, and others should shout, "Sit down, sit down."* AFİFE *eventually sees the* ACTOR's *signals; she is bewildered.*]

AFİFE: [*Whispering to the male* ACTOR.] Wait here a minute. Stop, I'll go and find out what's going on. I'll be back.

ACTOR: [*Surprised.*] What's happening?

AFİFE: I don't know. Maybe they're pounding on the door. Maybe some people came. I don't know. [*Exits running.*]

[*As the* ACTOR *on the stage looks around, bewildered, two* POLICEMEN *come running onto the stage. One of them is carrying a whip with a silver handle. He cracks the whip on his boot and yells toward the audience.*]

POLICEMAN: Where's that woman? That shameless and indecent creature? Where is she?

[*The curtain is drawn in a hurry. Actors run back and forth . . . voices.* HÜSEYİN SUAT *and* İBNÜRREFİK NURİ *come and stand in front of the curtain. They look sad and embarrassed and wring their hands.*]

İBNÜRREFİK NURİ: We are facing an unfortunate and regretful situation. Our theater, I regret to say, has been raided by the police. I believe that this happened because our distinguished actress, our beloved sister Afife Hanım, was on the stage. We are certain that this situation will be rectified; however, we cannot possibly continue our performance tonight. We hope that you will excuse us.

POLICEMAN: [*The one with the whip in front of the curtain.*] Where's that woman? Where is she? How did you let her escape?

İBNÜRREFİK NURİ: We're out here, sir; we don't know what's going on inside.

POLICEMAN: Gentlemen, I am arresting you both as the instigators of this unsavory situation. Sergeant, bring the handcuffs. [*Lights dim amidst the audience's hissing.*]

Scene 16

[*Üsküdar ferry pier.* AFİFE *and* METHİYE *are dressed in* çarşafs *and are heavily veiled. They talk in whispers. They are in a state of fear.*]

METHİYE: Look, Afife, the pier is full of policemen! Didn't I tell you not to go out, didn't I? You never listen!

AFİFE: Don't worry. They won't recognize us. How can they? I got a telegram from the theater telling me to go there immediately. If there were something to fear, they wouldn't have summoned me. Mother, don't be afraid; nobody will recognize Afife dressed in a black *çarşaf* and heavily veiled.

[*Two* POLICEMEN, *with a young,* FANCILY DRESSED WOMAN *between them approach slowly, but with determined steps.*]

FANCILY DRESSED WOMAN: Here! This is the woman you've been looking for! The one next to her must be her mother. This one is Afife Hanım!

FIRST POLICEMAN: Ladies, raise your veils.

METHİYE: I've never heard anything like this! No woman would raise her veil to two men and a strange woman she doesn't know.

SECOND POLICEMAN: We are performing our duty. We have the right.

FIRST POLICEMAN: If you don't raise your veils, we'll do it.

AFİFE: All right, here, I'll raise my veil. What do you want?

SECOND POLICEMAN: [To the WOMAN.] Is she the one?

FANCILY DRESSED WOMAN: Yes, she is Afife Hanım, who tarnishes our honor and our dignity.

METHİYE: Your honor and your dignity?

AFİFE: Mother, Mother, please be quiet.

FIRST POLICEMAN: Which one of you is Afife?

METHİYE and AFİFE: Me!

AFİFE: This lady is my mother. [*Her head erect.*] Officer, go ahead. What do you want?

FIRST POLICEMAN: We have an arrest warrant for you. In the name of the law, I arrest you and will take you to the police precinct. [*Takes the handcuffs from his pocket.* AFİFE, *holding her head high, stretches out her hands.*]

METHİYE: Oh, Afife! Afife!

AFİFE: Please try to be calm. Go to the theater right away and tell them about the situation.

Scene 17

[*The room of the* POLICE CHIEF *of the Kadıköy precinct.* HÜSEYİN SUAT *and* İBNÜRREFİK NURİ *are handcuffed and being questioned.*]

KADIKÖY POLICE CHIEF: [*Paces the floor and cracks his whip on his boots.*] So, you're not going to tell me where Afife is; you're are determined not to, right?

HÜSEYİN SUAT: If we did know her whereabouts, we would tell you, sir, but we just don't know. You put the handcuffs on us at the theater in front of the audience. How can we know where Afife Hanım is? [*The door opens quietly, and the two* POLICEMEN *bring* AFİFE *in, pushing her from behind.* AFİFE *stumbles and takes her place between her friends.*]

FIRST POLICEMAN: We found her and brought her here, sir.

KADIKÖY POLICE CHIEF: Where did you find her?

SECOND POLICEMAN: At the Kadıköy pier. She and her mother were waiting for the ferry to go to Istanbul.

KADIKÖY POLICE CHIEF: Like the grasshopper, you're caught. Let's see what you can do now.

AFİFE: [*Holds her head high.*] I'll complain about you to the chief of police, Tahsin Bey.

KADIKÖY POLICE CHIEF: What . . . what did you say?

AFİFE: Tahsin Bey sent you a communiqué informing you of his permission.

İBNÜRREFİK NURİ: Perhaps you didn't receive it.

KADIKÖY POLICE CHIEF: Yes, I received it. You forget your religion, your nation, and your honor by performing on the stage. And I have to say "Yes, sir" to Tahsin Bey's communiqué and let you get away with blasphemy, right?

HÜSEYİN SUAT: You have to follow the order given to you, sir.

KADIKÖY POLICE CHIEF: No, sir, I don't follow such orders. It is among the duties of the police to prosecute those who act contrary to the precepts of Islam. You shameless men, when you make the women go on the stage, I feel as if my own mother and my own wife are exhibited there. Aren't you ashamed?

AFİFE: You shouldn't talk to us in this manner!

KADIKÖY POLICE CHIEF: [*Slaps* AFİFE.] Look at her, how she talks back without fear! Whore!

İBNÜRREFİK NURİ: Sir, you cannot slap a woman.

HÜSEYİN SUAT: This will not be good for you. You have us handcuffed, so we can't defend ourselves. But you should know that these handcuffs will be taken off eventually.

AFİFE: I'll file a complaint against you.

KADIKÖY POLICE CHIEF: Is that so? To whom, honey?

AFİFE: I'll tell them how disrespectfully you treat honorable Turkish women, how you handcuff them unjustly, how you insult them, and . . .

İBNÜRREFİK NURİ: Afife, don't waste your time; don't talk too much.

KADIKÖY POLICE CHIEF: Yeah, don't talk too much! He's right: the more you talk, the deeper you sink. You whore, you harlot, you hooker . . .

AFİFE: [*Screaming.*] No!

CURTAIN

ACT II

Scene 1

[*A section of the room in the luxury hotel where* MINISTER OF THE INTERIOR MEHMET ALİ, *receives guests. A young* OFFICIAL *enters and bows.*]

OFFICIAL: Eliza Hanım is here, sir.

MINISTER: [*Takes off his glasses.*] Let her come in, bring her in. [*Gets up and waits by the end of the table.* BİNEMECİYAN *enters. She is very elegant, wears long gloves and a hat decorated with lace and flowers, and carries a parasol and a tasseled bag. She is in high spirits and full of confidence. The* MINISTER *kisses her hand and, still holding it, asks her to sit in an armchair. He settles in the armchair across from her.*] Wonderful, wonderful, at last you're back.

ELİZA BİNEMECİYAN: Yes, sir, I was unhappy in Paris. I felt homesick for Istanbul. I was restless and nervous.

MINISTER: Well, Istanbul does that to you, doesn't it? It won't let you go away. Istanbul was missing you, too. A couple of Muslim actresses tried to appear on the stage, but the public did not tolerate it. In fact, the Office of Religious Affairs didn't want to give them permission to act. The grand vizier, too, doesn't want Muslim women to go on the stage at this time.

ELİZA BİNEMECİYAN: I can understand that, sir. You know I am an actress. Acting is in my blood. I couldn't stay away from it even in Paris. I appeared in a couple of plays in a small theater while I was there. I was hoping to act in the Dramatic Arts Theater again when I got back to Istanbul. But when I came back, I found out that in my temple there is a young lady called Afife Hanım. Kınar Hanım says she is very successful.

MINISTER: But, Eliza Hanım, we want to see you perform at the Dramatic Arts Theater. That way we'll have the pleasure of having you back on the stage, and at the same time we'll be relieved of this constant, annoying pressure the Office of Religious Affairs is putting on us. The grand vizier's wishes, too, will be fulfilled.

ELİZA BİNEMECİYAN: I'm really sorry, sir, but as long as Afife Hanım is at the Dramatic Arts Theater, I won't be able to act there. You understand . . .

MINISTER: Leave that to me. We'll take care of those minor matters. I'll send my instructions. After the dust settles and the way is clear, you can start acting. It'll be a great pleasure for all of us to see you on stage. And this unpleasant matter of Muslim women acting on the stage will come to an end. [ELİZA BİNEMECİYAN *gets up, smoothes her skirt, picks up her parasol, and extends her hand to the* MINISTER.]

ELİZA BİNEMECİYAN: All these matters are over my head. I have no opinion whatsoever. I am an actress; I would like to perform where I belong. Sir, I thank you for your kind invitation. With my respects, sir . . .

Scene 2

[*The executive board of the Dramatic Arts Theater is meeting. The* BOARD MEMBERS *are sitting around the table.* AFİFE, *her face unveiled, is standing up. She is frightened and agitated, but determined. She walks slowly toward them and looks as though she is about to faint.*]

CHAIRMAN: Afife Hanım, the Municipal Council of Istanbul sent us a written order dated 27 February 1921, number 204. I regret to tell you that this directive concerns you, which is why we asked you to attend our meeting today. Unfortunately, this directive is a blemish on our theater's history and a disgraceful act against progress. We are ordered that from now on no Muslim woman will perform on our stage and that Afife Hanım is to be dismissed from the company. Today is 8 March. At our meetings, we have debated for nine days how to deal with this most unfortunate order, and finally, feeling helpless, we have decided to obey it. Otherwise, we would have no choice but to close the theater. We wanted to inform you, hoping that you will understand this decision. May God forgive us. [*Everybody hangs his head low.*]

AFİFE: I understand, sir.

CHAIRMAN: You may see the treasurer to receive what is owed to you.

AFİFE: I will not go to the treasurer, sir. [*Walks away, and as she is about to exit, she turns with tears in her eyes.*] You have told me about your decision. You are relieved now. You have gotten rid of a problem, or at least you think so. In another country, this action would have created a huge outcry. Now I realize I am alone in this fight. If you allow me, sir, I will tell you my decision. You can get rid of me, you can throw me out, but I will continue in my efforts, fighting on alone. [*Holds her head high and walks away with tears streaming down her face.*]

Scene 3

[AFİFE's *living room. She is reclining on the velvet chaise longue. Her eyes are covered with a band of black cloth. She moves her head from side to side and moans.*]

AFİFE: Oh, my head . . . my head. I can't stand it anymore. I can't. Mother, my head . . . [METHİYE *comes slowly, holding a bottle of eau de cologne.*]

METHİYE: Let me rub your temples a little; it'll make you feel better.

AFİFE: I can't touch my head it hurts so much.

METHİYE: Let me rub . . . I won't hurt, my father taught me how. [*Starts rubbing* AFİFE's *temples with cologne.*]

AFİFE: My grandfather the doctor . . . I miss him so much. Mother, where's the doctor who was supposed to come?

METHİYE: He'll come. When I got to his place, he had already left to visit a patient. I left a message; he'll come.

AFİFE: Why should I have such a terrible headache?

METHİYE: You're aggravating yourself. You're killing yourself. What's there to cry about like this and be so upset?

AFİFE: Mother, they threw me out of the Dramatic Arts Theater . . . threw me out by written order number 204 of 27 February. With one stroke, I was dismissed from the company. The Dramatic Arts Theater ordered this. Why shouldn't I cry and be distraught?

METHİYE: Look, you're sick. Is it worth it? There's a cure for every ailment. If it isn't the Dramatic Arts Theater, it can be the company of Burhanettin Bey. And if not that, you can join İbnürrefik Nuri Bey's New Theater.

AFİFE: They'll all be censored. Nobody will dare to let me join his company, you'll see. Mother, it's as if I'm cursed. Oh, my head, my eyes . . . I'm dying. I think it's better that I die; I should die.

METHİYE: Don't talk like that. It's not like you; you're strong, brave, and determined. [*The doorbell rings.*] Oh, it's the door. It must be the doctor. I'll go and see. [*Goes out and returns with* DR. SUAT, *an elegant, handsome, and dark man around thirty to thirty-five years old. He is carrying his doctor's bag.*]

DR. SUAT: How's the patient?

METHİYE: Come here, Doctor.

DR. SUAT: What's our patient's complaint?

METHİYE: She has an unbearable headache. She feels nauseated every now and then. Her eyes are very sensitive to light. Light feels like pins and needles in her eyes.

DR. SUAT: Yes. [*Puts his chair near the chaise longue and takes* AFİFE'*s pulse and counts.*] She has a slight fever. Let's take her temperature.

METHİYE: I'll bring the thermometer.

DR. SUAT: Don't bother, I have one. [*Takes the thermometer from his bag and hands it to* METHİYE, *who puts it under* AFİFE'*s arm.*]

AFİFE: Gently, don't shake me.

DR. SUAT: Can I open your eyes for one second? I have to see your pupils. [*Removes the black cloth.*]

AFİFE: [*Closes her eyes.*] Ah, they're burning.

DR. SUAT: Oh, aren't you Afife Jale Hanım? [*She becomes more animated, looks at him, and seems to like him.*] Ah, Afife Hanım, should I tell you that I am one of your admirers? What's the matter with you? Did they make you unhappy? Did they wear you out? What's happened? [*As he talks, he examines* AFİFE'*s eyelids and peers into her eyes.*]

AFİFE: They fired me from the Dramatic Arts Theater on the orders of the Ministry of the Interior and the orders of the head of religious affairs and also at Eliza Binemeciyan's insistence. [*Imitates her.*] "If Afife is there, count me out."

DR. SUAT: It's a shame. You're right to be unhappy, but not this much. Nothing is as important as your health, nor should it be.

AFİFE: I don't want to live anymore. Life has no meaning for me.

DR. SUAT: No, no . . . I can't believe it. Your nerves are at the point of breaking. You have no resistance left. We have to make you rest. You have to calm down.

METHİYE: If one doesn't eat, doesn't drink, and doesn't sleep for twenty-four hours and only cries . . .

DR. SUAT: [*Fills a needle with medicine.*] It'll pass. We'll make Afife Hanım feel relaxed. She'll understand that nothing in life is worth so much unhappiness. She is very young. She is very beautiful, even more beautiful than she is on the stage. [*Gives her an injection in her arm.*] Now you are going to feel better. Lie down on your back. Close your beautiful eyes again. Let yourself go as though you're immersed in warm water. [*Spreads the blanket over* AFİFE, *takes out the prescription pad, and talks gently with* METHİYE *as he writes.*] I'm going to prescribe two medicines. She can start taking them tomorrow. Let her sleep today. Don't let anybody come near her. She shouldn't talk about her problems. The medicine may have an adverse reaction; it might affect her mind. [*Hands the prescription to* METHİYE.] There's nothing to worry about. You shouldn't worry so much either. I'll drop in tomorrow evening.

METHİYE: We thank you, Doctor. She's calmer already. [*Hands him an envelope.*] Sir, this is what we owe you.

DR. SUAT: No, no, I won't take it. I haven't done anything yet. Let our patient be on her feet and feel as fit as a fiddle first. With your permission . . . [*Picks up his bag.*] Look, she's already asleep.

Scene 4

[*Same place.* AFİFE *is sitting on the sofa and feeling better.* BURHANETTİN TEPSİ *is sitting in an armchair across from her.* AFİFE *is happy because they have reached an agreement. She will be able to act in his company.*]

BURHANETTİN: We have a deal. So I must get going, and you try to get well as soon as possible, OK?

AFİFE: Yes, sir. Burhanettin Bey, shall I bring Seniye along? You ought to try her. I think she's a very talented girl. We've been together since we were children. We used to put up a curtain at home and act together.

BURHANETTİN: Bring her along, but she has to act in a comedy, *Hamit, the Miser.* It's a good play. [*Gets up.*] When you come, you'll get an advance on your salary. Try to have a good sleep tonight. Don't worry about anything. I don't want to see you looking like a ghost ever again.

AFİFE: Yes, sir. Thank you.

BURHANETTİN: You should know that you'll be the leading star in my company. [*Exits.*]

[AFİFE *takes a hand mirror from under her pillow and looks at herself.* METHİYE *walks in with excitement.*]

METHİYE: Afife, look who came to visit you. [KINAR *and* ANAİS *enter noisily, carrying flowers and boxes of chocolates.*]

KINAR: I hope you feel well now.

AFİFE: [*Elatedly.*] Ah, thank God! You brought me good health. You've made my day.

ANAİS: Your mother gave us the good news. You've joined Burhanettin Bey's company.

KINAR: Well, that's how it is—just mention Afife's name, and the whole world will be at your feet. You acted in *The Patches, The Sweet Secret,* and *The Odalisque* so well . . . even better than our Eliza Hanım.

ANAİS: Acted? She created those roles, my dear.

KINAR: My mother, let her soul rest in peace, taught me all about the theater. She certainly had a life. The whole world adored Bercuhi. Fasulyacıyan's company was Bercuhi. But she also suffered so much. Did you know about it? Actresses don't talk much; they live both Heaven and Hell in this world. Now, come to your senses and stop worrying. I, too, have suffered from Eliza Binemeciyan's inflated ego. If I told my story, it would fill volumes. One can write a play about the tricks she played to snatch the role of the baker's wife from me. I'm not joking.

ANAÏS: She's a beautiful woman. She has a lovely voice and is articulate. Her fame rests on her beauty, and she gets along well with the Ottoman bigwigs, so, in turn, they support her.

KINAR: Anais, we've chattered too much. Look at this girl. She's so thin and pale and exhausted. Let's leave.

AFİFE: [*Sadly.*] You have to leave for the rehearsal, right?

KINAR: We hope so, but we have to see. If it's like yesterday, we won't be able to rehearse.

AFİFE: What are you going to perform?

ANAÏS: Kınar Hanım will act in *Gülnihal*. I don't know what role I'll have. To have any fun we have to start rehearsing before that Binemeciyan woman starts tooting her own horn. But she won't step into the theater before her trunks arrive from Paris.

KINAR: Let's go. [KINAR, ANAİS, and METHİYE *exit amid the sounds of "bye-bye, get well," and so on.* AFİFE *returns to the room and sits on the sofa. She holds her head in her hands. The guests were too exciting and exhausting for her.* METHİYE *reenters.*]

METHİYE: What's the matter, dear?

AFİFE: It came back.

METHİYE: [*Absentmindedly.*] What came back?

AFİFE: My headache. I was afraid it would happen again. It came back, from here . . . from my temples. [*Points.*] It's piercing both my eyes and my head. It's like a drill.

METHİYE: Afife, you're tired, you're depressed. The girls talked too much and made you excited. Don't panic, just lie down here. Close your eyes. This dim light will be soothing for you. I'll give you an aspirin.

AFİFE: [*Nervously.*] No. Send a message to the doctor, tell him that it came back, that it's terrible.

METHİYE: I'll go right away . . . but you call him so often, and he doesn't accept any money. What are we going to do?

AFİFE: Mother! [METHİYE *closes the door gently.*]

Scene 5

[*Same place.* AFİFE *is nicely dressed, sparkling, sitting with magazines on her lap. The lamps are lit.* METHİYE *walks back and forth in the room and then sits down.*]

AFİFE: [*Outwardly cheerful, but restless and nervous.*] I'm scared to death that my headache will come back. Mother, is it the doorbell? Mother, it's the door. Hurry up. [METHİYE *exits. The door opens and* DR. SUAT *enters.*]

DR. SUAT: Good evening, how's our patient today?

AFİFE: [*Gets up and shakes* DR. SUAT'*s hand.*] If one has a gentle doctor like you, sickness goes away. Doctor, that day, when I had that excruciating pain, you gave me a shot with your magic hand and made me alive again. I can't forget the wonderful relaxed feeling it gave me. I wonder if you would write a prescription that I can keep and have it filled at the pharmacy whenever I need it. I dread these headaches. Then we won't bother you so often. [METHİYE *enters with the coffee tray.*]

METHİYE: Since that day she's been so agitated, she keeps repeating, "If it comes back, if it comes back." Doctor, she herself is forcing the pain to come back.

DR. SUAT: No, Afife Hanım, what you asked for can't be done. I can't hand you the prescription. You have to be under a doctor's care; otherwise, we'll have trouble. But I hope you won't need it anymore. Don't worry about it.

AFİFE: If you drop in once in a while and say, "Here I am," I may not get my headaches.

METHİYE: Well, well . . . isn't that just like my daughter—whatever she thinks, she blurts out. She doesn't have an evil streak in her.

DR. SUAT: There can't be anything bad in her anyway. If you kindly ask me to show up once in a while, I'll be honored and delighted to visit you.

METHİYE: You two sit here. I have to go to the kitchen to finish my chores. [*Picks up the coffee cups and exits.*]

Scene 6

[MINISTER OF THE INTERIOR MEHMET ALİ, *is sitting at his desk. He is very haughty and condescending. He keeps hitting the writing pad with a ruler.*]

MINISTER: Burhanettin Bey, I have to discuss something with you. Which play are you putting on now?

BURHANETTİN: We're rehearsing *Napoleon,* sir. Once a week we perform *Hamit, the Miser.*

MINISTER: *Napoleon!* Are there women in it?

BURHANETTİN: Of course, sir. Josephine is the leading one.

MINISTER: Yes, yes. Who is playing Josephine?

BURHANETTİN: Afife Hanım, sir. She's a great actress. I'm sure you've heard of her fame.

MINISTER: Didn't they fire her from the Dramatic Arts Theater?

BURHANETTİN: [*Stiffening.*] She's working for us now.

MINISTER: Burhanettin Bey, what I'm going to tell you now is not my personal opinion. Not at all. His Excellency the grand vizier doesn't want Muslim women to appear on stage. I'm just telling you that before it's too late to prevent trouble. It would be advisable to dismiss the Muslim women in your company. I'm only telling you the grand vizier's wishes, as a friend.

BURHANETTİN: I am grateful, sir, but I would like to know what would happen if I don't fire the Muslim actresses.

MINISTER: [*As if joking.*] Then we'll have trouble.

BURHANETTİN: His Excellency the grand vizier may personally think so, but I . . .

MINISTER: Look, Burhanettin Bey, if you don't heed my advice, you should know that we'll solve this problem by resorting to the police.

BURHANETTIN: [*Bowing his head respectfully in an exaggerated manner.*] I pay my respects, sir.

Scene 7

[*The same part of* AFİFE's *living room as in Act II, Scene 5.* METHİYE *and* HÜSEYİN KEMAL *sit facing each other.* HÜSEYİN KEMAL *is holding a cup of tea in his hand.*]

HÜSEYİN KEMAL: [*Engrossed in thought.*] Well . . . since when?

METHİYE: She had always complained of headaches, but since the day she learned that she was fired from the Dramatic Arts Theater, they became worse. She's been suffering from excruciatingly painful headaches, one after the other. Dr. Suat, a man of Syrian origin, is treating her. I think he is sentimentally attached to her, too. He comes often. His medicine gives Afife temporary relief, but then . . . afterward she is again . . . you won't be able to recognize her. She's become so thin, so frail, so emaciated. [AFİFE's *bedroom door opens. Wearing a nightgown, she enters the living room. At first, she doesn't see* HÜSEYİN KEMAL.]

AFİFE: Mother! Suat Bey should come and give me a shot. I can't bear it anymore.

HÜSEYİN KEMAL: [*Stands up.*] Afife Hanım . . .

AFİFE: [*Looks at him as though she doesn't recognize him.*] Oh! Hüseyin Kemal Bey . . . why did you bother to come all the way here? [*Collapses in the chair.*] I am suffering so much. [*Smiling.*] Maybe I have a brain tumor, though I always thought I had a tumor in my heart. It was a theater tumor. Right now I have a terrible headache, Kemal Bey, terrible. Mother, the doctor has to . . .

METHİYE: He said he would come this evening.

AFİFE: Now, now . . .

METHİYE: My dear, he's not home now; he's visiting his patients. We have to wait a little.

AFİFE: [*Very nervous.*] I'm dying; I can't stand it anymore. He has to come right now. He knows how to handle it; let him do whatever has to be done. He brings me relief.

HÜSEYİN KEMAL: I think I'm disturbing you. I should leave . . . with your permission . . .

METHİYE: [*Pleadingly.*] Please stay, please, please.

AFİFE: I'll put on a sweater and come back; I'm freezing. Why should you be disturbing us, Kemal Bey? Please don't go. [*Goes out.*]

METHİYE: [*Lowers her voice.*] That medicine he injects, whatever it is, makes my daughter feel really good, but I'm very worried. I think of terrible things. Please sit down. You've helped us so much. You're like an older brother to her. Ah, a young woman cannot be put under so much pressure. Please sit down. Maybe you will help me a little. [AFİFE *enters. At this moment, the distant sounds of a lute and a song come through the window. It is* SELÂHATTİN's *music.*]

AFİFE: [*Listens to the music for a moment.*] Isn't it beautiful? It's a young musician named Selâhattin.

THE SONG:

> *Months have gone by, but you still haven't come to me,*
> *Isn't this separation long enough? Should it last forever?*
> *The source of my inspiration is a fresh flower;*
> *Oh, don't make me wait; you, too, may fade and perish.*

HÜSEYİN KEMAL: Indeed, very beautiful. He must be living near here.

AFİFE: [*Rubs her temples.*] I don't know where exactly. Obviously very near us. [*Tries to smile.*] I sometimes think he composed these songs for me; I dream about it, and I'm pleased.

METHİYE: Why should you fade and perish? You never harmed anybody. They've always done you in.

AFİFE: Kemal Bey, you must have heard; they sent a written order to Burhanettin Bey that states categorically that no Muslim woman can perform on the stage. It was sent by the minister of the interior on the grand vizier's orders. It is his command.

HÜSEYİN KEMAL: Was it a British officer of the occupation army who brought the letter?

AFİFE: Yes, as if the instructions weren't enough, they also sent a letter. Where did you hear that?

HÜSEYİN KEMAL: Then the play about Napoleon is going to be canceled? Such news spreads fast.

AFİFE: [*With haste.*] Nooo! After that letter, Burhanettin Bey said, "If they resort to such manipulation, then I'll go to the French occupation headquarters and ask for their protection to put *Napoleon* on the stage." But probably nobody knows about it.

HÜSEYİN KEMAL: Did he do it?

AFİFE: Yes, he did. They promised to put the theater under their protection tomorrow.

HÜSEYİN KEMAL: God help you. Well, I have to leave. [*To* METHİYE.] There's nothing to worry about. Thank God, Afife is doing well. Look, after seeing me, her headache stopped bothering her.

AFİFE: It's true . . . really, then why do you have to leave?

HÜSEYİN KEMAL: It's time to go. [*As he walks toward* METHİYE.] Tell me if there's anything I can do for you. Good-bye. [*Leans to kiss* METHİYE's *hand.*]

Scene 8

[*Same place,* AFİFE *and* DR. SUAT.]

DR. SUAT: Don't be afraid, Afife Hanım. In the shots I give you, there is a minimum dose of morphine. We give this to many of our patients.

AFİFE: Morphine?

DR. SUAT: That was the only way to stop your pain. I, too, have frequent headaches and give myself the same injection when I have to. There's nothing wrong with it.

AFİFE: But if I become dependent on it . . .

DR. SUAT: This dosage doesn't create dependence. Not usually. When your problems are straightened out, you won't want it anymore. Your nerves will be calmed, and your headaches will stop.

AFİFE: My problems won't be straightened out. I won't be able to work in any theater. Our money is about to run out. If I become dependent on it, how can I find it, with what money, from which pharmacy . . .

DR. SUAT: [*Holds* AFİFE's *hands.*] My dear Afife—let me call you that, as though you are a part of me—Afife, what am I good for? I already confessed before, but let me do it again. I love you. I adore you. My father is a Syrian silk trader. He is as rich as Croesus, and I am his only heir. Marry me. Be my wife. You and your mother can be . . .

AFİFE: Doctor, please, first give me a shot. Please, quick . . .

DR. SUAT: Your haste, your rashness, your irritability worry me. You must calm down a bit. You'll upset people who are close to you.

AFİFE: Doctor, I don't care if anybody is upset. Come on, I can't stand the pain anymore. Look, my hands are shaking. See, I'm breaking out in a cold sweat. Doctor, please . . . I'm going to scream now. Mother will come and see me like this. She'll be devastated. Please, please. [*Starts crying.*] Please help me.

DR. SUAT: [*Without any feeling of sympathy.*] Afife, are you going to marry me? Promise me, promise!

AFİFE: You're so cruel. What's the use of a promise I give you now?

DR. SUAT: It's OK. Just say "I promise." I'm ready. [*Shows her the hypodermic needle.*]

AFİFE: All right, all right, I promise.

DR. SUAT: Well . . . then in your honor I'll give myself a treat, too. Afife, we'll have a high together.

Scene 9

[AFİFE's *living room.* METHİYE *is snoozing on the sofa. The door opens suddenly;* AFİFE, BURHANETTİN, *and* SENİYE *enter.* METHİYE *jumps up.*]

AFİFE: I'm sorry, Mother. I woke you up.

METHİYE: Never mind, I was dozing a little. What's happening?

BURHANETTİN: Excuse us, madam. We're sorry.

SENİYE: We were thoughtless.

METHİYE: Doesn't matter. I'll make you a nice cup of tea. [*Looks for her slippers.*] You came back safe and sound.

BURHANETTİN: The performance was excellent, but to save these ladies from the police we had to escape through the cemetery in the dark. Afife was scared to death.

AFİFE: When the branches of the trees touched my face, I thought the dead were caressing me. I'm terribly afraid of the dead.

BURHANETTİN: But none of the dead will harm you as much as these living people.

SENİYE: Are you still shaking and trembling?

AFİFE: What will they do to us tomorrow morning?

BURHANETTİN: The theater will be closed. That's it. They can't do much else.

AFİFE: What else, what else?

BURHANETTİN: You're crying!

AFİFE: [*Wiping off her tears.*] Yes, because my theater is closed again. But this time it isn't just that. Tonight, for the first time, I'm crying for another reason—because I'm without work and penniless.

BURHANETTİN: [*Anxiously and emphatically.*] Afife, my dear, I can help you.

SENİYE: Come with us to Egypt. We'll go there soon after we get married.

AFİFE: One can't accept money if one doesn't earn it.

BURHANETTİN: You can't think like that in the world of the theater.

AFİFE: I believe in the dignity of my profession. I can't live there on charity.

SENİYE: We'll perform in Egypt, and you'll pay back Burhanettin. Come with us!

AFİFE: Seniye, my dear, I don't know why, but I cannot leave Istanbul. [*The sounds of lute and song are heard from afar.*] Oh, the lute player . . . that young man . . .

SENİYE: He has such a sweet voice.

BURHANETTİN: Young ladies, permit me to go. I'm very tired tonight.

AFİFE: Aren't you going to have a cup of tea with us?

BURHANETTİN: I'd rather have something stronger, but you two don't know anything about that. Well . . . I say good night to you. [METHİYE *enters with the tea tray.*]

METHİYE: Oh, are you going away? The tea is ready, nicely brewed.

BURHANETTİN: Let the young ladies drink. God be with you. [*Exits.* AFİFE *accompanies him to the door.*]

METHİYE: It's wonderful that you're going to marry Burhanettin Bey. My daughter is incapable of doing something like that. Her mind is so occupied with the blasted theater that she sees nothing else.

SENİYE: She's still so young.

METHİYE: Yes, but time flies by before you know it. [AFİFE *enters and understands that they are talking about her; she is upset.*]

AFİFE: Mother, you should go to bed, it's getting late.

METHİYE: Seniye Hanım's bed . . .

AFİFE: I'll make it.

METHİYE: I was going to say that I made it. Good night, children. [*Exits. The two young women hold their teacups and seem to be deep in thought.*]

AFİFE: [*Sadly.*] So the company is going to break up. I feel as if I'm like a slate, constantly being written on and constantly being erased. My splitting headaches don't let me rest. There's no one, no money, no work. I've had enough, enough, enough.

SENİYE: [*Startled.*] Afife, be sensible, your mother will hear. What's the matter with you?

AFİFE: [*More subdued.*] I can't stand it anymore. I'm unable to do anything I want. I can't even scream to my heart's content.

SENİYE: Look, I'm telling you again, you're a great actress; you're wasted here.

AFİFE: But if I'm going to do something, I want to do it here. That's it.

SENİYE: Afife, I want to tell you something, but please don't be mad at me.

AFİFE: Go ahead.

SENİYE: Afife, Dr. Suat can't find a cure for your trouble.

AFİFE: [*Disturbed.*] I have terrible headaches.

SENİYE: So . . .

AFİFE: So . . . he's the doctor.

SENİYE: I want to go to Egypt with my heart at ease. You know how much I love you, ever since the days we set up a curtain and acted in your parents' home. I want to help you. I feel uneasy.

AFİFE: [*Coolly.*] Why? Anyway, I'll find work.

SENİYE: I'm not worried that you'll be without work. Burhanettin Bey talked to İbnürrefik Bey and told him to employ you in case his company broke up. They'll get in touch with you soon.

AFİFE: [*Becoming more spirited.*] Really? Why didn't you tell me before?

SENİYE: What if you don't see this Dr. Suat and see another doctor?

AFİFE: You talk like my mother!

SENİYE: Is it impossible?

AFİFE: I don't know what to say. Let's go to sleep.

SENİYE: I understand.

AFİFE: [*Puts the tea service on the tray and walks away.*] Good night, dear.

Scene 10

[DR. SUAT's *office.* AFİFE *is sitting in an armchair.* DR. SUAT *is sitting on the corner of the table. He hands her the cigarette he takes from the corner of his mouth.*]

DR. SUAT: Here, take it, take a puff, you'll feel better.

AFİFE: [*Takes the cigarette and inhales.*] There's no hope, right? For days, I've been having nightmares. I've fought the whole world. I've tried not to come to you. Why did you do this to me? Why, Doctor? Didn't you take the Hippocratic oath?

DR. SUAT: You were suffering too much. You couldn't stand the pain.

AFİFE: I wish I were dead. You did this to me deliberately. Why? Don't tell me that I was suffering. Now I'm suffering much more. I'm ashamed besides, and I hate both you and myself.

DR. SUAT: Then you shouldn't have come. I didn't invite you.

AFİFE: I can't help it. I can't stand the pain.

DR. SUAT: What do you want?

AFİFE: You know what I want.

DR. SUAT: What about your promise? Is it still there?

AFİFE: Yes, please, or do something else . . . kill me, please.

DR. SUAT: Why? Why should you be wasted, Afife? I loved you from the first day I saw you. I wanted you to be mine. For you to be dependent on me. Perhaps I wanted you to be like me. Maybe so that I could dominate you. Don't you understand?

AFİFE: Oh, come on, I don't want to hear anything now. Please, hurry up and give me a shot.

DR. SUAT: [*Hugs* AFİFE.] Will you be mine?

AFİFE: [*Violently.*] No, no! Why? [*Frees herself from* DR. SUAT. *He tries to look her in the eye.*]

DR. SUAT: Be mine. If not, I can't give you anything. I won't. Marry me . . . and everything will be all right. If you don't want to get married, let's live together . . . the two of us . . .

AFİFE: [*Cries.*] No, no, no. I can't bring myself to do that, never.

DR. SUAT: Then leave at once. I can't control myself any longer. I'm warning you.

AFİFE: Please . . . have a little pity . . . only a little . . . just so I can pull myself together. I'll never disturb you again. Tomorrow I'm starting to act in a new play, with a new company and new players. Please!

DR. SUAT: If you don't belong to me, I won't do it.

AFİFE: I'll give you all my money. [*Takes a piece of jewelry out of her pocketbook.*] Look, this is a keepsake from my grandfather. It has great meaning for me, but it's also very valuable. I'll give it to you. [*Begins to rage.*] If you don't give me a shot, I'll scream. I'll tell everyone about you . . . tell everything . . . to your patients out there.

DR. SUAT: Be quiet! [*Holds* AFİFE's *arms and shakes her.*] Shut up or I'll smash your face. [*Lets go of her angrily.*] Last time! I don't ever want to see you here again. [*Prepares the injection.*] Last time. Goddamn it . . . take that damn piece of jewelry and get out. I'm not a usurer.

AFİFE: [*Somewhat relieved.*] You're a murderer!

Scene 11

[*The same part of* HIDAYET's *house as in Act I, Scene 6.* WOMEN NEIGHBORS *are sitting and talking in whispers.* METHİYE *and the* AUNT *are pacing the floor.* HİDAYET BEY *is dead; his coffin is carried out by some men.* AFİFE *enters the room looking distraught, sees the people, and withdraws.*]

FIRST WOMAN: Isn't that his daughter . . . the actress Afife?

AUNT: Yes, the poor man died of grief because of her.

SECOND WOMAN: [*Whispers in the* FIRST WOMAN's *ear.*] She's no beauty. I wonder why they make such a fuss about her.

AUNT: We never got along well. My late brother spoiled her.

METHİYE: She's still your niece, Aunt! How can you talk like this in front of strangers?

AUNT: She ruined herself. She became the laughingstock of the whole world.

FIRST WOMAN: I guess the men are coming back. A carriage stopped outside. Let's go. [*Gets up to go.*]

SECOND WOMAN: May God give a long life to the ones he left behind. [*As she walks out, she turns to* METHİYE.] My deepest sympathies for your grief.

METHİYE: [*Following the* WOMEN.] I wish I were dead. Oh my, my . . . [*Exits.*]

[AFİFE *slowly opens the door, quietly enters, and drops into an armchair. She is lonely and distressed. A little later* ZİYA *comes in and goes to her as soon as he sees her.*]

ZİYA: At last, I found you alone.

AFİFE: How could you? I don't exist anymore. I'm nothing.

ZİYA: There's not much time to waste. Come on, give up this useless game.

AFİFE: Where's Salâh?

ZİYA: He'll have a drink and come back. Afife, what's happened, what's going on? Please tell me. Why didn't you answer my letters and my telegrams?

AFİFE: Awful things happened, and awful things are still happening. [*Cries.*]

ZİYA: You have to tell me everything.

AFİFE: You won't be able to understand me.

ZİYA: So let it be. I'll still love you. You know that, don't you?

AFİFE: Yes, yes. And this fact is the source of our happiness as well as our sorrow.

ZİYA: I'm waiting for you.

AFİFE: When you went to the pond, you always said, "I'm waiting for you." Did we really live those days?

ZİYA: Whatever happens, just tell me if you still love me.

AFİFE: [*Talks uninhibitedly.*] I don't know anything anymore. The only thing I know is that I'm not what I used to be. My past, my present, and my whole being are full of you, yet it won't be possible for us to be together. My mother doesn't want it, either. She's right; we can never again be together. We shouldn't be. There's been only one happy night in my life—the first night I acted on the stage. I think God is stingy and thinks that this much happiness is enough for me.

ZİYA: Afife, stop this nonsense.

AFİFE: [*As if she doesn't hear.*] Sometimes I have nightmares. I say to myself, "I wish I never knew you." Perhaps like the expulsion of Eve from the Garden of Eden, my fall could have been easier. But then I think: How is it possible? If he didn't exist, if he didn't love me and didn't caress my hair and tell me "Afife, I love you," I might not have been able to endure all this. Don't blame me.

ZİYA: My dear Afife.

AFİFE: Don't blame me, my dear, I'm innocent.

ZİYA: Who's blaming you? It is I who has to be blamed. But my sin is not loving you; it's my inability to understand you. I can't figure you out.

AFİFE: Yes, just like the whole world.

ZİYA: Leave the whole world out of it. The theater, your mother, my mother, everything. Let's you and I, just the two of us, start everything anew. Come with me, darling, please come.

AFİFE: [*Talks like a child.*] I can't do it. I'm going to the theater to play a comedy. On the night Hidayet Bey died. I have no more right to choose. I'll play whatever luck brings along. Beggars can't be choosers. What would my grandfather have said? It's absurd. [*Exits.*]

Scene 12

[*The chief of police,* TAHSİN BEY, *at his desk examining the papers in front of him. Across from him, a young officer is standing at attention and waiting for the papers to be signed.* MINISTER OF THE INTERIOR MEHMET ALİ *suddenly and angrily rushes into the room.* TAHSİN *gets up respectfully, but is surprised.*]

TAHSİN: I'm at your service, sir.

MINISTER: Damn it. What are you up to?

TAHSİN: I've already explained, sir.

MINISTER: What do you mean I can't stop the play? I'm ordering it now. Raid the theater, stop the play, and arrest those two whores. That's all.

TAHSİN: Excuse me, sir. [*Raises his head higher.*] I can't do it. [*More resolutely.*] I won't.

MINISTER: Then get the hell out of this position.

TAHSİN: As you order, sir. I'll immediately offer my resignation.

MINISTER: There's no need to resign . . . you are fired!

[*Lights dim.*]

[*When the lights go on again, another man is sitting at the desk, with two women sitting across from him:* AFİFE *and* ŞAZİYE.]

POLICEMAN: Ladies, I'm sorry, but you are under arrest on the order of the new chief of police.

AFİFE: What are you waiting for? Go ahead and do what is required.

ŞAZİYE: [*Whispers.*] Afife, calm down a bit. [*Sounds from the outside are heard.*]

POLICEMAN: If you can pay, perhaps you can be released on bail. [İBNÜRREFİK NURİ *and three* MEN *enter suddenly.*] What's up? Who are you? You think this is just anybody's stopping place? Why did you barge in like this?

İBNÜRREFİK NURİ: Oh, we were afraid we would be late. Sir, we brought the money for the ladies' bail. [*Points to one of the* MEN.] This gentleman has the power of attorney to represent the ladies.

POLICEMAN: Good, then you're prepared.

İBNÜRREFİK NURİ: Sir, please give your instructions for the legal procedure.

POLICEMAN: OK, OK. Anyway I was wondering about what to do with these strange women. [AFİFE *and* ŞAZİYE *get up happily.*] Go and deposit the bail money with the treasurer. [*To* AFİFE *and* ŞAZİYE.] You two wait here; I'll be back. [*Except for* AFİFE *and* ŞAZİYE, *they all exit.*]

ŞAZİYE: [*Hugs* AFİFE.] Congratulations! It's over!

AFİFE: Again a game of chase. Again police precincts. You know what? I've forgotten how many times and why. The price of crime. Again out of work and broke. We don't even have anything left to sell.

ŞAZİYE: Would you like to come with me?

AFİFE: Where?

ŞAZİYE: You're my mentor; you got me started in this profession. I have friends who will help me escape to Anatolia. There's the bail, but we'll pay it back to our friends. Mustafa Kemal Pasha has come a long way. The government here is in its death throes. There's a small company that's preparing for the Anatolian tour. We can join them. Please come.

AFİFE: One never changes. As long as one is alive, one's nature never changes. As usual, I hope to do something right here. Mother is insisting on going to Kastamonu for a few weeks to visit my sister. I'll take her there. I may be able to rest a little there, think things over, and come to a decision. Thank you very much, but I can't come. [*With more emphasis.*] I cannot.

Scene 13

[AFİFE *is in her room in the late hours of the night. She is pacing the floor nervously and wringing her hands. She seems to be suffering. Some of it is due to her craving for the morphine, but she is also physically ill and in pain. She finally sits on the chaise longue, covers her face with her hands, and cries. The doorbell rings. She lifts her head and listens to the sound, then goes to open the door, wiping away her tears. When she returns, she is with* ZİYA. *She is bewildered, full of emotion, frightened. It is as if she is about to run away, but is indecisive.* ZİYA *is wearing a raincoat and sunglasses and has an attaché case. As he enters the room, he takes off his sunglasses and the raincoat.*]

AFİFE: Is that really you?

ZİYA: [*Looks at her intently.*] You have become so thin.

AFİFE: I'm unable to pull myself together.

ZİYA: What's bothering you?

AFİFE: [*Sadly.*] You always ask me the same question—"What's bothering you?" What are you doing here, in Istanbul?

ZİYA: I came here on a mission for Mustafa Kemal Pasha. I have to get back soon, but I couldn't leave without seeing you.

AFİFE: [*Sobs quietly.*] I wish you hadn't. I have no strength left to bear all this. [*Wipes her tears with the handkerchief* ZİYA *hands to her.*] Are you all right?

ZİYA: Except for life without you, I'm all right.

AFİFE: Mother told me you're going to get married.

ZİYA: I bet my mother spread that news. She has her own plans, but as far as I'm concerned, such a thing is possible only with you.

AFİFE: But I'm out of it. I stopped existing. I couldn't cope . . . I've been fired so many times. I'm without work again and broke. I'm about to lose my mind.

ZİYA: [*Holds* AFİFE's *arms gently with sympathy.*] Afife, who is it? Who's the person who harmed you? What did he do to you? I'm dying to know. Could it be me? My burning passion for you?

AFİFE: [*Laughs like a child.*] Are you mad? Please, dear, don't ask. You're so precious, so important, and so unattainable for me. Ziya, dear, go away from here. I don't want you to get mixed up in all this mess.

ZİYA: What does that mean? We don't have to start our journey until 2:00 A.M. I have time. I can't leave you like this.

AFİFE: But you have to go anyway.

ZİYA: Where's your mother?

AFİFE: She went to Üsküdar to say good-bye. She'll take me to Kastamonu. She's exhausted, too. I'm going there to please her.

ZİYA: It may be a good change. Will you work for Fikret Şadi's company?

AFİFE: If you can call that working.

ZİYA: Look, you have to know one thing for sure. You must believe me. Whatever you are . . . whatever happened in the past, nothing can change my feelings about you. Whatever you may think about yourself, your place in my heart remains the same. You are untarnished and pure. I'm not going to ask you about the past if you don't want to tell me. You might have gone through a lot, Afife, but to me you're the same innocent little girl—naughty, stubborn, and rebellious. You're free to be what you want to be, but don't get sick and don't be unhappy. I love you. [*Embraces and kisses* AFİFE.]. My dearest, my only one. [AFİFE *embraces him, crying at the same time.*]

Scene 14

[GOVERNOR FUAT BEY's *residence in Kastamonu.* METHİYE *and* BEHİYE *are sitting in armchairs in front of the window in a large sitting room.* METHİYE *is sad.* BEHİYE *is confused and a little angry.*]

BEHİYE: I hope it's true. I don't know, but these things aren't that simple.

METHİYE: But, my dear, we came here ten days ago. She has neither complained of headaches nor asked for the injections. If she didn't feel well, she wouldn't be able to act like this.

BEHİYE: Everything is because of the damned theater. Everything. All instead of getting married nicely and having children . . . she should have been concerned with a home, a husband—a true vocation.

METHİYE: Maybe it wasn't her fate to be like that.

BEHİYE: Mother! You've supported and protected her too much. You abandoned Father because of her. You two made him die of grief.

METHİYE: You talk like your aunt. If I had abandoned her and kicked her out like you did, what would she have done? She's my child. She didn't ask for something bad. What she wanted to do was a beautiful thing, but she couldn't do it. The whole world was against her.

BEHİYE: [*Listens to the sound coming from the street.*] Oh, well . . . I think Fuat Bey's coming. Where's Afife?

METHİYE: She was lying down in the room where we're sleeping. Please, Behiye, keep your mouth shut. Please, my dear.

BEHİYE: Mother, it isn't what you think. I'm not Afife's enemy. [*Gets up and walks toward the door.*] I love her.

FUAT: [*Enters with a long face, looking serious.*] Good evening, Mother!

METHİYE: [*Gets up.*] Good evening, my son.

BEHİYE: Would you like a cup of coffee?

FUAT: Yes, my dear wife. [BEHİYE *exits.*] Today I had to face a terribly annoying problem in my office. I didn't know what to do; I couldn't believe my ears. I was dumbfounded. I was furious, and I shouted. The people around me were stunned, too.

METHİYE: Good heavens, can you tell me what happened?

FUAT: It concerns Afife. An unbelievable thing! Perhaps you know about it.

METHİYE: [*Very frightened.*] About what? [BEHİYE *walks in with the coffee tray and remains standing.*]

FUAT: [*Addresses both of them.*] The pharmacist Salih came. It seems he wanted to see me alone. I couldn't understand why, but I let him come in. He noticed recently that morphine had been stolen from his pharmacy. For a few days, he followed his assistant and caught the man red-handed. When he grilled him, the assistant started crying and got on his knees and told him he was doing it for the governor's sister-in-law. He said that she was forcing him, begging him, and paying a lot of money. Do you know how serious this is? The sister-in-law of the honorable governor of Kastamonu is an addict. She used my title to bring that horrible stuff into my house. What will happen to me if this news gets around?

METHİYE: [*Stands up.*] My dear Fuat, believe me, I know nothing, I swear. I was just telling Behiye what we went through. She had terrible headaches. My God . . . that's what I was afraid of. Believe me, Afife is not a bad person. Forgive her.

FUAT: I didn't say anything, but what she did was bad. She got me into trouble.

METHİYE: We'll go back to Istanbul right away.

FUAT: Mother, don't be so rash. Your return to Istanbul will solve nothing. If this story is true, then she should immediately get good treatment. If you have patience, we'll have her treated here, and you don't have to worry about its cost. I don't say this to create panic here. I'm looking for ways to save her from this scourge. You can't go to Istanbul in a hurry like that. Where's Afife now?

BEHİYE: In her room.

FUAT: Can I talk to her? Only the two of us?

BEHİYE: I'll go and get her. [METHİYE *and* BEHİYE *exit*. FUAT *is looking out the window when* AFİFE *enters. She is high, under the drug's influence, pretty and sure of herself.*]

AFİFE: My dear brother-in-law, did you decide to open a theater in Kastamonu after our conversation last night?

FUAT: Afife, sit down, here. I talked to the pharmacist today. I know everything. Don't do anything foolish. We have to save you from this trouble. You have to do what I tell you. I talked to a doctor friend. I'll be locking you up in the library for a few days, and you won't be allowed to go out. We'll go to your room now and get your things—your night-gown, your towel, your comb. I'm doing this for your own good. Behiye will remove all the dangerous things from the library, the book opener and the scissors. Your mother can help us to sort your things. I'll bring your breakfast and dinner myself. The library has its own bathroom. Nobody will open the door. This captivity will last only for a week or so, not longer. Tomorrow I'll bring the doctor. It's better like this than being the slave of that horrible poison for a lifetime. Don't you agree, my dear? Come, let's go to your room. I don't want my two sons or the servants to find out about this. Am I making myself clear? [*Walks, pulling* AFİFE *by the arm. She is completely shaken.*]

AFİFE: Dear Fuat, please kill me, please, please.

Scene 15

[BEHİYE's *sitting room at night. There is a feeling of silence and loneliness. Only a small light is on.* METHİYE *enters in her nightgown, her hair tousled. She is agitated, scared, and startled.* BEHİYE *enters from another door.*]

BEHİYE: Mother, what's going on? What happened?

METHİYE: Behiye, Afife escaped.

BEHİYE: Escaped? Don't tell me that. The door is locked; she's inside. Fuat locked the door. I saw it with my own eyes. He's got the key.

METHİYE: She's not in there. I know it.

BEHİYE: Mother, that's nonsense. She can't get out of there.

METHİYE: Come, look from this window. You can see the library's windows from here. [*They open the window and lean out.* BEHİYE *turns with her fist covering her mouth.*

She is trembling.] Didn't you see the sheets? The window is open. I knocked on the door—there was no answer. I wanted to check before I went to bed, to see if her light was on. She escaped, and this is the note she pinned on the door.

BEHİYE: [*Reads.*] "My dearest mother, I am going to face my fate. I know what I'm doing. After all the bad luck I've gone through, to be imprisoned is humiliating. I've endured it for four days. I can't say anything against Fuat; he was right. But I can't take it anymore. I was forced to take the sixty lira from your pocketbook. Do forgive me. I've made you and all the others so unhappy. Forgive me. Stay with Behiye, try to rest and relax a little."

Scene 16

[*Under the Bozdoğan Kemeri,[7] a small dilapidated wooden house belonging to* SALÂH. *There are only a few pieces of old furniture. The curtains are old, the floor is warped, and so on.* SALÂH *and* AFİFE *are standing. Both are sad and tired.*]

SALÂH: What do you mean by "exploiting me"? I'm your older brother. I stay in this house only a couple of times a year when I come from Izmir. It's your house. I'll be your guest when I come here.

AFİFE: Thank you, dear brother.

SALÂH: I thank you for telling me everything as it is. I think you need a little stove. I'll get one for you before I leave. If you want, you can write Mother to join you soon.

AFİFE: No, let her have a little rest at my sister's place. I've made her very unhappy and very tired.

SALÂH: Anyway, write a letter. Don't put it off.

AFİFE: I wrote a letter and mailed it this morning. I wrote that I've found work, and you've let me have your house.

SALÂH: And about going to the doctor?

AFİFE: I'll write about it as soon as I go.

SALÂH: Write me, too. If you need anything, don't be shy. Whenever you feel like it, come to Izmir. I'll introduce you to your future sister-in-law.

AFİFE: My dear, you're so good. Now I have a job; I even managed to get an advance against my salary. We're starting on Thursday, believe it or not.

SALÂH: I sure know you! Well . . . it's time for my train. I've got to go. [*Embraces* AFİFE.] May God protect you. Write me.

AFİFE: [*About to cry, covers her face with her hands.*] Dear Salâh, good-bye.

---

7. Bozdoğan Kemeri: Turkish name for the ruins of the Aqueduct of Valens. The aqueduct was built by the Emperor Valens around A.D. 375 as part of the new water-supply system constructed during his reign. It spanned a deep valley to connect the Third and Fourth Hills of Constantinople, crowned today by the University of Istanbul and the Fatih Camii, respectively.

Scene 17

[AFİFE *has pulled herself together. She is putting her new house in order. There are some familiar pieces of furniture from the previous house and the same pictures on the walls. But there is an air of shabbiness all over. Only the antique brazier stands out as a witness of the earlier times. On a small table there is a delightful pot with flowers.* AFİFE *is memorizing her role as she goes around straightening up her room. When she forgets lines, she looks at the papers on the small table. She is really acting.* SENİYE *enters quietly, watches her with a smile on her lips, and applauds her.*]

SENİYE: Bravo! As always, it's wonderful.

AFİFE: Seniye, dear, I didn't hear you come in.

SENİYE: The key was in the door.

AFİFE: Oh no! I forgot it. [*Takes the key and embraces* SENİYE.]

SENİYE: How are you? Busy, busy cleaning the house?

AFİFE: Not at all! Tonight there's no performance, so I have a visitor coming. I'm trying to tidy up a bit. Look at this mess.

SENİYE: Never mind. Why no performance tonight, Afife?

AFİFE: We performed ten days in a row. Unheard of! All the tickets for next week's performances are sold out. Mr. Bogos took us to Maxim's last night as a treat.

SENİYE: Let's tell all this to Burhanettin.

AFİFE: Do you know whom I met last night?

SENİYE: Who, who?

AFİFE: Selâhattin, the lute player.

SENİYE: Is he the one who's going to visit you tonight?

AFİFE: You're very smart. He brought me home last night. He lives in Fatih. He wanted to come inside. I said, "Come tomorrow, not in the middle of the night like this."

SENİYE: [*Kisses* AFİFE.] Good for you. Get out of this rut. Isn't he a nice man?

AFİFE: I don't know. He has bulging eyes, but he is warm and understanding. He's affectionate.

SENİYE: Then I should leave. Anyway, I have to get my ticket.

AFİFE: [*With curiosity.*] When are you leaving?

SENİYE: Every Friday there's a boat sailing to Alexandria. Burhanettin Bey wrote to me and told me to come as soon as possible.

AFİFE: "Come as soon as possible." If Mother were here, she would have said, "Nobody said this to you, Afife"—much to her regret. [*The doorbell rings;* AFİFE *and* SENİYE *speak at the same time.*] The doorbell.

SENİYE: Let me go; I'll open the door. [*Walks to the door, opens it, and goes out* as SELÂHATTİN *walks in hesitantly. He is timid and smiling.*]

AFİFE: Hello, come in please.

SELÂHATTİN: I hope she didn't leave because of me. I think it was Seniye Hanım.

AFİFE: No . . . not at all. She has to return to Cairo. She has to buy her ticket. [*Smiling.*] This place isn't like a home; it's more like a desolate stage setting, isn't it? Please, don't be turned off by it. It isn't important for me at all. Not anymore. I sold everything before I went on the tour. I was ill, very ill. Now I'm back. This house belongs to my brother. [SELÂHATTİN *holds* AFİFE's *hands with sympathy and warmth.*]

SELÂHATTİN: If one day you'll be kind enough to visit my place, you'll see that I don't even have a flower pot. This antique Beykoz tumbler . . .

AFİFE: It's cracked.

SELÂHATTİN: This Yıldız porcelain . . .

AFİFE: The lid is gone.

SELÂHATTİN: This Tophane inkwell . . .

AFİFE: Odds and ends from my parents' house. Sit down, please. I'll make you some coffee. [*Makes coffee on the alcohol burner and brings it. They sit on the sofa.*]

SELÂHATTİN: Did you like our concert last night?

AFİFE: It was beautiful, exquisite. But I had heard your lute playing before—many, many times.

SELÂHATTİN: It's impossible. I never saw you before.

AFİFE: I didn't see you, either, but many years ago when you lived in that Tozkoparan rooming house, we lived across from you.

[*The sounds become muted, shapes become blurred, and it gets darker. Music appropriate to the change is heard. Everything disappears in the dark. The light of dawn gradually appears. It is early morning.*]

Oh, we stayed up until dawn. If I hadn't heard the voice of the *simit*[8] seller, I wouldn't have noticed. Let's buy some *simit*s and have breakfast.

SELÂHATTİN: [*Gets up.*] I make very good tea.

AFİFE: OK, you make the tea. [*Opens the window.*] *Simit* seller! [*Lowers a basket.*] Two *simit*s. [*Pulls the basket up.*] Oh, they're piping hot.

SELÂHATTİN: The tea is brewing. Young lady, sit here. It'll be my pleasure to serve you.

AFİFE: [*Sits down, follows* SELÂHATTİN *with her eyes and thinks.*] What do you think?

SELÂHATTİN: About what?

AFİFE: All night you listened to the story of the girl you want to marry.

SELÂHATTİN: Yes, I did.

AFİFE: I told you everything, without lying, without skipping anything.

SELÂHATTİN: Yes, I heard it.

AFİFE: Why should you marry me? I'll ruin your life, too. Maybe I'm a woman of ill omen. I bring bad luck to people around me.

---

8. *Simit:* A bread roll in the shape of a large ring, covered with sesame seeds.

SELÂHATTİN: My dear girl, don't accuse yourself. People around you brought you unhappiness. First of all . . . that Syrian doctor. If I ever find him, I'll tear him to pieces. That man is without any scruples or conscience. But . . . didn't your mother abandon you, too?

AFİFE: [*Perturbed.*] No! How could that be? Mother returned to Istanbul soon after I did. She was ill and unhappy. I couldn't bear to see her like that. What little money she had, she put it in the Ottoman Bank in my name. I don't think I can touch that money. A week ago she went to see Salâh, my older brother, who is going to get married. My mother is the sweetest, the most generous, but also the most unhappy woman in the world.

SELÂHATTİN: Fine. Then I repeat my marriage proposal. Do you dare to marry a man like me, with little money and modest means, but with a big heart—a nonconforming, bohemian vagabond, a passionate lover of music and art, and an admirer and lover of Afife Jale? [*Gets up and opens his arms.* AFİFE *falls into them.*]

AFİFE: How sweet of you. But what about your father and especially your mother?

SELÂHATTİN: Afife, my love, let's get married as soon as possible without letting anybody know, except for the witnesses.

AFİFE: Won't they be more angry with you?

SELÂHATTİN: My father, Sadık Bey, is a professor of law, and my mother is İsmet Hanım. They are proud, haughty, and extraordinary people. But they know when they see a good person. Don't worry; they're going to like you.

AFİFE: Frankly, I am worried.

SELÂHATTİN: Look, Father never liked anything I did up until now, but he didn't hide this, either. Perhaps in the beginning he'll disapprove of my marrying you. That's the way he is, but it has nothing to do with you.

AFİFE: You love your father very much.

SELÂHATTİN: And you . . . didn't you, too?

AFİFE: [*Her eyes distant and full of tears.*] In those days, I was full of hope. I was optimistic, and I believed in myself and in what I wanted to do. I was naive. Father rejected me, saying, "I don't have a daughter called Afife." [*Hangs her head.*] He regarded me as a prostitute.

SELÂHATTİN: We're in love, the two rejected ones—that's the most important thing. Come, my dear, say yes. Let's get married. There's no other way.

AFİFE: Now you know everything about me—everything, right?

SELÂHATTİN: Except one thing—your cousin Ziya's place in your life.

AFİFE: [*Bites her lip.*] And you still want to marry me?

SELÂHATTİN: I have great respect for people who can live without the fear of guilt and sin, who can live their lives bravely, especially if they are women. I love you, Afife, but I respect you even more. We may be able to help each other and lighten our burdens.

AFİFE: Maybe, but we may also drag each other into the quagmire. I fear for you. You are too sensitive, too vulnerable, and too delicate to endure if such a thing happens.

SELÂHATTİN: I want to marry you. I want you to be mine.

AFİFE: Then promise me that when you get tired of me, when you can no longer be with me, you will leave like a gentleman.

SELÂHATTİN: I love you.

AFİFE: Promise me.

SELÂHATTİN: Will you marry me?

AFİFE: Yes, my darling, but I feel very sorry for you.

Scene 18

[AFİFE's *house.* AFİFE, *wearing a heavy sweater, is warming her hands over a brazier. She is shivering. She is holding a cigarette that looks hand rolled. She is preoccupied, gloomy, and tense. Next to the brazier are used coffee cups, a coffeepot, and so on. The antique brass brazier stands there as if to mock the shabbiness of the place.* SELÂHATTİN *walks in with his lute. He has on a shirt with an open neck and rolled-up sleeves, and over that a vest.* AFİFE *does not see him.*]

SELÂHATTİN: Ah, what is my beautiful one musing about so deep in thought? [AFİFE *doesn't seem to understand at first and gazes strangely.*] Afife!

AFİFE: They closed the theater. The letter came.

SELÂHATTİN: So what can we do? There are other theaters. [*Puts the lute on the sofa, comes to her side, and holds her hand.*] Would you like to apply to the Dramatic Arts Theater?

AFİFE: [*Emphatically.*] No! They threw me out.

SELÂHATTİN: They had to.

AFİFE: No! They threw me out not because I was a bad actress, but because I was a woman. That makes all the difference.

SELÂHATTİN: Then why are you crying now, my dear child?

AFİFE: Nothing is working out for me; everything is against me. Even you are against me.

SELÂHATTİN: Me? How can you say that?

AFİFE: In the early hours of the morning, you shut yourself up with friends and make music. It goes on for hours. I feel bored, I get fed up, I feel suffocated. [*Weeps.*]

SELÂHATTİN: [*Takes out of his shirt pocket a cigarette holder with a half-smoked cigarette, relights it, takes a puff, and offers it to* AFİFE. *She takes a puff. With a little effort, he murmurs.*]

I met you on a spring evening,
Your gaiety had a touch of melancholy.
Why did you lower your head,
When I gazed deeply into your eyes?

AFİFE: You liberated me from hanging my head low. I can't deny it. You gave me self-esteem and helped me to have more confidence in myself. But I can't go on anymore.

SELÂHATTİN: What do you mean by that?

AFİFE: I told you that it would be like this.

SELÂHATTİN: Told me what?

AFİFE: That you couldn't bear this togetherness.

SELÂHATTİN: Can you take it?

AFİFE: If the man I love sings this every day:

> Come and see how she made me feel weary of life,
> Because I loved you, both friends and enemies
> Kept throwing stones at us.

You compose songs like this, and I listen to them every day. A little while ago, when I was slicing onions in the kitchen, I decided not to listen to them anymore. I don't want to listen.

SELÂHATTİN: I can shut up. I know how to keep quiet.

AFİFE: No, dear, it isn't necessary because you won't be with me anymore. You have to leave.

SELÂHATTİN: Afife!

AFİFE: Perhaps you haven't noticed yet . . . [*Stands up, now truly an actress. Walks and stops in front of* SELÂHATTİN.]

> Because of you I became the talk of the town,
> All the eyebrows were raised against me.
> As for your bitter reproaches,
> I have no more tears to shed.
> But isn't it sad for you?

SELÂHATTİN: Afife!

AFİFE: There's also this one:

> Why did I love that cruel woman?
> She made my life turn into poison.

SELÂHATTİN: Enough, enough! I can't take all these reproaches. It confuses me.

AFİFE: Me, too. Listen, your father heard about everything. Your sister told me. About our marriage and our addiction. Is that why you say, "I became the talk of the town"? Your mother, too, is going around telling everybody, "Afife made my son an addict."

SELÂHATTİN: It isn't true, not true at all. Long before I met you . . .

AFİFE: I want you to leave here today and divorce me immediately. I'm not going to change my mind.

SELÂHATTİN: Afife, I can't live without you.

AFİFE: Why did you love that cruel woman?

SELÂHATTİN: I'm not acting. I'm very serious.

AFİFE: She made your life turn into poison.

SELÂHATTİN: Afife, you can't live without me, either.

AFİFE: Neither with you nor without you. Now you know my only passion and my only support. If you have a little money you can give me, just leave it and go.

SELÂHATTİN: What will you do later on?

AFİFE: I'll wrap my love with the wails of the night.

SELÂHATTİN: Afife, please, don't play games with me.

AFİFE: Why? Isn't life a game? When I started out, I was already a dead player.

SELÂHATTİN: Forget all this . . . if you have the stuff . . . get it. Let's forget everything. Even if it is a lie, it brings us happiness. Come on, Afife, please.

AFİFE: I've got nothing. Not even money.

SELÂHATTİN: [*Emptying his pockets.*] Take all of this, dear.

AFİFE: I won't say it again: you must leave. If you don't leave, I will. Be sure of that. [SELÂHATTİN *covers his face with his hands; we understand that he is crying.*] I'm doing this so as not to drag you farther into the quagmire. [*Exits.* SELÂHATTİN *continues to weep. A little later he raises his head and sees that* AFİFE *is gone. The voice of the singer Fikriye Hanım comes over an old gramophone.*]

THE SONG:

> You have left me all alone,
> Where can I find you now
> To ask for forgiveness?

Scene 19

[AFİFE *in her brother's little wooden house, curled up on a mattress on the floor. She is reduced to skin and bones. Her young nephew* MESUT *enters the room quietly, kneels down by her side, and strokes her hair.*]

MESUT: Aunt, I'm here. How are you?

AFİFE: Ah!

MESUT: Look, I brought something to eat. Would you like to try some?

AFİFE: What did you bring?

MESUT: Chicken and rice and a pudding.

AFİFE: [*Trying to sit up in bed.*] Where is it?

MESUT: It's here, dear. [*Opens the package.*] I'll find a fork.

AFİFE: There's a tray, too. Bring it quickly. There must be some bread.

MESUT: [*From the kitchen.*] I brought fresh bread.

[MESUT *puts a pillow behind her back and covers her shoulders with a shawl. He puts the tray on her lap.* AFİFE *devours the food ravenously. This mad hunger greatly upsets* MESUT. *Finally,* AFİFE *feels a little better.*]

AFİFE: Thank you. Thank you very much.

MESUT: You're welcome, Aunt. I wish I could help you more.

AFİFE: What's your name?

MESUT: Mesut. Have you forgotten? I'm your sister Behiye's son.

AFİFE: Mesut, my dear, what news from Mother? Why doesn't she write me anymore? Does my sister say anything? Mother should come back. I can't take it anymore. I haven't got much time left. I want her. [*Talks faster.*] I want her. I want to see that she hasn't abandoned me, like everybody else. [*Pounds the quilt with her fists.*] I want to know, I have the right to know. Don't I? I'm scared . . . I don't want to die alone. I want my mother.

MESUT: Aunt, Aunt, please. Grandmother didn't abandon you, didn't give you up. She wouldn't do that.

AFİFE: Then what happened? What . . .

MESUT: Grandmother died two months ago, Aunt. We didn't want to tell you this and make you sad.

AFİFE: [*Lets out a terrible shriek, pulls her hair.*] It can't be. No, no, no!

Scene 20

[*Same place.* AFİFE *is alone, hallucinating and talking to herself.*]

AFİFE: Oh, come, come, please come . . . I said I wouldn't go to that hellish place again, but if you take me there, Ziya dear, I'll go . . . come . . . see me . . . come, feel . . . [*The door opens.* ZİYA *enters, walking with muffled steps, and kneels down by her bed.*]

ZİYA: Afife my dear!

AFİFE: [*Very calmly.*] Ah, it's you. I knew you would come.

ZİYA: I told you yesterday that I would come.

AFİFE: Yesterday? When was that?

ZİYA: Are you hungry? I brought you soup. Have some. Take a spoonful. [*Puts the soup in a bowl and brings it.* AFİFE *eats it and feels better.* ZİYA *keeps feeding her by spoonfuls.*]

AFİFE: Is there a little bread?

ZİYA: Yes, there's also rice.

AFİFE: I can't eat it; you eat it.

ZİYA: Do you remember . . . I used to eat your tarts.

AFİFE: I used to buy them for a penny, but you never paid me. [*Sits up straight.*] Ziya, now I know everything. I was agonizing about why Mother never came, never wrote to me, why she abandoned me. You knew about it, too, didn't you? She's dead. Mother is dead. Nobody told me. Nobody. I didn't want to die alone, but why did Mother leave me alone? I don't want to die alone.

ZİYA: Afife, calm down.

AFİFE: Everybody abandoned me.

ZİYA: No, it isn't true. Why should they?

AFİFE: Then where have all of you been?

ZİYA: I'm right here. I'll always be by your side. I'll never leave you.

AFİFE: Yes, I remember.

ZİYA: Remember what, dear?

AFİFE: Why you look after me.

ZİYA: Didn't you ask me to come? Don't you always ask me?

AFİFE: I have no one else to ask.

ZİYA: Fine. I have no one else to look after, either.

AFİFE: Ziya, my dear, I wore you out. I made you so unhappy.

ZİYA: I always loved you. You know that, don't you?

AFİFE: You loved that little girl. You cannot love me. You can't bear such filth.

ZİYA: I loved Afife, no matter what she was. I always loved her, and I always will.

AFİFE: [*Cries.*] Why couldn't we find happiness, why?

ZİYA: Your desires and our reality couldn't go together.

AFİFE: Forgive me.

ZİYA: I told you I love you.

AFİFE: Tell me again.

ZİYA: I'll always tell you. Never forget that. [*Holds her hands.*]

AFİFE: Now I remember why I called you. Look, we both know the truth. This is my last wish. I won't behave like I did last time. I promise. Take me there again, please. I really want this. You did everything I asked you to do. Please, take me to the hospital. [*They embrace.*]

ZİYA: OK, OK.

AFİFE: Who else is here?

ZİYA: You and I, little girl, no one else is here.

AFİFE: Ah, but there are others . . . others . . . they want to take me to that hospital. Ziya, Ziya! Don't take me there. For God's sake! I was there before. I'm not crazy! I'm not! Believe me. Throw me into any dump, kill me, but don't take me there.

ZİYA: [*Hugs* AFİFE.] Don't be scared, dear, don't, don't. We're not taking you there. You're here. You'll stay here. I promise, dear, I do. [AFİFE *calms down. Two* MEN *standing at the door watch this scene.* ZİYA *makes* AFİFE *lie down and covers her. When he stands up, he sees the two* MEN.] Hello, Doctor. Hello, Kemal Bey.

DOCTOR: We shouldn't torture the poor child anymore. Let's leave her here and try to take care of her at home. Ziya Bey, is there anybody else besides you who can attend to her? By the way, what's your relationship?

ZİYA: I'm her cousin, sir.

DOCTOR: Any friends from the theater, besides Kemal Bey?

HÜSEYİN KEMAL: There are many friends from the theater, many.

AFİFE: [*Sits up.*] Theater friends . . . who are they, where are they? When did you come, Kemal Bey? Why are you standing up?

HÜSEYİN KEMAL: We just walked in and were about to sit down. The doctor wanted to see you, Afife. [*They sit down.*]

AFİFE: The doctor? There's nothing wrong with me.

DOCTOR: I just wanted to visit you.

AFİFE: [*Very calm and lucid.*] Kemal Bey, I hear there's is an actress called Neyire Hanım who is very good. They say she looks a little like me. I'm so curious. Tell me a little about her. Oh, I wish I could see her act. I love her without seeing her. Neyire Neyir! The woman who achieved what I could not. The woman who completed the unfinished work. [*Tries to get up.* ZİYA *and* HÜSEYİN KEMAL *help her. When she is standing, the audience can see she is wearing the same white dress as in Act I, Scene 1, of the play.*] Neyire . . . and many, many more women . . . actresses like Bedia, Şaziye, Melek, Muazzez, Ayten, Gülriz, Yıldız, and all the others. What's important is not their names. What's important is that there have been many Afifes. Many, many. The thorns have been cleared away, and the road is open. There are those who achieved what I could not. So I can say farewell to you. I think, now, we know each other well . . . very well. I am Afife Jale. Ziya, my dear, let's go to the hospital. [*As they walk slowly, a deep, sonorous, and powerful voice comes over the loudspeaker.*]

THE VOICE: Afife Jale died in Bakırköy Mental Hospital on 24 July 1941. At her funeral, there were only a young actor, Sait, and an unidentified young man. She was thirty-nine years old.

CURTAIN

◆　　◆　　◆

Vladimir Komarov

An Optimistic Play on Death

MEMET BAYDUR

An Editor's Note

By the age of fifty, Memet Baydur, the best original talent in the field of playwriting to emerge in Turkey in the 1980s, had reached an impressive level of maturity. Death in 2001 cut his creative life short. He had written more than twenty plays in less than twenty years. Each one exhibited unconventional techniques in presenting whimsical plots with unusual, sometimes eccentric characters and uncommon themes. If his creativity were to have lasted fifteen or twenty more years, chances are Baydur would have revolutionized Turkish theater and probably achieved international recognition.

Unlike most Turkish playwrights, Baydur spent the better part of his adult life abroad in such cities as London, Paris, Nairobi, Madrid, and Washington, D.C. He was proficient in English, French, and Spanish and occasionally wrote essays in these languages. He taught courses in cinema at Kenya's Mass Communications School, was a member of Madrid's International Mediterranean Theater Institute, and served as the Turkish consultant for the Bonn Theater Biennial.

The French version of Baydur's play *Kadın İstasyonu* (Women's Station) was produced at the Richard Martin Theater in Marseilles, directed by the playwright himself. *Doğum* (Birth) and *Çin Kelebeği* (Chinese Butterfly) were staged in Bretagne and at the Avignon Theater Festival.

His translations of works into Turkish include *Master Class* by Terrence McNally, which had two separate, highly successful productions in Istanbul and Ankara.

Baydur was also a fine short-story writer. His short fiction shared some characteristics of the virtuosity that marked his plays—fanciful plots and persons, a fluid and colorful style, unaccustomed themes. The short stories he wrote between 1974 and 1994 were collected in a volume that came out in 1995.

A collection of his essays was published in 1996, and another collection was released posthumously. Baydur wrote a sophisticated and stimulating weekly column for the daily *Cumhuriyet* in his last years. Many of his essays have yet to appear in book form.

Baydur's plays won seven major drama awards. The present work, *Vladimir Komarov*, earned the prestigious Avni Dilligil Best Play Award in 1993.

Vladimir Komarov appears here in a version prepared in English by Memet Baydur himself. The editors have checked it against the original and introduced some judicious modifications. The playwright gave this version the subtitle *An Optimistic Play on Death*. The play is set in 1967 and is based on a true event. Russian (Soviet) cosmonaut Vladimir Komarov perished in his space capsule on 24 April 1967. Toward the end, the play refers optimistically to the year 2000: "in thirty-three years we will be in the year 2000.... The world is moving toward better times." The year 2000 is many years behind us now, and Baydur lived to see it, dying just a year later. Do the intervening years prove his "optimism" right? That is for the reader or the spectator to decide.—TSH

Characters

VLADIMIR KOMAROV (IVAN), a handsome colonel, cosmonaut, and scientist

MAXIM KLIMT, a weary, bureaucratic, bored scientist

ELENA VELIOVITCH, a perhaps too serious, austere, and sentimental physics professor

LEONARD TOMKIN (LEO), young, charming, untidy-looking, incredulous scientist; a loving man full of hope

ANNA NATASHA KOMAROVA, Colonel Komarov's wife; a good-looking woman, calm but somewhat distracted

BORIS KUKAKOV, general manager, statesman; serious, thick eyebrows, reddish smiling face; both head and deputy, master and servant

ANDREI (MIKI), Komarov's elder son, an actor

ACT I

[*Light. We see the night sky on the stage. A silent magical sky with thousands of moving, twinkling stars. The stage is divided in two by an invisible line. There is a big, spectacular white space capsule on the right side of the spectators' view. The side of the capsule visible to the audience is open and covered by glass. Inside the space capsule, there is a white reclining chair. On the control panel, there are many luminous dials, switches, and so on. It is a one-person space capsule. During the entire play, the actor playing* VLADIMIR KOMAROV *will move only a short distance around the reclining chair. He wears his space suit and helmet, and most of the time sits immobile. The green, red, and yellow dial lights of the space capsule keep blinking. One gets the impression that the vehicle is moving in space.* Mobilis in mobili. *On the left side of the stage, on a level lower than the capsule, we observe the Communications Room of the Space Research Center near Moscow. Here, there are also many luminous dials, computers, computer screens, and so on. There is a long, thin table with three microphones on it. The place is encumbered by screens, switches, and buttons. A man wearing a gray suit is sitting at the table. From a glass, he drinks something like water. He gazes at the dials, rather worried. There is a lit cigarette in an ashtray nearby. The man looking at the computer screen flicks a few switches. He frowns. He is* MAXIM KLIMT, *one of the Space Research Center's head scientists. The clock on the wall shows 2:30 A.M. KLIMT stands up, holding the glass in his hand, and looks at the clock. He touches a button on the control panel and turns a switch. Suddenly, music by Tchaikovsky is played at a high volume. KOMAROV moves his feet a little inside the space capsule. He stops. Earth has started to broadcast music into the space capsule. KOMAROV, on his third day in space, is woken up at around 2:30 A.M., Earth time. Music, with all its beauty, covers the entire stage, the backstage, and the theater. KOMAROV first moves his hands, then his head. He resembles a prehistoric monster waking up from a thousand-year slumber. A good-hearted monster. The door to the Communications Room opens and DR. VELIOVITCH enters. She is wearing a white lab coat.]*

ELENA: It's two-thirty.

MAXIM: I just turned on the music. [*Pause.*]

ELENA: Does he know?

MAXIM: I can't tell. Yet . . . there's still some hope, Elena. All isn't finished; it's not all gone yet.

ELENA: Oh, hope . . . hope is always there. [*Pauses.*] *Swan Lake.* He loves this music. You know his wife is a ballerina. They have two sons. One is an actor. The other is a university student, becoming an agricultural engineer.

MAXIM: Is Anna Komarova still dancing?

ELENA: I think she's only teaching now. Anna was a real beauty.

MAXIM: It's been twenty years since I last saw a ballet.

ELENA: Ivan loves this music.

[Silence. While they were chatting, VLADIMIR wakes up. He slowly removes his helmet. A handsome middle-aged man appears. He looks sad and tired, but very intelligent. He opens his eyes, yawns. He swings the chair a little and looks at the control panel without getting up; he fiddles with a few buttons and switches, then stops. For an instant, he listens to the music. Smiles. On the other half of the stage, MAXIM turns a button, leans toward the microphone, and speaks.]

MAXIM: Hello, Vladimir. This is Maxim calling from Earth. You've slept for four hours and two minutes. Here it's half past two. 24 April 1967. Vladimir? [*Short pause.*]

VLADIMIR: I had a funny dream, but . . . [*Smiles.*] I'm not tired or anything like that.

MAXIM: Vladimir? Ivan? [*Presses another button.*] Can you hear me?

VLADIMIR: Yes, I hear you. [*Smiles.*] Can you all hear me? It's you who can't hear me. [*Reaches out and pushes a button.*] Cosmonaut Colonel Vladimir Komarov is at your command in the brightness of the cosmos.

MAXIM: Oh . . . is everything all right?

VLADIMIR: Almost. Nothing seems to be wrong. For the moment. [*Silence.*]

MAXIM: Shall we turn off the music?

VLADIMIR: Yes, turn it off. [*Looks to his left, smiles.*] Earth looks very pretty and much smaller when you look at it from here. Like a blue orange.

MAXIM: We can't yet solve the problem we have on channel four. [*Silence.*]

VLADIMIR: It's the seventeenth tangent of the fourth channel. Never mind, Maxim, it's nothing too important. The computer just shows a small deviation—nothing to be worried about. These things happen, you know.

[*Silence.* ELENA *and* MAXIM *look at each other.*]

MAXIM: How? What kind of a deviation?

VLADIMIR: Like, like I'm going farther away from Earth.

MAXIM: Like what?

VLADIMIR: Actually, my wording was wrong—not me, but the vehicle you have built seems to be drifting away from Earth. Whatever you want to call it seems to be slowly moving away from Earth.

[MAXIM *and* ELENA *exchange a look of pity.*]

MAXIM: The hydraulic system locked up. [*Pauses.*] Ah . . . we're trying to get to the root of it. Vladimir?

VLADIMIR: Yes?

MAXIM: Ah . . . are you all right? That is, apart from the malfunction, do you have any other problems?

VLADIMIR: No, none at all.

MAXIM: Come again?

VLADIMIR: I have no problem whatsoever except for the malfunction. I'm in an extraordinarily beautiful state. One feels guilty falling asleep here in space. Maxim, are you there?

MAXIM: Yes? I'm here.

VLADIMIR: Yes?

MAXIM: Ah . . . are you all right? Eh, apart from the malfunction . . . any complaints?

VLADIMIR: No.

MAXIM: What's that?

VLADIMIR: No . . . no complaints. Except for the malfunction, nothing to worry about. I feel just wonderful. As I said, one feels guilty about falling asleep out here in space. Maxim, are you there?

MAXIM: Yes, I'm here.

VLADIMIR: It's about time you started making space capsules for two. [*Silence.*]

MAXIM: Yes.

VLADIMIR: For a minimum of two. Maxim, can you hear me?

MAXIM: Yes, your message is received.

VLADIMIR: [*Laughs.*] Good. No problem, then. As long as you got the message . . . all is in order, then. [*Looks at the dials facing him and smiles.*] This deviation is not insignificant.

MAXIM: What's that? [*Leans over the microphone.*] Couldn't hear you. Vladimir Komarov, can you repeat, please?

VLADIMIR: [*Plays with a few buttons and switches.*] This is not a small deviation off the course. [*Silence.*]

MAXIM: Yes . . . ah . . . maybe we can correct it. [*Silence.*]

VLADIMIR: Did you say "maybe," Maxim?

MAXIM: I said we'll correct it.

ELENA: [*Sits in front of one of the microphones.*] Vladimir?

VLADIMIR: [*Happily.*] Dr. Elena Veliovitch! How nice to hear you, you sound so near.

ELENA: We're talking about a problem in the hydraulic system. Something seems to be clogged up.

VLADIMIR: Yes, I understand. The steering gear is gone, then.

ELENA: [*Smiles.*] Yes, something like that. [*Silence.*]

VLADIMIR: I was going to orbit Earth.

ELENA: Yes.

VLADIMIR: But now I have started to shift away from Earth. Am I wrong?

ELENA: Ivan?

VLADIMIR: Yes?

ELENA: Don't be frightened.

VLADIMIR: I'm not frightened. Why should I be frightened?

ELENA: [*Speaking to* MAXIM.] Oh my God!

VLADIMIR: Yes? What did you say?

MAXIM: [*Into the microphone.*] Nothing we can't cope with; we're working on it.

VLADIMIR: Good. Work on it. Everything is . . . so lovely out here.

MAXIM: You'll start your return to Earth in two hours.

VLADIMIR: [*Joking.*] I'll return and stay on Earth this time.

ELENA: All is not lost yet.

VLADIMIR: In that case, there still must be some hope. I'm worried about the time when we run out of hope as well. Think about that, Elena.

ELENA: Vladimir Komarov, please be serious.

VLADIMIR: I'm dead serious. When all hope is gone . . . imagine how boring it would be to live in an environment without cheese. Or a place where there are no postal services. I would even have to give up my drunken retired self-made engineer pen pal Igor Bulatovitch in Odessa. Can you imagine what a catastrophe this would be, my lovely friend Elena? Believe me, dear Elena, it would be terribly boring. No, all is not over yet. Must not be over. Of course, some things may be over. But everything? No. They're not. They mustn't be. The plums, cherries, oak trees, willows, children and old people, theaters, poetry, science, and everything related to these things. Also, technology that serves peasants with smiling eyes. In Tajikistan, I met someone who made the best fishing lines in the world; for him and many others like him, these people and all the things they make cannot be over, must not be over.

MAXIM: Vladimir Komarov?

VLADIMIR: Elena? [*Silence.*]

ELENA: Yes? [*Pauses.*] I'm listening to you.

VLADIMIR: Nothing is over; on the contrary, something is about to begin.

MAXIM: We'll make the repairs. Carry on with your observations. We'll be in touch with you soon.

VLADIMIR: Elena?

ELENA: Yes?

VLADIMIR: A place without strawberry ice cream is no good.

ELENA: Of course not, Ivan. You haven't changed a bit.

VLADIMIR: I had no time.

ELENA: For what?

VLADIMIR: To change.

ELENA: You were always like this.

VLADIMIR: Like what?

ELENA: Always joking, happy, full of life and love, and a little crazy.

VLADIMIR: How do you become a scientist otherwise, Elena? [*Silence.*]

MAXIM: There are scientists who aren't quite like that, Vladimir.

VLADIMIR: Are there really? [*Pauses.*] Science is a lovely thing. It constantly changes.

ELENA: [*Laughing.*] Years ago in New York, I saw an American film called *Love Is a Many-Splendored Thing*. [*Pauses.*] Three years ago.

MAXIM: Good. Now you're watching a film called *Science Is a Very-Splendored Thing!* Even as this magnificent capsule happens to be pointing its nose to a very far destination, science is a lovely subject! Ivan, do you feel like talking to us?

VLADIMIR: [*Silence.*] Not to you. [*Pauses.*] Not "talk" to you, Maxim. I want to tell you something. Someone, an author, wrote that science is for the benefit and development of humankind. Why?

MAXIM: Why?

VLADIMIR: Science extends human life. It eliminates diseases; it diminishes pain.

ELENA: Yes?

VLADIMIR: It augments the productivity of the soil. Science . . . [*Hushes.*]

ELENA: We're listening to you, Ivan.

VLADIMIR: It enabled us to make lighthouses.

MAXIM: What?

ELENA: Lighthouses?

VLADIMIR: Lighthouses. Have you ever stayed in a lighthouse? At one time, a lighthouse was as important as this space capsule. Based on science.

MAXIM: Yes.

VLADIMIR: Based on science, we are able to offer new weapons to warriors!

MAXIM: Your presence there is for the sake of peace, Vladimir Komarov.

VLADIMIR: My presence here is for the purpose of constructing a bridge unknown to our ancestors, over a river not crossed by them. Peace can only follow behind me. Science is the guide for thunderbolts. It illuminates our nights; not only that, but it also improves our sight, its sharpness; it enlarges our vision. And we owe our muscle power to it! [*Pauses.*] To science!

ELENA: It speeds evolution, brings what is remote closer.

VLADIMIR: Annihilates distances. Enables lovemaking!

MAXIM: What does that mean?

ELENA: Communicating, writing, all the other related things!

VLADIMIR: Enabling man to dive in the sea, fly in the sky . . .

ELENA: Go in unexplored caves or underground without fear . . .

VLADIMIR: Science is an endless philosophy! It can't be completed, and it will never reach perfection. It can't! Because . . .

ELENA: Ivan?

VLADIMIR: Because the only rule it has is evolution. A point beyond reach. Yesterday is today's target. Tomorrow, the same point will become the beginning.

MAXIM: Vladimir Komarov?

VLADIMIR: What? What do you want? [*Silence.*]

MAXIM: Do you want something?

VLADIMIR: Yes. [*Pauses.*] I want to return.

[ELENA *and* MAXIM *look at each other in pain. Music. Lights dim.* MAXIM *leaves.*]

[*Light. Only the Communications Room, which is on the left side of the stage, is illuminated.* ELENA, *looking at the sky, stands in the room. After a moment, she lights a cigarette, blows the smoke in the air, smiles. The telephone rings.* ELENA, *still smoking, just looks at the telephone at first, then eventually answers it.*]

ELENA: Hello, Dr. Veliovitch speaking. [*Listens for a moment.*] Yes. . . . No. It's not even technical; it's a mechanical failure! . . . Yes, mechanical. Nothing can be done! The space craft has already started to go farther away from Earth. It's going. We aren't happy at all, of course; this is the first time we are experiencing such a thing. In any case, how many such flights have we had? It's not a simple deviation; we're talking about a serious, final departure. . . . Yes. For the moment, it seems slow, but in eighteen hours he'll be out of our range, and we won't even hear him, let alone see him. . . .

An accident, yes, but we are about to lose one of our country's best physicists. . . . No, that's not my only worry, sir! He used to be my lover when we were at the university. . . . Vladimir Komarov! . . . Yes, sir. . . . No, sir. His return is impossible. That is to say . . . to our knowledge, approximately eighteen hours from now, our contact with Colonel Komarov will come to an end. But . . . the vehicle's oxygen supply will last for thirty-six hours. This means that if Vladimir Komarov does not commit suicide, he may survive eighteen more hours after he gets out of our range.

Yes, he can. He's supplied with a small pill. For such eventualities. I don't think he'll use it. He'd rather die first. . . . Yes, he is dying. You're right, sir. Vladimir Komarov is one of the most inquisitive people in this country. He wasn't angry. . . . No, he didn't swear. He spoke about very pleasant things. It's a mechanical failure, sir. I'm sorry to say so. . . . No, I don't think he'll be interested in such things. Someone seeing the world from where he is might not be too interested in having a statue of himself erected in his hometown. . . . Yes. I understand. Naturally. [*Looks at her watch.*] We'll reestablish contact in ten minutes. Unfortunately, only voice contact. [*Looks at her watch.*] He's got seventeen hours and thirty-three minutes with us. . . . Yes, all right. . . . Possibly. Good night, sir. [*Puts the telephone down. Sadly stands in the middle of that wretched, dark room.*]

[MAXIM *enters the room from her left. He is accompanied by a tall, funny-looking youngish man with a beard.* LEONARD TOMKIN *looks a little scruffy and is wearing a white lab coat and glasses. His hair is messy, but he looks charming.*].

MAXIM: Did they call?

ELENA: I just put the phone down.

MAXIM: What did they say?

ELENA: Everyone is puzzled. Surprised, sad . . . and a little angry maybe. Rightly so! A mechanical failure. A screw, a shitty bolt, will cause the death of Vladimir Komarov. How can this be possible?

MAXIM: One can't control everything.

ELENA: [*After a brief pause.*] What are you saying? What . . . what did you say, dear Maxim?

MAXIM: I said one cannot control everything.

ELENA: That's right. How right you are, but . . . Vladimir is about to leave our space. This bit of righteousness will soon not be able to reach him. Just because he lost his brakes, he's heading for the heart of darkness at full speed.

MAXIM: Perhaps it's not so dark out there, Elena.

ELENA: He's got a supply of oxygen that will last him another thirty-two hours.

LEONARD: Will he die when the oxygen runs out? [*Silence.*]

[ELENA *stares at* LEONARD *as though seeing him for the first time. Turns to* MAXIM *and makes a hand gesture as if asking, "Who in the world is this man?"*]

MAXIM: Oh, I didn't introduce you. Elena Veliovitch . . . this is our young engineer friend Leonard Tomkin. Vladimir's best friend in the past few years. He recently joined us here. A year ago . . .

LEONARD: Hello. Pleased to meet you.

ELENA: [*To* MAXIM.] One cannot control everything. [*To* LEONARD.] Hello, pleased to meet you. What are you doing here?

LEONARD: Maxim said it would be useful if I spoke to him.

ELENA: Speak to whom?

LEONARD: [*Points at the ceiling.*] With him.

ELENA: In that case, you should go to church!

LEONARD: [*Chuckles.*] No, not with Him. [*Points at the direction of the space capsule.*] With that one.

ELENA: You mean you came here to have a chat with Vladimir Komarov?

MAXIM: Elena . . .

ELENA: You mean you came here as a friend to try to ease the pain of his disappearing into space? [*Almost in tears.*]

LEONARD: No. The thing is . . . he left me his aquarium to look after. [*Pauses.*] It's a long, thin aquarium. One meter by fifty centimeters. We arranged it together. There are forty-one fish in it. From Japan, Russia, Brazil, Gabon, France . . . all different species. They're all aquarium fish, so we planted only aquarium plants for them. In the end, what came about was a scene that could only be in an aquarium. Dr. Komarov loves his aquarium. [*Pauses.*] I heard he's not returning to Earth. On his way out, I thought he would like to know that the fish are doing very well.

ELENA: You . . . are you really an engineer?

LEONARD: [*Laughs, points at the space capsule.*] I'm as much an engineer as he is a real cosmonaut. No more, no less.

ELENA: [*To* MAXIM.] What's going on, Maxim? Are we out of our minds?

MAXIM: Elena! In two days' time, nationwide mourning will be declared. His name will be given to schools, museums, flowers, microbes, awards, submarines, rockets . . . he'll become subway stations . . . bus stops. On his way out, Vladimir Komarov is entering our lives forever!

ELENA: [*Points at* LEONARD.] What is this man doing here?

MAXIM: We thought Vladimir would go happier if he heard him on his way out.

ELENA: You thought?

MAXIM: Yes, we thought!

ELENA: Who are "we," Maxim?

MAXIM: Myself and Natasha Komarova.

ELENA: Anna Natasha Komarova?

MAXIM: I invited her here.

ELENA: [*Worried.*] Will she come?

MAXIM: She said he ought to speak to Leonard.

LEONARD: She apparently suggested that I have a chat with him.

ELENA: [*Looks at* MAXIM *and* LEONARD. *Lights a cigarette. Sits down, pushes a button.*] Vladimir, Vladimir Komarov?

[*The right side of the stage is slowly illuminated with a mixture of blue, mauve, orange, and yellow lights.* VLADIMIR *is standing. He is watching space through a porthole. He speaks without turning his head.*]

VLADIMIR: Now there's no difference between light and darkness. I'm at the most beautiful moment of my life. [*Pauses.*] I'm listening to you, Elena.

ELENA: Do you have anything to report, Vladimir Komarov? [*Silence.*]

VLADIMIR: Yes. [*Pauses.*] I do have something to report.

ELENA: What is it?

VLADIMIR: I'm happy because nothing can change my life!

MAXIM: What?

VLADIMIR: From now on, nothing, nobody can change my life!

ELENA: And what does that mean?

VLADIMIR: It means what it means.

MAXIM: [*To* ELENA.] We must be tolerant.

ELENA: Tolerant? Ridiculous.

LEONARD: [*Smiling because he heard* VLADIMIR's *voice.*] He's singing! [*Silence.*]

VLADIMIR: Leonard! My dear friend?

LEONARD: Dr. Komarov?

VLADIMIR: Here, Leo. I'm right here. How are you?

LEONARD: Not too bad. A bit annoyed, of course. I couldn't figure it out.

ELENA: Figure what out?

VLADIMIR: Leo? Are you there?

LEONARD: I'm here. What's going on, Dr. Komarov?

VLADIMIR: The bishop . . . should move to c6, Leo.

MAXIM: Vladimir?

VLADIMIR: Maxim! Are you there, too?

MAXIM: We're trying to repair the malfunction.

LEONARD: If the bishop moves to c6, the queen has a large open gap in front.

VLADIMIR: What are you talking about, Leo? The central knight's pawn is threatening the queen.

MAXIM: Vladimir?

VLADIMIR: Yeah?

MAXIM: This is no time for playing chess.

VLADIMIR: Who says?

ELENA: Maxim!

VLADIMIR: Elena!

ELENA: Yes?

VLADIMIR: A little earlier, then . . . were you the one who said tolerance is ridiculous?

ELENA: [*Pauses.*] Yes, it was me. [*Silence.* VLADIMIR KOMAROV *sits in his seat. With the ease of knowing he is going to die, he stretches his legs.*]

VLADIMIR: From now on, nothing can change my world.

ELENA: At this moment, everything, everything is changing your world.

LEONARD: Your fish are fine.

VLADIMIR: Have the sea horses arrived, Leo?

LEONARD: They did. Two of them.

VLADIMIR: How are they?

LEONARD: A little . . . how should I say it, like they are a little drunk.

VLADIMIR: Confused sea horses!

LEONARD: Different environment.

VLADIMIR: They'll get used to it. Oh, yes, they will. [*They laugh together.*]

MAXIM: Vladimir?

VLADIMIR: Yes, Maxim, my dear friend, I'm listening to you.

MAXIM: Uh . . . well . . . this is not the right time to discuss aquariums either.

VLADIMIR: All right, it isn't. Well, then, what is it right for? What? Not for chess, not for aquariums, not for this, not for that. When I was a student, I read a poetry book. The author was Turkish. The book was called "Now's the Time for Love."[1] Actually, the author was a story writer. He eventually got around to publishing a book of his poems. Now it's time for love—and here I am alone somewhere in space in my unsteerable spaceship. Even if it's the right time for making love, not much can be done about it. All right, then, can you tell me what the present is appropriate for?

In order to keep my dog's fur in a good state, mix an egg in a glass of milk and give him that once a week . . . must be done on Saturday mornings. Don't forget. You'll see: his fur will remain brilliant. Please note this, Leo.

LEONARD: I won't forget. Don't worry.

VLADIMIR: Tell Natasha that she must play a lot of music in the house. I can't let them take advantage of my absence and live in a quiet house.

MAXIM: We'll repair the malfunction, Vladimir.

VLADIMIR: Elena Veliovitch, do you remember the Pushkin Middle School? [*Silence.*]

ELENA: I . . . I didn't catch that.

LEONARD: Vladimir Komarov is asking about the Pushkin Middle School.

---

1. Sait Faik (1906–54), *Şimdi Sevişme Vakti* (Now's the Time for Love) (Istanbul: Yenilik, 1953).

MAXIM: It's one of the biggest schools in Leningrad.

VLADIMIR: That's right. It's a gigantic building. First, they constructed an extraordinarily high T-shaped complex. On either side of the T, they placed a soccer field, park, swimming pool, basketball and volleyball courts, you name it. When the number of students exceeded five thousand, they started to expand the complex with huge buildings on both sides. When they started to dig, the foundations of the old building opened up a little. Through a small hole, one had access to the foundations of the Pushkin Middle School. [*Pauses.*] One day, a couple of friends and I descended into the foundations of the school.

ELENA: Foundations of the school!

VLADIMIR: Yes, foundations of the school. All three of us were around eleven to twelve years old. Dark corridors opened in front of us. It stunk. The hole in front of us was getting narrower and narrower. We got spooked. We ran—no, we dashed out! [*Pauses.*] The following day . . .

ELENA: How long ago was all this, Ivan?

VLADIMIR: [*Leans out of the space capsule toward the Communications Room and shouts.*] The following day we equipped ourselves with ropes tied around our waists, torches, candles, matches; we stuffed our pockets with dried fish, dried apricots, and other things; and again we went down into the foundations of the school.

LEONARD: We can hear you very well, Vladimir.

MAXIM: [*Leans over the microphone.*] Colonel Komarov?

VLADIMIR: Can you hear me?

MAXIM: [*In a sad tone.*] Yes, we hear you.

LEONARD: We're listening.

VLADIMIR: We promised each other not to return until we reached the other side of the school. We were determined to cross the Pushkin Middle School, underground, from one end to the other. We three were like Sinbad, the Lone Ranger, Odysseus, and Barbarossa.

MAXIM: Who in hell is the Lone Ranger?

LEONARD: Don't know, never heard of him. He probably read it somewhere.

VLADIMIR: We entered underground through that little hole. We tied the end of the rope to the acacia tree that was near where we entered.

ELENA: Why? [*Silence.*]

VLADIMIR: Didn't receive. Repeat.

ELENA: I asked you why you tied the other end of the rope around your waists to a tree just outside the entrance.

VLADIMIR: Well . . . [*Laughs.*] because . . . because [*Scratches his head.*] we were afraid of losing our way back. [*Laughs.*] In case we got lost, we wanted someone to find us. We tied the rope to that acacia as a lead, a sign. To that acacia . . . [*Pauses.*] We were kids.

We were frightened; we didn't want to get lost. Although we wanted to disappear, we didn't want to get lost.

ELENA: What exactly does that mean now?

VLADIMIR: There no longer is a now, Elena! "Now" means nothing. I was eleven; I tied one end of the rope around my waist and the other to a tree—and entered the darkness. [*Silence. He leans over and calls again.*] Hey, can you hear me?

LEONARD: Yes. And how!

VLADIMIR: [*Laughs.*] Listen to me, Leo. We entered that corridor, which was almost large enough for an eleven-year-old, and before our forty-first step we were obliged to crawl. The foundations of the school kept getting lower.

MAXIM: Vladimir?

VLADIMIR: [*Carries on as if he heard nothing.*] We crawled for a considerable distance . . . for about two hours, which felt like eternity . . . then . . .

ELENA: What happened to the rope, Vladimir Komarov?

VLADIMIR: Which rope?

ELENA: The one you tied to a tree at the entrance.

VLADIMIR: We reached the end of that in ten minutes. We left it at a corner. It's amazing what can trouble your mind, dear Elena. We proceeded for more than an hour or two. The passage was so tight that even our knees were no longer usable. We kept crawling. It was dark; it stank of sewage. We went around too many corners and bends. How many, we couldn't count. We didn't know where we were underground. We couldn't return. The only direction to go was forward. We had gone too far, and it was dark. We didn't know which way was forward. There were too many corners in question, and there was no good reason for our being there. [*Pauses.*] We were kids. [*Smiles.*] Perhaps . . . that may have been a very good reason.

MAXIM: Vladimir Komarov? I temporarily have to interrupt this connection.

VLADIMIR: [*Laughs.*] Fine with me!

MAXIM: We have to contact the Ministry of Technology and consult them on how we can fix this malfunction.

VLADIMIR: [*Shouts.*] Enough . . . grow up now!

ELENA: How did you get out of the foundations?

VLADIMIR: We didn't. [*Long silence.*]

MAXIM: Couldn't receive, Vladimir Komarov. Please repeat.

VLADIMIR: Leo?

LEONARD: Yes, Ivan, I'm listening.

VLADIMIR: I've told you something about my dog's coat.

LEONARD: Yes, I know, once a week a mixture of egg and milk.

VLADIMIR: Don't try to apply it externally. Dear Teteryov has to drink that mixture.

MAXIM: Teteryov?

LEONARD: Name of his dog.

MAXIM: Vladimir?

VLADIMIR: Yes, yes, yes?

MAXIM: You must have a rest.

VLADIMIR: All right. You contact the ministry.

ELENA: How did you get out of those foundations?

MAXIM: Elena Veliovitch, if . . . if you please . . .

ELENA: But we must know!

MAXIM: Know! But why "we," why plural? I couldn't care less what Vladimir and his eleven-year-old friends did down in the foundations. What interests me now is how we can get out of this terrible situation we're all in!

VLADIMIR: How right you are, my dear Maxim Klimt!

ELENA: How did you get out of there?

VLADIMIR: [*Sits down and stretches his legs, happy with himself.*] I told you. We didn't get out.

ELENA: What happened then?

VLADIMIR: We got lost. We weren't able to advance or return. We were going in circles underground!

ELENA: And, and then what happened?

VLADIMIR: We were found by construction workers seventeen hours later. They dragged us out of there with our matches, candles, dried food, and bleeding knees and elbows. We didn't get out; those lovely people got us out of there. [*Pauses.*] Thousands of brilliant people . . . thousands of workmen! [*Silence.*]

MAXIM: Colonel Komarov, I'm temporarily interrupting the contact.

VLADIMIR: Yes, do that. Somehow I feel tired now.

[MAXIM *pushes a button, turns a switch. Silence. In the Communications Room, everyone exchanges glances.* VLADIMIR *stands up in the capsule. Through the porthole, he watches Earth. Now he feels dreamy, nervous, cynical, and childish—in short, clever and stupid at the same time.*]

LEONARD: One egg to be mixed in a glass of milk . . .

ELENA: You are a close friend of his, aren't you?

LEONARD: Not really. I've known him only a few years. You see, we play chess together. He also got me hooked on aquariums. I now have three in my study. You know, they are very relaxing to observe. The colonel and I go on long walks. He can name all the species of squirrels. Not only that, he'll tell you all about what each species eats. From there, he may go on to talk about the nineteenth century.

ELENA: Oh, yes, Vladimir has always been very interested in the nineteenth century.

LEONARD: Agriculture and theater! [*Pause.*]

ELENA: I'm not with you.

LEONARD: Agriculture, theater, and space geometry!

ELENA: What are you talking about?

LEONARD: Agriculture, theater, space geometry, and music!

MAXIM: Comrade Veliovitch?

ELENA: Yes?

MAXIM: [*Looks at his watch.*] We must be on our way.

ELENA: [*Points to Leonard.*] But what does he mean?

LEONARD: Agriculture, theater, space geometry, music, and quantum physics!

ELENA: Komarov must have really impressed you!

LEONARD: The answer to a perfect fur coat is an egg mixed in a glass of milk!

ELENA: You'll have to answer some questions on this for us!

LEONARD: Please don't pluralize yourself, madam!

ELENA: A little earlier you were pluralizing me!

LEONARD: Now you're playing on words and telling me that I put you in the same place with a dog.

MAXIM: She's not playing on words!

ELENA: No, I'm not!

LEONARD: What questions will I have to answer, then?

ELENA: What questions?

LEONARD: You mentioned the questions, not me!

ELENA: Who did?

LEONARD: You did!

ELENA: I did not!

LEONARD: You did.

ELENA: You know, you're funny.

LEONARD: I hope I am!

MAXIM: Elena, we must go. Boris Kukakov is waiting for us.

LEONARD: What in the world is that fatso doing here tonight?

ELENA: That fatso happens to be in charge of bilateral meetings concerning space research.

LEONARD: This is a scientific research center. What's he got to do here?

ELENA: The situation Colonel Komarov's in is beyond the limits of science. This tragedy concerns our entire country.

LEONARD: Why is that?

MAXIM: Elena, we must go!

LEONARD: No situation can go beyond the limits of science! [*Pause.*]

MAXIM: Let's go.

ELENA: Some situations involving people can go beyond the limits of science.

LEONARD: That's impossible. Science does not have limits. Also, we are not confronting a national tragedy.

ELENA: What then?

LEONARD: This tragedy involves dear Ivan and a handful of scientists who work at the center. It's a tragicomedy. A comical satire.

MAXIM: We're leaving, Leonard. Please wait here.

LEONARD: I'll be here. Don't worry, I'm not going anywhere.

ELENA: [*Comes near* LEONARD, *puts her hand lovingly on his shoulder.*] We're all nervous. We're trying not to lose him. That's all.

LEONARD: His return is almost impossible.

ELENA: You said nothing was impossible, or something along those lines, didn't you?

LEONARD: I'll feel very lonely without him!

MAXIM: [*Escorting* ELENA *out, he turns around and addresses* LEONARD.] This meeting may last a long time. There are things to eat in the cupboard.

LEONARD: I'll be here, Maxim. Till the end.

[ELENA *and* MAXIM *go out.* LEONARD *sits down, stretches his legs.* VLADIMIR *does exactly the same in the space capsule. From here onward, their movements are synchronized. A strong blue light falls on the space capsule. The right side of the stage suddenly comes alive with stars, moving meteorites, and so on.* LEONARD *reaches out and touches a button, and simultaneously* VLADIMIR *does the same. Music is heard: perhaps the first movement of Beethoven's Symphony no. 8 or the second movement of Mozart's "Jupiter" Symphony or Brahms or any movement of Tchaikovsky's Symphony no. 6 or even Mahler. Whatever is chosen must be played loudly.*

LEONARD *gets up and goes to a window.* VLADIMIR *gets up and goes to his porthole. They remain at their specific positions for a while and simultaneously go back and sit in their seats. Both take their heads in their hands and remain in that position for a while. They simultaneously touch a button, and the music stops—not suddenly, but slowly fading away. The synchronization between them fades away with the music.* VLADIMIR *takes out a red leather-covered book and starts reading it.* LEONARD *gets up, approaches a cabinet, takes out a brown file and a bottle of vodka, places them on the table. Goes back to the cupboard, takes out a glass, pours the vodka into it, starts to study the file.*

He lights a cigarette and laughs while reading the file. As the light on the space capsule dims, the light in the Communications Room increases. As LEONARD *casually turns the pages, he suddenly perks up. Puts his glass down, puts out his cigarette. He starts to read the file very carefully and suddenly finds the page he's interested in. After reading it, he slams the table, closes the file, pours himself another drink, and lights a cigarette. The door opens;* ANNA NATASHA KOMAROVA *enters. A good-looking, pretty blonde with blue eyes, she is very well dressed, simple but striking.*]

Natasha!

NATASHA: Hello, Leo, anything new?

LEONARD: [*Shakes his head, finishes his vodka.*] No, nothing new!

NATASHA: An ever-increasing deviation is in question.

LEONARD: That's right. But in twelve hours that deviation will create a ninety-degree angle in his course.

NATASHA: That means Ivan will be getting farther away from Earth.

LEONARD: Yes . . . and at a very rapid pace, goddamn it!

NATASHA: Don't act like this, Leo. It would really upset Ivan.

[*Silence.* NATASHA *starts to cry quietly; at the same time, she carries on with her conversation.*] You know he gets upset with people who lose their sense of humor. The weapon, the deadliest weapon, is to be able to laugh, you know this.

LEONARD: [*Takes a handkerchief out of his pocket, gives it to* NATASHA.] Yes, you're right.

NATASHA: He used to tell me that humans are entitled to everything. He used to say this when I cried. He used to say this when I felt sentimental.

LEONARD: Natasha, do you want to speak to him?

NATASHA: I . . . I don't know. [*Breaks down, starts crying, hugs* LEO.] I want to be with him, Leo. I want to touch him. I want to play with his hair, I want to kiss him, I want to feel dizzy watching him going around our house. I want to hear his voice. Although I don't necessarily listen to what he says, I want him to tell me stories, get all excited about what he's been telling me, see that childish expression of a storyteller on his face, and see him sulk when he realizes that I've heard the story before. Leo, why? Why, Leo, why, why, why?

LEONARD: Calm down. Do the boys know what's going on?

NATASHA: I called Andrei at the theater. I told him as much as one can on the telephone. He picked up everything instantly. He's like his father, you know. I called and left a message for Anton at the university. I told him to call here or home. They're not really too attached to their father. They both love him very much, but he managed to teach them how to be indifferent when the worst comes to the worst.

LEONARD: [*Pours a vodka, drinks it, looks at his glass.*] Do you want one?

NATASHA: [*Wipes her tears, passes the handkerchief to* LEO.] Yes, I wouldn't mind one.

LEONARD: [*Takes the handkerchief, plays as if he's wiping off his tears.*] If he saw us like this, he would really make fun of us. This is unheard of. This isn't possible!

[BORIS KUKAKOV *enters the room. Wearing a brown suit, he looks suave, like a very experienced fox, a fat fox with thick eyebrows.*]

BORIS: Yes, yes, this isn't possible. Please accept my respects, Anna Komarova. I don't know what to say!

LEONARD: Boris Kukakov?

BORIS: Director of the Bilateral Discussions Division for Space Matters. Who are you, young man?

LEONARD: Leonard Tomkin. I happen to be Vladimir Komarov's assistant.

BORIS: [*Puts his hand out.*] Aah, aah, how nice. Pleased to meet you.

LEONARD: [*Hands over the vodka he prepared for* NATASHA.] How about a drink, comrade?

BORIS: [*Takes it and drinks it in one gulp.*] We're very sorry!

LEONARD: Yes, the quality of vodka is going down every day. [NATASHA *laughs and turns around to conceal her chuckling.*]

BORIS: [*Did not register the joke.*] I have given the necessary orders to enable Vladimir Komarov's safe return. They will be carried out immediately. Everything possible is being done. Feel relaxed, Comrade Anna Komarova!

LEONARD: Comrade Kukakov, weren't you supposed to be at a meeting?

BORIS: How do you know? What are you doing here, you . . . what was your name, anyway?

LEONARD: Leonard Tomkin.

BORIS: Comrade Tomkin. Tell me, what is your job?

LEONARD: I told you. I'm Vladimir Komarov's assistant.

BORIS: Yeah, yes, you told me, but for the moment the world doesn't . . . yes, it doesn't know what kind of a scientist Colonel Komarov is . . . or was. [*Pauses.*] They are not aware yet. [*Looks at his watch.*] They'll find out tomorrow or the day after at the latest! [*Takes a red handkerchief out of his pocket and wipes his forehead.*] Anna Komarova!

NATASHA: Be calm, Mr. Kukakov.

BORIS: Anna Komarova! I came here to correct this terrible mistake.

LEONARD: And how are you going to do that?

BORIS: Do what?

LEONARD: How are you going to stop the space capsule from turning its nose toward outer space after every eighth revolution around Earth? It should turn toward Earth, you know.

BORIS: [*Takes the red handkerchief out again.*] Is that what is happening?

LEONARD: Yeah, that's what's happening.

BORIS: Anna Komarova! We will severely punish those responsible. Statues of your husband will be erected all over the country. I have ordered that.

LEONARD: And what's going to happen to Vladimir Komarov? [*Silence.*]

BORIS: [*Addresses* LEO.] And who are you?

LEONARD: Leonard Tomkin.

BORIS: Ah, oh yeah, I heard the name. What are you doing here, Comrade Tomkin?

LEONARD: Didn't you have a meeting?

BORIS: Yes, I was supposed to have a secret meeting with Comrades Klimt and Veliovitch.

LEONARD: Yeah, if it was secret, it couldn't have been very important.

BORIS: I don't get it.

LEONARD: It's not important.

BORIS: [*Trembles. The red handkerchief appears again.*] Anna Komarova, we will do everything possible.

NATASHA: I have no doubt, Boris Kukakov.

[ELENA *and* MAXIM *enter. They are harried, angry, and tired.*]

MAXIM: Comrade Kukakov! We've been looking all over for you for at least an hour.

BORIS: And I've been looking for you.

LEONARD: You all look like you're lost in the depths of space, not in this building! [*Pause.*]

ELENA: Natasha.

NATASHA: Elena.

[*Silence.* LEONARD *lights another cigarette.* MAXIM *bows his head.* ELENA *and* NATASHA *shake hands.* BORIS KUKAKOV *watches the situation in amazement.*]

BORIS: I welcome you all. [*Pauses.*] Here . . . the main reason to get us together under the roof of science, on the eve of a tragedy that involves the entire nation, . . . yes . . . shows our togetherness, which has not diminished a bit for half a century! [*Red handkerchief again.*] My friends! Vladimir Komarov, a great man, a marvelous creation of the revolution, a cosmonaut, an invincible knight, a perfect scientist . . . for reasons beyond our control . . . is in an undesirable situation . . . at this moment.

LEONARD: Yes?

BORIS: Yes, what?

LEONARD: We're all listening.

BORIS: [*Looks around him.*] Aah . . . yes . . . we are going to talk about a matter that deeply concerns national security.

LEONARD: Good.

BORIS: We can even get into details you are not supposed to know.

NATASHA: Understood.

LEONARD: I don't understand.

MAXIM: Leonard, will you please take Anna Komarova into the guest room? We'll call you two as soon as the meeting is over.

LEONARD: I must remain here, Maxim.

BORIS: And why is that? Look here, young man, if you don't want to leave this room feet first, take Mrs. Komarova with you and get out of here. [*Pauses.*] Please.

LEONARD: Excuse me?

BORIS: If you please.

NATASHA: Let's go, Leo.

MAXIM: We'll call you as soon as the meeting is over.

LEONARD: [*On their way out, stops at the door, addresses* MAXIM.] I've got things to say, but I see that saying them to you people won't do any good.

MAXIM: Please don't do this, Leo.

BORIS: What is it? What is he going to say?

LEONARD: [*To* BORIS.] You wouldn't understand. [*To* MAXIM.] Read file number 4. Read it carefully.

ELENA: Leonard Tomkin!

BORIS: What's file number 4? Which file? How many files are there?

ELENA: You must keep out of other people's business.

BORIS: Are you talking to me?

LEONARD: I am a scientist. Nothing in the world is beyond a scientist's reach. [*Short pause.*] Vladimir Komarov . . . all right, he's not within my reach or on this world, but as you all can see, I'm very concerned about him and his present situation. [*Short pause.*] And there's nothing to get all worked up about. My concern is to find out more about this mistake in order to avoid a chain of such mistakes in the future. [*Bows, saluting everyone.*] I, Leonard Tomkin, and Anna Komarova will wait in the guest room for the announcement of the end of your meeting. Good luck! [LEONARD *and* NATASHA *go out. The room remains silent. Everyone looks at one another.*]

CURTAIN

ACT II

[*With the light coming on,* ELENA *slams to the floor the file she's holding in her hand.* MAXIM *is standing in the middle of the room. He looks very tired.* BORIS *has taken his jacket off. He is sitting down, red handkerchief in one hand and a glass of vodka in the other.*]

ELENA: Tomkin is right. This is unbelievable! How could you approve such a thing?

BORIS: How many times do I have to repeat myself? State security has priority over the security of a space capsule.

ELENA: A human life, a very valuable human life, is in question!

BORIS: A human life. Yes, a single human life. The life of an individual standing high on the shoulders of a great nation. I am obliged to consider the national benefits before personal benefits.

ELENA: Who is obliging you to think like this?

BORIS: I don't understand.

ELENA: He's obliged! Hah! Ivan is perishing because of your obligations!

BORIS: [*Stands up.*] I didn't hear this . . . you didn't say anything like this . . . [*Pauses.*] I warn you! [*Pauses.*] Cosmonaut Colonel Vladimir Komarov, professor of physics at the Military Academy, the most popular member of our Space Research Center, is going to become an unfortunate hero of our nation after an incredible accident. The most popular member of the Space Research Center will be the unforgettable hero in the heart of the nation. A source of pride. We are the most powerful and developed country in the world. A little accident or one-time bad luck can't change this fact. If the need arises, we can produce ten, a hundred, or a thousand spaceships. We will find ten, a hundred, or a thousand Vladimir Komarovs. This hallowed land is able to produce many things and a great many able people. Pampering individuals diminishes countries. Yes, right now we are face to face with a very annoying and unexpected accident.

ELENA: [*Laughs nervously.*] What? Did you say an accident is taking place?

BORIS: Is that what I said?

MAXIM: What are we going to do?

ELENA: [*Points to the file on the floor.*] We are going to make this information public and explain it.

BORIS: I haven't heard this. I'm not hearing this! We shall make that decision!

MAXIM: We will not expose it!

BORIS: Bravo! Comrade Maxim Klimt, I congratulate you on behalf of our nation!

ELENA: What are you saying—that we're going to hide this?

BORIS: What?

ELENA: This accident was easily avoidable. The trouble spot was mentioned as a weak point time and time again in the reports given to your office. The money allocated in the budget to correct it was always diverted and sucked up in other fields. A haven for scientists was crammed with personnel who couldn't even turn a vacuum cleaner on and off, who couldn't get employment elsewhere. Are we going to keep lying about this and just say, "Sorry, Vladimir Komarov had to vanish." Considering the social upheaval and public hysteria this statement will cause, we'll hide the truth and make a public declaration that all this happened because of a technical malfunction. [*Pause.*]

BORIS: [*Calmly.*] Yes.

ELENA: What are you saying?

BORIS: We're going to hide it.

MAXIM: We can't be frank about it. [BORIS *makes a gesture to* ELENA *as if saying, "That's the way it is."*]

ELENA: Maxim! [MAXIM *is helpless. He opens his mouth. Nothing comes out.*]

BORIS: Elena Veliovitch! My dear friend, sit down, calm down a little. Komarov . . . he wa . . . was very important . . . very important to you, wasn't he?

ELENA: What do you mean? Wasn't he important to you?

BORIS: I wanted to say that you were his lover.

MAXIM: Boris Kukakov!

ELENA: How does this relate to file number 4?

BORIS: There never was such a file. I didn't hear anything about it. Forget it altogether.

ELENA: [*Shouts.*] I will not forget anything. [*Pause.*]

MAXIM: [*Mumbles to himself.*] These files are in triplicate.

BORIS: [*Addresses* MAXIM.] What?

MAXIM: These files are always produced in triplicate. [ELENA *nervously laughs.*]

BORIS: [*Points at the file on the floor.*] This is one?

MAXIM: Yes.

BORIS: Where are copies two and three, Maxim Klimt?

MAXIM: A second copy is always dispatched to your office right away.

BORIS: Good, that means it's safe. How about the third copy?

MAXIM: That goes straight to archives, downstairs on the first floor. [*To* ELENA.] Go and get it now!

ELENA: No.

BORIS: Yes.

ELENA: We cannot erase the cause of Vladimir Komarov's disappearance from the records.

BORIS: And why is that?

ELENA: It's immoral!

[*Toward the end of this argument, some activity begins in the space capsule. The audience's attention is attracted to the capsule by lighting arrangements. As* VLADIMIR KO-MAROV's *figure is well lit, he stands up, looks at the dials, laughs, shakes his head, sits down, reaches for and pushes a button. He pauses, waiting.*]

BORIS: Why should science be immoral?

ELENA: Science can't be in conflict with morals.

BORIS: Your statement doesn't interest me at all.

ELENA: Why?

BORIS: Ivan Komarov is up there, where he is, under the auspices of science.

ELENA: But you're confused. You're mixing up science with technicalities.

BORIS: No, madam, I'm not confused, and I'm not getting my priorities mixed up. I'm only concerned about the benefits to and the welfare of my nation.

ELENA: Science has no benefits, profits, or welfare. [*Pause.*]

BORIS: I didn't hear that!

ELENA: Science is very different. It has no relation whatsoever to techniques. It's a different story.

BORIS: I prefer not to hear this.

ELENA: Science is a lovely, poetic thing. It's full of curiosity and goodness. Idiots, retarded bureaucrats, and technocrats have no place in it. They can't understand or even discuss it. Science is different.

BORIS: I wish I hadn't heard this.

MAXIM: [*Keeps an eye on the luminous dials on the table.*] Look here!

ELENA: Since science is like this, it can't hide anything from the people.

MAXIM: Look, look here!

BORIS: [*Ignores* MAXIM.] This time it will hide the other copies of file number 4. Whether you like it or not!

ELENA: I will tell everyone everything I know!

BORIS: I prefer not to hear you.

MAXIM: Would you please listen to me? [*Pauses.*] Vladimir Komarov wants to talk to Earth! [*Silence.*]

ELENA: Oh my God!

BORIS: I didn't hear that! [*To* MAXIM.] Please establish contact.

ELENA: What are you going to tell him?

BORIS: I don't know.

MAXIM: [*Reaches and pushes some buttons.*] Komarov? [*Silence.*]

ELENA: [*Speaks into a microphone.*] Ivan? Can you hear us? [*Silence.*]

BORIS: Comrade Komarov? Are you there?

VLADIMIR: [*Laughs.*] Where?

BORIS: Ohh . . . well, out there, in space.

VLADIMIR: I'm here. [*Silence.*]

ELENA: We're listening to you, Ivan.

VLADIMIR: How nice. I'm listening to you, too. [*Silence.*]

BORIS: And what does that mean?

VLADIMIR: Elena?

ELENA: Yes, I'm listening.

VLADIMIR: I hope the last voice I heard wasn't yours. [*Pauses.*] I mean the voice that growled, "And what does that mean?" wasn't you, was it?

ELENA: [*Looks at* BORIS.] It wasn't me. It was someone else. Ivan?

VLADIMIR: Yes?

ELENA: No, nothing.

VLADIMIR: Is Maxim there?

MAXIM: I'm here, Ivan, listening to you.

VLADIMIR: Is Leo with you? [*Pause;* VLADIMIR *gets up in anger.*] Leo! Leo! Where the hell are you?

MAXIM: He just stepped out, Vladimir; he'll be back any minute now.

VLADIMIR: All right, all right. [*Laughs.*] Is my wife there now? And my sons? [*Silence.*]

MAXIM: They're not here now. They'll . . . they'll be here soon!

ELENA: Ivan!

VLADIMIR: Elena! Can you hear me?

ELENA: Yes, I can hear you. [*Silence.*]

VLADIMIR: I . . . How should I put it? It's all moved beyond the situation I'm in. I was never frightened in the past. I'm not frightened now! I go, it goes—that is, the little thing that ticks within. [*Silence.*]

ELENA: I don't get it.

VLADIMIR: I'm talking about my heart. This is a Siberian guessing game: I go, it follows me within, ticking all the time we're together.

BORIS: Ticks within me, all the time. [*Mumbles to himself.*] Like a time bomb.

VLADIMIR: That's right. That's it. Elena, who is that intelligent individual? [*Silence.*]

BORIS: It's me.

VLADIMIR: [*Laughs.*] And who are you, sir?

BORIS: Boris.

VLADIMIR: Boris who? Boris Pasternak?

BORIS: [*Upset.*] What do you mean, Comrade Komarov?

VLADIMIR: Don't get upset. I'm only joking. You . . . which Boris are you? I just wondered.

BORIS: [*Wipes his face with the red handkerchief and reaches out to the microphone.*] Boris Kukakov. [*Moment of silence.*] Director of bilateral discussions between your department and mine. [*A moment's pause.*] Boris . . . Kukakov?

VLADIMIR: Maxim?

MAXIM: [*Shakes himself and comes around.*] Yes, yes, sir?

VLADIMIR: What's going on down there?

MAXIM: We're working. We're trying to get things done, Vladimir. Get things done. We're working.

VLADIMIR: It goes down laughing and comes up in tears. [*Silence.*]

MAXIM: I don't get it.

VLADIMIR: It goes down very happily and comes up in tears.

BORIS: That's a bucket in a well.

VLADIMIR: You got it right! Maxim?

MAXIM: Yes?

VLADIMIR: What in hell is Boris Kukakov doing there tonight?

MAXIM: Yes?

VLADIMIR: What the hell is Boris Kukakov doing there tonight? [*Silence.*]

MAXIM: Vladimir . . . look, you are a man of this world. Kukakov is simply here to explain our situation to the administrators. He's just doing some research. [*Silence.*]

BORIS: We all know that you will die and perish in space, Comrade Vladimir Komarov. We are here to find an acceptable way of telling this to our people and ourselves. I don't know; this is a very difficult task, but we're working on it. Very hard.

VLADIMIR: Elena?

ELENA: Yes, Ivan, I'm listening to you.

VLADIMIR: What do you say in this situation?

ELENA: Which situation?

VLADIMIR: He just said I will die, I will perish. I always thought I wasn't going to die or perish.

MAXIM: Ivan! One moment, please!

VLADIMIR: It's not possible to die and perish. One can't die and perish at the same time. One perishes while one is alive. When one dies, he remains there, dead! [*Pauses.*] My situation creates a lot of controversy. Naturally. I will be "going" rather "traveling" when I'm dead.

ELENA: Ivan!

VLADIMIR: There will always be a doubt concerning my death. I will expire talking. At least in your minds. I will be a receding voice. You won't even know if that voice is heard elsewhere. We can't know. Nobody can! [*Pauses.*] Nobody, Boris Kukakov.

BORIS: [*Shivers violently.*] Comrade Komarov, I'm listening to you.

VLADIMIR: Comrade Kukakov, I'm retreating from the official ideology at a great speed. I never had much to do with its unofficial version, either. Right now I'm going farther away from that incredible void you have created, watching the lovely Milky Way, my meteorites, in the darkness of my own space and getting out of that lovely setup of yours.

BORIS: I really would have liked to be accompanying you.

VLADIMIR: I don't want to hear that!

MAXIM: Ivan, my dear friend, we're doing all that's possible.

VLADIMIR: I'm sure of that, Maxim.

MAXIM: The secretary-general called. He's appalled. This is not possible.

VLADIMIR: Maxim, this is an adventure—a scientific adventure. Once we're involved in this, we mustn't expect too much and should take the unexpected into consideration in our calculations. Of all things, we mustn't be surprised when it happens.

MAXIM: I know. I know all this. But even when we launched into this adventure, we thought we knew the risks, and we thought we would come out of all this all right. Didn't we, Ivan?

VLADIMIR: Naturally we did. But along the same lines, we're still not sure this adventure will end up a failure, are we?

MAXIM: What do you mean by that, my dear friend?

VLADIMIR: In two hours, the deviation of the orbit will reach its limit, and I will start going farther and farther away . . . from you. From that moment on, my oxygen reserve will be sufficient for another eighteen to nineteen hours. Let us not forget that I will be traveling hundreds of thousands of kilometers per minute. When the orbital deviation is complete, within a couple of minutes, you will be unable to hear my voice—our communication will be cut off. But . . . I will still be very much alive. I will be the only one to know the last part of this adventure. I'll probably never be able to tell you all about it, but, all the same, I will live through the final part of this adventure. Very conscientiously. Maxim?

MAXIM: You are right, Vladimir! There's this side of the adventure as well. My sorrow, my sadness, has reached such a degree that talking like this is giving my heart tremendous pain.

VLADIMIR: It's no use at this moment. It's too late to get worried or nervous. It's too late. It won't help.

MAXIM: One gets awfully confused in this situation.

VLADIMIR: Are you in Communications Room number 1?

ELENA: Yes.

VLADIMIR: There should be a bottle of vodka in the cupboard. Why don't you have it? [*They all laugh together.*]

MAXIM: Leo already started; he offered us some, too.

VLADIMIR: Yeah, where is Leonard?

BORIS: He's coming, Comrade Komarov, any moment now. [*To* MAXIM.] Call him, please.

MAXIM: [*Picks up the telephone.*] Please ask Comrade Tomkin and Mrs. Komarova to come here. They are in the guest room. . . . Yes, right away. [*Silence.*]

VLADIMIR: Is Natasha there, too? What in the world are they doing in the guest room?

MAXIM: Mmmm, we were having a meeting here.

ELENA: Yes, we were having a very important meeting. Too important and confidential to have your wife and assistant present.

VLADIMIR: If it's that secret, it can't possibly be important.

BORIS: Colonel Komarov . . . the tragedy we are living through has great importance for our people. That is . . . how this tragedy will be announced to our nation, that's very important. What I want to say is, how will our people receive this?

VLADIMIR: I understand.

ELENA: What, Ivan? What do you understand?

VLADIMIR: Elena . . . my precious friend . . . I understand the way you feel. After all, it's not easy to be about to lose a wonderful, nice, intelligent, humble, dependable person, friend, and colleague like me. It certainly isn't easy. But keep calm. Please don't be aggressive.

ELENA: Ivan, there are facts you don't know.

MAXIM: Elena!

BORIS: Comrade Veliovitch, you are going beyond the limits of your job!

ELENA: I resign!

BORIS: Good. Your resignation is accepted. Please leave this room and the premises immediately. Come on, quickly, right now!

ELENA: We have to tell him!

BORIS: We will tell him.

ELENA: What are you going to tell him?

BORIS: We'll tell him that he will always live in our hearts. Newborn babies will be named after him. What a great hero he is . . . who loved his people more than he loved himself . . . and this never will be forgotten. We will tell him all, everything.

ELENA: Will you also tell him why he's there?

VLADIMIR: You say I don't know why I'm here?

BORIS: How can a great person like Colonel Komarov ignore such a thing? Of course he knows. He has been decorated ever so many times. He's a cosmonaut.

MAXIM: Elena, please calm down.

BORIS: [*To* ELENA.] And who the hell are you to tell and explain things to a great person like Vladimir Komarov? My God, she's trouble—this woman!

ELENA: Vladimir, listen to me!

VLADIMIR: Calm down, Elena. I'll miss you, too.

[*At some point during this conversation—perhaps when* BORIS *addresses* ELENA*—the door opens, and* LEO, NATASHA, *and* ANDREI *enter the Communications Room.*]

LEONARD: Hello, Ivan, good evening.

VLADIMIR: Leonard, you're there. Good, listen to me: Read Mandelbrot's book again. He explains the solution in chapter 17.

BORIS: Who is this Mandelbrot? Never heard of him.

LEONARD: Yes, Ivan. I'll read it again, first thing tomorrow morning. How are you, all right?

VLADIMIR: I'm fine—in fact, very well. But what a mess, a tremendous, ugly mess I'm in— in fact, that we're all in. Leo, people like us are made for other kinds of messes and difficulties, aren't we?

LEONARD: Everything can be repeated over and over, but there must be slight differences in every version!

VLADIMIR: As long as we're aware of that little difference between the versions and search for it, we'll be able to understand what's going on and what's to come!

LEONARD: Benoit will be very pleased to hear this.

BORIS: Who is Benoit? Does he work here?

ELENA: You're all mad!

MAXIM: Elena!

NATASHA: Ivan? [*Silence.*]

VLADIMIR: [*Sits down, sad.*] My love! At the beginning, when the foundation of the Space Research Center was being laid, I told you what a great adventure I was entering, remember? Andrei was already born. You were pregnant with Anton, do you remember?

NATASHA: Yes.

VLADIMIR: It was during one of our long walks; we sat down on the grass, where I told this to you. You kissed me; actually, you kissed my eyes when we were there on the grass, and you said you understood. Really, really, that was my happiest moment, down to the deepest particle of my body. That cool April evening, your kissing my eyes. I was thoroughly happy.

NATASHA: Ivan?

VLADIMIR: Yes, Natasha? Yes, my love, my darling wife, my precious friend?

NATASHA: Is there anything in particular you want me to do?

VLADIMIR: Yes, of course. Just act natural. Don't rub it in too much. Everyone will have to make a remark. Everyone will have something to say. I don't want you to think I'm dead. [*Giggles.*] Because I'm not dying. I'm going. This is a scientific departure. I want it to be a poetic way of going.

NATASHA: Very well, then.

VLADIMIR: There, in that room, in the presence of others, you won't be able to tell me all you intended to. I know. I also know what you're telling me now.

NATASHA: Yes, that's right.

VLADIMIR: Please give all my writings to Leo.

BORIS: Comrade Komarov?

VLADIMIR: Who's talking?

BORIS: Boris Kukakov. I'm talking as a responsible and authorized person.

VLADIMIR: Where I happen to be, I assume all the responsibility and authority. What's your name again?

BORIS: Kukakov.

VLADIMIR: Kukakov, I'm listening to you all the same.

BORIS: Wouldn't it be better if all your writings, notes, and personal library went to the Space Research Center archives?

VLADIMIR: No, it wouldn't.

ELENA: Vladimir Komarov?

BORIS: Just think of our people. You're like a lantern illuminating, enlightening, them now!

VLADIMIR: Aah, yes . . . light . . . how's that, Leo?

LEONARD: Light is invisible. We can see only the things illuminated by it.

BORIS: How nice. [*Claps.*] Bravo, all the same, I'm saying . . .

NATASHA: Ivan? [*Silence.*]

VLADIMIR: I'm listening, my darling.

NATASHA: Andrei is here, too.

VLADIMIR: Miki?

ANDREI: Yes, I'm here.

VLADIMIR: How's the theater going these days?

ANDREI: Very well.

VLADIMIR: What are you playing in now?

ANDREI: *Hamlet.*

VLADIMIR: You don't say! Really?

ANDREI: Yes.

VLADIMIR: How nice! I love Shakespeare.

ANDREI: I know, Dad.

VLADIMIR: I know that you know. Miki?

ANDREI: Yes, Dad?

VLADIMIR: Do whatever you feel like doing. [*Pauses.*] I know that you are very kind to the ones you care for, but also be kind to the ones you don't like. Don't let them see right away that you don't care for them. Be a good actor. That's if you're going to make a living as an actor; at least, play well.

ANDREI: Yes, Dad.

VLADIMIR: Learn to listen to what the other actors are saying to you, Miki. If you want your words to be meaningful and considered, you must listen and understand what the others are telling you. Don't ever forget this.

ANDREI: [*Smiles.*] I understand, Dad.

VLADIMIR: If you don't grasp the meaning of what's being said to you, your answer will vanish into thin air!

ANDREI: I know, Dad.

VLADIMIR: Good. [*Takes a deep breath, wipes his forehead.*] What part are you playing in *Hamlet?*

ANDREI: Hamlet, Dad. [*Silence.*]

VLADIMIR: Andrei?

ANDREI: Yes, Dad?

VLADIMIR: You . . . I'll miss you a lot.

ANDREI: Thanks, Dad. I'll miss you very much, too. Can I speak now? [*Pauses.*] Can you hear me?

VLADIMIR: Yes, for the moment, yes.

ANDREI: Now . . . I don't know how to say this, but I know you'll . . . understand . . . all the same. [*Pauses.*] Anton and me, you have brought us up in such a way that we manage to laugh at the worst, the most horrendous happenings. We never have to open our inner selves to others even about death. That's thanks to your way of bringing us up. [*Silence.*]

VLADIMIR: [*Comfortably settles down in his seat.*] I'm listening, Miki.

ANDREI: Do you remember, your arm got burned in a fire? You kept saying it was burned in the fire of science. Do you remember? You weren't able to use it for a year? Your right arm!

VLADIMIR: [*Laughs.*] I remember it like yesterday, Miki. But what does that have to do with the present situation?

ANDREI: A lot.

BORIS: With what?

ANDREI: [*Shouts at* BORIS.] With everything!

VLADIMIR: Don't shout, Miki. I hear you very well. [*Silence.*]

ANDREI: There are things you don't know, Dad.

VLADIMIR: Naturally, I know there must be a lot of things I'm unaware of!

ANDREI: No, that's not what I mean.

VLADIMIR: For example, I'm not aware of what you're trying to tell me.

ANDREI: We'll miss you a lot, but our anger is not only related to losing you!

VLADIMIR: I hope it isn't, Son.

ANDREI: Listen to me, Dad!

VLADIMIR: By the way, I must remind you, I can't stand things like bad temper, anger, and such.

ANDREI: You're not listening to me!

VLADIMIR: I rather prefer people who live their lives like a sudden burst of anger, but without getting angry and violent.

ANDREI: Dad, this is way out of context. Although you're right.

VLADIMIR: Yes. [*Laughs.*] You're just like me—in this respect.

ANDREI: I wish I was there. With you.

VLADIMIR: Aah! I worked thirty-four years to get to where I am at this moment! By the way . . . all of you are with me here, you, Anton, Natasha, all of you are with me, beside me now. [*Silence.*]

LEONARD: Ivan.

VLADIMIR: Leo! Leo, you just can't imagine what an incredible, what a magnificent thing . . . I'm living through, experiencing. Leonard, I'm like someone who encounters his own ghost. Now I understand, I understand much better, a lot of people who mean a lot to me, whom I really love. I understand now.

LEONARD: Who are they, Ivan?

VLADIMIR: I understand Mayakovski . . . Eisenstein and Einstein, Charlie Parker and Gogol . . . Nazım Hikmet and everyone who loves these people.

LEONARD: Einstein and Eisenstein . . .

VLADIMIR: As long as they rhyme, you name them.

LEONARD: Vladimir? [*Laughs. Can't stop, goes on laughing.*] What do you mean by meeting your own ghost? That doesn't sound like you at all.

VLADIMIR: This place doesn't look very familiar, either. It's a beauty of a mess I'm witnessing, Leo. A beautiful, very big mess.

BORIS: Comrade Komarov [*Artificially coughs.*] . . . the thing is . . . sorry to say, but we down here are witnessing the misery of the same mess.

ELENA: You could have been alive, Ivan.

VLADIMIR: I am alive, damn it! Even if I happen to be in space, I am very much alive!

MAXIM: Elena, what do you think you're doing, you fool?

ELENA: [*Shouts at the top of her voice.*] I love him! [*Silence.*]

NATASHA: Me, too . . . I love him, too.

VLADIMIR: I thank you. Both of you.

LEONARD: Vladimir! You are up there in this situation because of a cheap trick! [*Silence.*] Do you hear me?

VLADIMIR: [*Smiles.*] I hear you, Leo.

ELENA: Tell him everything, Leonard!

BORIS: [*To* ELENA.] Didn't you resign?

ELENA: I withdraw my resignation.

BORIS: Withdrawal rejected.

MAXIM: Please don't be ridiculous.

BORIS: You can't speak like this to someone in charge!

ANDREI: But Dad should know everything!

LEONARD: I'm trying to explain. Please let me!

NATASHA: You're wasting your time. [*Silence.*]

LEONARD: Natasha?

NATASHA: I don't know what to say. I don't know anything, except . . .

BORIS: That you don't know anything! [*Everyone laughs, including* VLADIMIR KOMAROV.]

NATASHA: He already knows. He knows what you're trying to tell him.

MAXIM: Mrs. Komarova . . . please . . .

ELENA: Natasha, everything was classified.

ANDREI: That doesn't change anything!

LEONARD: Can I say something? Please!

BORIS: Yes, as long as you don't say something antirevolutionary.

LEONARD: I didn't ask you!

VLADIMIR: Leo? Leooo!

LEONARD: We're listening, Ivan.

VLADIMIR: Come on, shoot. Tell me. [*Silence.*]

LEONARD: Ivan . . . something like this was expected. These people weren't sure, but there was a possibility of this mission going wrong. Well, more or less . . .

VLADIMIR: Yes, and . . . ?

LEONARD: No one lifted a finger. They just signed whatever was put on their desks. They made everyone sign the acceptance of the mission in the darkness of a jungle of red tape. Even I signed two of them.

BORIS: There you are!

ELENA: Vladimir, you're not in this situation because of an accident. This is murder. Murder because of red tape.

VLADIMIR: Come on. My presence here is not murder or an accident!

ANDREI: Forgive me!

VLADIMIR: Andrei! What are you saying?

LEONARD: Vladimir! This malfunctioning could have been detected and corrected long ago.

BORIS: How do you know? Are you experts on this subject?

LEONARD and ELENA: [*Simultaneously.*] Yes, we are experts!

BORIS: Experts of what?

LEONARD: You could drive anyone crazy.

BORIS: Oh my. Oh my . . . well, well, well!

ELENA: Natasha?

NATASHA: Elena?

ELENA: What's happening must not be hidden—must not be kept secret.

BORIS: We won't keep it secret. We don't hide anything from our people!

ANDREI: "Something is rotten in the state of Denmark."[2]

VLADIMIR: Bravo, Andrei. I have no doubt you'll be great in the play!

BORIS: [*To* ANDREI.] Is this a good moment for theater?

ANDREI: Isn't it?

VLADIMIR: Through theater, you can change the world. You can stop wars. Through theater, you can make people look better! With theater, you can bring down inflation, correct the educational system, even improve the judicial system. Through theater, people once and for all realize that they are real people. Never to be forgotten. With theater, people can make their own elections and understand the importance of being able to say no! In theater, each person learns how to be humane and reject the inhumane! One can see only reality in the theater. Leooo?

LEONARD: [*Surprised.*] Yes, yes I'm here, sir.

VLADIMIR: One day we talked about the people who considered the sky only as a thing to fly in . . . do you remember?

LEONARD: Yes, very well. I remember very well.

VLADIMIR: To fly on, not in it . . .

LEONARD: Yes, yes . . . we discussed this for hours!

VLADIMIR: If . . . only you were with me now. I'm in an enormous bed, surrounded by orange, red, blue, and white bedcovers. I'm getting faster and faster, Leo. No, the sky is like a very inviting bed. Covers above and below me.

ELENA: Ivan! Ivan! Please listen to us, Ivan!

MAXIM: Leave him alone.

[*Silence. Everyone in the room looks at* MAXIM. *Ever since* LEONARD *told* VLADIMIR, *"This accident was expected,"* MAXIM KLIMT *has been silently sipping his vodka in the corner. By hand gestures and smiles, he makes sure that it's understood that he is very much involved in the situation and has listened to every word said.*]

VLADIMIR: Thank you, Maxim!

BORIS: [*To* MAXIM.] Thank you!

ELENA: Has everyone gone mad, Leo?

LEONARD: Vladimir! That's enough! Listen to me!

VLADIMIR: Hush! [*Silence.*] C'mon, what a shame. [*A moment's pause.*] Please forgive my selfishness, my friends! At present, I'm not in a magical loneliness. But I'm not lonely at all, either! Now I realize how right I was all along!

---

2. William Shakespeare, *Hamlet,* Act I, Scene iv, line 90.

BORIS: Is he right?

VLADIMIR: I look into the future with a great deal of hope. That's how I have viewed it all the time.

ELENA: Ivan, in a little more than eighteen hours your oxygen supply will run out.

VLADIMIR: Well, that means I'll be looking into the future with hope for eighteen more hours. I always said in my lectures that there is nothing beyond nature! I stated that one must not be afraid of the future. I repeated this thousands of times. For years, I advocated that the only thing of real value is morals achieved through the teachings of art and science. I was right. Right! [*A moment's pause.*] This is a lovely feeling!

ELENA: Ivan, you're drifting away from reality!

VLADIMIR: Isn't science a compilation of realities?

LEONARD: Bronowski!

VLADIMIR: Well done, Leo! Science only searches for the realities concealed in the great mixture offered us in the wild. When you look at it from this angle, theater is a science. Even painting is!

ELENA: Vladimir, you're going away; the remaining time is very limited.

VLADIMIR: On my way out, I'm learning how to have very high morals, my friends.

BORIS: What morals?

VLADIMIR: The morals of science. Or the immorality of the theater. In the end, they are one and the same.

BORIS: The same?

VLADIMIR: They may also reach the light of the sky or its limits. Like I'm about to do myself!

BORIS: I offer you my respects, Colonel Komarov!

ELENA: Ivan? [*Silence.*]

LEONARD: Vladimir? Can you hear me? I have something very important to tell you! Can you hear me? [*Silence.*]

VLADIMIR: It's not as important as all that, Leo. [*Silence.*]

LEONARD: You don't know what's going on.

VLADIMIR: That's not important . . . and by the way . . . may be the least important thing, Leo. [*Silence.*]

ELENA: I understand, I do understand your situation, Ivan.

LEONARD: All the same, you must listen to us!

VLADIMIR: [*Relaxed, smiling, tired.*] How many times have I told you, Leo?

LEONARD: Told me what?

VLADIMIR: How many times have I told you not to refer to yourself in the plural?

ELENA: We want to know how you think about a very important issue for the sake of our country and the world or for the sake of everything we believe in and defend, Vladimir!

VLADIMIR: Is my wife still there? And my son?

ANDREI: We're here, Dad, we're here!

BORIS: I'm also here, Comrade Komarov!

MAXIM: I'm not here.

VLADIMIR: Leo?

LEONARD: Yes, listening.

VLADIMIR: Yes, that's better. [*A moment's pause.*] I have a feeling the tension down there, where you are, is rather high. Am I right?

BORIS: It is. For some reason unknown to me!

VLADIMIR: Are you blaming each other because of file number 4?

> [*Long pause. They look at each other.* MAXIM *drinks;* BORIS *wipes his forehead with the red handkerchief;* ELENA *covers her face with her hands;* LEONARD *looks at the ceiling;* ANDREI *smiles; and* NATASHA *weeps quietly in a corner.*]

You are shortening my time in this magnificent period because of silly file number 4!

ELENA: Did you know?

VLADIMIR: I produced it, put it in order, and placed it in that cabinet for you to read.

ANDREI: Have a nice trip, Dad. I'm leaving now.

VLADIMIR: Have a nice trip yourself, Son! Become a well-established Hamlet! [ANDREI, *without looking at anyone, walks out, slams the door. Silence.*]

ELENA: We will expose what we know, Ivan!

BORIS: What are you going to expose, my dear?

ELENA: All the contents of file number 4 and how it came into being!

VLADIMIR: That will be a very stupid thing to do! Stupid and unnecessary. [*Pauses.*] This is a magnificent experience I'm having, the end of which will be unknown to you. How can you downgrade it to the level of a wretched file? How can that be right?

LEONARD: Ivan, there isn't anything more important than the world!

VLADIMIR: Right, Leo. You're right. Under the circumstances, we cannot possibly reduce this grain of reality to the level of the contents of a shitty file.

LEONARD: Shall we lie to the world?

VLADIMIR: Well, just tell them Vladimir Komarov is gone.

ELENA: They will ask why.

VLADIMIR: Because of a technical error that occurred in space.

LEONARD: A lot of people will want to know about the details.

VLADIMIR: Then you'll tell them about the details. File number 4 has nothing to do with the curious people or with the details!

BORIS: [*Whispers.*] Yes.

MAXIM: [*Takes a sip of his drink.*] Cheers!

ELENA: Although you were a legend among the students, I always envisaged you as someone to look up to. A legend . . .

VLADIMIR: In reality, I was only a mediocre scientist, a teacher, as I am now . . . at least among my students. As a living human being, I am already a legend. I'm curious, relaxed, phasing out, but at the same time very serious. I have not yet lost my sense of humor. I'm a man who likes experimenting.

LEONARD: Vladimir?

VLADIMIR: Take good care of the sea horses, Leonard; they're very delicate creatures!

ELENA: On your way out, you're becoming a part of this rotten system. [*Pauses.*] Just like a thin plastic bag inside the trash can—a refined one.

VLADIMIR: A refined trash can!

ELENA: Yes. Vladimir, you are bad . . . Vladimir Komarov, you are bad.

VLADIMIR: Elena. My darling Elena, at this moment we don't have the choice of being good or bad. Now I can only say whether I have some people in my life. And even this is not right. File number 4 has nothing to do with me.

LEONARD: It's got nothing to do . . . with us?

VLADIMIR: [*Sits down, relaxes, stretches his legs.*] That's right. It's got nothing to do with us, Leo.

ELENA: One has to account for everything. [*Silence.*]

VLADIMIR: Elena, why are we behaving like this? I am here, you are there, the situation is not reversible. Forget it.

NATASHA: [*To* ELENA.] You know, at times he wants to be all by himself. He's not like anyone else we know. Almost like he came here from another planet. He's funny. He's sad.

VLADIMIR: Natasha, my darling, do you remember?

NATASHA: You must give me everything, Ivan. Every detail.

VLADIMIR: Natasha, my darling, do you remember, do you remember everything?

LEONARD: Vladimir, you must let me, you must give me permission!

VLADIMIR: [*Recites a poem, rather distractedly.*[3]]

> *To hit the road. At the end.*
> *Toward the shining suds,*
> *—To disappear in the golden air of the summer*
> *—be blessed—and at the end—to leave*
> *everything to the waves.*
> *Release all the happy contractions of the muscles.*
> *For an instant, alone with the upcoming surge of the interior.*
> *To launch everything toward the dawn*
> *Launch everything, all the screams, bury yourself in*
> *eternity. Reborn all shining, untouched and yourself,*
> *unheard of and happy, fast, like a star.*
> *Light and all by yourself.*

LEONARD: Forgive me, Ivan.

BORIS: [*Wipes his forehead.*] What about file number 4?

---

3. From Jorge Guillén (1893–1984), Spanish poet.

VLADIMIR: It's in three copies. I suggest they give you all the copies, Comrade Kukakov.

ELENA: Do you really want us to do this, Ivan?

VLADIMIR: Yes, that's what I really want you to do.

LEONARD: Then that's what we'll do.

VLADIMIR: Thank you all very much, my friends.

ELENA: This is impossible!

LEONARD: Everything else was impossible, madam. Vladimir says his task is not over yet. He still has work to accomplish.

VLADIMIR: Hey! That's my Leonard Tomkin! I knew you would understand!

NATASHA: There are so many things I want to tell you and want you to understand. [*Silence.*]

VLADIMIR: Tell them to Leo, Natasha. Not a thing will go astray. [NATASHA KOMAROV *sits down at the table with many dials, facing the microphone. Lights a cigarette with shaking hands, has a sip of her vodka.*]

LEONARD: [*To* ELENA.] I personally think that you should turn the third copy over to Boris Kukakov right away.

MAXIM: Yes, let's go.

ELENA: [*Picks up the file, hands it to* KUKAKOV.] The final copy is downstairs in the archives. I'm ready to go when you are.

BORIS: [*Takes the file from* ELENA, *wipes his forehead, puts his jacket on.*] Eeeh, we better go right away. We've got a dinner party with the French. There is a visiting French scientist; the French ambassador will be there, too.

[LEONARD *and* VLADIMIR *start laughing, and* MAXIM *joins them.* BORIS *looks embarrassed.* ELENA *doesn't laugh.* NATASHA, *in the meantime, gazes at the microphone.*]

MAXIM: [*Stands up, a little tipsy.*] Have a nice trip, Ivan. I would have been a very happy man had I lived one day of my life like one of your ordinary days.

VLADIMIR: Or, my friend, if you understood that happiness is not a very important thing. Give my love and greetings to your wife and children. I embrace you, Maxim.

ELENA: [*Touches* NATASHA's *shoulder.*] Vladimir, everything will be done as you wish. Although I disagree and think otherwise, everything will be done your way. Don't worry.

VLADIMIR: Elena, even we should be allowed a few mistakes every now and then.

ELENA: As long as it doesn't cause harm to others . . .

VLADIMIR: What's happening is not causing harm to anyone but me.

ELENA: So be it. We will miss you. [*To* BORIS.] We can go now.

BORIS: Good night, Natasha Komarova. [*To* LEONARD.] Good night, young man.

LEONARD: Leonard Tomkin, professor of quantum physics!

BORIS: Do excuse me. Very pleased to meet you! You are one of the most distinguished people I have ever met. [*Coughs, clears his throat, looks up to the ceiling, and starts his speech.*] Colonel Komarov! Your life will continue not only in our hearts, but in the hearts of every human in this world! We . . . will . . . never forget you!

VLADIMIR: [*Joking.*] Boris Kukakov, are you threatening me?

BORIS: [*Gasps.*] What do you mean?

VLADIMIR: It's only a joke! Comrade Kukakov, in thirty-three years we will be in the year 2000. Who knows, I might be getting there thirty-three years ahead of you. The world is moving toward better times. Outmoded beliefs are becoming fewer by the day. Religion has a good relation between the believer and what he believes in. When I was on Earth, I was receiving good news from places like Prague and Paris. There is a lovely restlessness there. Now, I think, the time has come to have these places returned to their real beauty. No one should bang on anyone else's head just because he thinks differently.

BORIS: You are right, sir.

VLADIMIR: Before dealing with political differences, we must free ourselves from the mass vulgarities, ignorances, and stupidities embedded in our daily lives. You don't have to be perishing in space to realize this.

BORIS: You are right, sir. [*Pauses.*] We're leaving now, sir. [*Silence.*]

[*As he goes out with* MAXIM *and* ELENA, *he turns back.*] Vladimir Komarov?

VLADIMIR: Yes?

BORIS: I do like Pasternak myself. I just wanted you to know.

VLADIMIR: [*Laughs.*] Bless you!

[BORIS, ELENA, *and* MAXIM *go out. Silence.* NATASHA *sadly stares at the microphone in front of her.* LEONARD *approaches her from behind, touches her shoulders with both hands.* VLADIMIR *fiddles with the buttons and switches in front of him.*]

Leo, do we have a very short communication period left?

LEONARD: I'm here, Vladimir. Yes . . .

VLADIMIR: It will phase out slowly, won't it? My voice? What I want to say is: the moment will come when I will no longer be heard, right?

LEONARD: Yes.

VLADIMIR: Oh, God! I don't like that!

LEONARD: Neither do I!

VLADIMIR: I won't even know what my last word to reach you will be. Even if I told you something meaningful, poetic, significant, and beautiful or whatever, if it was followed by some words like "spinach pie," the last thing you will have heard in my voice will be "spinach pie." One day they'll ask you, "What were Vladimir Komarov's last words?" You can tell them "spinach pie." [*Laughs.*]

There's one other way of determining when our contact will be cut off. You will have to keep talking. Because I will have no idea when our contact is disrupted, neither will you. Whoever is talking loses! See if you can sort that out!

LEONARD: [*Leans forward and hugs* NATASHA, *then straightens up.*] It's a difficult situation, Ivan.

VLADIMIR: Natasha is there with you, isn't she?

LEONARD: Yes, she's here right beside me.

VLADIMIR: From now on, don't be away from each other for long periods. Leo?

LEONARD: Yes, I'm listening.

VLADIMIR: Keep whatever you find useful among my notebooks, files, and documents. The rest turn over to them.

LEONARD: Yes, I will.

VLADIMIR: Leo?

LEONARD: Yes, Vladimir.

VLADIMIR: It's very beautiful here! Shall I tell you how I feel? A poet[4] once said, "a village idiot threw a stone into the sea, and it landed thousands of miles away." I feel just like that stone. I'm like two individuals, Leo. One is weightless, and the other is sinking to the bottom. I'm completely together with myself now!

LEONARD: I will do everything you told me to do, Vladimir. [*Silence.*]

VLADIMIR: No, try to do everything you want to do yourself, not what I want! Try to do everything you want to do, and keep working at it, Leo! Until the very end, work non-stop at it because you want it, because you like it. Even try to dream things related to your goals. You know working like this is great fun.

LEONARD: If nothing improves in the malfunction of your space capsule . . . if you continue your present route . . .

VLADIMIR: Aah, bravo, Leo! I have always been fond of you! Yes, if I stay on this course, in twenty-five years I will be back at this same point over Earth again.

LEONARD: When did you figure that out?

VLADIMIR: Today. Twenty-five years later, Leo . . . one evening very unexpectedly you may hear a voice from outer space. It may say: "Got any spinach pie?" The year will be 1992. Most likely, though, I'll pass over you without a whisper.

LEONARD: Twenty-five years is a very short period, Vladimir.

VLADIMIR: That's right. Twenty-five years is even shorter than you think it is. One realizes that up here. There is no long time span. All time segments are brief. There is no such concept as a long time period. When you look at the whole thing like this, "spinach pie" . . .

[VLADIMIR KOMAROV *continues talking. His mouth moves, but his speech is not audible.* VLADIMIR *carries on in his lovely manner of speech, sagacious, funny, and lovable.* NATASHA *and* LEONARD *are taken aback.* LEONARD *leaves his seat next to* NATASHA, *gets up, throws some switches, turns buttons. They look at one another.* VLADIMIR

---

4. Edip Cansever (1928–86), a prominent Turkish poet.

carries on with his inaudible conversation. Light falling on the space capsule becomes stronger, then gains speed, and spins away. Now the right of the stage is completely dark. On the left, LEONARD *turns another button. Music comes on.* LEONARD *reaches and kisses* NATASHA.]

CURTAIN

♦   ♦   ♦

My Lovely Scarf

REFİK ERDURAN

An Editor's Note

Few Turkish playwrights have been as prolific as Refik Erduran (b. 1928). From his pen came dozens of plays after his *Kahramanlar* (The Heroes) had an impressive presentation at his alma mater, Robert College, in Istanbul in 1948. A new work, *Herşeye Rağmen (Elele)* (Despite All, Hand in Hand), had its premier at the christening of a glittering Ankara State Theater stage in 2006.

Erduran earned a master's degree at Cornell University, where he studied dramatic literature and history of the theater. He did his military service as a reserve officer and interpreter with the Turkish brigade in the Korean War. On his return to Turkey, he established a publishing firm, which became remarkably successful in the mid-1950s. He was also the publisher of a popular humor magazine at that time. In 1968, he was invited to the International Writers Workshop at the University of Iowa, following which he spent seven years in California.

In addition to his extensive work in the theater, Erduran has achieved renown as a novelist, humorist, and columnist. His journalistic work has won such major awards as the Best Columnist prize given to him in 1985 by the Turkish Newspaper Association.

Among some forty Erduran plays produced in Turkey's leading theaters, the works of social satire received the highest praise. His *Cengiz Han'ın Bisikleti* (Genghis Khan's Bicycle) is a masterly comedy about the tribulations of a husband with four wives in the aftermath of Turkey's precipitate banning of polygamy. Another Erduran succès d'estime was *Ayı Masalı* (The Bear's Fable), which spoofs compromises and concessions made by hypocrites determined to succeed. Many of Erduran's plays are deft exposés of human foibles and universal quandaries.

Refik Erduran's creative spectrum has included such diverse topics as the Byzantine emperor Justinian, about whom he wrote a conventional tragedy, and Istanbul's burlesque and musical comedy tradition, to which he gave a fanciful recasting.

Honors and awards for this virtuoso have come from the Turkish Ministry of Culture (Best Playwright Award, 1991, and Best Play Prize, 1995), from the Atatürk Cultural Center (1996), and from many other institutions.

Erduran has also distinguished himself on the strength of his television scripts and film scenarios. In 1985, a script he wrote in English was made into a film in the United States *(Moon in Scorpio)*.

In Turkey and abroad, Erduran has been active in theater organizations. For many years, he has served as president of the Turkish branch of the International Theater Institute (ITI) and represented Turkey at ITI congresses. He is currently the chairman of the Literary Committee of the Turkish State Theaters and executive editor of Istanbul Culture University Press.

My Lovely Scarf is Erduran's own English-language version of his 1999 play entitled *Yemenimin Uçları*, which was published in book form by the Turkish Ministry of Culture and produced by the City Theater of Istanbul. In 2000, *Yemenimin Uçları*, done in Turkish in Germany, won the Best Play Prize at the Brest International Drama Festival.—TSH

Characters

ZEHRA

NURSE

DOCTOR

ASSISTANT to the doctor

NUH, Zehra's husband

ECE, Zehra's daughter

BOYFRIEND, Ece's

EFE, Zehra's son

FIRST VOICE

NEF'Î

SECOND VOICE

THIRD VOICE

FOURTH VOICE

WOMAN, a patient

KEZBAN

FATHER'S VOICE, Zehra's father

EX-HUSBAND, Kezban's former husband

Scene 1

[*A hospital room. Surreal lighting. Human shapes move about in a nightmarish dance. Lighting returns to normal.* ZEHRA *sits up in her bed. A* NURSE *is attempting to attend to her.* ZEHRA *resists. The* DOCTOR *enters, followed by his* ASSISTANT.]

DOCTOR: Good morning, good morning! You know the nurse, and this young man is my assistant.

ZEHRA: Your assistant looks charming, but the nurse is an idiot.

DOCTOR: Really? Why?

ZEHRA: She spies on me. Through a hole. I don't know where it is. I looked everywhere. Can't find the damned thing.

DOCTOR: I see. How d'you know this nurse is spying on you?

ZEHRA: This morning, just before dawn, I tricked her. Hid under the bed. She rushed in. Ha! Was she terrified! Obviously, she thought I'd escaped. Imbecile. How d'you get out of this place? The doors are locked. Iron bars on the windows. Which, again, is ridiculous. Who can jump down from the fourth floor? Ah, I get it. It's to prevent suicide. That's right. There's nothing made of glass in this room. I might break something and cut my wrists.

DOCTOR: I agree with the lady; this room's too empty. Give her what she wants.

ZEHRA: Idiots, I said! I can do that with the windowpane. And look, there's a hook on the ceiling for the light. If I wanted to, I could push the bed over there, put this chest of drawers on top of it, make a rope of sheets, and hang myself quite nicely. You think I can't do it? Sure I can. Nothing easier. In the morning, you'll look through your hole and faint.

DOCTOR: You'll feel at home in a few days. Then you'll be sorry you said these things.

ZEHRA: But I won't do it. Why should I?

DOCTOR: Of course not. Why should you?

ZEHRA: I have no problems. No problems at all, except my son. Sure, he's gone . . . for a while. It doesn't mean he doesn't love his mother. He loves me very much. Drove me here himself. He's going to pay you lots of money. In dollars! He's going to work hard for those foreigners, and he's going to send you his hard-earned cash. That's how much he loves me. And he loves his country. You know what he said? "Mail me some Istanbul postcards every now and then so I won't be homesick." That's what he said.

DOCTOR: I've got plenty of beautiful Istanbul pictures. I'll bring you some tomorrow.

ZEHRA: You can bet your life he loves his country. Why did he leave it then? It's his father's doing. [*Pounds her pillow with her fists.*] Bastard! Bastard! Bastard!

NURSE: Madam, you must take your medicine.

ZEHRA: [*Begins to cry, stops, glares at the* NURSE.] Tell this bitch to go away.

DOCTOR: Why?

ZEHRA: Can't you see she's hostile? Doesn't believe a word I say.

DOCTOR: [*Nods at the* NURSE *and* ASSISTANT. *They leave.*] Don't mind her. No need to get upset.

ZEHRA: [*Walks around, goes to the window.*] Someone's pruned your trees very badly. Kezban would have done it much better. Do you know how many years it'll take for those branches to grow back? This is what comes from handing an axe to any old fool. [*Yells.*] Don't let just anyone who comes around have an axe, you fools!

DOCTOR: Who's Kezban?

ZEHRA: What?

DOCTOR: Who is Kezban?

ZEHRA: How d'you know her name?

DOCTOR: I didn't. You just mentioned it.

ZEHRA: You're going to testify against her, aren't you?

DOCTOR: My dear lady . . .

ZEHRA: Leave her alone! And don't let everybody have axes! You're all jackasses.

DOCTOR: All right, all right. Easy. We'll give you something to help you sleep.

NURSE: [*Enters when the* DOCTOR *signals. Approaches* ZEHRA.] If you'll allow me, madam . . .

ZEHRA: Don't touch me. And listen. I don't want my daughter to know I'm here. I told my son not to tell his sister, but she might hear about me from someone else. She might come to visit me. If she does, please tell her I'm not here. Please! My daughter has veiled herself. All covered up. You'll know her when you see her. But if she sees me here, she'll go completely mad. You understand? Completely. [*Suddenly snatches a small bottle from the* NURSE's *hand and runs to a corner. The* DOCTOR *and* NURSE *are panic-stricken. He shouts. The* ASSISTANT *runs in.*]

DOCTOR: Hey! Give me that bottle! Give it back and go back to your bed! Give me the bottle! Go back! Take the bottle from her! Take it!

NURSE: Madam . . .

ZEHRA: Don't touch me!

ASSISTANT: Madam, please don't be afraid. Look, I'm here. I wouldn't hurt you, would I? Now give me that bottle.

DOCTOR: Give him the bottle, damn it!

ZEHRA: [*Scrutinizes the* ASSISTANT.] You're not my son. [*Tries to gulp down the contents of the bottle.*]

[*With angry yells, the others fall upon* ZEHRA, *drag her to the bed, and subdue her with injections. When* ZEHRA *is motionless, the* ASSISTANT *and* NURSE *move away. As the lighting slowly becomes surreal, the* DOCTOR *changes his clothing and thus turns into Zehra's husband,* NUH.]

Scene 2

[NUH *sits on his suitcase, blowing bubbles nonchalantly.*]

NUH: Hello, Zehra. How are you, darling? Still comfortable in your beloved Istanbul? [*Hums and sings a popular American song.*] Here I am, sitting by the side of a pool, under palm trees enjoying myself, but I'm homesick. Homesick for the dirty air, sidewalks with potholes, crowds of invading peasants in the streets. Hey, what's that place you're staying at now? A hotel? Boarding house? Old folks home? No! A private hospital for the mentally unbalanced? So, finally, you're in a nuthouse. A posh nuthouse, but a nuthouse all the same. You have my sympathy, darling. However, I can't say I'm surprised. You always had a genius for achieving failure. I hear they washed out your stomach. So you didn't even manage to swallow something quietly. And with that bird's brain in your cranium, you have the nerve to expect our son to stay with you.

Our son the electrical engineer. You know why he came here, to my side? Not only to live in comfort. Not only to advance professionally, but also to get away from you. From your obsessions, your dead idols, your chains. He's going to be a citizen of the world here. A citizen of the world! All your life you fought me. Scorned me. The tension drove our daughter crazy. She wrapped herself up in black sheets, poor girl. But I'm saving our son from your clutches. I won! Now you're alone. All alone.

ZEHRA: [*Has left her bed and joined* NUH.] My charming, cheating, thieving rascal of a husband! In a way, you're right of course. I've always followed my own lead. So every now and then I hit a wall. But I'm not alone. You're the one who's alone. I know that country. Everyone's alone there. Lots of noise, lots of bustle, lots of hullabaloo. But everyone's busy by himself. As for our daughter, she's not crazy. She thinks we're crazy. I'm told she prays every day for us to get well. The world's full of mindless people. I watched that construction site this morning. Look at those workers. Like ants. They keep carrying things without once stopping to think. They're building a skyscraper. But when the thing is finished, they won't be allowed to set foot in it. What galls me is that our daughter's boyfriend died for those ants. He had a name for them. For those insects. It was his favorite word: *proletariat!* Remember how he lectured us all the time? Wrote slogans on walls: "Workers and Peasants, Unite!" "All Power to Labor!" "Revolutionary Youth to the Barricades!" Marched in front, carrying a red flag. Someone told the cops where he was hiding. It was you, wasn't it?

NUH: That's a lie.

Scene 3

[ECE *and her* BOYFRIEND *appear in the background.*]

BOYFRIEND: All right, comrades. Lock arms and let's go. We're late.

ECE: Yes, my love, we're late. We should've been married last summer. I'd have a lovely baby in my arms by now.

BOYFRIEND: Hey, cut it out. This is no time for jokes.

ECE: You're calling my wish for motherhood a joke? OK, let's march to our death, but don't tell me you love me.

BOYFRIEND: I do love you. Very much.

[*The two are pulling the ends of a large black sheet in opposite directions. The* BOY-FRIEND *backs off, step by step, and disappears from view. The taut sheet suddenly goes slack.* ECE *very slowly begins to wrap herself in it.*]

ZEHRA: What I said is no lie. Remember how those rallies and marches frightened you? You kept saying, "Next thing you know, this jerk's gonna poison our son's mind!" Our daughter is sure you were the informer.

[ECE, *now completely wrapped up, remains motionless in the background.* NUH *slinks away.* ZEHRA *addresses* ECE *without looking at her.*]

Darling. My sweet little girl. You're always trying to help everybody, aren't you? These days you're a big help to your mother. Oh, how I wish I could pray like you! I try, I try. [*Kneels and covers her head.*] Dear God, please help me. I have failed my father. His last wish was clear: "This land is in your hands now. Let it be in better shape when you hand it to your children." Well, it's not. And now I'm losing my son. Show me you care, dear God. Bring him back.

[*Rises, uncovers her head.*]

It's no use, darling. I can't pray like you because I don't believe like you do. How you acquired your faith is a mystery. After your young man died . . .

ECE: He didn't die. He was murdered.

ZEHRA: Yes.

ECE: In a dungeon.

ZEHRA: In a dungeon, yes. Did the change come over you right after that? You just disappeared. Where did you go, what did you see? Why won't you tell me, darling? I'll never forget the day you showed up. After months.

[ECE *slowly comes forward, still covered up.* ZEHRA *turns to her, looks stunned.*]

Ece, is that you?

ECE: It's me, Mother.

ZEHRA: What . . . what happened? Have you lost your mind? [ECE *turns to go.* ZEHRA *intercepts her.*] Where d'you think you're going? I said, "Are you in your right mind?"

ECE: Mother, do you love me?

ZEHRA: Of course I do!

ECE: Then, please, no questions.

ZEHRA: But . . .

ECE: There is no room for "buts" in love. I love you, too. Without conditions. Now I'm at peace, and I wish the same for you.

[ECE *exits. Lights change. She returns as the* NURSE.]

NURSE: All right, time for your medicine, madam. [ZEHRA *takes the medicine without objection.*] Thank you. [*Exits.*]

Scene 4

[*Surreal lighting again.* EFE *runs in, holding his hands behind him.*]

EFE: Mother, guess what I have in my hand?

ZEHRA: How would I know?

EFE: Clue: birthday present from Dad.

ZEHRA: Envelope full of money.

EFE: Close. Airline ticket. To go around the world. I can stay in any city as long as I like. And . . . and . . . look! To meet expenses, a . . . a . . . guess what? A credit card! Not just a gold card. Better than gold. Platinum!

ZEHRA: What does that mean? That you'll stay as long as you like?

EFE: It means as long as I like.

ZEHRA: That's to say . . . if you like a place so much that you'd want to stay there for good . . . you will. Is that it?

EFE: If I like the place that well, sure.

ZEHRA: Your birthday is two weeks away.

EFE: So?

ZEHRA: Don't you see your father's trying to bribe you?

EFE: Bribe me?

ZEHRA: He's decided to run away, and he wants to take you with him.

EFE: Look, if he wants his son to live in a good place, is that a bad thing?

ZEHRA: Remember, "Efe" means "brave warrior." My father gave you that name hoping his grandson would have a lion's heart. And now I look at you. Some lion! Oh, how I wish I were a man! I'd beat the shit out of you.

EFE: Mother, what the fuck are you talking about?

ZEHRA: Remember, there was a show at the end of your first year in grade school. You danced the Harmandalı,[1] pounding the floor with your little knees. I wanted to join you when you were rehearsing at home, and it made you angry. You said it was a man's dance, that only men were allowed to do it. Oh, the things I've been excluded from throughout my life just because I'm not a man! Every time I tried to fly, they broke my wings. And now I find myself jailed in this cage.

EFE: Mother, the only cage you're jailed in is this country. Dad wants to take you with him, but you say no. What on earth keeps you here? What d'you see in the boondocks?

ZEHRA: In the boondocks, as you choose to say, I see myself—my past, my future.

EFE: No one has a future here. You teach literature, but now it's time to get real. Look out the window. See the street, not the garden. Watch those hordes of two-legged cattle. They can be herded in any direction their master chooses. If the master is hanged, they won't say moo in protest. They don't know how to live; they don't know how to love. What future can you have among them? As for their past, it's full of nothing but brawls and blood. Am I wrong?

ZEHRA: You're more than wrong; you're blind to your riches. But it's my fault. I spent so much time teaching here and there, I forgot to educate my own son. No wonder his

---

1. Harmandalı: A folk dance of the Aegean region.

father the scoundrel owns him. [*Assumes a teacher's pose.*] Listen, Son. Don't judge the value of this land by the crowds in the streets. They are displaced newcomers, poor dears. The true value lies in the treasure chest of millennia past. It includes our poets. Yunus,[2] who's very much alive. Or should be. He has no use for Paradise with its silly houris, here or in the other world. All he wants is to reach his God.

EFE: [*Hums Yunus's song.*] "All I need is you . . ." OK, OK. Go on with the lesson.

ZEHRA: The lesson?

EFE: You're a born teacher. You need to be teaching all the time.

ZEHRA: Right now all I need is you, my son.

EFE: I'm afraid I can't return the compliment. My needs are a bit more extensive.

ZEHRA: Such as?

EFE: Don't talk to me about things I can't see, Mother. Those dead people you admire so much—actually, they led a dog's life.

ZEHRA: Our ancestors led dogs' lives? On this land?

EFE: That's right. Where I am now, people are enjoying themselves.

ZEHRA: It's hard to believe you're a college graduate. Tell me, what does enjoying oneself mean?

EFE: It means enjoying oneself. Having fun.

ZEHRA: The other day you went to a jazz concert. Beautiful sounds, you said. That's enjoyment, isn't it? A form of fun. Well, this land has produced some of the most beautiful sounds in the world. Just listen to our folk songs. But when your father deigns to lend an ear to our history, all he can hear are screams and the racket of battles. Just think, what people have a past free of screams and blood? The nation you're trying to join now—does it have a pretty history? The Crusaders said they were defending Christ and who slaughtered the Christians in this very city . . . the professional torturers of the Inquisition burned people alive, and spectators watched for fun . . . the colonialists tied resisting natives to the muzzles of cannons and blasted them to hell . . . the monstrosities of twentieth-century Europe. Why d'you see only minuses on our side and pluses on the other?

[EFE *does not reply, moves away, becomes the* ASSISTANT.]

Scene 5

[*Normal lighting. The* ASSISTANT *approaches* ZEHRA.]

ASSISTANT: Hello, hello, hello! How are we this morning? As good as we look?

---

2. Yunus Emre: An Anatolian mystic (ca. 1241–1321) whose poems and hymns have been very popular in rural Turkey and in modern times in Turkish cities. Many of his mystical love poems are used as lyrics of widely performed songs.

ZEHRA: I'm fine, Doctor. I sort of go away—and come back. Getting used to it by now. Hey, you're handsome. Are doctors supposed to be handsome? If Kezban saw you . . .

ASSISTANT: Who's Kezban?

ZEHRA: What?

ASSISTANT: Who is Kezban?

ZEHRA: How d'you know her name?

ASSISTANT: You just mentioned it.

ZEHRA: Did I? Maybe I did. Listen. I know we're not allowed to flirt, but can't we at least smoke together?

ASSISTANT: Smoke? Here?

ZEHRA: Please.

ASSISTANT: All right, but don't let anyone see you.

ZEHRA: I won't. Thanks. Let's sit down. Look, they think I got sick because my son went away. Don't you believe it. He left with my permission. I wanted him to get around a bit, see the world. It doesn't mean he won't come back. Is that what they're saying? That he won't come back?

ASSISTANT: No, no. Of course he'll come back. But let's discuss that some other time. Now tell me about yourself. Where were you educated?

ZEHRA: At the Sorbonne.

ASSISTANT: Really?

ZEHRA: Kidding. I went to small schools here and there. My father was a forestry engineer. He married a peasant girl. They spent all their savings putting me through college. Around the time I married Nuh, they settled in Istanbul just to be near me, but our two families saw very little of each other. Why? Because my husband's parents were very "refined."

[*Lights change on part of the stage.* NUH *appears there.*]

Sometimes they spoke French in their house. Even when they stooped to use their mother tongue, to them a passport was *"passeport."* My mother never managed to refine her speech. It embarrassed my husband terribly. He was scared to death that she might show up in polite society.

NUH: What about her attitude? She despised me.

ZEHRA: In the end, most everybody despised you. Even your parents.

ASSISTANT: Why are you turning away?

ZEHRA: Turning away?

ASSISTANT: You're looking at the wall.

ZEHRA: [*Laughs.*] Old habit. I look at walls. You may ask, "Why did you marry a man like that in the first place?" Brilliant young architect. Charming, witty, famous. He swept me off my feet. How could I know he'd end up being a brilliant con man?

NUH: I didn't con anyone. My company had a streak of bad luck, that's all.

ZEHRA: What did he need a company for? Promising to sell thousands of summer houses to foreigners. Breaking all promises. Living in disgrace for the rest of his life.

NUH: In disgrace? Ha! I'm in clover!

ZEHRA: The clover is the loot he took with him when he sneaked away. Now he can't come back. He'd be arrested if he did.

NUH: Who the hell wants to come back?

[*Distant music, slowly rising.*]

ZEHRA: Shhh! Do you hear the music? It's an old Turkish song. The words are by Nef'î, the Ottoman poet. Who's the most famous seeker of honesty? Diogenes, who with a lighted lamp in broad daylight searched Athens for an honest man. Nef'î went farther and died in the search. He simply couldn't stand any whiff of dishonesty. Satirized his own father when the old man did something he didn't approve of. Listen to what he says in this song.

[*The words of the song are heard: "Can't converse with you, Fortune. Your mirror is filthy."*]

Even fate is dishonest in his eyes. He almost quarrels with God and has no use at all for human beings, of course.

[*"How can we be heart-to-heart friends when your heart is not clean?" The music stops.* ZEHRA *walks around, agitated.*]

So he keeps looking and looking for someone he can trust and embrace. But there is no one. It drives him mad.

[*The light begins to turn red.* NUH *stands watching, looking alternately amused and angry.*]

He begins to curse everything and everyone. It's like a volcanic eruption. Not even the most powerful people in the empire are spared. His enemies multiply day by day. On the throne sits Murad IV, the most ferocious ruler in Ottoman history. Nef'î, with his pen, cuts down the sultan's top men one by one. Neither entreaties nor threats can stop him.

[ZEHRA *takes a file from the chest of drawers.*]

Look: I began to write a play about it. No one's seen it yet. You'll be the first. Here. Let's act out this scene. You read these parts. Out loud.

ASSISTANT: What's this? Voices? OK, here goes.

FIRST VOICE: "O Nef'î, I am your friend. Beware the danger that is coiling itself around you like a snake. Do not try to tread on the rulers of this land."

[ZEHRA *becomes* NEF'î.]

ZEHRA as NEF'Î: "Then let the bastards stop treading on the people of this land."

FIRST VOICE: "Are you mad? Hold your tongue, for heaven's sake!"

ZEHRA as NEF'Î: "I can't—not even for heaven's sake. Everyone has a problem with a body part that can't be controlled. Mine is the tongue."

SECOND VOICE: "Repent, infidel! Your accursed pen has defiled the holy name of our great *şeyhülislâm.*"[3]

ZEHRA as NEF'Î: "With his unholy greed, your fat *şeyhülislâm* defiles Islam every day. Tell him to repent."

SECOND VOICE: "O rabid devil! You have even dared malign our glorious sultan's *grand* vizier."

ZEHRA as NEF'Î: "I am the *grand* poet. I can tell the truth about any old pig."

THIRD VOICE: [*Quiet but very threatening.*] "Are you calling me a pig, Nef'î?"

ZEHRA as NEF'Î: "It matters not how rich or big, a fucking pig is still a pig."

THIRD VOICE: "I said, 'Are those beastly lines about me?'"

ZEHRA as NEF'Î: "No, no. Actually, pigs are charming beasts. I wouldn't insult them by hinting at any resemblance to you."

FOURTH VOICE: [*A deep, commanding voice.*] "Nef'î."

ZEHRA as NEF'Î: [*Prostrates herself.*] "Your Majesty!"

FOURTH VOICE: "I like you, but you go too far. Swear you won't satirize anyone again, and I will let you live." [ZEHRA *hesitates. The* VOICE *thunders.*] "Swear!"

ZEHRA as NEF'Î: "I swear, Your Majesty."

[*Silence.* ZEHRA *gets up and walks around slowly, looking ill at ease with herself. Sounds of pigs feeding are heard. The squeaks, grunts, and snorts get louder.* ZEHRA *listens to the din of the feeding frenzy with increasing annoyance, then can bear it no longer.*] "Cut it out, pigs! Gobble up your shit in silence!" [*The noise ceases.*]

FIRST VOICE: "Careful. You promised."

SECOND VOICE: "The people you insult are the faithful servants of His Majesty, enjoying his largesse."

ZEHRA as NEF'Î: "They're pigs eating shit."

[*A collective sigh of exasperation is heard.*]

THIRD VOICE: "As grand vizier, I try to be very tolerant. Tell me what you want, Nef'î."

ZEHRA as NEF'Î: "I want the impossible. I want you to be honest."

THIRD VOICE: "Ha ha! You know, I actually like your satire. It makes me smile. If you would only behave yourself a little, we could be friends."

ZEHRA as NEF'Î: "The grand vizier can zig and zag, can zag and zig. Behind his silly grinning face, he's still a pig."

---

3. *Şeyhülislâm:* Chief religious dignitary in the Ottoman Empire.

THIRD VOICE: "You stupid clown, you just broke your promise to His Majesty."

ZEHRA as NEF'î: "Majesty, my ass!"

[*Collective gasp of horror. Then hubbub of outrage.*]

FOURTH VOICE: "Silence." [*Silence.*] "Wring his neck."

[ZEHRA *clutches her neck as if in pain, sinks to the floor. Lighting slowly returns to normal as* NUH *laughs and applauds.* ZEHRA *gets up, turns to the* ASSISTANT.]

ZEHRA: My son, I didn't make up any of this. It all happened. Being strangled was the only way Nef'î could escape the filth of this world. So you see, Efe, there were some in our past who weren't "two-legged cattle."

ASSISTANT: You're calling me "Efe."

ZEHRA: Am I? Never mind. Hey, I like your acting. [NUH *laughs loudly.*] What's funny, Nuh?

NUH: Crazy bitch! What d'you think our son is—some kind of history nut? You really expect your little story to excite him? He's young. He wants to live now. To live and to have fun. "Joie de vivre." It was my father's favorite expression. "The joy of living." The glory of spring, not winter sleep.

ZEHRA: You ignorant merchant, you think there was no joy in the past? Haven't you heard of the Tulip Age?[4]

NUH: In the past, in the past! What does your country have to offer my son today?

ZEHRA: Today, most of my country is covered with slime, thanks to scum like you. Just one generation ago it was different. There was great beauty. There can be again. I remember our times together when we first met. How happy I was! And how surprised when the nonsense started. My husband the skirt chaser, the drunk, the former architect. Then the bankrupt. Finally the crook. It just doesn't make sense. Why did you throw away everything that was right and good?

[*The atmosphere suddenly becomes festive. Multicolored lights. Music starts: a tango.* ECE *runs in with drinks and presents. The* ASSISTANT *turns into* EFE. NUH *grabs* ZEHRA. *They all dance.*]

ECE: Hooray! Let's dance! Then we'll drink and cut the cake. Happy Birthday, Mother!

ZEHRA: [*When they stop dancing, takes a scarf from a box.*] Ah, a gift from my father-in-law! Purchased in Paris, no doubt. Look, I'm putting it next to the scarf I'm wearing. Another present—very dear to me. It's what you might call a peasant scarf. Now, which is more beautiful? The one from Paris is exquisite, of course. But this one's lovely, too, with bold colors, striking patterns. If you guys don't think so, it means you're totally alienated from your culture.

---

4. Tulip Age: A period of lavish festivities in the Ottoman capital, Istanbul, that lasted from about 1718 to 1730.

ECE: What are my dear brother's views on this vital subject?

EFE: The greatest triumph is to transcend the milieu you're born into. You can't do that, Mother. That's why you get stuck. And you refuse to get unstuck.

ECE: Let's hear from Daddy.

NUH: No one can get unstuck in a country that is itself stuck. In the end, everybody gives up trying.

ZEHRA: Everybody?

NUH: Wake up, woman! Join us in the new age. Happy Birthday, honey! [*They drink.* ZEHRA *looks sad.*]

EFE: Why the long face, Mother? No need to be sad. The only reason to be sad is if you're finished before you're dead. D'you feel finished?

ZEHRA: I don't know. I love all of you very much, but sometimes I feel so lonely . . .

EFE: Lonely? That's ridiculous. We're all here.

ZEHRA: You're here, but away.

[*The others laugh. Music rises.* EFE *dances with* ZEHRA, *and* NUH *with* ECE. *As* NUH *tries to take a present from his pocket, a roll of bills falls out. Music stops.*] What's this? Where'd you find all this money?

NUH: Your no-good husband managed to get the mother of all contracts. Who cares if the world's sinking? We're in Nuh's Ark, lady, but you're not coming aboard.

[*Lights dim.* NUH, EFE, *and* ECE *exit.*]

ZEHRA: [*Grows thoughtful, then picks up a phone.*] It's me. Did Efe get there? . . . Good. You could have called to let me know. . . . What? Permission for what? He's a grown man now. I don't think he needs my permission for anything. . . . What girl? Who is she? . . . I see. . . . No, it's not a shock. Many of my friends have foreign girls for daughters-in-law. But of course I'd like to meet her. Let me talk to him. . . . Darling, how was the trip? Oh, sorry about that. Try to get a good night's sleep now, and you'll be fine in the morning. . . . Yes, your father just told me. Why did you keep me in the dark? I'd love to meet her. When d'you think you might bring her here? . . . I understand. . . . I'm all right. They'll soon realize there's nothing wrong with me, and I'll go home. Don't worry about it. Just don't leave me in the dark about anything. OK?

[*Lights suddenly return to normal as the* ASSISTANT *enters.* ZEHRA *looks disconcerted for a second, then recovers her composure.*]

ASSISTANT: Time for your medicine. You look a little tense. Take this and relax.

ZEHRA: Will you do me a favor?

ASSISTANT: If it's in my power, I'd be delighted to oblige. Provided, of course, it's not something that might be harmful to you.

ZEHRA: Lend me your phone for a minute. I wish to speak with my son. I had decided not to call him, but now there's something I need to know. Urgently.

ASSISTANT: What is it?

ZEHRA: What is what?

ASSISTANT: What is it that you urgently need to know?

ZEHRA: I'm not sure. I'll tell you when I find out. Now hand me the phone.

ASSISTANT: Look, you know it's not good for you to be in touch with the outside world just yet. Let's wait for a few days; then we'll let you have your own phone, and you can use it whenever you want. Just be patient for a few days.

ZEHRA: Please. Let me have it.

ASSISTANT: Oh all right.

[ZEHRA *grabs the phone, moves away, begins to speak. Tense music, building up. The* AS-SISTANT *takes out a little notebook and takes notes, glancing at* ZEHRA *furtively. Music ends as she moves back toward him. Silence.*]

Well? Did you reach him? [ZEHRA *is silent.*] I warned you. I said you should wait a little.

ZEHRA: Doctor, why didn't you tell me my son had applied for citizenship in another country? You knew it, didn't you? You knew, and you kept it from me.

ASSISTANT: No, no. How would I know?

ZEHRA: You knew! Everybody knew, except me!

ASSISTANT: Please be calm. It's nothing to get upset about. Actually, it's good news. This might help your son professionally when he comes back.

ZEHRA: He won't come back! I'll never see him again!

[*A young* WOMAN, *another patient, looks in from the door.*]

WOMAN: Doc! This is it! My labor pains! You think it's a boy?

ASSISTANT: Hey! Who gave you permission to leave your room? Go back there!

WOMAN: No, no! There's no time! This is an emergency. I gotta do it now, right here. Sorry to bother you. Sorry, lady. I gotta have my baby right away. Will it be a boy or a girl, Doc? I want a girl. Oh my God! I can't stand it! Help me, please! Help me!

ASSISTANT: OK, OK. Take it easy. Don't shout. Now slowly. Take a deep breath. That's good. Push. Again. That's it! Bravo! [*Takes a pillow from under the* WOMAN's *robe and hands it to her.*]

WOMAN: Is it a girl?

ASSISTANT: Yes, a girl.

WOMAN: What shall we call her? Ayşe . . . Dilek . . . Demet . . .

ASSISTANT: Let's call her Kezban.

WOMAN: Right. That's a good name.

ASSISTANT: Now go back to your room.

WOMAN: Can I have another baby tomorrow?

ASSISTANT: Sure. Now do as I say. [*The* WOMAN *moves to the door, cuddling the pillow like a baby.* ZEHRA *runs after her and takes it.*]

ZEHRA: Look, they're fooling you. This is a pillow. A pillow! You understand? Don't be hoodwinked. A pillow! Get it through your thick skull. You do not have a baby!

WOMAN: [*Begins to cry.*] No! This is my baby. My daughter. I just had her. Ain't that right, Doc? I just had her, didn't I? What does this bad woman want from me? I ain't done nothin' to her. Don't you like people, lady? Don't you love your kids? Doc, this is my baby, right? Just had her, right?

ASSISTANT: Sure, sure. Here's some candy. One for you, one for the baby. Now go back to your room.

WOMAN: Can I have a cigarette?

ASSISTANT: Don't you know that cigarette smoke is bad for the baby? It's time for her nap. If you don't go, I'll give her to another mother.

WOMAN: I'll have another baby tomorrow, right?

ASSISTANT: Sure thing. [*The* WOMAN *exits.*] See, we have serious cases like this. Your problems are nothing compared to hers. They brought her from her village three months ago. She lost a baby late in her pregnancy and won't ever have a baby again, so her husband left her. Just like that.

ZEHRA: I knew a peasant girl. Loved her like my own daughter. Her name was Kezban. She cleaned our apartment every week. Gave me a scarf on my birthday. I still keep it. She had beautiful white teeth. Long, flowing hair she never covered. We lived on the ninth floor. She used to go out on the ledge to clean the windows. Her hair blew in the wind. I used to scream in terror. She just laughed and flashed her pearly teeth. [*Suddenly becomes aware that the* ASSISTANT *is taking notes.*] What are you writing? Poetry?

ASSISTANT: No. Nothing.

ZEHRA: Let me see.

ASSISTANT: You wouldn't understand it.

ZEHRA: I showed you my play because I trusted you. Now it's your turn. [*Snatches the notebook, quickly looks inside it.*] How interesting. So I'm a case study. For your research. That's why you need me, why you're being friendly. This is cold-blooded stuff. Almost hostile. So what's the diagnosis? And the prognosis? Does dear old medicine hold out any hope for me?

ASSISTANT: You'll be fine. Trust me. This is going to be my specialty.

ZEHRA: Really? How nice. You'll probably be going abroad to sharpen your skills.

ASSISTANT: If I can.

ZEHRA: Go, then.

ASSISTANT: What?

ZEHRA: Go!

ASSISTANT: Where?

ZEHRA: Home! Your work on this case is finished. [*The* ASSISTANT *exits sheepishly as* ZEHRA *turns away from him.*]

Scene 6

[KEZBAN *on a ledge, cleaning a window from the outside.* ZEHRA *is not visible in her bed.*]

KEZBAN: Don't worry, ma'am. I never fall. I've got an amulet around my neck, and I always look before I move. When I was little, I lived in treetops. The boys couldn't climb that high. They never tangled with me. If one cussed, I cussed right back. Used real bad language. That was my worst problem later in life. I couldn't take shit from nobody. Begging your pardon, ma'am. My husband's family was the richest in the village, but his father was a real asshole. Sorry, ma'am. Always riding his son. One day I got real mad, told him to go to hell. "I won't have my man bullied," I said. "Not even by his father." Then I told my husband to pack. We came here, stayed with his cousin. That guy had a coffeehouse, but sold funny stuff on the side. Little pills and things. And he had his eye on me. My husband looked for work. Couldn't find any. So he went to Germany. Then to Holland. I don't know where he is now. He'll send for me when he can. But the news is bad. They say some people in those places are giving our men trouble. I sent word to my husband. "Don't go begging," I said. "If they don't treat you right, come back," I said. See, I'm making enough for the two of us. So now I'm waiting. [*Comes in, moves away.* NUH *can be heard laughing.*]

ZEHRA'S VOICE: Don't laugh, Nuh!

KEZBAN: [*Returns.*] Morning, ma'am. Yes, he's here. [*Tries to smile.*] Seems like he missed me real bad. Got on top before I could say hi, didn't let me breathe till noon. [*Begins to dust.*] Yeah, we had a talk. In the afternoon. Things don't look too good. Seems he needs a paper. Without that paper, they treat him like dirt. So I said, "Let's find the money for that paper." He said, "No, can't be done with money." Seems there's only one way—he's gotta look like he's married to a local woman. So he's gotta divorce me first. What could I say? I said, "OK." He made me sign papers in an office. I don't know. I think it's called notary or something. No, I'm not worried. It's all government stuff. When they hand him his paper, we'll get married again. Yeah, I know it's not nice. But that's the way things are in those places. Without that paper, my man is of no account. [NUH's *laughter is heard.*]

ZEHRA'S VOICE: Nuh, don't laugh! [KEZBAN *exits.*]

KEZBAN: [*Comes back.*] Sorry, ma'am, I'm late today. No, I'm not sick. My stomach's kind of upset, that's all. I'll get some fresh air now, cleaning the windows. Only I need to make a call first. Yeah, still no word from him. It's been two months. He didn't leave his number. Just now I stopped by his cousin's place and got it. Can I please call from here? I'll make it short. [*Goes to the phone and dials, very excited.*] Hello? Hello? Anyone there who understands me? [*Prays silently as she waits. Then she jumps for joy.*]

It's me, it's me! . . . The number? Sure I found it. No problem. You've got a clever wife, remember? . . . What? What's wrong with me calling you? . . . What d'you mean, they don't like it? Who's they? Listen. If you're so scared, why d'you stay there? Just wanted to tell you something. I'm pregnant. . . . Yeah. Hello. Are you there? Can't hear you. . . . What? The what? . . . Timing? What's that mean? You said you'd have the paper in no time. . . . You mean, just because their government . . . then come back! Come back! . . . Oh, I get it. Yeah. Don't say anymore. Don't worry. I won't have your baby now even if you ask me on your knees. [*Hangs up.* NUH *is heard laughing again.*]

ZEHRA'S VOICE: Nuh! I said don't laugh!

KEZBAN: Sorry, ma'am, but I can't come here anymore. I think I'll be working in the coffee-house. Yeah, the one that guy's running. My husband's cousin. Only, it's not a coffee-house anymore. He calls it a nightclub. With a funny name. "Ecs" something. "Ec-sta" . . . yeah, "Ecstasy." I don't know. He said I could help the bartender. Seems there's good money in it. I'll be needing the money. For the doctor and things.

[*Loud laughter from* NUH. *Lively music starts.* KEZBAN *throws off her robe, revealing a scanty, sexy costume. She does a provocative dance. Then she walks the streets, heckling the passersby.*]

Hi, Johnny. Want some fun, handsome? You have a light, Hans? Wait. *Bitte.* Swine! Hey, Jacques! What's your hurry, monsieur? Where's the fire? Let's talk dollars, baby. Local money, no go. Hello, pretty darling. Looking for customers on my beat, eh? You a boy or a girl? Hey! What? I'll yell all I want. Fuck the cops. Oh, look who's here. Interested, Ivan? You think I'm one of your Natashas?[5] My name is Kezban. Hey, you people! You all look foreign to me. Is there one local man in this street? I mean a real man. Ha! [*Sees someone and stops short. Her bravado vanishes.*] Ma'am! It's me. Me! Yeah, I've changed. A lot. Tell me, how're you doin'? And the family? Good, good. Me? I'm OK. No, really, I'm fine. Worked at the nightclub for a while. Got used to lots of things. "Addicted," they call it. Takes heaps of money. But that's no problem. I'm doin' fine now. No, really. I can buy a house if I want. Maybe in Europe even. Well, bye. Oh, let me give you a card. Just call if you need me for anything. No, no, ma'am. Don't worry about me. I never fall, remember? Don't you worry. Bye now. Bye.

[KEZBAN *exits.* ZEHRA *sits up in her bed dejectedly. She looks around, glances at the ceiling, begins to make a rope of the bedsheets, tying the ends in knots.* NUH *appears, watches her, looks amused.*]

NUH: Careful. You made a mess of pill taking. If you break a leg now, you'll be the laugh-ingstock of the hospital.

ZEHRA: Is that all you have to say to me now?

5. Natasha: A foreign, usually Russian, prostitute.

NUH: No, I have a bit of advice. Make the knots strong.

ZEHRA: Ece, my sweet daughter, please pray for me. I know what I have in mind is a sin, but there's nothing else I can do. May God forgive me. Daddy! Hear me, please. What shall I do, Daddy?

FATHER'S VOICE: Laugh at yourself.

ZEHRA: Laugh? Oh, the universe has gone crazy! No one loves me, Dad.

FATHER'S VOICE: So what?

ZEHRA: So what?

FATHER'S VOICE: If others don't love you, is it the end of the world? Or the end of you?

ZEHRA: No. No, of course not. I remember what the poet says.

NUH: What does the poet say?

ZEHRA:

If you're a black sheep, love the color black.

Go your own way, forget the flock.

NUH: Talk, talk, talk! That's all you're capable of. Won't you ever act?

ZEHRA: Act?

NUH: Do something. Like me. Or like that silly bitch Kezban. She's a hooker, but at least she made a decision.

ZEHRA: I wonder what she's doing now.

[NUH *disappears as the lighting returns to normal.* ZEHRA *brings out the peasant scarf, removes a card that is attached to it with a needle, goes to the phone and dials.*]

Hello? May I speak to Kezban, please? . . . Yes, that Kezban. I'm an old friend. Is she there? . . . What! When? Why? I mean, how? What happened? . . . Oh, my God. With her baby? . . . What baby? . . . I see. What's his name, do you know? I don't believe it! No, it's just . . . an interesting coincidence. Thanks for the information.

[*Hangs up, looking stunned, moves away, turns and stares at the phone. Then she smiles.*]

Nuh! Did you hear, you stupid scoundrel? Did you hear what my Kezban has done? Her stupid scoundrel of an ex-husband called her names, so she slashed him with a jackknife. And she has a baby boy. He's with her in jail now.

[*Walks around with growing excitement.*]

You know what name she gave to the child? Efe! Oh, Kezban. Crazy girl. No, she wasn't crazy at all. They drove her mad.

Scene 7

[*Surreal lighting.* KEZBAN, *in her professional costume, sits on a bench. A big, open umbrella on the floor beside her. Her* EX-HUSBAND *approaches her gingerly.* ZEHRA *can be seen dimly in her bed in the background.* KEZBAN *turns and sees the man. They stare at each other.*]

EX-HUSBAND: Won't you say hello?

KEZBAN: No. We're strangers. Go away.

EX-HUSBAND: What's wrong with having a little talk?

KEZBAN: There's nothing to talk about. Get lost.

EX-HUSBAND: What're you doing here?

KEZBAN: What d'you think?

EX-HUSBAND: Look at that getup! I hear you've got a brat. Who's the father?

KEZBAN: None of your damn business.

EX-HUSBAND: All our friends are talking about you. [KEZBAN *does not reply.*] You don't want to know what they're saying?

KEZBAN: I ain't got no friends, and I don't give a shit what anyone's saying.

EX-HUSBAND: Your brat's gonna grow up. One day he'll ask, "Who's my dad?" What're you gonna tell him?

KEZBAN: My son ain't gonna need no dad. I'm saving lots of money for him.

EX-HUSBAND: Yeah? How're you making all that dough? Like this?

KEZBAN: That's right. Like this.

EX-HUSBAND: OK, then. Take 'em off.

KEZBAN: What?

EX-HUSBAND: You heard me. Go on. Strip. If you're selling, I'm buying. Right here.

KEZBAN: You can't be my customer. I don't serve all comers. No jerks.

EX-HUSBAND: You're calling me a jerk?

KEZBAN: That's right, jerk.

EX-HUSBAND: You'll be sorry.

KEZBAN: You're drunk. Beat it, or there'll be trouble.

EX-HUSBAND: Kezban . . .

KEZBAN: Listen, I wouldn't fuck you if they put a gun to my head.

EX-HUSBAND: I can't look anyone in the eye. You made a monkey of me, selling yourself.

KEZBAN: Ha! Look who's talkin'! "Selling yourself." You started it, jerk.

EX-HUSBAND: That's enough!

KEZBAN: Don't shout.

EX-HUSBAND: Bitch!

KEZBAN: I said don't shout.

EX-HUSBAND: Might scare away your customers, eh?

KEZBAN: That's right. They don't like jerks.

EX-HUSBAND: I'll go find your brat. I'll shout in his ear.

[*The light turns red.*]

KEZBAN: What's that? What did you say?

EX-HUSBAND: I'll shout in your little bastard's ear: "You're the son of a filthy whore!"

[KEZBAN *strikes her* EX-HUSBAND. *He grabs her, begins to tear off her clothes. They grapple and fall to the ground behind the umbrella.* ZEHRA *leaves her bed, approaches them with a jackknife.* KEZBAN's *hand comes up above the umbrella.* ZEHRA *puts the jackknife in it. The hand comes down. Lights out. Tense music. Then spotlight on* KEZBAN. *She is standing in court, addressing a judge.* ZEHRA *listens in the background.*]

KEZBAN: I ain't got nothin' to say, Judge. You wouldn't understand anyway. Sure, it's wrong to stab a guy, but he stabbed my soul. My baby? That's all I care about now.

[*The light turns soft blue as* ZEHRA *comes forward and goes to the phone. Music also softens.*]

ZEHRA: Hello? It's me again. We spoke a little while ago, about Kezban. I have a suggestion. Please tell her Zehra wants to take care of the baby boy while she's in jail. . . . No, I can't go there today, but I'll do so as soon as I can. Thank you.

[KEZBAN *smiles, picks up the baby, hands him to* ZEHRA, *and exits.* ZEHRA *sits on the bed, puts the baby down next to her, stares at him.* EFE *and* NUH *come in, sit, and read the letters in their hands.*]

EFE: "My dear son, I've decided to let go of you. It's up to you as a grown-up to correct any mistakes that you make. If you can be at peace with your own country, fine. If you're lost to it, I'll be sorry, of course, but it's your decision. I think I'm managing to cure myself here. I fervently wish the same for you. Your loving mother."

NUH: [*Laughs.*] "Dear rascal, I haven't heard from you for some time, which is a blessing. I'm not angry anymore, only sorry for you. Just think. Suppose Noah builds his ark, but there's no deluge. He shuts himself in his little ship all his life, expecting torrents any minute, thinking he's lucky to escape the danger. Wouldn't you feel sorry for the poor paranoiac? That's how I see you. For half a lifetime I lived in your shadow. Now I'm on my own, but free. End of nightmare! You stay there, enjoy your paradise. I'll go my way. Be thankful that I did not, as a parting present, stab your ass."

[NUH *laughs again. Music turns into the melody of the folk song "Elif."* ZEHRA *sings the words, then speaks to the baby while the music continues in the background.* ECE *returns as the* NURSE *with two white coats, which she hands to* NUH *and* EFE. *They put them on in slow motion as* ZEHRA *speaks.*]

ZEHRA: Baby, baby. Are you sorry you were born in this country? Some people will say it's the wrong place—with lots of anger and little love. Don't you believe it. Even on the slopes of our remotest mountains, romance flows like spring water. The song I just sang is about a young man's tender passion for a girl called Elif. He's so overjoyed with enchantment that there's nothing else in the world for him. The birds sing "Elif, Elif"; the wind whistles "Elif, Elif"; the wild flowers smell like "Elif." One day he sees her through the window of her room. The glittering buttons on the girl's silk blouse fascinate him, so he just stands there, unable to move. Elif sees him and frowns. But the childish adoration in his face softens her. On an impulse, she motions him to come in. Incredulously, he obeys, as in a trance. She notices him glancing at the bright buttons and averting his eyes. His innocent yearning charms her. On another impulse, she begins to unbutton her blouse. The young man closes his eyes. In his ears, the rustle of silk against skin whispers "Elif, Elif."

[ZEHRA *is smiling. The* DOCTOR, *the* ASSISTANT, *and the* NURSE, *all in white, surround her.*]

NURSE: How are you, madam?

ASSISTANT: Are you all right now?

DOCTOR: Tell me how you feel.

ZEHRA: I feel fine, Doctor. In fact, I think I can dance the Harmandalı. [*Proceeds to do so; the music follows suit.*]

CURTAIN

Biographical Notes

◆   ◆   ◆

Acknowledgments

◆   ◆   ◆

Biographical Notes

TALAT S. HALMAN is a critic, a scholar, and a leading translator of Turkish literature into English. His books in English include *Contemporary Turkish Literature, Modern Turkish Drama, Süleyman the Magnificent Poet*, three books on Yunus Emre, *Mevlana Celaleddin Rumi and the Whirling Dervishes* (with Metin And), *A Brave New Quest: 100 Modern Turkish Poems, Shadows of Love* (his original poems in English), *A Last Lullaby* (his English/Turkish poems), *Living Poets of Turkey, Turkish Legends and Folk Poems*, and many books featuring modern Turkish poets (Dağlarca, Kanık, Anday). He is the editor of *A Dot on the Map: Selected Stories and Poems* and *Sleeping in the Forest: Stories and Poems* by Sait Faik. His book *Nightingales and Pleasure Gardens: Turkish Love Poems* was named one of the ten best university press books of 2005 by *ForeWord Reviews.*

Among Halman's books in Turkish are eleven collections of his own poetry, including *Ümit Harmanı* (his complete poems); a massive volume of the poetry of ancient civilizations; the complete sonnets of Shakespeare; the poetry of ancient Anatolia and the Near East; Eskimo poems; ancient Egyptian poetry; the *rubai*s of Rumi; the quatrains of Baba Tahir Uryan; two anthologies of modern American poetry; and books of the selected poems of Wallace Stevens and Langston Hughes. Halman was William Faulkner's first Turkish translator; he has also translated works by Mark Twain and Eugene O'Neill.

Halman has published nearly three thousand articles, essays, and reviews in English and in Turkish. He has served as a columnist for the Turkish dailies *Milliyet, Akşam*, and *Cumhuriyet*. Many of his English articles on Turkish literature have been collected in *Rapture and Revolution: Essays on Turkish Literature*. Selections from Halman's Turkish articles and essays have been collected in two volumes, *Doğrusu* and *Çiçek Dürbünü*. His English reviews of works of Turkish literature have been collected in *The Turkish Muse: Views and Reviews, 1960s–1990s*. Some of his books have been translated into French, Hebrew, Persian, Urdu, Hindi, and Japanese. He won Columbia University's Thornton Wilder Prize for his work as a translator.

His translations of Robinson Jeffers's *Medea*; Jerome Kilty's *Dear Liar*, a play adaptation of the correspondence of George Bernard Shaw and Mrs. Patrick Campbell; Eugene O'Neill's *The Iceman Cometh*; and Neil Simon's *Lost in Yonkers* were produced in Turkey. *Dear Liar* and *The Iceman Cometh* won best-translation awards. His English version of Güngör Dilmen's one-woman play *I, Anatolia* was presented by Turkey's premier actress

369

Yıldız Kenter in North America, England, Europe, and Asia. Halman also wrote a one-actor Shakespeare-based play entitled *Kahramanlar ve Soytarılar* (Heroes and Clowns), which was presented in the 1986–87 season by the prominent actor Müşfik Kenter in Istanbul. It was published in book form in 1991. Later, Halman himself presented it as a dramatic reading. In recent years, he has been doing a revised version with Yıldız Kenter in both English and Turkish. The script was published as a book under the title *"Türk" Shakespeare* in 2003. Halman was chosen to write the 2006 World Theater Day proclamation for Turkey.

Talat Halman served as Turkey's first minister of culture and later as its ambassador for cultural affairs. He was a member of the UNESCO Executive Board. Between 1953 and 1997, he was on the faculties of Columbia University, Princeton University, the University of Pennsylvania, and New York University (where he was also chairman of the Department of Near Eastern Languages and Literatures). In 1998, he founded the Department of Turkish Literature at Bilkent University, Ankara, and has since then been its chairman. He also serves as Bilkent's dean of the Faculty of Humanities and Letters. He is currently the president of the Turkish National Committee for UNICEF and editor in chief of the *Journal of Turkish Literature*. He was also the general editor for a four-volume history of Turkish literature published in Turkish.

Halman's honors and awards include many literary prizes, two honorary doctorates, a Rockefeller Fellowship in the Humanities, the Distinguished Service Award of the Turkish Academy of Sciences, the UNESCO Medal, and Knight Grand Cross (GBE), the Most Excellent Order of the British Empire, conferred on him by Queen Elizabeth II.

JAYNE L. WARNER is director of research at the Institute for Aegean Prehistory in Greenwich, Connecticut. She holds a B.A. in classics, an M.A. in ancient history, and from Bryn Mawr College a Ph.D. in Near Eastern and Anatolian archaeology. Her publications include *Elmalı-Karataş II: The Early Bronze Age Village of Karataş*. Warner has served as assistant editor for the American School of Classical Studies at Athens and executive director of the Poetry Society of America (New York). She has also served as director of the American Turkish Society (New York) and director of the New York Office of the Board of Trustees of Robert College of Istanbul. She is the editor of *Cultural Horizons: A Festschrift in Honor of Talat S. Halman*, *The Turkish Muse: Views and Reviews, 1960s–1990s*, and *Rapture and Revolution: Essays on Turkish Literature*. She is the associate editor of *Sleeping in the Forest: Stories and Poems* by Sait Faik, *Nightingales and Pleasure Gardens: Turkish Love Poems*, and *A Brave New Quest: 100 Modern Turkish Poems*.

♦ ♦ ♦

Acknowledgments

The editors offer their thanks to the following individuals for their assistance with various aspects of the production of this book: Tuncel Acar, Ceyda Akpolat, Ahmet Baydur, Gönül Büyüklimanlı, Günil Özlem Ayaydın Cebe, Demet Güzelsoy Chafra, Attilâ Dorsay, Yıldız Kenter, Sevda Şener, and Ela Şengündüz.

The editors are also grateful to the following for permission to print these translations: Neriman Asena, Sina Baydur, Güngör Dilmen, Refik Erduran, John D. Norton, Turgut Özakman, Nilüfer Mizanoğlu Reddy, Yeşim Salman, and Dinçer Sümer.